The Sixties Spiritual Awakening

The Sixties Spiritual Awakening

American Religion Moving from Modern to Postmodern

Robert S. Ellwood

Rutgers University Press
New Brunswick, New Jersey

Library of Congress Cataloging-in-Publication Data

Ellwood, Robert S., 1933–
The sixties spiritual awakening : American religion moving from
modern to postmodern / Robert S. Ellwood.
p. cm.
Includes bibliographical references and index.
ISBN 0-8135-2093-2
1. United States—Religion—1960– 2. United States—Social life and
customs—1945–1970. 3. Postmodernism—United States—
Religious aspects. I. Title. II. Title: 60s spiritual awakening.

BL2525.E44 1994   93-44227
200'.973'09046—dc20   CIP

British Cataloging-in-Publication information available

Material from the *San Francisco Oracle* is reprinted in this book
by permission of Allen Cohen and the Regent Press,
Oakland, California.

Contents

Preface

This study of American religion in the 1960s is offered in the hope that it will find its niche in the growing edifice of books on that decade. The Sixties are a period on which any number of defining perspectives on religious life, as on political and social life, are possible and no doubt defensible. In most books on the Sixties, including this one, the protests, the bizarre apparitions, and the radical new departures may appear overemphasized among the farrago of spiritual events that made up that tumultuous and confusing time. Conservatives never tire of reminding us that the majority of Americans, even of American youth and American religionists, were neither countercultural nor protest minded in the days of Kennedy, Johnson, and Nixon. The truth in that contention was to some extent manifested as the traditionalist side of American life asserted itself in subsequent decades.

But if one sure law of history can be found, it is that change never ceases, and therefore agents of change have their place, even if it is also true that change rarely happens exactly as any particular agent would like to see it occur. In fact American religion, like American culture generally, has not been the same since the Sixties. In some respects that is in reaction against them, but to a greater extent it is as a continuation—sometimes under other names and on a cultural rather than political base—of what the Sixties were about. Attitudes toward race, sex, dress, beards, gender roles, demonstrations, and divergent life-styles are not and will never be again quite what they were before Selma and Haight-Ashbury. It is right, therefore, to look at the changers a little more than those who changed not. We shall do that, and we shall put the change in the context of the larger modernism/ postmodernism discussion.

This book was largely written at my home in Pasadena, California. Some of my most interesting ideas, however, especially on modernism and postmodernism, came while I was on a Buddhist retreat at which writing materials were not allowed. No doubt that proscription was for good reason. Still, I felt that to run the risk of losing those insights by trusting them only to frail memory would be the greater offense against Cosmic Law, so on several occasions I surreptitiously borrowed a pencil from the bath sign-up sheet and recorded them on both sides of a map of the grounds.

I recalled that my teacher in history of religions, the late Mircea Eliade, when once imprisoned for political reasons in his native Rumania, had been under a similar ban but had written a large part of one of his books with a smuggled pencil on toilet paper. When the map was exhausted, I had recourse to the same medium. Some readers may find this an apt metaphor for the contents of these pages, though I hope others will be more charitable.

The main inspiration for this effort, however, was a freshman seminar I have offered at the University of Southern California in recent years entitled "The Sixties Spiritual Awakening." Many of the data and ideas in this volume were first exchanged with these exceptional students. The remarkable enthusiasm that undergraduates of the late 1980s and early 1990s have shown for the Sixties, a decade that ended before most of them were born but to them a legendary era—already a myth becoming almost an Eliadean mythical time of beginnings—awakened anew my own never deeply buried interest in a brief era that did so much to shape my own life. To those students this book is dedicated with deep appreciation. It also seeks to honor the memory of Samuel Taylor Coleridge, certainly a Sixties type before the time, whose poetry has provided strikingly appropriate epigraphs for these chapters.

Finally, I would like to thank my colleagues in the School of Religion of the University of Southern California, particularly Henry Clark and John C. Crossley, and my wife Gracia Fay, who have read portions of this manuscript and discussed them with me, making numerous very helpful suggestions. Professor Jacob Neusner of the University of South Florida kindly read the section on Judaism and made very helpful comments and suggestions. I am also grateful to Kenneth Arnold, former director of Rutgers University Press, for constant friendship, support, and good advice. I am, of course, solely responsible for the eventual contents of this book.

Abbreviations for Organizations

CALCAV	Clergy and Laity Concerned About Vietnam
COCU	Consultation on Church Union
COFO	Council of Federated Organizations
CORE	Congress of Racial Equality
FOR	Fellowship of Reconciliation
HUAC	House Un-American Activities Committee
IFIF	International Federation for Internal Freedom
IHM	Immaculate Heart of Mary (religious order)
LSD	League for Spiritual Discovery
MFDP	Mississippi Freedom Democratic Party
NAACP	National Association for the Advancement of Colored People
NCC	National Council of Churches
SCLC	Southern Christian Leadership Council
SDS	Students for a Democratic Society
SNCC	Student Nonviolent Coordinating Committee
WCC	World Council of Churches

The Sixties Spiritual Awakening

Magic Is Afoot,
War Is Prophesied:
Foundations of the Sixties

Beware! Beware!
His flashing eyes, his floating hair!
Weave a circle round him thrice

And close your eyes with holy dread,
For he on honey-dew hath fed,
And drunk the milk of Paradise.
Coleridge, "Kubla Khan"

Memories of Magic

Memories of the Sixties

I recall an evening, at the very height of the counterculture, that my wife Gracia Fay and I spent in a large ramshackle Victorian house near downtown Los Angeles. The visit had been arranged by a couple of students who were well known there. I was, back then, a fairly young historian of religion who, in 1967, had found himself suddenly warped into an amazing world where the old magic of which he wrote and taught in his dusty libraries and classrooms had exploded back to life on the streets around him in roman candles of living color. A new store near campus called the Eye of Horus sold real magic wands, and I knew people who thought nothing of spending an evening excursioning out of the body or conversing with Shiva in one of his higher heavens. It was a little frustrating that all I could do was talk about the history of the idea of Shiva. My docents caught this, sensed my fascination with our tempestuous day and its apprentice alchemists, and wanted me to see them at their best. They sent me to the old Victorian, a counterculture temple on Temple Street. (Around the same time, I also got to know a neo-Gnostic bishop who lived, appropriately, on Alexandria Street in Hollywood.)

The chief druid in this inner-city sanctuary was a celebrated "hippie astrologer" rumored to have well-placed and well-heeled Hollywood clients but now more visibly surrounded by a colony of dropouts who had crashed in the manor and made it a sort of commune. When we arrived, about a dozen of these "free people," as one insisted we should call them, were lounging in the living room. (They were mostly males; the womenfolk, as still happened in those days, were back in the kitchen fixing supper.)

The sacred spice of incense was in the air, wafting in cloudlets past magic posters giving on eternity, bright cloth-of-India hangings, Tibetan *tankas*, meditating buddhas, and many-armed escapees from the Hindu pantheon. The holy aroma was also striving, without notable success, to cover the racier fumes of marijuana.

There they were at their ease, these volunteers of the new class proudly displaying their insignia: soft, fringed leather boots, bell-bottoms, paisley shirts and ornamental vests, beads and headbands, even tinted glasses and gold-painted eyelashes. Corsairs from Xanadu they seemed, a shipload from Somewhere Else deposited on the trim republican streets of Fifties America, terrorizing the natives and subverting their young.

But here they appeared regular folk behind the exotica. They talked about regular things like cars and pets, as well as about the price and quality of certain street goods, and about various mind-blowing philosophical perceptions. A few, still in college, even talked assignments and grades.

One young man talked about nothing at all. He simply sat there, staring wide-eyed straight ahead at some beauty or terror beyond our ken. But the others took kindly care of him. He had had a bad trip, we were told.

The astrologer made his entry down the winding oak staircase a little later in the evening. He wore sandals and a stunning plain white ankle-length robe. With his long brown hair and beard, and above all his wide dark luminous eyes, he bore a striking resemblance to conventional portraits of a certain well known first-century figure. It was those eyes that held one. They were wise; they had seen visions, known ecstasy, and scanned with compassion the world's wounds. A lifetime was in them, despite his scant twenty-some years. When he spoke, one was not disappointed; his voice, as he interpreted someone's chart, was rich, caring, and resonant with long thoughts. He gave everyone who came to him a copy of the old Chinese classic, the *Tao te ching*, because he thought this was a book everybody should read. He also thought everyone should take vitamin C tablets, which he distributed free like Johnny Appleseed broadcasting seeds to frontier folk.

He was clearly an Old Soul embodied in one of those youthful magi who appeared from out of whatever depths of space and time they had reincarnated to hold sway in the deepest heart centers of the counterculture for its few years. It was as though they were envoyed to fulfill some cosmic mission that could be assayed on our planet only rarely, during a brief opening like the Sixties, after centuries of darkness. Then they vanished as mysteriously as they had come, and youth were once again just callow youth. (A little later I heard the astrologer had moved to Tucson, where he worked in an occult bookshop, but I was unable to trace him there.)

At the wizard's side as he descended the stairs was his lady companion, another pure Sixties type: incredibly young, fresh-faced, and lovely in her delicate, pink-cheeked, almost vulnerable way, with a trace in her carriage and unconscious finishing-school politesse of the moneyed background from which she had come—and dropped out. She was also earthy, saying without words that she enjoyed parties, baking wholesome whole-grain bread, and sex. She was in bare feet, squarish old-fashioned glasses, and a long-skirted lacy off-white dress, supposed to look homemade whether it was or came from a pricey each-garment-one-of-its-kind boutique. She was sweet and authentic, and I liked her a lot.

We then took dinner around a long table, the astrologer holding court at the head. Food in this house was basically a huge steady-state vegetarian stewpot—at mealtime a sufficient amount was ladled out, and in due course more water, onions, potatoes, beans, and other ingredients were tossed in. But there was also fresh bread, hearty red wine, salad, and of course magical brownies.

After dinner not much came down. It was the age of the unplanned society. Either a spontaneous happening happened, or you just kicked back and hung out. The menage dribbled down into small rap groups or solitary meditations. Gracia Fay and I talked with the astrologer about our charts and were given the *Tao te ching* of old Lao-tzu, reputedly the greatest dropout of them all. Then, sensing that as a professor and an over-thirty I could never be more than a participant observer, and neither of us wishing to be intrusive, we left.

College Days

A second memory is from the campus where I taught. It was May 1970, a moment at once the climax and the end of the Sixties, the campus uprisings after the Cambodian "incursion" announced on April 30 and the May 4 shootings at Kent State. My private California university was no Berkeley and had taken a long time to get aroused, though by '68 or '69 good-sized antiwar—or more to the point antidraft—demonstrations were reasonably common. But when Kent State hit, it was all over for everyday academics. So it was at some 30 percent of U.S. universities, disproportionately at the larger and more elite ones. Probably a million students demonstrated for the first times in their lives during May 1970.[1]

As I was trying to teach, groups of student activists rushed up and down the halls, sticking their heads in classrooms and shouting, "On strike! Shut it down!" Before long the university had effectively ceased to function, classes giving way to teach-ins and endless meetings. These went on well into the night, in the student union, in dorms, in religious centers, talking about the war and the shootings, deciding what students could and should do in this desperate national crisis. The Protestant, Catholic, and Jewish campus chaplains were busy as perhaps never before or since, attending, advising, and counseling. More than one student broke into hysteria from the supercharged tension and emotionality of the evening, particularly after (false) rumors of more campus shootings around the country came in.

It was the next morning, as I recall it, that a vast rally was held on the campus's central park. An emergent student leadership stood on the library steps facing thousands of their fellows, more people than I had ever seen there before. Needless to say, city and campus police were also present in force around the perimeters, nightsticks ready and expensive radio equipment chattering. And so were legions of reporters and television news camera people, with all their expensive equipment. Southern California's oldest university was going to be on the six o'clock news tonight.

The son of a Lutheran pastor and chief student speaker, who had taken some of our religious studies courses and was now a Students for a Democratic Society (SDS) activist, was shouting through a bullhorn. He laid out the demands—similar to those made at numerous other campuses—that the lengthy conferences of the evening before had come up with: close the university for the rest of the semester, give students their grades to date, liberate them all to work full-time against the war and the draft. They would leaflet their neighborhoods, lobby Congress members, and go to the huge May 9 demonstration in Washington.

He then, amid immense cheers of consensus, raised his hand, fist clenched, and made a dramatic personal vow never to return to normal studies or to ordinary life till peace had come. As he finished speaking, he kept his hand aloft, but in the manner of the black power salute let his head fall as though in prayer or reverie, or merely overcome by the awesomeness of the occasion.

A day or two later, the issue was decided at a big faculty-student conclave in the auditorium. After much debate, the president of the university, a highly respected personage on the verge of retirement and far from a radical, acceded to the demands, only allowing students who wished to continue classes till the end of the semester to do so. Some seventy-five other schools across the country similarly closed. My classes dwindled to perhaps a fifth of their original size. As for the other students, my hunch is that as the month of May wore on most of them spent more time on the beach or back home than in peace activism. For that matter, the leader was seen back in the classroom well before the last helicopters had left the roof of the American embassy in Saigon in 1975. But the point had been made. President Nixon was compelled by the massiveness and effectiveness of the demonstrations to declare that U.S. troops would penetrate no more than twenty-one miles into Cambodia and would all be out by July 1.[2]

In 1961 and 1962, I had been a Navy chaplain with a batallion of Marines stationed on the island of Okinawa. Though these were the opening years of the Sixties, it was still politically and spiritually the Fifties so far as I personally was concerned. In hindsight, and from the Okinawan perspective, perhaps those first two years of the Kennedy administration—though they were after Sputnik—represented a sort of apex of postwar America's power and glory.

Over there, on this insular outpost in a conquered nation, one had little sense of anything changing at home. The Officers Club, where our meals and drinks were served by smiling natives, was splendidly situated on high ground overlooking a vast panorama of barracks, rice paddies, thatched-roof villages, and the sparkling waters of the South Pacific. It was the most solid, permanent-looking building on the base. One felt this clubhouse could well have been in Kipling's India, at the heyday of another empire. Now, over cocktails on the verandah, one could hear twice-told reminiscences of the great and good war that had ended a decade and a half before, and sometimes there were uproarious drunken parties with tinsely Japanese-lantern decorations, probably unchanged since that war's end.

I returned and started graduate studies in Chicago the next year. Before the year was out news came of the young president's murder. He had said we Americans would "pay any price, bear any burden, support any friend, oppose any foe" for the sake of liberty. Though it had not been any great burden for a young bachelor, I had gone a great distance on that mission, I supposed, and for its sake heard strange tongues and watched the sun set over alien seas. I had been there, but now . . .

Where was America's mission to be found? At home or in steaming faraway jungles? On earth or on the moon? Here and now amid the muck of everyday politics, or in the eschatological coming of an Aquarian Age? And who were the true questers of this grail? Visionary dropouts, antiwar protesters, patriotic soldiers, civil rights blacks, or the "silent majority"?

There are more memories. Visiting the Roman Catholic church with friends, I worshipped at a traditional Latin mass at the beginning of the decade, and by decade's end, after Vatican II, a charismatic one in English, with guitar accompaniment, people standing informally around the altar, and the babble of glossolalia in the background. Though I am not a Roman Catholic, my devout friends virtually insisted I receive communion, as though to prove a point.

I could go on to mention encounters with Zen centers and the Hare Krishnas, a stint as faculty adviser to a campus transcendental meditation group, and chats with a student who had innocently found himself sharing a rooming house with novices in a demanding ceremonial magic order. I heard the Maharishi Mahesh Yogi of transcendental meditation speak, with his infectious giggle full of holy joy and his hair and beard hanging down like old vines, and Maharaji, the plump teenage Lord of the Universe, and a few other gurus, some good, some bad. Though I was not physically present, I saw on TV the great Washington dramas of the decade: the 1963 jobs and freedom march at which Martin Luther King made his magnificent "I Have a Dream" speech; the 1965 antiwar march; the 1967 Pentagon demonstration. And the Berkeley dramas, from Free Speech to People's Park.

Histories Sacred and Profane

I have cited Sixties activities from both the spiritual and political wings of the spectrum, though neither was conventionally so. The astrologer's house was no more an ordinary church than the demonstration was an ordinary election. I would like to suggest that, on the other hand, the two had much more in common than might appear on the surface, and that both were manifestations of a Sixties mentality. That mentality was nothing simple, but certain strong and deep features of it can be isolated and analyzed.

Understanding the Sixties mind may, in turn, lead to new ways of understanding what the Sixties were and how they shaped American life. That decade was really a time of transition between two styles of spiritual life that I shall call, not originally, modern and postmodern. This terminology intentionally connects this discussion with the thought of several recent French writers, Jean-François Lyotard, Michel Foucault, and Jacques Derrida, that I have found helpful in coming to terms with the Sixties. But first let's name some other texts.

A few histories have looked at the spiritual, or at least the psychological, Sixties in some depth: Walter Anderson in his fascinating story of Esalen, *The Upstart Spring: Esalen and the American Awakening* (1983), or Peter Clecak in *America's Quest for the Ideal Self: Dissent and Fulfillment in the 60s and 70s* (1983), or, in a backhanded sense, Steven Tipton in *Getting Saved from the Sixties* (1982). So have memoirists, whether they highlight the spiritual dimensions of the drug scene like Timothy Leary in *Flashbacks* (1983) or of music as does Charles Perry in *The Haight-Ashbury: A History* (1984).

But most so-called serious historians have seen a different Sixties than did many of the participants. Rejecting the counterculture and the hippies as a clownish sideshow, and the drug scene as an embarrassment, they have zeroed in on what appears in hindsight to have been really important, the political side of the decade's experience: the dramatic free speech, civil rights, antiwar, black power, and other protest and revolutionary movements. This has, to date, been the main thrust of books with historical perspective written ten years or more later: W. J. Rorabaugh, *Berkeley at War* (1989); Todd Gitlin, *The Sixties: Years of Hope, Days of Rage* (1987); Irving Horowitz, *Ideology and Utopia in the U.S., 1956–1976* (1977); Taylor Branch, *Parting the Waters: America in the King Years, 1954–63* (1988), Myra McPherson, *Long Time Passing: Vietnam and the Haunted Generation* (1984), and others.

Yet on the other hand, some very important books on the Sixties written *in* the Sixties, or in 1970, make it sound as though what was really going on was not political but religious or spiritual revolution. One thinks of Timothy Leary, *The Politics of Ecstasy* (1968); William Braden, *The Age of Aquarius* (1970); Lewis Yablonsky, *The Hippie Trip* (1968); Charles Reich, *The Greening of America* (1970); Theodore Roszak, *The Making of a Counter Culture* (1969); Rasa Gustaitis, *Turning On* (1969); Jacob Needleman, *The New Religions* (1970); Paul Goodman, *The New Reformation* (1970); and all those about Vatican II and the Death of God.

To these popular on-the-scene writers and prophets, the crucial current event was not the campus conflicts or the Pentagon sieges—though they might be symptoms of real revolution—but the emergence of a wholly new culture, based on a new spirituality. A new world was gestating in the Haight-Ashbury, or the nurseries of scattered remote communes, or an East-West lamasery in Colorado, or at least in the collective wombs of the old churches. Despite all appearances, the great event was the coming of the Love Generation, the Aquarian Age, or secular Christianity, and in the last analysis that eschatological event would be wrought not by street revolutionaries but by those who dropped out and turned on.

Since an Aquarian Age of love and peace seems still, unfortunately, not at hand, it is easy to dismiss this side of the Sixties and concentrate on those political struggles whose course can be traced in yellowing newspapers and newsmagazines. Failed prophets, as most of the more exuberant spiritual or eschatological Sixties writers appear to be, have few friends the morning after. Though a hint of the spiritual Sixties has resurfaced in the New Age, most of what presents around us is other than what the utopian Sixties foretold.

Instead of the Aquarian Age we got the Reagan Age, instead of secular Christianity an evangelical revival. Why not then concentrate on the civil rights movement, which did powerfully change the lives of millions of African Americans, and the antiwar movement with its somewhat more ambivalent success?

Yet the long-term impacts of spiritual movements are less easily read in the morning headlines than those of political movements. Walter H. Capps, in his thoughtful book on Vietnam, *The Unfinished War* (1982), deals with the spiritual connotations of that struggle at home and abroad for the American soul but does not treat directly of other aspects of Sixties religion. Timothy Miller, in *The Hippies and American Values: The Utopian Ethics of the Counterculture, 1965–1970* (1991), has argued that the hippie counterculture changed America more than did the ambiguous political Sixties.

The case can certainly be made that the hippies, bringing a fresh perspective on everything from dress and hair to life-style and the "sexual revolution," actually wrought more deeply seated results in some arenas than the radical (and sometimes quasi- or crypto-spiritual) politics of the decade. At the same time, it must be observed that the political side won on civil rights (if not on black power) and at least modified the terms of discussion on war, while the counterculture, though it changed many things, lost on the acceptance of visionary or recreational drugs by the general culture.

Widespread changes throughout American religion followed in the wake of the Sixties and though not always radical were certainly aftershocks from the earthquakes of that era. Phillip Hammond, in *Religion and Personal Autonomy* (1992), has made the case, to be examined a little more fully in the concluding chapter, that since the Sixties American religion has been far less a matter of traditional kinds of denominationalism and parish activity, and much more one of "personal autonomy" involving readiness to switch religions and church affiliations for subjective reasons. In short, external religious authority is widely rejected in favor of one's right to find a religion that meets one's own perceived needs—though, paradoxically but understandably, sometimes that religion of choice is conservative and demanding.

Wade Clark Roof, in *A Generation of Seekers: The Spiritual Journeys of the Baby Boom Generation* (1993), has comparably shown that the spiritual quests of people who came of age in the Sixties, though on one level dividing sharply between those who returned to some sort of orthodoxy and those who kept to the free, eclectic Sixties style, also evidence distinctive commonalities. Pluralism was "now for real"—whether one elected a conservative or radical path, religion was now "whatever one *chose* as one's own," without benefit of a hegemonic national or (very often) family tradition. Religion was also "multilayered" in belief and practice, meaning that one could, and often did, combine items from several sources in one's personal religious style. New patterns of religious community were emerging on all sides, with emphasis in practice less on doctrine than on "sharing, caring, accepting, belonging." Finally, the real value, for both conservatives and radicals, was the power of religion to effect personal transformation, a pragmatic "what works for me" approach, though often combined with a subjectivity-centered 1990s-style social and political activism. An emphasis on "open heart" and "feeling," that is, the self and its fulfillment, is very much at the center of the discussion of commitment, whether to personal or social goals. Somehow, all of this seems for Roof to connect to the boomer generation's liking of the flexible, open-ended term *spirituality*, which it frequently seems to prefer to *religion*.[3]

We will note later that Andrew Greeley found changes in post-Sixties Catholic "religious imagination" that had moved from severe and judgmental concepts of God to emphasis on divine love and forgiveness. All this was an aftereffect of the Sixties.

My contention is that the religious and political sides of the Sixties should not be set against each other so much as seen as bands in a single spectrum. Both are spiritual in that they touch on values of ultimate significance. What they have in common is much more important than what sets them apart. They can *both* be understood through categories from out of the phenomenology of religion—mythology, apocalyptic, transcendental symbols of community, and the like. We will be especially thinking here of religious features that mark times of profound social transition, for it is precisely then that nonreligious perspectives—now undergoing overhaul—are superseded by those pointing toward timeless ultimates, or so it seems to many in that day.

In America the Sixties were fundamentally a time of transition from modern to postmodern ways of thinking and being. We will look at the meaning of these terms in a moment. I propose that the story of religion, and religious consciousness, in that decade offers an indispensible key to understanding changes wrought by the Sixties in society as a whole.

Why? Because in America religion has generally been the most available language for that which is of unconditioned importance. The ultimate level of significance is especially highlighted in moments of transition from one consciousness era to another. For an era is a particular conversation, a finite province of discourse conditioned by its specific horizons, and as Nietzsche said, every age has a limit or horizon that can be seen as horizon only when it has been transcended.

The moment of transition, though, appears as a time between one horizon and the next. It is an unconditioned time, a transliminal state in which nothing but the language of unconditionality seems adequate to the task of explaining what is happening. In the American cultural milieu, deeply molded by countless religious quests, that can only be the language of religion.

Modernism and Postmodernism

Michel Foucault, a founding carpenter of the postmodern discussion, has spoken of his books as toolboxes from which one may extract what one can use. They are not finished cabinets in which everything can be put in a readymade pigeonhole. I would like to pull out of the box a postmodern jigsaw with which to cut up the spiritual Sixties, and then put them back together as a time when American religion, rather dramatically and on a large scale, made the wrenching transit from modern to postmodern modes of spiritual existence. That idea will be the harness trying to keep the bricolage of a book like this pulling in one direction.

What exactly then is meant by modernism and postmodernism? First let it be observed that one finds little consensus on the exact contours of the two blocs, or for that matter on when the modern began and when it commenced to give way to the postmodern. A case can be made that the postmodern began not in 1967, as I shall half-seriously propose, but with the Second World War, the First World War, or even in 1900.

In regard to artistic and intellectual history an early date is understandable, although I am inclined to think that such movements as surrealism, cubism, Marxism, or Freudianism, while they undercut aspects of what was meant by the modern in the nineteenth century, still express similar assumptions in a radically different and more "advanced" way. By criticizing the world modernism had made, they nonetheless gave testimony to its dominance. By advancing radically new world hypotheses, they nonetheless adhered to the modern vision of universal truth.

But when we come to American religion, surely its Fifties style represented the culmination of what it meant to be religious in a "modern" way compatible with the same in the political, economic, and educational realms—a way that was severely challenged in the Sixties. More on this in a moment.

The locus of investigation by those seeking to sort out the postmodern from the modern also varies: some savants work with science, some with literature, some with political and social phenomena. Even greater is the diversity of tone in interpretations of postmodernism. There are those who find it profoundly liberating and therefore hopeful, while others view with the bleakest pessimism the way it seems to be sucking humanity into a black hole of nihilism.

Doubtless that is as it should be. To make postmodernism into a catechism, or to apply it dogmatically as a univocal touchstone of interpretation for the Sixties or anything else, would be a grotesque contradiction in terms. For if there is any fundamental point to the whole business, it is that postmodernism means no universal truth, only various conversations, and no one right interpretation of anything, only personal perspectives. I would certainly not want to be read as presenting modernism/postmodernism as *the* interpretation of American religion in the Sixties. The dichotomy is, as I said, just a tool I am taking out of the box. It has a good blade, but it will cut some things better than others, and it may be pretty worn by the time the job is done. It affords some ways of looking at the Sixties that I think are interesting and that may be helpful in understanding not only where we were then but also where we are now. But don't hold me to believing that what follows is *true*.

Let us now advance the modernism/postmodernism argument by noting that a premier interpreter of the issue, Jean-François Lyotard, has insisted that a key definition of postmodernism is its "incredulity toward metanarratives"—grand, overarching stories by which countless lesser stories are interpreted. Surely such incredulity would mark an hour of transition between two great ages of the spirit. He identified the two great "metanarratives" of modernism as, first, the emancipation of humanity by progress, both political and scientific; and, second, the unity of knowledge in a way amenable to rational, "scientific" abstraction and technological implementation.[4]

Thus the modern university, so much a center of Sixties conflict, was founded on these metanarratives. On the other hand, knowledge (and experience) that did not fit them was excluded or marginalized. At the same time, the "modern" observer was supposed to have a privileged position from which to view the cultures of the past or of less advanced corners of the globe. From this high conning tower the observer could classify and explain their stumbling struggles toward the truth. As for nonstory ideas and concepts, like those of the sciences, Lyotard notes that despite science's notorious "conflict with narratives" all ideas and concepts are really inseparable from the stories that are used to legitimate them, those of science as well as any others.

The university was the embodiment and dispenser of the metanarrative of an expressible, universal knowledge, largely attained through progress and science, or its equivalents in "critical" humanistic studies. It was therefore the bastion or educator of modernism's elites and had a distinct prestigious role in modern societies or those striving to become modern. The serious questioning of the university and its metanarratives of general truth in the Sixties was therefore very significant for the modernism to postmodernism transition. The Sixties revolution began with civil rights, then carried over to Vietnam, then spread to religion and life-style issues when the modern elite did not seem to be doing what they were supposed to do even by modern standards.

The problem was that to those elite who best embody and perpetuate modernism's leading values, all other people are marginalized to varying degrees. The marginal comprise a much larger circle than the elite, though they are the latter's principal clients. If the elite are the business and professional classes, the marginalized are the usually more-laggard poor or various minorities; if the elite are European settlers, the marginalized are indigenes; if the elite are those well-enough trained to use advanced technologies, the marginalized are those who must depend on the expertise of others; if the elite are military officers and the bureaucratic planners and rationalizers of war, the marginalized are the conscript troops who fight it. But the modern elite were supposed to make life better for everyone by making everyone more like themselves in all essentials. The moment they seemed more concerned instead with their own power and privilege as the elite, incredulity toward their stories could set in.

In a word, the epitome of modernism was unity: unity of truth, unity of self, unity of words and meaning, a unified state, a view of history as unitary and moving in one direction, relative conformity in the way of life and the views of those who count. In the modern period languages became more standardized, economies more integrated; elites around the world increasingly dressed the same (in coat and tie rather than a colorful array of native garb) and talked in the same way about "development." In fact, the ideal modern unitary state also often required symbols beyond bureaucracy of its unity and authority, the king or the strongman.

Furthermore, as we have seen, in the United States and apparently also in the Soviet Union, the military draft, in some sense the logical ultimate extension of the modernist dream of a planned society and a unitary state, has been the "over the top" expression of modernism that turned significant numbers against it, arousing in them "incredulity toward metanarratives," at least those that have legitimated putting them in a position of armed servitude. That was certainly the case in the Sixties in the United States. For a mass army, especially an involuntary one, is the epitome of that most provocatively self-contradictory aspect of modernism, elite control in the face of professed democratic ideals. In modernism the bureaucratic and military elite necessary to maintain progress and the requisite social control are typically idealized as dedicated, well trained, and at the cutting edge of a better world—the brightest and the best. But the conscription called for to feed its military side drew lightning in the Sixties; with it an unflattering light, leading to incredulity, was cast on the broader metanarratives of modernity as well.

Postmodernism has meant the breakdown of all kinds of unities, starting with that of the self; it has meant the discovery of half-forgotten identities submerged by modernist ways of being. In Japan and the former Soviet Union, for example, one may note a revived interest in unique local, even village, traditions once suppressed for the sake of the modern. In the United States and elsewhere, once marginalized groups, from Native Americans to gays, are seeking equality in a society that no longer has to have a dominant elite on the leading edge of progress. New—and far more intricate—boundaries are being cut.

"Incredulity" toward the "metanarratives" that had sustained religion along with the reigning political and scientific paradigms up through the 1950s was thus distinctly on the rise in the Sixties. It took many guises and not seldom brought forth polarized articulations, from extreme Right to extreme Left, from radical traditionalism to radical utopianism. At times Sixties causes seemed on the surface to be perpetuating myths of modernism, such as those of the Marxist left

13

or the conservative anti-Communist right. But increasingly, differences betrayed the old narratives, building them toward critical mass, finally shattering them and revealing the embryo of something new. The mood was therefore religious—revivalistic, apocalyptic, nostalgic for paradise.

I would now like to lay out my own modernism-postmodernism chart. Bear in mind that this table is not about postmodernism in the Sixties but at greater maturity in the Nineties. The entries do not therefore directly reflect the way postmodernism appeared at its first glimmerings, but after its defining features had moved above the horizon: the collapse of Marxism and the end of the Cold War, virulently resurgent nationalism, and a world population racing toward six billion, much of it on the edge of famine or beyond. But one cannot move from left to right on this chart without thinking of the Sixties, when one typically first saw the entry in the left-hand column in extreme silhouette, and behind it the dawning light of what lies opposite on the right.

Modern	Postmodern
Rationalistic science	Alienation from objective knowledge; uncertainty principle; chaos theory
Psychologies of the self as a single ego with a true nature or identity beneath its several roles	The self as plural, moving freely among a number of independent identities
Technology	Ecology
Ideal of progress	Pessimism about future
Ideal of social justice	Pluralization of society into fragments; declining sense of common identity or goals
Large unitary states based on ideology or sense of national purpose, often supported by large standing armies and draft	Breakup of empires; rise of societies rooted in nationalism or localism
Ideal of universal public education	Ideal of universal public education under pressure from pluralism and democracy
Linear media: reading, books, public libraries	Visual, episodic multimedia: videos, computerization
Ideal of universal public health	Pluralism of healing methods and economic constraints

Modern	Postmodern
Liberal and conservative politics	New alignments
Large corporations and state economic planning based on consumerism, assumption of growing affluence	Economies of technology plus cheap labor; growing gulf between rich and poor
Belief in universal, general truths, usually capable of abstract or scientific statement	Skepticism; tendency toward relative or personal truths

Religion Modern and Postmodern

Now what of religion and modernism/postmodernism? First we must observe that religion, or more to the point the great institutional founder religions, is the ultimate forebear of modernism. The founder religions—Confucianism, Buddhism, Christianity, and Islam, and the Judaism out of which the last two branch—are religions of history and of the written word. They are thus of a piece with the metanarratives of progress and of universal truth, for they presume that time can and will be a venue for the progressive spread of truth and right living, and that truth can be put into universally valid verbal form.

This is not surprising, for the founder religions emerged in a time of the discovery of history, or rather in a time when we discovered that we live in historical time—what Karl Jaspers called the "Axial Age."[5] This was the discovery that the onrushing stream of time is irreversible; things change and do not change back. The realization was certainly related to the invention of writing, which made possible chronicle as well as myth. The founder religions were like counterfoils to Mircea Eliade's "terror of history"—the fear of living in open-ended time in which anything could happen and whose end, if it had one, was impenetrable by ordinary means. These religions, in brief, made history meaningful by offering a central pivot—the coming of the founder with plenary revelation—in the midst of its stream, a moment in which "the hopes and fears of all the years are met."

The historical founder faiths made individual life meaningful by providing the model of an ideal spiritual person living in the midst of history, and also by offering with new emphasis individual judgment and individual salvation—concomitants of new emphasis on the individual in an increasingly complex world. By greatly heightening emphasis on the religious self—personal salvation, personal karma, personal devotional feeling, and moral values held even against the

15

world and to the point of martyrdom—they reinforced the notion of the self, now the soul, as an independent entity with a true nature that would be weighed in the balance, as over against the protean polytheistic self or tribal self. They thereby laid the foundation for ego psychology of the modern sort. (Even Buddhism, though theoretically denying separate selfhood, managed also to reinforce it with its emphasis on individual asceticism, karma, and responsibility.) They usually looked toward a far-off eschatological—or near-at-hand apocalyptic—end of history, replete with individual judgment. And they made the idea of truth meaningful by offering the written word, written scriptures containing universal truths, which one was supposed personally to read, know, and believe.

The great religions, then, came into the world as religions of historical meaning, personal life, and universal truth. They were born of history, unlike the timeless cosmic religions that referred back to mythic time. Soon enough they became religions with a historical mission: to disseminate themselves and their paradigms of human life. Finally they became religions with a history, their own metanarratives legitimating themselves with exemplary stories of martyrs, saints, and triumphs, painting their histories as all in all a tale of progress and portraying their institutions as archetypes of unity and the unitary state.

But if the great religions were the prototypes of modernism, they also early on began to sense the tremors of its dissolution. Like all human institutions—if possible, even more than most—a great religion is a house of words. It depends on a unifying language that resonates with the inner experience and institutional needs of its adherents. But words and sentences, like organisms, can become exhausted. By making the religion's original revelation historical, words make it distanced in time. Though the faith may have a grand narrative telling how we got from then to now, what happened "then" is nonetheless only a mediated experience. In Paul Ricoeur's phrase, the "immediacy of belief" is "irremediably lost"; the "primitive naïveté" is forever gone, and we can at best only "aim at a second naïveté in and through criticism."[6] Indeed, it finally dawns upon the learned of the religion that words themselves fictionalize, a point that can also be made about the modern universal knowledge ideal.

What the historical words of a metanarrative of a religion create is not the past but a separate reality, which for that reason may have great power but is not the same as a literal past. That this allure is constructed of an Indra's net of words will sooner or later come through to those who approach the tradition mainly in terms of words. The coming of this observation is the faith's own foredoomed nemesis; though its dark advent may wait centuries or millennia, it is embedded in the religon's own operating premises from the beginning, like hidden canker eggs whose spawn will eventually devour their host. A great religion, born of the discovery of history and knowing human life as historical existence—witnessed to by narratives and institutions—likewise *dies* in history, the cause of death the engorgement of too much historical time and exposure to historical awareness. In the meantime, though, the great religions interacted with great cultures.

Religion as ally of culture was, for long, enough to enable religion to survive and even flourish in the modern world. Whether or not it still could claim unmediated truth, so long as it lived in symbiosis with the great, seemingly stable institutions of modernity it shared their life in abundant measure—the unitary state, the great corporation, universal education, and health care. Religion did this in the most flattering way possible, by imitation in its denominations and parishes of modernism's large-scale unitary structures and elite professionalism. Except for marginalized sectarians, modern religion did not attack the university or the hospital head-on but placed chaplaincies on their boundaries.

Modern religion, then, set itself up as a parallel institution to the modern state, university, hospital, and the like, it was hoped with no hint of inferiority. In the United States, a denominational society, the great denominations were in effect unitary states within a unitary state, with local centers as outposts of a headquarters, each parish retailing the denomination's own version of universal truth. Many churches established universities, schools, and hospitals in parallelism with the state.

But, as we shall see, in the Sixties many denominations began seriously to be decentralized and such ambitious institutions laicized or abandoned, as religion found new foci in localism, or in social or partisan rather than denominational causes.

Perhaps it is worth an aside to note that the overthrow of those mighty institutions was not by comparable forces so much as by powers that seemed small and weak at first. In each age, one can see contrary motifs that are, or may be, precursors of the next, like those small furry mammals that ran around the feet of the dinosaurs in their hour of triumph; if it were not so, nothing would ever change.

Such a mammal in the heyday of modernism was G. K. Chesterton. He wrote in 1905, "It is not fashionable to say much nowadays of the advantages of the small community. We are told that we must go in for large empires and large ideas. There is one advantage, however, in the small state, the city, or the village, which only the wilfully blind can overlook. . . . In a large community we can choose our companions. In a small community our companions are chosen for us."[7] As we shall see, Harvey Cox, in the late modern mode of his *Secular City*, celebrated the great modern city for precisely the freedom of its anonymity and the choice of associates it permits. But Chesterton noted that when people are free to choose their companions they choose those like themselves, and so "a big society is a society for the promotion of narrowness," while a small natural one forces one to be as catholic as the real world in one's associates.

Similarly Herbert Marcuse, that Sixties icon who was probably voguishly overappreciated then and has been underappreciated since, observed the deceptive nature of most of modernism's vaunted democratic freedoms, as we shall note later. He limned the subtle but compelling ways modern societies, with their omnipresent media and models, contrive to bring most individuals—of their own free will, as they think—into conformity with the norms promoted by the economic and cultural elite, and above all by technological "progress" as a blind, self-perpetuating force. The only hope, he said, is again in the small—in those minorities, rebels, bohemians, seemingly so oppressed or marginal as to be bypassed by the juggernaut, but who for that reason have not bowed the knee to the new Baal and so provide a source for new growth. In the Sixties that countercommunity commenced to achieve significant proportions, find a voice, and construct postmodern pluralism—even as, in the Vietnam War and all its works, the modernist steamroller appeared first to be overachieving and then began to rattle. Noon is born at midnight.

Symbols, Gestures, and Communities of Light and Darkness

Now we may look at some of the quasi-religious ways the modern to postmodern transition played out in Sixties America. The first thing to come to mind is the extraordinary importance of symbols, gestures, and the roles they demarcate for Sixties actors. This is characteristic of such times of major transition. People said who they were, and were defined by, dress and hair—hence the remarkable importance attached to whether the former was hip or straight, the latter long or short. The great demonstrations for civil rights or against the war and the draft took on a quality that was almost liturgical in their ultimate, climactic use of charged symbols to sum up in a moment what might take an hour to explain in a teach-in. One still almost hears the litanylike chants and slogans and sees the Birmingham "Children's Crusade," the candlelight vigils, the raised fists, the street processions, the theatrical blockings of munitions trains and recruitment centers.

It was G. K. Chesterton who also once remarked that America was "a nation with the soul of the church," and if so the churchly part of it was still very much alive in the 1960s. It was a time of religious discovery and change as well as police dogs and change. Even at their scruffiest the Sixties seemed to be taking place in an invisible cathedral. For all the talk of secularity, the Sixties still belonged to the Age of Faith, which lingered long in America. The Sixties did not so much secularize the sacred as sacralize the secular, turning its causes into crusades and its activism into liturgies, with their initiatory ordeals and their benedictions at the end. Its dropouts were monks and nuns, complete with habit and reverse tonsure (though, it may be, friars as much of the flesh as the spirit), and they knew no dearth of sacraments and sacramentals.

Add to this the spiritual visionary aspect of psychedelic drugs, and the related apertures to occult and Eastern spiritualities. No less important were the great changes in the Roman Catholic church, and the rise of radical social activism in several traditions. As different as these are, they have in common a sense of the importance of religious vision, and an instinctive awareness that ultimate values and the issues to which they relate are religious, so must be expressed in a religious way.

That is, they work through language and gestures that take a set form because they are codes, or condensed symbols, for large ranges of experience and meaning. A sit-in, a beard, a psychedelic poster, or the peace sign declaimed, in a particularly sharp and clear way for those who got the code, a stance toward the world and feelings to go with it. Getting the code made a community out of those who shared the secret. So it was that the psychedelic experience created communities of people defined by dress and jargon, and that the changes in Catholic consciousness effected by Vatican II would have been lost without corresponding dramatic changes in the way mass was celebrated in the ordinary parish.

Of equal interest is the way in which even the secular wing of the Sixties placed the same virtually religious emphasis on symbol, gesture, language, and community. The whole, in other words, amounted to a new spiritual awakening, certainly worthy of compare with the colonial Great Awakening, the frontier revivals, or the Spiritualist vogue of the 1850s, perhaps closest of all in its combination of radically new and experiential religion and utopian vision, against the familiar backdrop of a nation increasingly polarized over race and war.

Yet nothing has been quite like the traumatic and epoch-making decade of the 1960s. It wrought immense changes in social and political life, but perhaps on a profound level nowhere was the change greater than in religious life, or more precisely in the way religious paradigms were shifted, redirected, and recharged in both formally religious settings and in nominally secular ones. Sixties folk seemed strongly impelled to create and to symbolically define (through such means as dress and hair) communities that were essentially the "children of light" engaged in apocalyptic war against the "children of darkness." This passion for bifurcation matches a basic modern characteristic, the yearning to see issues in dualistic, polar terms—old versus new, truth versus superstition, and the like—the flip side of the ideals of progress and the unity of knowledge.

The great division model may be tracked back to the Cold War image of communism versus "Americanism," the Second World War model of freedom versus fascism, or—and this is not to be minimized—lingering internal U.S. attitudes going back a hundred years to the passions and righteous absolutes of the antislavery and Civil War struggles. But in the Sixties, the original model was the "natural" African American community of the early decade's civil rights movement set against such opponents as "Bull" Connor, Ross Barnett, and George Wallace; this natural community of children of light was easily transferred to symbolically constructed intentional communities of light in the antiwar movement, the counterculture, or communalism.

In these Aquarian Age eschatological battles combatants put great store in quasi-magical media of change: chanted rhetoric, demonstrations, symbols, liturgical reform, rejection of materialism, the power of will. The Love Generation people emphasized the sacred importance of music—with dance, probably the oldest means of religious expression—of visionary and mystical experience, of art that spoke to the spirit as well as to the eye.

But the Sixties finally ended up with so much pluralism that dualism was defeated. This triumph of pluralism was evident by around 1970, when the Sixties causes and campaigns based on a dualistic, light-versus-darkness vision of the world seemed suddenly to dissipate. Something else was in the air instead, what we like others have called postmodernism. But perhaps postmodernism means, in Jean Gebser's phrase, a "world without opposites." It may be, as John W. Murphy insists, that dualism spawned dehumanization, and this prompted the move toward postmodernism.[8] Certainly, in very practical terms, the Sixties charge that the (modern) system was dehumanized was a major postmodern wedge. The desire of the back-to-nature wing of the Sixties to live without opposites was a foundation of postmodern ecological criticism of exploitative models of the human relationship with nature. But at the same time, the lack of dualism—or to put it more bluntly, the lack of a clearly defined enemy—has weakened postmodernism as a force; whatever it says becomes muffled amid the endless liquid ripples of private opinions in pluralistic puddles. (Arnold Toynbee once remarked that American audiences to whom he spoke in Cold War days became glum when he mentioned the gulf between the Communist powers Russia and China, as though they really yearned for a single monolithic enemy.)

On its most profound level, the postmodern world without opposites, but rather of many oblique facets, is internal. The modern tendency to see the world in terms of dualism and polarization was one side of a mutual objectification process; the other side was seeing the self as a single ego with a beginning, a single personal narrative history (such as that uncovered by psychoanalysis), and a single true nature—one's real self, "who I really am," beneath all the roles and acquired attitudes one carries around. This was an assumption underlying virtually all the modern psychologies and concepts of self, despite their kaleidoscopic variety, from the classic "faculties" psychology and the Victorian notion of "character" to Freudianism and Jungianism. The world is polarized because the self is a single solid entity set against the world of challenges and stimuli; some things out there are congruous with it, and some are not.

But now postmodern psychology like that of James Hillman tells us we are in fact legion, different identities following each other, that we consort with many polytheistic gods day after day with none more real or true than any other. We become Robert J. Lifton's "Protean Man," whose life-style is "characterized by an interminable series of experiments and explorations—some shallow, some profound—each of which may be readily abandoned in favor of still new psychological quests." Or we are Orr and Nicholson's "expansive man," who views the self as process created out of a series of experiences and is eclectic, drawing experiences from things new and old with casual freedom.[9] The best we can do is animate and enjoy each in its time, and not let them get in each other's way. The spiritual histories of many Sixties, not to mention postmodern Seventies, people through a long series of political and religious experiments bears that out. I can recall talking with students in those days who, before they were twenty-one, had been into five or six radically different faiths, from Catholicism to

Scientology or witchcraft. Sometimes, with a true postmodern triumph of experience over logical consistency, they were able to do all at once.

What Happened in the Sixties?

What happened in the Sixties then? At first, the Sixties were like an ultimate expression of modernism. There was an accelerating drive to complete the progressive agenda. Civil rights, Great Society and even the Vietnam War were seen as expressing a "universal" commitment to American-style democracy. The modernist scientific agenda was displayed in the no less significant race, at fabulous expense, for the moon. John F. Kennedy and Martin Luther King were the essence of progressivist schoolbook history centered on great men or heroes devoted to high ideals. The mainline churches were largely synchronized with this drive, an avant garde carrying it to the extreme of secular theology and the Death of God theology; the Roman Catholics pursued their own version of modernization at Vatican II.

Then cracks began to appear in those modernist dreams. An absolutely fundamental feature of modernism, as we have seen—long a strength but in the end a fatal flaw—is that it requires an elite vanguard that most completely fulfills its requisites for education, scientific/technological expertise, and the management of a complex unitary state, marginalizing many other people in terms of where the action is, and where the rewards are. When modernism has sufficiently advanced that these others are aware of the discrepancies and are not content to be merely in awe of their betters, trouble is afoot.

That trouble started in the Sixties when blacks and their numerous white sympathizers, fully awakened, began to require progress faster than the modern machine could grind it out. A little later the modern democratic ideal found itself at violent odds with the modern unitary state ideal over Vietnam and soon enough, the tension unsustainable, began shifting into postmodern pluralism and privatization. The same transition came more or less simultaneously in several other less immediately conspicuous but significant shifts: the decline of reading in favor of other media, moves from industrial to postindustrial modes of work and production.

Sixties Themes

These preliminaries suggest motifs we will be looking for as we trace the religious life of the Sixties decade; we need now to begin listing some ways in which they will emerge. Here are some Sixties themes to be explored in this book, starting with those of late afternoon modernism.

The Myth of American Uniqueness

The Sixties tacitly accepted the post–World War II and Cold War–era assumptions that the United States was a nation uniquely powerful, uniquely affluent, and possessed of a uniquely moralistic heritage and self-image; it was therefore uniquely capable of radical good or evil—a rampant example of modernist dualism, dehumanizing and virilely empowering. In the context of this society, therefore, issues were easily seen in Manichaean, light-versus-darkness terms; though the Cold War dualism might be turned on its head, the model was not so easily abandoned. John H. Redekop, writing about the American far right in the Sixties, commented:

> Perhaps it is correct to say that the United States sprouted more Rightism, and more Far Rightists, simply because more Americans, compared to Britishers, Frenchmen, or Canadians, project morality into foreign affairs, promote ideological crusades, and actually possess more of an ideological commitment. Let us remember that fundamentalism was, and still is, largely an American phenomenon, and that no other democratic nation has developed a notion paralleling the concepts of Americanism and un-Americanism. No other nation seems to have infused its patriotism and nationalism with so much moral righteousness, and none has been quite as ready to label a purely power-political venture as an "ideological crusade."[10]

Although the specifics of this statement are now partially dated, they offer a valuable Sixties perception. The fundamentalistic moralizing and crusade mentality were conspicuously visible on all hands. The American far left, especially the "New Left" as it emerged in the Sixties maelstrom of civil rights and antiwar activism, came very close to reverse-mirroring those sentiments at the opposite extreme. America was either the best or the worst; either the proud, triumphantly screaming eagle of those with "Love It or Leave It" bumper stickers and flags on their hardhats; or the fascist, imperialist "Amerika" of those who chanted "Ho, Ho, Ho Chi Minh" and burned draft cards. Or so it seemed, though undoubtedly real "quiet Americans" in their millions were somewhere in between.

Then there was American affluence. The underlying premise of John Kenneth Galbraith's much-discussed Fifties book, *The Affluent Society*, that more people were making more money than ever before, was generally accepted.[11] In the Sixties the United States still seemed conspicuously wealthier than Japan, Europe, or virtually anywhere else, and the much-vaunted American standard of living was still talked about, even though the poverty line—demarcating millions who hardly shared it—was also in the news, and the gap with other First World countries was beginning to close. But affluence is as much a state of mind as anything else, and in the Sixties, despite all the troubles, real wages and profits were going up, and prosperity was in the air as universities expanded and freeways elongated. But whether this affluence was divine blessing on a righteous nation or ill-gotten loot was another gods and demons issue. Affluence in the secular city meant that all things were possible, all could be made new, material-ism (paradoxically) shucked in favor of more humane values. It also meant wealth for war, and coin in the coffers of those sucking the lifeblood of the Third World.

Mario Savio, leader of the Berkeley free speech movement, noted that for his elders the America that had been won in the epic victory of 1945 was the way America should be for all time. There was noth-ing left to do postwar but enjoy the American way of life amidst ever-expanding affluence and freedom, while of course fending off the Red enemy that lusted to destroy all this. Savio then assessed the situation for Sixties youth aptly by indicating that for this new, huge, and restless generation just plucking the fruits in their fathers' gardens was not enough. "I'm tired of reading history," he added. "Now I want to make it."

It is important to realize that, in the world of the early Sixties particularly, so differently from the later Sixties, liberal Democrats— heirs of the Roosevelt-Truman economic and military triumphs and inclined to see the new world they had made in rosy terms—most epitomized the elders' quintessentially modern mentality. People com-fortable with power, they believed in big government and big educa-tion, trusting these two together could solve any remaining problems through bureaucratic programs while keeping big business adequately regulated. Afraid of neither large budgets nor the outside world, they favored more military spending than did Eisenhower and tempera-mentally were activist and internationalist in foreign affairs. Any dis-sent from the best of all pragmatically possible worlds they perceived around them was virtually incomprehensible.

Among them were Clark Kerr, the mild-appearing Quaker who as president of the California "multiversity" the first half of the decade was the uncomprehending nemesis of Berkeley's free speech move-ment and other tumultuous, disruptive causes; Pat Brown, governor of California the same years; perhaps John F. Kennedy; certainly Lyndon Johnson. Walter Capps records how Lyndon Johnson, the erstwhile

New Deal Democrat, explained the vision behind the disastrous Vietnam War in precisely such terms, saying of the Vietnamese:

> The task is nothing less than to enrich the hopes and existence of more than a hundred million people. And there is much to be done.
>
> The vast Mekong River can provide food and water on a scale to dwarf even our own TVA [Tennessee Valley Authority].
>
> For centuries, nations have struggled among each other. But we dream of a world where disputes are settled by law and reason. And we will try to make it so.[12]

This was to justify what turned out to be interminable war!

Some radicals, like Savio, preferred honest conservatives to such—as they saw them—complacent and compromising liberals. "The reason why liberals don't understand us," he said, "is because they don't realize there is evil in the world."[13]

The New Community

As it moved gingerly toward postmodern pluralism without opposites, the Sixties in its several natural communities—the young, blacks, students—and in its intentional communities had a strong community-creating drive. These modern to postmodern transitional sets of communities were often apocalyptic and polarity-minded groups that strongly delineated the good from the bad, the children of light from the children of darkness, whether in terms of age, class, life-style, shared goals, or shared experiences like drug-induced visions and rock music. Communities were defined by clear symbols of identity and separation in clothes, hairstyles, life-styles, common "in" language and rhetoric, sometimes place of residence.

The natural community of the new awareness was only now rising, like some sunken Atlantis, out of a prosaic sea. One of its major voices was the *San Francisco Oracle*, published to serve the Haight-Ashbury–based counterculture community there from late 1966 until early 1968. Here is something from it on that emergence:

> Dick Alpert keeps assuring us that the conscious Community is, like the iceberg, mostly submerged. There exists, we are told, a great number of conscious, turned-on, and enlightened people hidden beneath the waves of anonymity on the Great Bourgeois Sea. If this is so . . . there remains the big job of opening up lines of community between the enlightened members of the American Middle-Class and the open subcultural communities.[14]

To demonstrate how the emergence of the submerged becomes intentional and symbol finding, here are the *Oracle* words of Allen Ginsberg:

What can the young do with themselves faced with this American version of the planet? The most sensitive among the "best minds" do drop out. They wander over the body of the nation looking into the faces of their elders, they wear long Adamic hair and form Keristan communities in the slums, they pilgrimage to Big Sur and live naked in forests seeking natural vision and meditation, they dwell in the Lower East Side as if it were an hermetic forest. And they assemble thousands together as they have done this year in Golden Gate Park, San Francisco, or Thompkins [sic] Park in New York to manifest their peaceableness in demonstrations of Fantasy and transcend protest against—or for—the hostilities of Vietnam. Young men and women in speckled clothes, minstrel's garb, jester's robes carrying balloons, signs, "President Johnson we are praying for you," gathered chanting Hindu and Buddhist mantras to calm their fellow citizens who are otherwise entrapped in a planetary barroom brawl.[15]

The new community, in Ginsberg's eyes, defined itself not only by being prophetic in the biblical sense, thus linking its causes to the moralism in the American Puritan heritage, but also by flaunting exotic religion and highly visible tokens of playful fantasy, gestures clearly intended to go against the grain of righteousness past and bespeak all things made new.

The Power of the Weak

Within the newly defined communities, and in the new generation's vision of society as a whole, traditional hierarchical structures were under much pressure to give way to more collegial kinds of management. That move represented the breakdown of the modernist bureaucratic ideal based on the model of the unitary state, which in turn is what it is because it assumes a universal truth and a universal human nature, comparable to rational or scientific truth. This was evident in the Roman Catholic church after Vatican II, in the university after student insistence on participation in decision making, in new less-patriarchal styles of family life, in the breakdown of party discipline in government, in the emergent or collective leadership of many new communes or movements. Although this change was occasionally deceptive, for spontaneous, charismatic, or group leadership can become as authoritarian as any other, changes of consciousness—in expectations as to what leadership ought to be and how human beings ought to relate in making decisions—were real as real estate.

No small part of the new inversion of hierarchy was the affirmation of the power of the weak, the marginal, and the eternally young who, like Peter Pan, have their own magic. The power of such is a continual theme of religion. Time and again it is the David who defeats the mighty, it is the despised by whose stripes we are healed, it is the beggar and the outcast who are discovered to be gods incognito.

All the liminal roles of weakness, dropout, and child came together in the counterculture. Its power lay in the reversal of the ordinary, modernist, structural symbols of power; it employed instead symbols of what Victor Turner has called *communitas*, the nonstructural, nonhierarchical I-Thou sort of relationship that lies at one pole of the human social dream.[16]

The Power of Magic

The Sixties made extraordinary use of symbolic "magical" means to articulate worldviews and achieve goals, as the preceding should make clear. Magic is in obvious reaction to scientific, progressive modernism, for which all such things are superstition. But now they come back as condensed symbols and also as tokens of another world behind and beyond the modern. From Panhandle Park to the capital, from right-wing "patriots" to protesters, from Vietnam and its rhetoric to the Aquarian Age, it was a great era for the manipulation of symbols before the eyes and the ears. It was indeed a time of magic, if by that we mean the use of nonrational means toward this-worldly ends. The decade's love-ins, demonstrations, chants, peace symbols, assassinations, psychedelic art, and Berkeley street battles—like its flag-waving and shows of force over Hanoi—all seem eager to assert the persuasive power of dreamlike free association or raw tribal emotion over cool reason and, like all magic, want to affirm the ability of will forcefully expressed to prevail over stubborn realities. Rock music was a part of the magic making the new order. The *Oracle* told us "that rock is a vital agent in breaking down absolute & arbitrary distinctions" and warned the world "that today's teenyboppers will be voting tomorrow and running for office the day after."[17]

The Clarification of Archetypes

The Sixties were also a time of the clarification of archetypes. A period of transition from one horizon to another will inevitably be one in which archetypal images, like the condensed symbols that are the essence of magic, stand out against a mottled sky. By archetypes I mean, in a quasi-Jungian sense, identities that clearly relate to standard mythical or stereotypical roles, though they may be presented with a twist that makes them rebellious and seemingly marginalized actors. The Student Radical, the Soldier, the Rock Star, the "Traveler" to Katmandu, the Hippie defied modernist concepts of what an elite ought to look like, instead provocatively exalting the marginal and individualistic. But these identities were also potent on the archetypal level, subtly becoming also Prometheus, Achilles, Orpheus, Odysseus, or Dionysus.

The Celebration of Childhood

The Peter Pan aspect of the Sixties mentality seemed to want to perpetuate childhood, or to enact some adult role as perceived by children, and perhaps more subtly to preserve or rediscover the easy pluralistic selfhood thought to be enjoyed by children in their moods and games. This is obviously related to the characteristic adolescent waver between child and adult self-images and roles. Thus many Sixties styles: short childish dresses or sailor suits like boys used to wear, "wise woman" granny dresses, dress-up soldier or pioneer outfits, or psychedelic visions in sartorial form. No doubt these self-presentations are connected with magical ways of thinking and acting, which some would categorize—perhaps with too much mock maturity—as childish. Certainly they are related to the generation's self-perception as a new culture comprised of those under thirty and not afraid to maintain childhood innocence and primal wisdom. They were not seldom connected to the desire to reverse the myth of progress and find equal immediacy of access to the distant and the past.

Perhaps the Peter Pan aspect was related as well to the counterculture's love of synaesthesia and multisensory perception, since that recalls young children's modes of experiencing the world, their need to touch, sniff, taste, and make a noise with the block as well as look at it. Chester Anderson, following McLuhan, tells us in the *Oracle*: "Synthesis & synaesthesia; non-typographic, non-linear, basically mosaic & mythic modes of perception; involvement of the whole sensorium; roles instead of jobs; participation in depth; extended awareness; preoccupation with textures, with tactility, with multisensory experiences—put 'em all together & you have a weekend on Haight Street."[18]

Pluralistic Modes of Being

The Sixties were an age of the opening up of pluralistic and protean modes of being and of life-styles. The *Oracle* described the Human Be-In in Golden Gate Park, January 14, 1967, in characteristically grandiose terms as "a gathering of the tribes" that would reflect the new vision:

> Now in the evolving generation of America's young the humanization of the American man and woman can begin in joy and embrace without fear, dogma, suspicion, or dialectical righteousness. A new concert of human relations being developed within the youthful un-

derground must emerge, become conscious, and be shared so that a
revolution of form can be filled with a Renaissance of compassion,
awareness, and love in the Revelation of the unity of mankind. The
Human Be-In is the joyful, face-to-face beginning of the new epoch.[19]

Heretofore even utopias had been perceived as monochrome, the
slaves of a single vision of absolute perfection. But now it seemed
there could be many subcultures or countercultures with varying values and symbols. But in the end most Sixties factions were less willing than their ideological forebears to live only in a realm of
disembodied doctrine or permanent division, and they happily or
grudgingly came to terms with a new America of postmodern pluralism far less segregated by race, class, or gender than before, and far
more accommodating to pluralism; even political reaction after 1968
has not seriously threatened the permanence of change on these fronts.

The Human vs. the System

A major Sixties theme was the human against the System, or the
Establishment. This theme is obviously postmodern in that the System inevitably meant what was created by modern ideals of unity,
rationalization, and scientific/technological progress—all of which were
now seen, as in Vietnam, as having become a mechanical monster out
of all human control. It is usually argued that the cultural/political
Sixties really started to come together with the free speech movement
in Berkeley, essentially a student protest against the authoritarianism
and impersonality of a mass university. As Mario Savio, the movement's
most articulate spokesperson, put it in a dramatic contrast of steel and
human flesh:

> There is a time when the operation of the machine becomes so odi-
> ous, makes you so sick at heart, that you can't take part; you can't
> even passively take part, and you've got to put your bodies upon the
> gears and upon the wheels, upon the levers, upon all the apparatus
> and you've got to make it stop. And you've got to indicate to the
> people who run it, to the people that own it, that unless you're free,
> the machines will be prevented from working at all.[20]

Important wings of the counterculture went on to protest corporations, computerization, technology, and the world they made. Certainly there was a fascination with and idealization of primitive ways
of life. Allen Ginsberg tells us in the *Oracle* that

> Among the young we find a new breed of White Indians in California
> communing with illuminated desert redskins; we find our teenagers
> dancing Nigerian Yoruba dances & entering trance states to the electric

29

vibration of the Beatles who have borrowed shamanism from Afric sources. . . . All the available traditions of U.S. Indian vision-quest, peyote ritual, dancing, Oriental pranayama, east Indian ear music are becoming available to the U.S. unconscious through the spiritual search of the young.[21]

Nothing is harder to assess a generation later than this Sixties facet. Alan Watts, at the famous Houseboat Summit that brought him together with Snyder, Ginsberg, and Timothy Leary in February 1967, opened by saying that "the whole problem is whether to drop out or take over," but in the end the Sixties generation did not quite do either.[22] At the same time, the Sixties maelstrom did spin off ecology and concern for the Third World, and even corporations—like universities—are said now to be more flexible about human beings than they once were. But though the Sixties brought about the final capitulation of such hated subsystems as Jim Crow and later the draft, the decade brought no major establishment to its knees as later happened, say, in Eastern Europe in 1989. Like most millenarian movements, after the initial failure of the world to fall before its Jericho trumpets, it transferred a large part of its energies to personal salvation and "working within the System" instead. This it may still be doing.

Politics as Shamanism and Magic

The Sixties were preeminently a time of social ideas, though these ranged from modernist dualistic to transitional shamanistic-mystical to postmodern mellow. Often these ideas were deeply dyed with psychological thought; it was also an age of various kinds of psychoanalytic interpretations of political and social processes. Social psychology or psychohistory provided vehicles for linking the world to the subjective sources of meaning that are so important when all else is crumbling. One view of this process was expressed in the Sixties by Paul A. Robinson, summarizing the position of the Freudian anthropologist Géza Róheim:

> For Róheim, politics was a kind of black magic. The political leader, far from being descended from the gods (as in traditional hierarchical theory), had risen from the depths of hell. The politician was the modern descendant of the sorcerer, and political science, therefore, was most accurately treated as a branch of demonology.[23]

One will never truly understand the politics and metapolitics of the Sixties unless one can approach it as a kind of shamanism or sorcery, if not a branch of demonology. It was sometimes a benign sorcery like that of those early biblical prophets still close to their ancestry in the maven and the mutterer, less concerned with writing than with signs and summonses. But, for all that, its best practicioners were wizards casting spells, not politicians counting votes. That is to say, they were manipulators of images, even when, among the righteous, what was practiced was the politics of the Holy Ghost rather than of demons or of ordinary sinners.

The use of a psychoanalytic thinker like Róheim to cast light on the Sixties is not inappropriate. The decade itself thought in such terms much more than any since. Norman O. Brown and Herbert Marcuse were among the fashionable intellectuals, and however far they tortured their theories away from classical Freudianism, they were in the psychoanalytic tradition. Though Brown might call for the "resurrection of the body" to a life of "polymorphous perversity" in the service of love, and Marcuse combine Marx and Freud in an unlikely but popular alliance, they essentially taught Freudianism with the repressions off. Philip Rieff, in *The Triumph of the Therapeutic: Uses of Faith after Freud* (the very title of this book suggests something important about postmodernism), drew attention to the conservatism (though with radical potential) of Freud and to a large extent Jung. But he contrasted a passing-away "culture of denial" with an incoming "therapeutic," adumbrated by Nietzsche, Reich, and D. H. Lawrence. The old "commitment" therapies supposed that denials of knowledge and pleasure could contribute to spiritual health. The therapeutic, instead, helped people to see nothing but "dis-ease" in denial, suggesting one can or should be as unrepressed as one liked.[24]

The sage of Vienna, with his old-world pessimism about the mutability of human nature, may have held repression and civilization inseparable, but those cantankerous radicals and their Aquarian disciples were willing to try sloughing the encrustations off in one tremendous revolutionary spasm.

Nor did the popular artists and cartoonists on the left shy away from a psychoanalytic view of the decade's political heavyweights, not excluding endowing them with the "castrating phallus." Satirical images of Lyndon Johnson and other Vietnam warriors with upraised cannons or missiles between the legs were common fare in the leftist and underground press. Jungian, Marxist, Aquarian, and other ideological packagings were no less common, but the decade must be remembered as the last golden age of popular social thought in the psychoanalytic tradition.

Layered Reality and a New Romanticism

The cultural Sixties evoked a new consciousness that seemed always open to levels of reality behind the phenomenal, levels that are just as important for meaning as the surface, and that may be labyrinthine in complexity. They are not amenable to ordinary language and call for insider slang: "out of sight," "blowing your mind," and so on. The layered texture of periodicals like the *Oracle*, with the text superimposed on or bracketed in art at various degrees of representationalism, could make for virtual illegibility on the level of linear, typographical discourse but made the metaphysical point effectively. The jargon and the layeredness both made for Lyotardian language games that went against any idea of unified truth, at least any conveyable in linear rational language rather than impressionism or wordless mystical experience.

As was often said, a new romanticism was around, even a new Pre-Raphaelitism, which disdained the linguistic and other canons of classicism and emphasized the unspeakableness of experienced reality and the aesthetics of the proximity senses, touch, taste, and smell.

Religions can be divided into those that exalt the distance senses, seeing and hearing, while disparaging the religious worth of much that pertains to the proximity senses, and those that affirm or even exalt the latter. Psychoanalytic interpreters of religiosity will no doubt want to make much of the fact that the proximity senses are those highly active in early childhood and in sex, while the distance counterparts are refined only more gradually and partly in connection with education, thus bearing overtones of a presumptive adult maturity about their functions. Protestant Christianity and Islam, with their emphasis on hearing the word of God, and reading, chanting, or singing the sacred text, while disdaining such accoutrements of worship as incense, icon kissing, or excessive sacramentalism, are clearly seeing-and-hearing, distance-sense religions.

Roman Catholicism and Eastern Orthodoxy, and normative Hinduism and Buddhism, with their ceremonial burning of incense and restrained, sacramental tasting, touching, and kissing, might be said to be tilted more toward a decorous use of the proximity senses. But it is fair to say that modernism in all religions has usually been weighted heavily toward the distance senses, as it has toward verbalism and concepts of objective verbal truth generally. Much archaic religion, with its sacred feasts, dances, and occasional orgies, together with such pungent, potent underground spiritualities as Tantrism and ceremonial magic, clearly put heaviest reliance on the proximity senses instead.

Certainly one strand of the incipient postmodernism of Sixties religion was a recovery of the sacred use of the proximity senses, if not quite as magic or tantra, at least as dancing and hugging. Even mainline churches often revived the eucharistic kiss of peace in sensuous form and replaced flat, tasteless communion bread and wine with heartier fare. A good many Eastern imports and other new religions not only confronted their adherents with exotic sights and sounds, but also with nimbuses of incense, the Zen taste of tea or the spicier cuisine of Krishna, and the sensual feel of soft robes and cushions, of rosaries, and of one's body in yogic pose.

Planned synaesthesia then was in the air. But the Sixties also exalted the aesthetic of the spontaneous—the happening—and of the thrown together—the collage and the musical jam session. The drug experience had a major role in shaping the new sensuality, but so did other forms of rediscovered romanticism and mysticism. Sixties people loved a playful use of double meaning, as in the names of rock groups: Beatles, Grateful Dead, Led Zeppelin. No doubt this nomenclature suggested that one can make child's play of reality and all the solemn assumptions of the earth plane and find freedom as well as confusion in a world of relativity and duplicity.

The Recovery of the Past

A further important theme was the recovery of the lost and the past, as though the total experience for which the age yearned could only be complete when one had experienced all of the past as well as all of the present—a postmodernist rejection, as we have suggested, of the modern observer's privileged position in favor of level placement in the marketplace of ideas of all wares past and present. The *Time* magazine cover story of March 21, 1969, "Astrology and the New Cult of the Occult," opened with an impressive evocation of an ancient Babylonian seer scanning the zodiac and advising the king whether the hour was opportune for a move against the Assyrians, then noted with some astonishment that counsel based on the same celestial signs and wonders was being proffered in the trendier circles of contemporary society, and even Woolworth's was moving in with a full line of zodiacal highball glasses and paper napkins.

The glamour of astrology probably lay not just in its antiquity but also in the very fact of its being an outcast from the worlds of establishment science and religion. Sentiment in favor of excluded systems grew with the sense that scientific modernism was beginning to pall. Thus astrology's seductiveness for anyone who felt similarly put off, even if only vaguely, by the pretensions of the modern elite. The

astrologer's arcane jargon and colorful symbols, with the hint of immense mysterious deeps of space and time behind them, also had
their appeal, as did the craft's implication that, however vast, the
universe resonates with meaning for frail human life. The science of
the stars combined personal interest psychology with the fun of a
cypher puzzle and the naughty delight of doing something frowned
upon by pompous know-it-alls.

But the recovery of the past was a significant part of astrology's
appeal for two reasons. First, scenes from the past of wizards and
wonders, often envisioned in psychedelic splendor, were a stock-in-
trade of the generation's romantic expansion of consciousness and
search for alternatives, anywhere, anywhen, to the System. Second,
the past was of help in the counterculture's quest for legitimation and
authority; it had the true classicist's surmise that those whose words
have endured must have something to say.

Sources such as the *Oracle*, then, are replete with the wisdom of
such sages as Whitman and Thoreau, Hesse and Blake, as well as of
wellsprings more distant and past, the Heart Sutra and the *Tao te
ching*. Whether well understood from the scholar's perspective or not,
texts such as these and others, from the kabbala to the tantras, were
ransacked for the seed mantras of a new way of life.

The Sixties: Their Four Periods

The religious Sixties in America divide themselves into four sets
of years, which shall each constitute a chapter of this study. The first,
1960–1963, essentially up to the assassination of John F. Kennedy,
may be thought of as the Fifties under pressure. Religious motifs and
power positions—mainstream Protestant preeminence, Cardinal
Spellman–style Roman Catholicism—were initially carried over from
the preceding decade. But they were under mounting strain from the
tensions of the civil rights movement, the Catholic-Protestant stresses
engendered by the Kennedy presidential campaign, Catholics anxiously
or eagerly anticipating change from the Vatican Council getting under
way, and radical new theological and practical challenges reaching
the churches in the form of books like Gabriel Vahanian's *Death of
God* or Gibson Winter's *Suburban Captivity of the Church*.

The second period, 1964–1966, may be called the years of secular
hope. It is epitomized by the iconoclastic, world-affirming, yet profoundly religious tone of Harvey Cox's remarkable 1965 book, *The
Secular City*. These were years of declining church attendance, but at
the same time of brave new experiments in ministry based on the

"servant church" concept, of highly visible religious participation in such social justice activities as the Selma march and—by 1966—of explosive interest in radical theology, in Bishop Pike, and in the Death of God movement. It was also a time of growing interest in the spiritual effects of LSD and other psychedelic drugs. Escalation in Vietnam was continuing apace, race riots hit Watts in Los Angeles and elsewhere, and talk of changing sexual mores was in the air.

The third period is a single year, 1967, the year of the avatars. The hippie counterculture with its drugs, mysticism, and New Left radicalism descended into full public view; the quasi-liturgical antiwar demonstrations became large-scale as the nation divided deeply on the issue; the full impact of Vatican II on Roman Catholic worship and attitudes hit home. It was the year of the *Oracle*. New religious movements or practices, Eastern or occult or out on the far fringes of psychotherapy, attracted followers and publicity. A sense that immense revolutionary changes of some sort were about to happen shook the religious, political, and cultural worlds.

The fourth and final phase, 1968–1970, may be called the bitter years. It was when those changes didn't happen. But the war, and the rhetoric of the Nixon-Agnew administration, polarized the country even further. The King and Robert Kennedy assassinations, together with more riots, suggested to many that the country was tearing itself apart with violence, but responses seemed only to generate more polarization. The counterculture lost its idealistic sheen as it was riven by violence, such as the Tate-La Bianca murders, and by drug-related problems. The radical, black power, and antiwar movements, though they mounted larger demonstrations than ever before, acquired a tinge of revolutionary hardness that increasingly antagonized the nonhip and nonrevolutionary people now called Middle Americans. But Woodstock gave the memorable Sixties a final memory. Religion tried to help, but by now it seemed to be following more than leading and was itself torn between idealistic radical commitments from the servant-church era, and nostalgic appeals to church and God as they were before things seemed to fall apart. Catholic priests and nuns leaving the church were much in the news, as was the arrest of the Berrigan brothers—as priests—for antiwar civil disobedience. Also in the papers and the magazines were black theology, the "sex explosion," and a resurgence of evangelical Christianity, including the "Jesus movement" among ex-hippie young people.

Let us now turn to the Sixties themselves.

Chapter 2

1960–1963:
The Fifties under Pressure

> . . . already had I dreamed
> Of my sweet birth-place, and the old church-tower,
> Whose bells, the poor man's only music, rang
> From morn to evening, all the hot Fair-day
> So sweetly, that they stirred and haunted me
> With a wild pleasure, falling on mine ear
> Most like articulate sounds of things to come!
> *Coleridge, "Frost at Midnight"*

The Starting Lineup

In 1960, as the decade began, the United States counted 63 million Protestants, 42 million Roman Catholics, 2.7 million Eastern Orthodox, 589,000 Old Catholic and other Christians outside those categories, and 5.3 million Jews. Enumerated Buddhists, Muslims, and other "others" were negligible. This was out of a total U.S. population, according to the 1960 census, of 179.2 million.

Of the Protestants, nearly half (about 30 million) belonged to mainline denominations—Episcopal, Presbyterian, Congregational, Methodist, Disciples, and others who, with several Eastern Orthodox churches, were members of the National Council of the Churches of Christ in the U.S.A., the NCC. This body was founded in 1950 on the basis of the 1908 Federal Council of Churches and a dozen or so other "cooperative" organizations. The NCC was an American manifestation of the burgeoning ecumenical movement that had produced the World Council of Churches (WCC) in Amsterdam in 1948.

Many of the other denominations were in the fundamentalist camp, with all that implied culturally in the midcentury American context, though a few nonmembers like the Missouri Synod Lutherans and the Christan Reformed Church, linked to conservative evangelical traditions with strong European intellectual roots, were culturally rather different. A small number, like the Unitarian and Universalist churches, were too liberal for the National Council.

This was the heritage left by the 1950s, a time in which churchgoing had reached levels probably unprecedented in American history (49 percent of the population in an average week in the high years,

1955 and 1958, according to Gallup polls; in my view, these figures are probably too high, but certainly attendance was strong). In that banner decade the Roman Catholic and mainline churches, at least, enjoyed no small prestige, and their leaders social and even political power. In fact, for several decades afterward, the 1950s, the first full postwar decade, were considered as a sort of norm in American religion against which subsequent aberrations could be measured. Full, well-budgeted churches, with lots of baby boom children from newly affluent suburban-type families, hummed with activity and became pillars of a certain American life-style archetype, of a piece with the "Ozzie and Harriet" image of the American family.

The style was well portrayed in that Fifties sociological classic, *The Organization Man*, by William H. Whyte, Jr. The United Protestant Church in a new suburban community he describes had a spectacular "plant" and a full schedule of social activities. The minister, who saw himself chiefly as a pastoral problem solver, delivered upbeat messages designed not to offend anyone of whatever denominational background. Human relations, he said, were what was most important: "I think this is the basic need—the need to belong to a group. You find this fellowship in a church better than anywhere else."[1] At the same time, prominent theologians, preachers, and bishops were virtually household names, their fame spread by glamorous accounts in the newspapers and newsmagazines (particulary Henry Luce's *Time*, then very serious about religion stories) and by interviews on the new medium called television.

Roman Catholics were laying cornerstones for new churches, schools, and hospitals once a week in some places, while still enjoying their proverbial Latin-rite, Tridentine conservatism and exclusiveness, eating fish on Friday and condemning even slightly suspect movies. Jewish temples and synagogues were almost ostentatiously respected by nearly all other Americans, their people having earned acceptance in the famous Protestant-Catholic-Jew triad of American religion after their immense sufferings in the war.

The mainline Protestant churches of colonial American background, however, still held an indefinable but special place in American life, gauged by such criteria as treatment in the news media, the relation of some of their seminaries to the oldest and most prestigious universities, the still disproportionate number of their old-family adherents in the higher levels of business and politics.

Episcopalians, Presbyterians, and Congregationalists still basked in the glow of their supposed special role in the shaping of American values. Episcopal presiding bishops or Presbyterian stated clerks could make a special sort of news, even though they shepherded churches numbering each no more than 2 percent of the total population. The mainline churches were, perhaps more to the point, reputedly chaplains to the class that held the ultimate levers of political and economic power and also were the pillars of what was left—after the depression and the war—of "society." All this made them not only custodians of a heritage from the past but also of the still-dominant modern values in religion, from bureaucratic organization on the model of a democratic but unitary state, to broad sympathy for the reformist, progressive concerns of the social gospel.

But there were other sides to Fifties religion. First, at least as they were reported and talked about, and in many cases viewed themselves, the religions of a good segment of that total population were not meaningfully part of the triad but were marginalized in relation to the modern-style religious elite. Fundamentalist churches, African American churches, Eastern Orthodox churches, Hasidic Jews, not to mention Buddhists and others outside the Jewish-Christian spectrum altogether, at best ministered effectively to their own people, but—apart from the anomalously public role of the fundamentalist Billy Graham's crusades—had little if any place in the larger society. Evangelicals made news only if they did something the mainstream considered disturbing or quaint, including the singularly large numbers they often chalked up for revivals or as members of their cardinal churches. But moving up religiously, say from Southern Baptist to Episcopalian, still often happened as a concomitant of one's moving up in one's career, or transplanting from the country to the sparkling new suburbs.

The leaders of the mainstream, NCC denominations were characteristically persons with North European names, educated in recognized universities and divinity schools, and possessed of a certain savoir faire that marked them as serious, moderate, world-class ecclesiastical statesmen who could talk without discomfort to a European colleague out of Oxford or Uppsala. (In the Fifties, we must remember, many cultured Americans were still beset by a rather colonial obsequiousness toward the better class of Europeans, the dramas and tragedies of the war years notwithstanding. Americans tended to think of themselves as morally superior but culturally inferior to Europe or, in the eyes of a few, Asia; in the countercultural Sixties the perception was virtually reversed.)

For that matter, the mainstream leaders and they alone among religionists could talk as equals to the intelligentsia of the leading universities, the captains of industry, and the people who still, from the higher ranks of the State Department, the army and navy, and even Congress, kept tabs on how things went in Washington. But challenges were gathering force. People like Dean Acheson (son of an Episcopal bishop of Connecticut) were shaken by early-Fifties McCarthyism. Their sort, often derided at the time as "cookie-pushers" with effete manners and compromising minds, seemed to be especially irritating to Senator Joseph McCarthy and his allies.[2] When that roughneck lawmaker of Irish Catholic background targeted elite, Harvard-groomed Alger Hiss, spoke of Dean Acheson as a "pompous diplomat in striped pants, with a phony British accent," and decried from his invisible "lists" the "traitorous actions of those who have been treated so well by this Nation," "the bright young men who are born with silver spoons in their mouths," one has no doubt that class and regional lines were being drawn. Those lines would be drawn again with a vengeance in the Sixties as the John Birch Society surged and Middle America squared off against the counterculture and the antiwar activists and would contribute much to the political careers of Richard Nixon and Ronald Reagan.[3] But by 1960 the Ivy League elite had recouped their losses for the moment, all the more in 1961 as Harvard came to Washington with the Kennedy administration.

Roman Catholics and Jews, not yet fully assimilated into the heart of the American establishment but often modern in their own way, had anomalous positions. Catholics, under leaders like Fulton Sheen of television eminence or Cardinal Spellman (whose aggressive forays into the political and financial worlds challenged the Protestant mainstream's power base), together with intellectuals possessing *gravitas* like John Courtney Murray or Gustave Weigel, showed they could hold their own by any visible, objective definition of parity. Judaism, helped by such outstanding figures as Abraham Heschel or Will Herberg and by enthusiasm for the new state of Israel, grew and changed; in the years between 1937 and 1952, according to Nathan Glazer, "hundreds of tiny Orthodox congregations in the slum areas of cities had closed; they had been replaced by hundreds of large and vigorous synagogues—Conservative and Reform, as well as Orthodox— on the outskirts."[4] African Americans, encouraged by the Supreme Court's disallowing of school segregation in 1954, were gathering strength to demand their rightful place in society.

By the Fifties tolerance was in the air, and such institutions as Brotherhood Week were important civil religion events, though not a few practical restrictions in housing, education, and social life endured. (As late as 1963, a B'nai B'rith study found that 72 percent of 803 country clubs surveyed practiced definite religious as well as

39

racial discrimination. The manager of one club near Detroit put it this way: "Jews don't make application at our club and we don't apply at theirs"; as we shall see, racial integregation met even greater resistance).[5] And as the 1960 presidential campaign was to demonstrate in the case of Roman Catholicism, the political status of non-WASP religion at the highest level was still unresolved.

Even in the most liberal circles, the discussion around the collective American table implied that these African, Jewish, and Roman Catholic fellow diners were less owners of the house than long-term lodgers. They were familiars who paid their rent, usually, and in turn one granted them tolerance and goodwill, then both much-touted virtues. One listened to them out of courtesy, or even genuine interest, for it was true they had some worthwhile things to contribute, as well as a few peculiar crotchets and, at least in the case of the Roman Catholics, an unfortunate air of finality to their words. (In regard to the latter, none other than Reinhold Niebuhr was once exasperated enough to remark, "It is not easy to cooperate with an institution that claims to be a perfect society.") Nonetheless, in the Fifties a great many Americans assumed, rather prematurely, that most serious social problems at home were behind them, that the ship of state had found its way into a great calm sea of democratic tolerance, where the only danger would be torpedoes from a distant warship bearing a red flag.

The Underside of the Fifties

There were other aspects to the Fifties than the famous Protestant-Catholic-Jew troika on the public scene. Religious awakenings like those of the Sixties do not spring entirely de novo from barren ground; underground rivers, at the least, have been feeding the channels through which the new fountains surface. Standard interpretations of the Sixties tend to emphasize the drab, fearful, conformist nature of the previous decade in order to showcase against it the rebel yells and psychedelic hues of the successor. But all revolutions have a need to justify themselves by painting what went before in the bleakest colors; memory and some reference to the literature of the times suggests a Fifties decade with at least some variety.

I was an undergraduate at the University of Colorado in Boulder early in the Fifties. This was well before that pleasant little city at the foot of the Rockies had become home to a Tibetan Buddhist seminary and other countercultural monuments, but the student population was far from monochrome. I recall several self-designated existentialists, an individual who would go into the mountains to perform ceremonial magic rites, and the creepy thrill some of us gave ourselves by going into Denver to visit a dark, Left Bankish espresso shop allegedly operated by satanists. (In the men's room under a portrait of Satan ran the words, "Who shall deliver me from this body of death?")

I myself was heavily involved at the time with an Anglo-Catholic set, wrapped up in the romance and rigidity of that Anglican sect, yearning amidst the spiritual aridity (as we saw it) of Protestant or philistine Roman Catholic America for an idealized medieval Christendom of friars, pilgrim shrines, and Gothic towers, and we loved to worship with things like incense, bells, and genuflections. I am of the opinion myself that although this Fifties Anglo-Catholicism was ensconced within the ultraestablishment Episcopal church and certainly did not espouse Sixties-type liberation in matters sexual or sartorial, in some ways it was for us, as it had been much earlier for certain aesthetes of the Mauve Decade, the 1890s, a kind of inner spiritual counterculture. Like the hippies to come we rejected a humdrum world by creating around ourselves an infinitely more colorful and exciting alternative reality. By dint of the Middle America-defying vestures and gestures of our medieval European rites we experienced expansion of consciousness across great gulfs of space and time, liberating ourselves at soul level from the one-dimensionality of the present. Like members of the League in Hermann Hesse's paradigmatic *Journey to the East* we were in the world yet not entirely of it as we wandered from festival to festival and from century to century and did not pass a church (of our persuasion) without entering its dim cool interior to whisper a prayer amid the saints and sanctuary lights.

Anglo-Catholicism was not the only, nor the most important, alternative spiritual culture of the Eisenhower era. Four writers whose names were common coin and whose books sold remarkably well in those years of supposed broad but shallow religious revival say as much. They are the perennial philosopher and psychedelic pioneer (as well as first-rate novelist) Aldous Huxley; the one-time Anglo-Catholic priest who gave it up in favor of Zen, free love, and spiritual free-lancing Alan Watts; the worldling turned Trappist monk Thomas Merton; and the Beat chronicler Jack Kerouac.

Perhaps significantly, all four of these writers were of backgrounds that gave them a certain insider/outsider perspective on the American scene—a not inappropriate perspective in a nation of immigrants and for precursors of the intentional alienated native stance of Sixties counterculture observers. Huxley and Watts were transplanted Englishmen. Merton was born in France of New Zealand/American parents and spent a rather chaotic childhood and youth in several countries. Kerouac was born in Lowell, Massachusetts, of French-Canadian, ultimately Breton, descent; he spoke French before he spoke the language in which he became a lively voice of the American outsider, and from his Breton legacy he brought more than a little of the Celtic romantic's love of wandering, words, and wonders.

Merton's *Seven Story Mountain* appeared as early as 1948, and to the delighted amazement of the publishers remained on the bestseller lists for months. This narrative of the author's conversion to Catholicism and decision to enter an austere contemplative order commences with an unforgettable portrayal of a late-Thirties intellectual world, represented for him by Columbia University where he was a student, in which it almost seemed that everyone was defined as a partisan of some highly doctrinaire and loudly argued cause—Fascist, Trotskyite, orthodox Communist, Socialist, Vedantist, Catholic, whatever; amid these clamorous options Merton made his choice and then the even more provocative monastic turn that apparently rejected almost all in which America thought it believed—except God.[6]

Something about Merton's testimony appealed to the war-weary and nostalgic, at once backward-looking and forward-looking, immediate postwar generation, a people wanting fresh sacred experience but not yet ready to create a new spiritual culture, the world of my Anglo-Catholicism too. Merton was read, and thousands of young Americans dropped out and entered strict monasteries after his example; the cloistral explosion was still news in the early Sixties, right up to the rather sudden implosion of such traditionalist Catholicism. (As late as January 5, 1962, *Time* ran an article in the religion section entitled "The Affluent Monasteries" on the growth of U.S. contemplative religious orders such as the Benedictines, Trappists, Carthusians, and Camaldolese over the past five or six years, highlighting their relative wealth through the production of items like jams and cheeses.)

Aldous Huxley's *Perennial Philosophy* appeared even earlier, in 1946. This elegant book is essentially an argument for Advaita Vedanta, which Huxley together with two other immigrant English writers, Christopher Isherwood and Gerald Heard, had studied at the Vedanta Society of Southern California. Huxley displays wide familiarity with the mystical literature of many traditions, however, and is concerned to show that they concur in proclaiming a timeless, changeless reality behind the realm of appearances, and that only in knowing it can a person find true peace or meaning.[7]

The attention that this book, like Merton's, received suggests there were cadres in the postwar religious boom prepared to mine the deeper veins of mystical spirituality, as well as build churches for burgeoning suburbia. Both the mining and the building sectors of the movement were conservative in the sense that they assumed the requisite answers to the world's spiritual emptiness could be found within existing traditions, including traditional, institutionally sanctioned modes of contemplation and worship. Even Huxley, though more sceptical than Merton (at that time) of institutional religion and its leadership, was fully ready to embrace the authority of a highly traditionalist, though cross-cultural, canon of saints and spiritual writers.

The mood in religion was to do what we've always done, but to do it now, in the affluent society, with more money, more bricks and mortar, more books and airwave time, than ever before. Voices calling for serious ecclesiological or liturgical reform, or for mystics in a new mold, were still scattered; their *kairos* had not yet come.

It was Aldous Huxley himself who, in his slim but influential 1954 essay *The Doors of Perception*, began to break the mold. Here the author decribes the experience of taking four-tenths of a gram of mescaline. As he relates it, the drug enabled him to *see* what he had only written about before. Reality itself flared like the burning bush out of every common hedge, and the Clear Light of the *Tibetan Book of the Dead* (in the 1927 Evans Wentz version, another longstanding classic of the mystical underground) arose with the sun. In *The Perennial Philosophy* and especially *The Doors of Perception*, this erudite, abstemious Britisher, who was to die the same day as John F. Kennedy, left a sort of charter for Sixties mysticism: the inner planes of reality, as penned by exotic sages in the Shangri-Las of the past, could *now* be directly known, seen, and experienced on the streets of a new world, in part with the help of magic potions known to the wise.[8]

Alan Watts also experimented enthusiastically with the new alchemy, his trips being retailed in *The Joyous Cosmology* (1962). But his main contribution to the subterranean Fifties vectoring toward the Sixties was undoubtedly *The Way of Zen* (1957), which definitively collated popular Western Zen in the D. T. Suzuki tradition.[9] That Zen was not only the radishes and rice of the Beat Generation, but also an important ingredient of the heartier Eastern cuisine to come.

During his years (1944–1950) as an Episcopal priest and chaplain at Northwestern University, Watts had written a couple of books in the already cited creative-conservative mood of reviving and rearranging ancient traditions. *Behold the Spirit* (1947) was an uneven but sometimes brilliant endeavor to draw the best of the East into a richly sacramental, incarnational, and mystical vision of Christianity. In *The Supreme Identity* (1950) Watts presented, on behalf of a radical

Christian monism, the most sustained theological argument of any of his books; it is a scholarly and impressive piece of work, though the young priest-intellectual who wrote it is now likely to be forever lost behind the tipsy, hedonistic mystic and "philosophical entertainer" of the Sixties he was to become.[10]

After leaving the Episcopal ministry for both creedal and personal reasons, Watts had to scramble for a living through assorted teaching, writing, and lecturing stints; one fruit of this was *The Way of Zen*, which propounds, without Christianization, the wisdom of spontaneity, "direct pointing" to reality beyond words, and artistic creativity he saw in that tradition. He believed the West, so self-tortured by its dualistic and moralistic credos, and so ridden by its humorless patriarchal God, desperately needed a little quiet time with the wise and whimsical old Zen masters across the Pacific. The timing of this message was right, and Watts gained quite a few companions on his journey to the East. Some GIs returning from Occupation duty in Japan had been moved by the lovely eaved temples and enigmatic rock gardens in the land of the former enemy; a few, like Richard Kapleau, author of *The Three Pillars of Zen* (1967), a more practice-oriented but no less important American Zen classic than Watts's, took serious Zen training in Japan.[11] Even more broadly, the emergent generation wanted its own spirituality, just as it wanted its own politics, music, and lifestyle, and the East was a good place to start looking.

Among those who looked were Jack Kerouac and his Beat friends. *The Dharma Bums* (1958), an autobiographical novel featuring the leading Beat lights thinly disguised behind pseudonyms, recounts the Zen side of their quest. It is dedicated to Han Shan, "Cold Mountain," the old-time Chinese poet, mountaineer, and monk, whom "Japhy Ryder" (the poet Gary Snyder) is translating, and who is presented as the greatest "Zen Lunatic" of them all. Living their own version of the Zen lunatic life, the protagonists party, climb mountains, hitchhike, drink too much, and endlessly talk philosophy, Buddhism, and life, and occasionally read from sacred texts of their faith like the Diamond Sutra.

Over the whole of the year traced in this story lies the fact that at its end Japhy, by far the most advanced woodsman, Zennist, and lover of life of them all, a sort of Mark Trail and reborn Henry Thoreau, Walt Whitman, and Han Shan rolled into one, will leave to go to Japan to study in a real Zen monastery. (Alan Watts, who knew them all and who makes a cameo appearance in *The Dharma Bums* as "Arthur Whane," thought that Gary Snyder's role as Japhy Ryder "did not begin to do him justice," that "he *is* just exactly what I have been trying to *say*." Watts then paid Snyder what must be one of the most remarkable compliments in all literature: "I can only say that a universe which has manifested Gary Snyder could never be called a failure.")[12]

The Dharma Bums has its literary flaws, but it is good reading and cumulatively offers a vividly hued montage of bright, adventurous, uninhibited young men engaged in the simultaneous exploration of travel, experience, ideas, and spirituality. Some passages are unforgettable. No treatise from the East that I know of sums up the profound sense of cosmic wonder that is at the very heart of Mahayana Buddhism as well as these lines, recounting a night when Kerouac was hitchhiking and camping out on the desert near El Paso:

> There just isn't any kind of night's sleep in the world that can compare with the night's sleep you get in the desert winter night, providing you're good and warm in a duck-down bag. The silence is so intense that you can hear your own blood roar in your ears but louder than that by far is the mysterious roar which I always identify with the roaring of the diamond of wisdom, the mysterious roar of silence itself, which is a great Shhhh reminding you of something you've seemed to have forgotten in the stress of your days since birth. I wished I could explain it to those I loved, to my mother, to Japhy, but there just weren't any words to describe the nothingness and purity of it. "Is there a certain and definite teaching to be given to all living creatures?" was the question probably asked to beetlebrowed snowy Dipankara [the Buddha of the previous universe], and his answer was the roaring silence of the diamond.[13]

Or this grand-slam sentence, set near the University of California at Berkeley:

> Japhy and I were kind of outlandish-looking on the campus in our old clothes in fact Japhy was considered an eccentric around the campus, which is the usual thing for campuses and college people to think whenever a real man appears on the scene—colleges being nothing but grooming schools for the middle-class non-identity which usually finds its perfect expression on the outskirts of the campus in rows of well-to-do houses with lawns and television sets in each living room with everybody looking at the same thing and thinking the same thing at the same time while the Japhies of the world go prowling in the wilderness to hear the voice crying in the wilderness, to find the ecstasy of the stars, to find the dark mysterious secret of the origin of faceless wonderless crapulous civilization. (38–39)

It is mind-boggling to realize he is talking about *Berkeley*, of all places, which less than a decade later would be prowling with thousands of Japhies, or would-be Japhies. But the point is that Kerouac here presented a template, a prototype, of the revolution to come, and there would be those who would remember.

When the sun rose on New Year's Day, 1960, the wintry sky colors were still in appropriate strata and the major weather signs suggested a stable barometer. But, though not many noticed at the time, a few clouds were billowing and fraying around the edges before the first mild gusts of a distant storm, and straws of race, creed, and culture were blowing in the wind.

The Opening Rounds

The positioning of the several religious teams as the decade got under way is made quite clear by contemporary newsmagazine stories. Thus in *Newsweek* for January 4, 1960, a major story on the religion page tells us that Dr. John Vernon Butler, rector of Trinity Episcopal Church in Princeton, New Jersey, would become dean of the mighty Cathedral of St. John the Divine in New York, succeeding the Right Reverend James A. Pike—of whom much, *much* more will be heard as the Sixties advance—who had left it upon his election as bishop of California.

A second religion story informs the reader that in Mount Moriah, Missouri, the small town's three clergymen had united in opposition to dances at the local high school.[14] The Southern Baptist minister declared of dance that "it's evil—it's the tool of the Devil," and his Methodist colleague opined that "many unwed mothers across the nation . . . are victims of the school dance." But the dances continued and were popular.

One cannot help but contemplate exactly what is being said by the juxtaposition of these two stories. First, it seems that in 1960—whether that would be the case today or not—a simple change of prominent appointments in the Episcopal church was national news, presumably just because that denomination was in fact a quintessentially modern elite religion, and hence its affairs were on a par with those of the top elites in government, business, and society. The story was, on a deep level, a clarification of hierarchy, and any such clarification usually entails the setting up of entities to represent opposite poles.

Thus the Mount Moriah fracas was news not because any church in that town was a co-player with a St. John the Divine, or even a Trinity, Princeton, much less because the Reverends Butler or Pike would have likely concurred in those clergy's views of school dances, but for a very different reason. *Newsweek* presumably thought that readers seriously interested in major New York mainline church appointments would find Mount Moriah entertaining, and at the same time reassuring in that it subtly reinforced the difference they wanted to sense between themselves and second- or third-stringers in places like rural Missouri.

Indeed, the Episcopal church seems generally to have had an oddly privileged place in the religion columns of those days. To be sure, in 1960 that denomination attained a membership of 3,444,000, nearly 2 percent of the population. (The statistical high was 3,647,000 in 1966. Three decades later, in 1991, Episcopal membership was down over a million to 2,433,000, less than 1 percent of a much more populous and pluralized nation.) But one doubts that the prominence of the Church of England's American auxiliary was based only on its numbers.

In fact, Episcopalian events seemed to make news that would go unreported in larger but apparently less interesting denominations. *Time* on August 25, 1961, for example, went so far as to run a story on a dispute between the Episcopal church in Marble, Colorado, a town of fifty-eight souls, and its bishop over whether its edifice could be used for interdenominational services. (Baptist churches, in contrast, appear to be newsworthy chiefly in connection with great numbers. *Newsweek* on August 8, 1960, ran an item on Dr. Dallas Billington of Akron, Ohio, a champion preacher who delivered old-time fire-and-brimstone religion to an independent Baptist congregation of some 16,000; and on October 10 the magazine described First Baptist in Dallas, Texas, the Southern Baptist church with the largest membership and biggest budget of all in that burgeoning denomination.)

Several stories appeared in 1960 on the Reverend Dennis J. Bennett of the Episcopal church in Van Nuys, California, who deeply divided his parish and was finally forced to resign because his ministry included speaking in tongues. Bishop Pike, in retrospect a man of more surf than depth, was constantly in the news during the Sixties, including a *Time* cover story, for his assorted forays into church union, heresy, and spiritualism and his penchant for outrageous statements. One has a distinct feeling that these items did not see print because someone, or even some member of the clergy, was practicing Pentecostalism or saying controversial things, but because it was an *Episcopal priest* or *Episcopal bishop*.

Like *Newsweek's*, *Time's* religion page for its first issue of the decade (January 4, 1960) was true to its team. We read that five leading members of the Protestant clergy of upscale, exurbanite New Canaan, Connecticut, joined in denouncing Young Life, an extra-denominational, evangelical teenage movement from the hinterland that had invaded their community. In contrast to the Mount Moriah case, we sense that here the religion editor is in sympathy with the denouncing clerics as they decry Young Life as a "separate teenage church, financed and led by adults not answerable to any local group"; the Episcopal rector goes on to complain that the movement "tends in the direction of Fundamentalism. They give easy answers to life's most difficult problems . . . their workers . . . are not well trained"— meaning they did not hold elite academic credentials.

Prominent theologians and preachers of the mainline churches continued to be news. On March 16, 1962, *Time* ran a story on "The Changing Sermon," citing as among the great preachers of the day not megachurch Baptists but more fashionable figures like David Read of Madison Avenue Presbyterian Church, New York; James Pike, Episcopal bishop of California; Theodore Ferris of Trinity Episcopal, Boston; and Los Angeles Methodist bishop Gerald Kennedy. The story claimed that sermons were shorter, more low-key but penetrating analyses of faith compared to the stemwinders of yore. On May 24 *Time* identified the major younger Protestant theologians, among them five who would be much heard from in the Sixties and after: Jaroslav Pelikan, 39; Robert McAfee Brown, 41; Langdon Gilkey, 43; Roger Shinn, 45; and Schubert Ogden, 34.

Here are a few other religion stories from the decade's opening weeks. *Time*, on January 25, did a sensitive, reverential piece on Evelyn Waugh's new biography of Msgr. Ronald Knox, the son of an Anglican bishop who had become a Catholic convert and writer noted for his acerbic wit and intellectual gifts, and who had died in 1957. The same page carried a lighter piece on a festival in Japan for a definitely non-elite figure, Ebisu, the "fat-faced Shinto god of wealth."

Finally, we read of a talk by Bishop G. Bromley Oxnam, the distinguished Methodist and embodiment of mainstream liberal Protestantism, remembered for his confrontation with the House Un-American Activities Committee in the previous decade. Before looking at his remarks, we need to recall that outer space, its exploration, and the possibility of life on other worlds were important Sixties themes. On January 4, on the same page as the hue and cry over Young Life, *Time* presented the opinion of Cornell astronomer Thomas Gold, a proponent of steady-state cosmology, that life may have been brought to Earth by spaceships, having existed elsewhere for uncounted billions of years.

The excitement over Sputnik was still in the air. Plans were in preparation for the manned Mercury spaceflights commencing the next year, and the unmanned Mariner flights to Venus and Mars. The media were full of future-is-now stories on the emergent Space Age, ranging from nuts-and-bolts technology to speculations about life on other worlds, and it was anticipated that going into space would somehow change the nature and quality of human life forever. *Newsweek*, February 22, 1960, had as a cover story "Life in Outer Space? The Search Begins," and the July 11 cover story was "Dawn of the Spaceman."

Space, in fact, was a pervasive Sixties theme, culminating in the 1969 moon landing, and served as a kind of counterpoint to the turmoil, the antitechnology and anti-Americanism, of much of life below the clouds. Unlike its cities and its war, America's space projects by and large worked; the astronauts, military men and archetypes all, were short-haired, clean-shaven, straight types who looked and talked like hometown boys who had made it; as though to spite the dissidents and counterculturalists, their successes seemed to keep vindicating Middle American values and capabilities.

Against this background, we can digest the lighthearted comments by which Bishop Oxnam, on the 175th birthday of American Methodism, seemed ready to take the spirit of liberal Protestantism into the universe: "Before another 175 years have passed, we will have conquered space and come to know the thinking, the culture, the dreams, the problems, the limitations of the people who inhabit the great planets of the universe. . . . Are Methodist seminaries preparing men and women for these conversations and conferences? . . . Are we ready to hear them?"

Here is another name in the news. According to *Newsweek* for January 11, 1960, Billy Graham was at a Youth for Christ convention in Washington, D.C., which also included pop-drinking and pie-eating contests; a couple of months later, Graham's trip to the Near East, including a controversial visit to Israel, made the papers. A prominent religious figure all through the Sixties though hardly a Sixties type, Graham is not easy to fit into the picture. One can, of course, see him as a sort of counterpoint to the burning and tripping Sixties, like the astronauts of a piece with the Middle America that was momentarily at bay but would reassert itself at the end of the decade with the election of Richard Nixon, Graham's friend. But there is more to Graham than that.

He is a deeply American figure, heir to the legacy of the frontier revivals and last in an apostolic succession of premier national evangelists: Charles Finney, Dwight Moody, Billy Sunday, Billy Graham. As such he does not conform to any modern category; he is obviously not elite yet is clearly much bigger than the marginal evangelicalism of his day. He is an independent, but also, because of the heritage he embodies, a national figure, almost what the Japanese would call a living national treasure, who incarnates a tradition and craft vital to the culture as a whole.

He may be criticized, as he was by the likes of Reinhold Niebuhr, but he is not handled by the media in the jocular or alarmist manner reserved for lesser fundamentalists like those of biblically named Mount Moriah or New Canaan. He brings the spiritual heritage of the American past, or at least one wing of it, into the present visibly; sociologists have commented on the way his great crusades and their harvests of conversions have a ritual quality. Like a shaman, he evoked and personified symbols facilitating movement outside the one-dimensional present—movement toward God, toward the past, toward the people.

With him on *Newsweek*'s January 11, 1960, religion page: the large new Church of Religious Science on Sixth Street in Los Angeles was opened, flagship of that New Thought denomination; and back in the Episcopal church, an Episcopal Society for Cultural and Racial Unity was formed to promote racial integration. Here we point, of course, toward one of the great issues of the decade, and we will hear more of ESCRU.

On February 15, *Newsweek* tells us that Ralph Abernathy is succeeding Martin Luther King as leader of the Montgomery (Alabama) Improvement Association; King was moving to Atlanta to continue his civil rights work from that city. (In 1954, King had become pastor of Dexter Avenue Baptist Church in Montgomery. After Rosa Parks was arrested in Montgomery for refusing to give up her bus seat to a white man on December 1, 1955, the city's black leadership had formed the Montgomery Improvement Association and selected King to lead a bus boycott. King's home was bombed; he was nonetheless indicted with eighty-eight others and found guilty of conspiracy in connection with the boycott. But in late 1956 the U.S. Supreme Court upheld a lower federal court's ruling that segregation in public transportation was unconstitutional, and King was vindicated, though violence continued against him, and against black churches and businesses.) In April he would convene a meeting of student activists in Raleigh, North Carolina, leading to the formation of the Student Nonviolent Coordinating Committee (SNCC), which endeavored to coordinate the sit-ins that had begun in February. The same issue of *Newsweek* tells of another Alabama pastor doing battle against evil—he had, over the years, set afloat some 27,800 whiskey bottles containing messages of salvation.

The February 22 *Newsweek* cover story on life in outer space presented the words of several theologians, including C. S. Lewis and Hla Bu, a Buddhist, on what the religious meaning of contact with strange flesh on other worlds might be. Contact with those of other persuasions—as well as of other skin pigmentations—here on Earth also remained a problem. Protestant-Catholic dialogue was a much-discussed topic in religion circles in 1960 and would be more so as the possibility, and finally the actuality, of a Catholic candidate in the presidential election of that year greatly raised the interreligious stakes.

Pre–Vatican II attitudes still prevailed on each side, at least officially, but the personality of Pope John XXIII had changed the atmosphere, as had the three-faiths mentality of postwar America. As Protestants and Catholics gradually approached practical as well as theoretical parity, and such issues as state and federal aid to education (How would parochial schools be dealt with?) became hot political topics, both camps more and more felt the need to talk. Chiefly associated with this dialogue was Robert McAfee Brown, later prominent in anti–Vietnam War activism and liberation theology. In *Newsweek* for February 29, 1960, he is cited as offering six rules for Catholic-Protestant dialogue.

A foretaste of the future in the April 4 *Newsweek*: an article on the draft indicated that though that harsh lottery now picked out just one young man out of ninety-nine, it hung over every male's head until he reached the magic age of twenty-six; no man could make absolute and final plans for his life until he knew it had passed over him for good.

The April 18, 1960, Easter issues of *Time* and *Newsweek* present an interesting contrast. The *Newsweek* cover story was here and now: "Could the Religious Vote Swing It? The 'Pros' Rate Kennedy's Chances." But the *Time* cover portrait was of St. Paul, and the story was on Christian missionaries: "From St. Paul to 1960." The article described the life and times of the great missionary apostle; then, with the help of vividly colored photographs, it surveyed the work of missionaries in the world of 1960.

The generally upbeat, laudatory tone, the obvious favoritism toward Christianity and its American mainline denominations, the unobtrusive but respectable academic scholarship behind its portrayal of the first century, all make the *Time* article not only a monument to Henry Luce's values but also a kind of capstone and epitaph for Fifties-style, public, self-assured, modernist religion, confidently working out of unquestioned great traditions and, like America generally, thought to be doing good on a global scale. It was much in contrast to other famous *Time* cover pieces on religion that were to appear only a few years later, such as the "Is God Dead?" of Easter 1966, or the

"Astrology and the New Cult of the Occult" of March 21, 1969. Before coming to those matters, however, we must examine the lingering great tradition in the early Sixties.

The modern, NCC Protestant mainstream enjoyed a lingering sense early in the decade of spiritual primacy. But awareness was growing that this hegemony was no longer to be taken for granted. Changes were in the wind to challenge and caution the immediate postwar religious world. The very first year of the decade under study, 1960, powerfully presented three such challenges and cautions, in the form of a serious Church Union proposal, the Catholic President debate, and a rapidly accelerating civil rights movement. More were to come.

Church Union: The Blake-Pike Proposal

The Church Union proposal refers to the overture made by Eugene Carson Blake, stated clerk of the United Presbyterian Church U.S.A., in a sermon preached at Grace Episcopal Cathedral, San Francisco, on December 4, 1960. This sermon was followed by a statement of enthusiastic endorsement by the Right Reverend James A. Pike, Episcopal bishop of California; hence the product is sometimes called the Blake-Pike proposal. The document called for a church "both catholic and reformed," with provision for episcopal, presbyterian, and congregational features in its governance, and for the use of both the ancient Catholic and the Reformation creeds and confessions of faith. The new Great Church would allow for diversity in worship while generally favoring modest simplicity and would encourage a collegial rather than hierarchical spirit of ministry. Blake called on the Episcopal, Presbyterian, Methodist, and United Church of Christ denominations to inaugurate talks on a plan of church union based on the principles he articulated in this sermon.

Coming on the heels of the final creation of the United Church of Christ, combining Congregational with Evangelical and Reformed traditions, and the hopeful 1948 founding of the World Council of Churches, as well as the 1950 National Council of Churches, Blake-Pike could well have seemed an idea whose time had arrived. It will be noted that it was a thoroughly modern, in contrast to postmodern, proposal in every sense: the new domination was to be progressive, bureaucratic, democratic, universalist; it seemed to fulfill the promise of the Fifties' United Protestant suburban church described by William Whyte in *The Organization Man* that was enthusiastically received because it combined resources and offended nobody. But times were changing.

The ambitious reunion scheme turned out to be an idea whose time had come and gone. The UCC was the last merger to join churches of different lineages, and although later important intratradition mergers took place—Unitarian-Universalist, Presbyterian, Lutheran—the processes often brought as much pain as joy and did little of themselves to solve the deep-seated problems of mainstream American religion.

The cathedral sermon was, of course, followed up. In 1962, representatives of the four original churches gathered in Washington for the first COCU (Consultation on Church Union) plenary, establishing commissions to deal with faith, order, and polity; liturgy and sacraments; sociological and cultural factors; and organization and power sharing. These produced *Principles of Church Union* (1966), offering a consensus on scripture, faith, ministry and sacraments. But its concrete proposals for reunion evoked little enthusiasm.

While some spirited and principled opposition arose from the conservatives of various denominations, what really did in Blake-Pike and COCU was a more widespread if inarticulate Sixties apathy toward the whole prospect of large-scale organic church union, and all the interminable meetings, arguments, and labors it would undoubtedly entail. The immense diversion of time and energy would merely sap vitality from the rest of the church's mission, while reunion of itself, it was widely believed, would do little to meet the urgent spiritual needs of the day at other than bureaucratic levels. And in response to those needs, a new generation of clergy and laity was already living reunion where it counted: in campus ministries, in the inner cities, on the frontlines of the civil rights movement.

New theologies of the servant church and secular Christianity paid small attention to the ecclesiological disputes that had so preoccupied earlier generations of church leaders—so little that, in a paradoxical way, it hardly mattered if episcopacy or presbyteries survived, for they were scarcely worth the trouble, in the face of more pressing ministerial tasks, of dismantling or rearranging. Nonetheless, Blake-Pike was a most important early Sixties indicator, simply because in the end it brought to high visibility how different the religious world of the Sixties was from that of 1948 and 1950, when, in the glow of immediate postwar ecumenism, the World Council of Churches and National Council of Churches were founded.

But institutional church reunion did not excite the Sixties, even the churchly Sixties, as an important spiritual ideal in the way it might have the preceding generation. It was not an imperative for the same reason that the various renewed traditionalisms of Merton, Watts, and Huxley in the Forties and Fifties did not entirely suit the self-consciously new world of the Sixties. The Sixties did not simply want bigger and better religious institutions, however streamlined in administration and inclusive in creed. Rather, they wanted to take a hard new look at religious institutions from the ground up, so to speak, not necessarily to jettison them altogether, but certainly to reassess their precise relation to spiritual experience, to valid religious leadership, and to the mission of religion in society.

In quite different ways, and with differing results, this reassessment was undertaken by mainline and evangelical Protestants, by Roman Catholicism in the Vatican II era, by the growing numbers attempting to transplant Buddhism and other Eastern religions into American soil, and by the burgeoning ranks of at least temporarily independent seekers. What was coming was religious decentralization and local-level diversity, with favor going to ways of the spirit that produced direct, felt experience and perceptible social change. Few expected that a union of nine gray-flannel denominations would produce anything but more of the same, and it was a decade yearning instead for psychedelic rainbows. (Eugene Carson Blake himself some four turbulent years later owned to "second thoughts" about the proposal, holding, in language that echoed contemporaneous Catholic second thoughts swirling around Vatican II, that the union could be an "outmoded triumphalism.")[15]

Finally, COCU failed because, in the end, the Sixties brought nothing less than a sea change in the character of America as a *denominational society*. The term refers to a religious polity, of which the United States is no doubt the world's premier example, in which it is tacitly understood that the spiritual function is shared by several independent and coequal organizations or denominations. Each has its own unique history and emphases and is chiefly devoted to the care of its own people, at the same time acknowledging through both competition and cooperation the existence of others of broadly comparable strength and secular standing.

The century and a half leading up to 1960 was a golden age for denominations, and it is not accidental that it was also the heyday of the modern mood. Aided by great advances in transportation and communication, by publishing houses and educational foundations, denominations became religious parallels to the other major local, state, and national insitutions of society: government, the educational establishment, the great corporations. The major denominations established public identities, national headquarters, bureaucracies, and local branches comparable to those of a state, a supermarket or department store chain, or a school system. They took their modern shape over more or less the same years as these bodies were taking theirs, and often quite deliberately in imitation of them. The Fifties mainline denomination, like Fifties Roman Catholicism in America, was the culmination of this trend, and COCU was to be its capstone.

Instead, the system began breaking down in the Sixties with the movement from modernism to postmodernism, leaving the COCU ideal high and dry. Initiative on important issues, like civil rights, was local or individual or led by extradenominational organizations like the Southern Christian Leadership Conference—the politics of the Holy Ghost rather than of institutions. Budgets for national church offices declined, and tensions between them and parish churches increased; at local levels the well-modulated liberal policies characteristic of headquarters satisfied neither the can't-wait radicals nor the increasingly outspoken and embittered conservatives. Denominational loyalty in any case was clearly less important to many Sixties generation people than to their parents and grandparents; if they went to church, it was often not so much because of denomination as convenience or the particular style of local ministry.

As early as 1960, a survey of college students showed that, while a majority felt a need for religion, almost half of these meant by religion nothing more than "some sincere working philosophy or code of ethics, not necessarily a religious belief." Secular values or pragmatic reasons for belonging to a church, such as "personal adjustment," "an anchor for family life," and "intellectual clarity" were more important than traditional doctrines.[16] Although needs such as these could undoubtedly have been well met in a vast ecumenical church, one wonders if such unpassionate believers would have the motivation to create one.

The important splits, such as those between liberals and evangelicals, or liturgicals and charismatics, were often as much intradenominational as interdenominational. In a word, religion was reverting to its ultimate base, localism. I have suggested elsewhere that this midcentury process can also be thought of as a reversion of religion to the style of a folk religion, rather than of a great tradition.[17]

It is worth noting that, if denominationalism shifting into reverse does represent a large-scale and long-range trend, it will be one of major religious-historical importance. It will indicate a reversal of the dominant trend in most great religions over the past 2,000 years, above all, as I have indicated, the last 150 up to 1960. But actually the great founder religions like Christianity, as we saw in the first chapter, were the real precursors and paradigms of modernism. Over the last two millenia their trend has been broadly toward augmenting the power of national or international religious structures—papal, royal, caliphal, denominational, whatever—to which the local is distinctly subordinate. This has meant not only hierarchical control of local appointments, but also long-term pressures toward standardizing forms of worship, toward the imposition of universal creeds and confessions, and toward the homogenization of religious cultural and moral values over against the local.

Even when such centralization has been formally denied, as in churches of congregational and baptist type, the prestige of a general, that is, denominational, religious culture within a church, of the whole over the branches, has been apparent. Significantly, that wider culture has usually been defined preeminently in relation to the major elite of the society or region. As we have seen, denominational leaders have characteristically been educated in elite universities and seminaries, in interaction with potential leaders of the other major institutions, government, business, education. The upshot is that, one way or another, a typical church was a local outpost for the dissemination of a great tradition, rather than primarily a place for the independent creation or definition of local-level spirituality.

The concept of local religion as "branch" and derivative from something else wider, older, and truer is far from completely undermined and perhaps can never be in a world in which the local is under so much unfriendly pressure from mass media, multinational business, and heavy-handed governments. But one facet of the Sixties spirit seemed to want to make religion a refuge from homogenization rather than another arena for it. Local prayer groups, meditation groups, charismatic groups, religious social action groups, and house churches, not to mention new and independent religions, sprang up alongside the standard brands. Activists of the religious left and right, often tangential to mainline denominations, went their own conspicuous ways. The elite leaders seemed, like Blake and Pike after 1960, to be following more often than leading. A new kind of postmodern American religious reality was emerging in the 1960s, and in the course of this study we will try to ascertain better just what it was and is.

The tension is by no means new in American religion. One thinks of such extra- or antidenominational awakenings as the frontier revivals, spiritualism, or Pentecostalism, which no less challenged existing denominations to find vessels able to contain their new wine. As we shall see, Martin Marty believed that "awakenings" marking the end of a phase of American religion are a recurrent phenomenon. But in the end the pattern breakers came to terms with denominationalism in principle, either accommodating themselves to existing churches or forming new ones. Now, though it is too early to say certainly, it is possible that in the rise of postmodernism the traditional denomination itself, in the sense of an institutionalized religious subculture with bureaucracy and local branches such as we have described, is in recess, and that now denominationalism will decrease as the age of the spirit, and of localism, increases. The fate of Blake-Pike was an important early indicator of all this.

The trend was powerfully backed up by several other general Sixties themes we have cited: antihierarchicalism; favoring charismatics against institutional knowledge-holders; favoring sharply defined intentional communities (usually concrete, immediate, and so local); accepting pluralistic modes of being and life-style; and supporting the particular human against the system—any system. Only the theme of recovering the romantic past might favor religious systems and hierarchies with an especially evocative aura of ancient wisdom almost lost and now once more found. In all this, the laurels went to shamans, to marginal people, and to those able to profit from the equalized postmodern marketplace of spiritualities.

The New Conservatism and the Protestant Future

In light of all that happened after 1964, it is easy to forget that, at the time, the early Sixties were perceived not as an era of rising radicalism—except for the civil rights movement in one segment of the population—but as two or three years of growing conservatism, and even of an alarming upsurge of right-wing extremism. Newspapers and magazines commented on an alleged increase in conservative views on campus. Senator Barry Goldwater was a popular speaker in colleges as elsewhere, and his book *The Conscience of a Conservative* and syndicated columns were widely read and discussed.[18]

In religion, the new conservatives, including a rising breed of extremists, strongly challenged the Blake-Pike kind of Protestant establishment. The National Council of Churches was especially attacked by such groups as the John Birch Society, the Christian Anti-Communism Crusade, and the Methodist Circuit Riders, who accused it of being a kind of superchurch led by "pinks" and Communist infiltrators, of speaking for members without consulting them, and of taking stands favoring admitting Red China to the United Nations and abolishing the House Un-American Activities Committee (HUAC).[19] Some churches and church gatherings were flooded with slick, expensively produced extremist literature and divided by bitter struggles between Rightists and moderates. The showing of HUAC's highly partisan movie

57

Operation Abolition, which in its original form (later modified) contained attacks on the NCC and liberal members of the clergy, was often a flashpoint. A 1960 furor arose over the air force manual *Guide for Security Indoctrination*, which contained a section, "How to Stop Communism in America," repeating as authoritative the ultra-Right allegations that Communists had infiltrated the nation's Protestant churches and especially, of course, the NCC. Defense Secretary Thomas S. Gates was said to be "furious" about the manual and wrote letters of apology to the appropriate churches and the council. But anti-Communist believers continued to believe.[20]

It must be noted that the conservative extremists of the Sixties, no less than their counterparts on the Left, were characteristically obscure people with no elite credentials and minimal visibility. Frederick Schwarz of the Christian Anti-Communism Crusade was an Australian physician, the son of an immigrant Viennese convert from Judaism to Pentecostalism who had done well in Sydney in the war-surplus business. John A. Stormer, author of one of the most influential extreme Right books of the period, *None Dare Call It Treason*, was the child of a plumber and a 1954 graduate of San Jose State College in California rather than of a prestigious Ivy League school. His short-haired, clean-shaven unsmiling face gazing resolutely from the book's back cover suggests the position he then held, chairman of the Missouri Federation of Young Republicans; the cover also states that he attended a "fundamental" church.[21] Billy James Hargis, son of a truck driver, headquartered his Christian Crusade in Tulsa and flaunted a diploma mill doctorate.

But the followers of these and other such prophets of the Right, typically from dusty small cities of the South and West, had this much in common with civil rights blacks and the soon-to-come student rebels at prestige universities they despised: all were people who had long felt patronized but marginalized by the elite establishment, and who were not going to take it any longer. The Sixties were a time of the breaking of many such molds, on the Right and on the Left. On both flanks one finds the typical Sixties politics of the Holy Ghost, animated by potent archetypes and self-images, overwhelming the conventional and compromising established institutions.

The charges of the anti-Communists were answered in editorials like "Back the National Council!" and "Religion and the Radical Right" in the *Christian Century* (July 12, 1961; April 11, 1962).[22] On the Catholic side, in 1962 the Reverend John Cronin of the National Catholic Welfare Conference published *Communism: Threat to Freedom*, a pamphlet that along with its assaults on communism attacked the extreme anti-Communists, such as the Birch Society, for "giving aid and comfort to the enemy" by their distortions and divisiveness. The booklet drew negative reaction from some Catholic rightists but was endorsed by most bishops and widely circulated.

It is important to recover the atmosphere of those stormy years. An editorial article in the *Christian Century* of May 16, 1962, "Rightist Weather Map," reports bitter and divisive battles in small towns and heartland cities all over the country after the appearance of extreme anti-Communist groups.[23] Those vigilantes split churches and communities over sermons, schoolbooks, showing the HUAC movie, and the relation of local churches to the NCC. The extremists did not, in the end, always or even often win, but neighbor had been set against neighbor, once friendly communities left ugly and suspicious, and ministerial careers jeopardized. Archetypes had been raised into high relief, and, as one might expect, polarization set in like a winter freeze.

This scene was only a counterpoint to the better-known new progressive visions of the Kennedy era. The Kennedy victory may actually have prepared the way for the 1961–1962 rightist upsurge, the most potent since the McCarthy era a decade before. In the interval the presence of a Republican administration had ameliorated all but the most rabid of the ultras, like Robert Welch of the Birchers in his famous claim that Dwight Eisenhower was "a dedicated and conscious agent of the Communist conspiracy." But an administration like Kennedy's, suspect to the Right in any case, together with the even more suspect burgeoning civil rights movement and the discreditable Cuba crisis, again set the extremists full tilt against Washington and left them free to unleash their tactics of total polarization.

But the deepest reason for the radical Right was certainly the pervasive deep-level fear—of a changing world, new values, a new kind of open culture, racial integration, international tensions—that seemed to affect a sizable part of the population in those tense postwar, Cold War years, and that led them to yearn almost religiously for conformity, solidarity in a cause, and a purifying purge of society. No one put it better than one of the chief religious rightists himself. According to Mark Sherwin, Billy James Hargis once boasted that he had "the feel of the people" and went on to comment, "They wanted to join something. They wanted to belong to some united group. They loved Jesus, but they also had a great fear. When I told them that this fear was Communism, it was like a revelation. They knew I was right, but they had never known before what that fear was."[24]

There the rightists were in the early Sixties, strongest in the growing Sun Belt states of the South and Southwest—areas less under the grip of the liberal, intellectual wing of the modern elite than the North and East, and now asserting their new political and social importance, an importance to be consummated in the careers of Nixon, Goldwater, and Reagan. In the next chapter we shall note how the unsuccessful Goldwater crusade of 1964 was perceived to be, for a great many of its supporters, more like a religious revival than an ordinary political campaign. Often honed by the "Christian" anticommunism of the decade's early years, they brought to it attitudes reminiscent of un-compromising religious belief.

The far Right was not the only disruptive force confronted by traditional faith. Not a few unfamiliar and much-criticized forms of religion were now being observed by an apprehensive public. In 1960 the first U.S. chapter of Soka Gakkai was formed; as Nichiren Shoshu, that controversial high-pressure, this-worldly school of Japanese Buddhism would grow exuberantly during the Sixties. The Black Muslims were increasingly visible in the cities, and Eric Lincoln's valuable 1961 book on them, *The Black Muslims in America*, increased awareness of this militant movement.[25] In 1963 officers of the U.S. Food and Drug Administration raided the Washington, D.C., Church of Scientology and seized its E-meters, electrical devices used to measure responses in "auditing," or Scientological counseling. (They were returned in 1969 after a decision that auditing with E-meters was a validly religious procedure.)

Amid all the frenzy around the religious perimeters, the once-solid center itself seemed to be giving way. Protestants were becoming aware that the boom years of the early Fifties were past. In 1960 it was reported that between 1958 and 1959 Catholic church membership had gone up 3.4 percent, but the Protestant increase at 1.7 percent lagged behind an overall population growth of 1.8 percent.[26] Mainline Protestants were doing even less well, and seminary enrollments were declining.[27] Between 1960 and 1962 the membership of six quintessentially mainline, predominantly WASP churches—Episcopal, Presbyterian, United Church of Christ, Disciples of Christ, Methodist, and American Baptist—together grew by only 128,000, less than several important but less centrist denominations garnered on their own. In the same years the Missouri Synod Lutherans gained 131,000 members, the Latter-Day Saints, 195,000, and the Southern Baptists 460,000, while Roman Catholicism added 1,743,000 to its parish rolls.

Most of the 1960–1962 mainline growth was Methodist, and in 1961 the United Methodist Church topped ten million. After much study, Methodist statisticians determined that the ten millionth member was a blue-eyed, blonde, ten-year-old girl in Wilson, North Carolina, who upon being interviewed said that when she grew up she wanted to be a kindergarten teacher in the morning, a housewife in the afternoon, and a Sunday school teacher on Sunday.

Methodism was for the moment the largest Protestant denomination, and it was a moment of Methodist glory. A May 25, 1960, editorial in the *Christian Century* had praised the Methodist church as "nationally our most inclusive church," with a more representative racial and regional balance than any other. But it was not to last, and all too soon the malaise that had afflicted the other WASP mainliners would reach Methodism. The Southern Baptists were catching up fast and would surpass the Methodist church in numbers in 1962; by 1991 Methodism had fallen from ten to just over nine million.

A Catholic President?

Sparked by the candidacy of John F. Kennedy, changing religious perceptions and contours were profiled in the 1960 debate over the appropriateness of electing a Roman Catholic to the presidency of the United States.[28] The debate in the early months of the year, as Kennedy approached closer and closer to the Democratic nomination, was as much over whether religion would be a factor as whether it should be. Some Protestants, especially parsons of more conservative denominations, felt nagging doubts based on a belief that in case of conflict a Catholic as president would have to put the moral and institutional demands of his church ahead of his duties to the nation in a way that a Protestant would not.

The Reverend Robert G. Borgwardt, pastor of the First Lutheran Church of Sioux Falls, South Dakota, summed up the conundrum this way: "The potential candidacy of Senator Kennedy leaves most Protestant churchmen with schizophrenia. Certainly any citizen of the United States should have an opportunity for the highest office in the land, regardless of race or creed. This is so fundamental to our democratic way that it is agonizing to have any sort of hesitancy on this point. However, I must admit that I do."[29]

Norman Vincent Peale, with some 150 other Protestants, organized a National Conference of Citizens for Religious Freedom. Though in fact a pro-Nixon campaign front, it presented itself as "an intelligent approach to the religious issue on a high philosophical level," from which heights it cast doubts that a Catholic president could separate his duties from his commitment to mother church. (Later, Peale expressed regret at his involvement in this group.)

The issue was endlessly discussed. Bishop Pike produced a slim

Counterpoint: Another California Quaker

Clark Kerr, president of the University of California, was the subject of an October 17, 1960, cover story in *Time* that highlighted rapidly expanding higher education in the United States. A few years later, the balding, witty administrator was to become the quasi-innocent demon of the Berkeley free speech movement as he sought to enforce regulations originally adopted as an improvement over a McCarthy-era ban on Communist speakers but that equally restricted all political activity on campus. Yet Kerr was a true liberal of the New Deal era, and virtually an archetype of both the virtues and blindspots of modernism. He had gone to Swarthmore College where he became a Quaker and social activitist. He delivered street-corner lectures on behalf of pacifism for the American Friends Service Committee. Later he made for himself an honorable liberal reputation as a labor economist and skilled strike arbitrator. He had done his part to make modern industrialized society work fairly; perhaps it would be too much to expect him fully to understand those young people spawned by the Sixties who were disaffected by its shiny blueprints.

In 1960 the economist turned university president published *Industrialism and Industrialized Man*, which argued that, in time, high technology tears down dictatorships instead of strengthening them and creates, through market forces and their educational requirements, democratic "industrial pluralism."* Events in the late twentieth century have suggested that, in the very long run, he was probably right. His critics on campus and off, however, increasingly contended that Kerr saw the university itself as little more than an industry, and even more to the point as no more than a feeder of trained talent into the vast industrial system that was the U.S. economy. Kerr argued that business, government, and education all needed each other and had to meet each other's needs; the campus could no longer live apart from the world when high tech everywhere required the mass training of skilled hands and minds. It was all to the greater good; together higher education and high technology can create a true liberal paradise. To this immense task politics on campus could only be a distraction, poisoning the requisite trusting partnership between business, government, and education. Clark Kerr still meant well, but he had come a long way since the days he was a pacifist street preacher.

*Clark Kerr et al., *Industrialism and Industrialized Man* (Cambridge, Mass.: Harvard University Press, 1960).

book on the subject.[30] A few people also raised the issue of the Republican candidate's Quaker religion, asking whether Richard Nixon as a member of that traditionally pacifist church would be prepared to use armed force if necessary, despite his having served as a navy officer during the war and not being known to have attended a Quaker meeting in years.

In the end, most lay people in 1960 decided that religion should not be an electoral factor, and it probably was not.[31] The election was thus the first great advance in the dramatic Sixties march toward a vastly expanded American pluralism with power sharing. Ironically, those who knew John F. Kennedy personally were aware that he wore his familial religion very lightly, as Nixon did his Quakerism. Kennedy pointedly avoided being seen with Roman Catholic bishops or other hierarchs, or appearing at any public function in a Catholic capacity. It was an open secret that some very prominent Catholic ecclesiastics, including Francis Cardinal Spellman and Egidio Vagnozzi, the apostolic delegate, preferred Nixon to Kennedy, both because they felt the Quaker was sounder on anticommunism and other values important to them, and because they reckoned, no doubt rightly, that they would gain more from a Protestant president indebted to the church than from a lukewarm Catholic resentful of its pressure.

Kennedy had declared that if he were president he would observe strict separation of church and state. The Massachusetts Democrat flatly opposed federal aid to parochial schools and promised he would never appoint an ambassador to the Vatican—both burning issues that put him in opposition to Rome and the American hierarchy generally. A Protestant politician, on the other hand, might well have felt himself free to show greater flexibility on those points and wish to in order to ingratiate himself with twenty million or so votes.

In late October 1960, just before the election, a curious episode occurred in Puerto Rico that briefly reheated the religion issue. The archbishop of San Juan and two other bishops of the island dependency issued a pastoral letter forbidding church members to vote for the Popular Democratic party of Governor Luis Muñoz Marín, ostensibly on the grounds that it supported public funding for birth control services. The letter produced as fervent a reaction in the mainland United States as in Puerto Rico, raising new doubts about Kennedy and the Catholic church's role in politics. "They said it couldn't happen in America, but it did," declared the *Baptist Standard*, and others joined suit. Nonetheless, Muñoz won, as did Kennedy, and the Puerto Rican bishops quickly backpedaled from their excommunication threats. John Cooney, Cardinal Spellman's biographer, believes that the whole affair was one of the New York prelate's "Machiavellian maneuvers," intended to weaken Kennedy's position on the eve of the election. He points out that Spellman was in Puerto Rico October 12–14, just before the letter was issued and, though disclaiming it, seemed to have "enjoyed the uproar."[32]

In the event, it was Protestant hopes and prelatic Catholic fears that were borne out. A 1962 *Newsweek* article observed that, after a year in office, Kennedy had "lost some Catholic support but won wide Protestant approval." The Jesuit weekly *America*, at the same time, complained that the first Catholic president "has not only gone out of his way *not* to ingratiate himself with a specifically Catholic constituency; he has regularly bent over backwards so as to make it dramatically clear to any Southern Baptist who might be watching that he doesn't give an inch."[33] Specifically, *America*, like many other Catholic voices, was sharply critical of Kennedy's stand against parochial school aid, though others of his faith remained supportive, recognizing the political and constitutional box he was in. (In the end, after intense lobbying on both sides, but especially by Catholics who opposed it as discriminatory if parochial schools were not to benefit from it, federal aid to public education was defeated in Congress.) On the other hand, Protestant leaders, including some who had opposed Kennedy on religious grounds in 1960, expressed approval, at least on the separation of church and state issue.

Church and State

On other levels, however, Roman Catholic attitudes on church and state were in movement. The Jesuit John Courtney Murray was an important figure, the subject of a December 12, 1960, *Time* cover story on "U.S. Catholics and the State" based on his book of the same year, *We Hold These Truths: Catholic Reflections on the American Proposition*. It is a sober, serious, pre–Vatican II address to the question, Is American democracy compatible with Catholicism? Despite the Roman Catholic church's claim to absolute truth, and traditional insistence on the obligation of the state to favor truth, Murray contends that the answer is yes. Following the teaching of the fifth-century pope Gelasius I, who presented a doctrine of the ecclesiastical and political realms as two distinct societies, Murray argued that the American separation of church and state is acceptable to Catholics, provided there is a "public consensus" on the principles and values underlying American society, and this consensus is based on natural law, not "rationalism" or a notion of "natural rights" emphasizing only human autonomy, as in the philosophies of Locke or Dewey.

64

Natural law upholds the responsible individual freedom intrinsic to working democracy but also embraces the rights of groups, such as the church, to recognition as integral though nonstate actors in society; churches can then seek to fill the spiritual emptiness that the merely autonomous modern person feels. The church confronts the state only through individuals, in terms of their obligations and rights. Thus, on the hotly debated parochial school aid issue, Murray contended that the denial of aid to religious schools denies distributive justice and "does not square with the fact of our pluralist social structure" by not reckoning fairly with its diverse individual educational needs.[34]

The Catholic world in which cautious, balanced statements like Murray's could look advanced was to pass away sooner than anyone in 1960 would have expected. (The Catholic church ten years later was virtually unrecognizable as the one out of which Murray wrote in 1960; a 1970 *Time* cover story ran on "The Catholic Exodus: Why Priests and Nuns Are Quitting.") The Decree on Religious Liberty of Vatican II, in the formulation of which John Courtney Murray had a large part, swept away his church's longstanding willingness to associate itself with the secular sword. It renounced external force in matters of religion, and affirmed the dignity of even an erring conscience; some council speakers explicitly rejected the claim, which had so irritated Reinhold Niebuhr, that the church is a perfect society.[35] (Vatican II, and the pontificate of John XXIII, would go a long way to bring American Catholicism into virtual religious parity with Protestantism and Judaism by undermining old perfectionist and separatist attitudes and practices; after 1965 Catholic priests, nuns, and laity suddenly possessed something like a new culture, looking and talking, even sharing doubts and institutional criticisms, like anyone else.)

John XXIII's great social encyclical, *Mater et Magistra*, dated May 15, 1961, argued even earlier for the right of all persons, wherever and of whatever class, to equal dignity and a fair portion of the world's goods. It called for the state not to restrict the freedom of individuals to take responsibility for their own lives, to own property, and to form cooperative relationships, if within the bounds of equal justice and humanity.

John's even more important encyclical *Pacem in Terris* was dated April 11, 1963, less than two months before the pontiff's passing, his "last will and testament," as his biographer Peter Hebblethwaite called it. Unlike certain predecessor popes, John pointedly emphasized a positive assessment of the modern world's achievements: the rising standard of living for the working class, the emancipation of women, the demise of imperialism. He reiterated even more strongly his theme of the ultimate importance of the individual person and his or her freedom, including full freedom of conscience; he called for peace based on trust rather than fear, on the ending of the arms race, and on the interdependence of nations.[36]

The dominant religious figure of the early Sixties, in the United States as in the world, was certainly Pope John XXIII. He was greater than any one encyclical, in a sense greater even than the Vatican Council, for he had summoned it. His calls for *aggiornamento* or up- dating in the life of the church, and his openings to the East, glad- dened the hearts of all except the most hardened conservatives, but the true revolution that he wrought in the papacy and the church as a whole was based less on any particular action or policy than on the warm, spontaneous, natural personality of the man himself. The im- age of a pontiff who clearly understood and lived the priority of grace over gravity, and Christian love over legalism, compellingly suggested the possibility of a new kind of church in which the same virtues were expressed freely in styles of worship and ministry, in liberty of thought and collegiality in governance. The implementation of those ideals was the burden of Vatican II, in which John was even more present, if possible, after his death than when he officially opened the council October 11, 1962.

Not all Catholic hopes were realized, and much was lost as well as gained. The great exodus of priests and nuns in the late Sixties and early Seventies from the church Pope John and the council had made testifies to that melancholy reality. Perhaps the advance was too rapid and unsettling. But the pope who reigned at the onset of the tumultu- ous decade was, like the decade itself, made of soul stuff, not spirit only. (His book was called *Journal of a Soul*; in it he had written, on November 25, 1940, amid the horrors of war, "What is happening in the world on a grand scale is reproduced on a small scale in every man's soul, is reproduced in mine.")[37] To Sixties people, whether of his faith or not, he was a holy father. When he died on June 3, 1963, the outpouring of sorrow worldwide was immense.

At the time he wrote *We Hold These Truths*, John Courtney Murray feared that the "public consensus" upholding the "American proposi- tion" was crumbling more and more. That was one reason he urged that the Republic's polity be explicitly founded on the deep bedrock of natural law, rather than on mere human reason or "natural rights." He could hardly have known at the time how much more the Ameri- can body politic would crumble, in the sense of becoming ever more pluralistic and divested of symbols of spiritual cohesion, in the next decade. In the eyes of many, one major signifier of that decline of "civil religion"—whether viewed with alarm or satisfaction—was the Supreme Court school prayer decision of July 1962.

In a six-to-one vote, the U.S. Supreme Court ruled that mandatory prayer in public schools, such as the nondenominational classroom prayers with which numerous teachers had heretofore begun the school day, trespassed freedom of religion, violated separation of church and state, and was an unconstitutional "establishment of religion." The outcry was immense; the ruling was compared to tearing a star or stripe off the flag, there were those who were sure it was Communist inspired, and some observers thought it could only lead to such further rulings as removing the motto "In God We Trust" from coins or abolishing military chaplaincies. Bishop Pike, throwing himself as usual into the thick of things, proposed a constitutional amendment seeking a "middle way" between "Church-state union" and the "secularization of public life"; the amendment would define clearly what Pike believed to be the original intent of the First Amendment by stating that "Establishment" meant support of a particular "denomination, sect, or organized religious association." This clarification would permit the recitation of presumably nondenominational and nonsectarian prayers in public schools and other public settings, but no religious favoritism. His proposal, however, went nowhere.[38]

Though the controversy was soon off the front pages, pushed out by even more dramatic and unsettling civil rights events, school prayer has remained a staple of conservative politics ever since. Undoubtedly its role as an issue has been more symbolic than substantive; a minute of bland generalized devotion may or may not have warmed many childish hearts, but it meant the arbitrary-seeming removal of even the semblance of a common piety, and many found disturbing the insistence that the American state—unlike most others past and many others present—must avoid even the appearance of being other than a purely secular entity. It suggested we were entering waters as new and uncharted as those in race relations and (in the wake of the Catholic president issue) religious pluralism. As forcefully as Harvey Cox's book of three years later, the prayer decision said we were now come of age in a secular city and would have to make the best of it. On June 17 of the next year, 1963, the Court ruled further that recitation of the Lord's Prayer or the reading of Bible verses in public schools was also unconstitutional. The Sixties drive toward pluralism, and the deconstruction of hegemonic institutions, pushed on.

Counterpoint: Mater et Media

The election of a Catholic president and the almost contemporaneous commencement of Vatican II boded change in two institutions, the U.S. government and the Roman Catholic church—though the change was much less than expected in the former, and far more in the latter. In one respect, however, there was no real change at all. Both before and after 1963 both institutions were almost entirely male dominated, as for that matter were Judaism and virtually all Protestant churches as well. That reality was not yet under serious challenge in 1960, but the deep background of challenges to come was starting to be painted in.

Valerie Saiving Goldstein, a "nondenominational Protestant" writing in the *Journal of Religion*, complained that contemporary theologians "are making the mistake of assuming that a thinking man's theology is equally good for a thinking woman." Men, she said, have to achieve and are therefore more anxious and assertive, while women are taught to be more passive and waiting. Their "specifically feminine forms of sin . . . , outgrowths of the basic feminine character structure," are suggested by such terms as *triviality, distractability,* and *diffuseness*; lack of an organizing center or focus; dependence on the other for one's self-definition—all the opposite of ego-centered masculine sinfulness. The ideal of selfless love, held up by masculine religion as the hard but necessary negation of natural human pride, for women can instead easily become a temptation that appeals to their weakness, their yearning for approval and lack of a firm ego center, more than it is a real sign of spiritual maturity. If it is true, Goldstein concluded, that society is becoming more feminine, then theology ought to reconsider its view of what sinfulness means; a feminine society would have its own special potentials for both good and evil.*

Later religious feminists may find as much to jeer as to cheer in Goldstein's pioneer statement, but she does suggest that the mothers of the baby boom years, and within a few years their daughters even more, were not entirely content with a religious or social world that looked at them largely through male eyes. In the same year, the topic was also examined by *Newsweek* in a "Special Science Report" on "Young Wives." (Significantly, the story was not written by a woman journalist but by *Newsweek*'s science editor, Edwin Diamond, who "put [the] girl-who-has-everything under the microscope and offers an analysis of the young American wife in the 1960s.") "Who could ask for anything more?" the tale begins. "The educated American woman has her brains, her good looks, her car, her freedom. Come next November, she will outvote the American male—for the first time in history there are 3 million more registered woman voters than men voters.

Counterpoint: Mater et Media *Continued*

"Yet she often complains that she is not completely happy."

The report focused entirely on women in the "upper income bracket," "the product of good obstetrics, good nutrition, and good living." She is, therefore, "*a woman freed from the tyranny of her body*" (italics in original). Yet she is unhappy, and "her discontent is deep, pervasive, and impervious to the superficial remedies which are offered at every hand." Diamond appears to have had some difficulty in figuring out the reasons for this ungrateful response to "a lot that women of other lands can only dream of." But, in a wise move, he turned in the end to the wisdom of Margaret Mead, then doyenne of American womanhood, who pointed out that postwar America, reacting against the unsettled Twenties and Thirties and the war years, had rushed too far in the direction of overdomesticity and the cult of "togetherness."

"Togetherness, you know," the anthropologist said. "Marriage is supposed to be the apex of the woman's existence—in fact, the only purpose in life." But where does this leave a woman when the glamor years of courtship and young marriage are gone, the children are going away to college, the nuptial relationship has perhaps become humdrum, and a mind and a set of feelings are wasting? Margaret Mead concluded, "Remember, family life is not an end in itself. A woman's career should last longer than a boxer's or a ballet dancer's. Her goal should be development of herself as an individual, not because she is a wife or mother, but because she is a human being."

The article praised women in their late thirties and early forties who were reenrolling in "Barnard, Hood, and the California junior colleges."**

*Valerie Saiving Goldstein, "The Human Situation: A Feminine View," *Journal of Religion* 40, 2 (April 1960): 100–112. See also the article on Goldstein in *Time*, June 27, 1960, 76–77. This article has been anthologized under the name Valerie Saiving in *Womanspirit Rising*, ed. Carol P. Christ and Judith Plaskow (San Francisco: Harper and Row, 1979), 25–42.

**Edwin Diamond, "Young Wives," *Newsweek*, March 7, 1960, 57.

New Beginnings

Why did that electorate with a plurality of women voters elect Kennedy? William Hamilton did a postelection piece in the *Christian Century* called "The Victory Was Video's," in which he argued that the TV debates between Kennedy and Nixon were decisive.[39] But probably no one could say for sure whether it was the young Catholic candidate's greater wit, sex appeal, mastery of material, and much-touted charisma; or the subtler and deeper way his calls for a new beginning matched a widespread deep discontent like that of the young wives who, according to *Newsweek* in 1960, had "everything."

In any case, it was probably that discontent that, behind the scenes, pushed Protestantism into what Martin Marty, around inauguration day, called its third phase: "Inauguration Day 1961 can serve symbolically as marking the end of Protestantism as a national religion and its advent as the distinctive faith of a creative minority." This was an application of Marty's thesis in *The New Shape of American Religion* (1959) that in American history a religious revival, like the Fifties revival of "interest" in religion, actually marks the *end* of a religious phase, in that case the Protestant "Pietist" age begun with the Great Awakening; it was to be supplanted by a "post-Protestant" era—no doubt what we have been calling postmodernism.[40]

Civil Rights

By 1960 there were many for whom the American dream now had to include equal civil rights for all, and explicitly for African Americans. The movement for equal rights for blacks, to end segregation and gain full voting rights in the South and equality in jobs and education everywhere, was preeminently a story of the early Sixties. Its time of greatest glory, both morally and politically, was the years of principled nonviolent sit-ins, freedom rides, voter registration, and the march on Washington under Martin Luther King leading up to the Civil Rights Act of 1964 and the Voting Rights Act of 1965. Thereafter, in an atmosphere increasingly marred by inner-city riots, extremism like that of the Black Panthers, and resurgent violence including the assassinations of King and Malcolm X, gains were fewer and polarization greater. But no setbacks can ever mar the spiritual splendor of the civil rights movement in its best hours or diminish it as, after Gandhi, probably the clearest example in history of successful nonviolent political activism based on spiritual commitment.

Galvanized by a sense of clear-cut right and wrong, thousands of black and white students first experienced several important Sixties things in connection with civil rights: forming activist communities, violating unjust laws, feeling moral outrage and a sense of themselves as morally and spiritually different from the older generation, taking risks and traveling to where the action was—all based on fundamentally religious values.

Out of civil rights arose the politics of the obscure individual led by the spirit, and in these spiritual politics noninstitutional voices can sound louder than those of hierarchies. In civil rights a natural community (blacks) supplemented by an intentional community (white supporters) sharply defined its frontiers by symbols of dress (at first, the conspicuously neat outfits of the sit-ins and freedom riders) and action (sit-ins, marches). It was civil rights that first brought Sixties-style leveling and pluralizing pressures to bear on a moral/political issue, and that first set the righteous young—as children of light, students of both races, Peter Pans, and their believers—solidly against the armies of darkness.

Actually, the civil rights struggle began as a tremendous upsurge of modernism, in the sense of believing in progress and in endeavoring to implement the democratic modernist agenda now—but it ended by undercutting modernism through its leveling of the elite and marginalized, and its leading to more demands for more equality and more pluralism than could be met by modernist means.

The situation was evident enough. Early in 1960 much talk centered around a series of articles by John Howard Griffin in *Sepia*, later published as a book called *Black Like Me*. Griffin, though white, had dyed his skin and spent four weeks traveling around the Deep South as a black. He suffered much abuse from white segregationists, and his stories rang all too true for African Americans. He vividly spoke of what it was like to travel at the back of an interstate bus and not be able to get off at a white rest stop after a long ride to grab a snack or use the bathroom or even get a drink of water. He was once picked up by a white truck driver who asked him if his wife had ever slept with a white man and added that "you'd be doing your race a favor to get some white blood into your kids." (Griffin noted that the southern white male, whenever he got a chance to talk man-to-man with a man of the other race, often revealed a near obsessive interest in the sexual lives of blacks.) When Griffin offered his seat on a bus to a white woman, all he got was a "hate stare" in return.[41]

To counter the grossest of those evils, the civil rights movement first sought to compel desegregation. Then it sought to gain equal education and voting rights for blacks, in order to insure that equality at the lunch counter would be lasting and would lead to equality in the boardroom and the state legislature. In the early Sixties, each year had a special motif: 1960 was the year of the sit-ins, 1961 of the freedom riders, 1962 of the universities, 1963 of the Washington march.[42]

The Year of the Sit-Ins, 1960

After the Montgomery bus boycott of 1955, already mentioned, the next major civil rights move was on February 1, 1960, when four black students sat at a whites-only lunch counter in Greensboro, North Carolina, and politely requested service, prepared to wait patiently for hours to receive it. The nonviolent gesture caught the public imagination and was imitated thousands of times across the South, and in the North too. In New Haven, two hundred Yale Divinity School students demonstrated in support of the sit-ins. Overwhelmed, such public service facilities began to desegregate on a large scale.

One place sit-ins were imitated was in Nashville. The first sit-ins there, on February 20, were quiet. Lunch counters closed when the demonstrators approached. But on the afternoon of Saturday, February 27, the demonstrators were joined by about eighty students from Fisk University, Tennessee Agricultural and Industrial University, and American Baptist Theological Seminary. At this point some rowdy white boys began jeering and hurling epithets at the students, finally attacking them violently. Arrests were made, mostly of the black demonstrators, and considerable tension arose in the city. Despite the efforts of black ministers at dialogue, Nashville was racially divided, and the white establishment seemed determined to prosecute the protesters. On March 3 a warrant was issued for the arrest of a particular suspect, James M. Lawson.

Lawson was a Methodist minister, a senior at Vanderbilt University Divinity school, a representative of the pacifist Fellowship of Reconciliation, a project chair for the Nashville Christian Leadership Council, and an African American who had counseled students in methods of nonviolent resistance. As a consequence of his role in the sit-ins, he was expelled from Vanderbilt University, though he had replied to charges that he had encouraged students to violate the law with a statement that declared:

> Under no circumstances have I ever made, or will I ever make, the categorical statement that students should violate the law. These are not my words. Defiant violation of the law is a contradiction of my entire understanding of and loyalty to Christian nonviolence. When the Christian considers the concept of civil disobedience as an aspect of nonviolence, it is only within the context of a law or a law enforcement agency which has in reality ceased to be the law, and then the Christian does so only in fear and trembling before God. Furthermore, the issue completely overlooked is that throughout the demonstrations, particularly and foremost the last one on Saturday, the students remained wholly loving and nonviolent even though the violence directed against them was beyond anyone's imagination.[43]

72

Nonetheless, Lawson was dismissed; the university chancellor told the press that "the issue is whether or not the university can be identified with a continuing campaign of mass disobedience of law as a means of protest." Divinity school students and hundreds of Vanderbilt faculty members pledged Lawson their support. On May 30, 1960, after the chancellor had further refused to permit Lawson to enroll in the summer session of the divinity school, J. Robert Nelson, dean of the divinity school, and eleven other of the school's sixteen faculty members resigned.

In the meantime a number of lunch counters in Nashville had been opened to customers regardless of race, but the board of trustees of Vanderbilt University supported the chancellor. In the end a compromise was reached by which Lawson would be permitted to return, take examinations, and earn the B.D. degree without actually enrolling, and the resigned professors would be given ten days within which they could withdraw their resignations. Declaring this a victory, nine divinity school faculty returned. Dean Nelson, who was to be dismissed in any case, and two others stayed away.[44] In the first year of the Sixties, then, a doleful pattern was wheeled into place. First comes the waffling of well-meaning but anxious knowledge-holding institutions, church and university. Then power and glory goes instead to erstwhile marginal persons—the young, the black—whose eyes are single, and who prevail not by dint of many words but as shamanic masters of silent symbols like the sit-in, and by the power of their sufferings.

In the April 13, 1960, *Christian Century*, Martin Luther King published an article for the "How My Mind Has Changed" series called "Pilgrimage to Nonviolence." He referred to reading Walter Rauschenbusch and Gandhi but said that the experience of Montgomery had clarified his thinking on nonviolence more than anything else.

April 15–17 also saw the convening of the Leadership Conference on Nonviolent Resistance at Shaw University in Raleigh, North Carolina. Speakers included Lawson and King, and the upshot was the forming of the Student Nonviolent Coordinating Council, or SNCC. A second SNCC conference was held in October 1960 in Atlanta, where the organization had established itself in the headquarters of the Southern Christian Leadership conference (SCLC); Martin Oppenheimer says that by the time of this meeting sit-ins had reached a "semi-institutional" stage. They were by now supported by a number of semiofficial church bodies—the NCC General Board, ESCRU (the independent Episcopal group), the (Northern) Presbyterian Church U.S.A., the Congregationalist Home Mission Board, and others.[45]

SNCC was to have a curious history. It was formed to coordinate the sit-in activities of 1960, which were paradigms of nonviolent activism in the Gandhian tradition, and the group's original statement, written by Lawson, was an eloquent affirmation of pacifist principles. Yet Lawson himself was never active in SNCC. After the sit-in movement wound down in 1961, SNCC would have died too but for its decision to move on to other labors in the Deep South, specifically organizational and voter registration work among black people. After 1962 it was no longer a student movement but dependent on a poorly paid staff of around sixty and a large number of volunteers. It became more radical, even revolutionary, at best seeing nonviolent activity as a means of creating tension out of which revolutionary consciousness could arise; this caused tension with SCLC, and by 1966 charges of SNCC "paronoia" even by the group's friends.[46] The increasing radicalization and eventual demise of originally pacifist, or otherwise deeply spiritual, Sixties activist groups is a theme to which we will return.

August brought the first widely publicized kneel-ins. In 1959 Liston Pope of Yale Divinity School had called the church the most segregated institution in America, and eleven o'clock Sunday morning was often said to be the most segregated hour of the week. That ancient pattern began to end on August 7, when some twenty-five "courteous Negro college students" attended six of Atlanta's white churches. They were welcomed at all but two, both Baptist, and another barrier was falling.[47]

By this time the presidential campaign and the Catholic president issue had begun to push the civil rights movement temporarily off the front pages and the religion page. The two matters of contention, White House Catholicism and Southern civil rights, however, returned in tandem that October when Robert Kennedy, brother of the embattled candidate, intervened with a Georgia judge to obtain bail for Martin Luther King, who was imprisoned as a result of an Atlanta department store sit-in. At the end of the year some 3,600 students had been arrested for sitting in, and one or more lunch counters had been desegregated in 108 southern communities. But the struggle was far from over.

Newsweek on November 28, 1960, contained a grimly prophetic item on a race riot in New Orleans, perhaps the first but far from the last such story of the new decade. It was in curious juxtaposition with the cover story, "Today's Parents: Trapped in a Child-centered World." "They are disobedient, impossible to control, why can't they be like we were? What's the matter with KIDS today?" Not a few white grown-ups were asking the same question about American blacks—and the two questions would be threads running through the Sixties from here on out.

The Year of the Freedom Riders, 1961

The early Sixties were a time of coffeehouses and folk songs. Bob Dylan and Pete Seeger did much to create the ethos of those years, singing verses like "I'll be sittin' at the front of the bus . . . , / Come on over to the front of the bus, / I'll be sittin' right there." A radical idea has to be conceptualized in simple, appealing form before it can truly take hold. The civil rights folk song brought freedom down home, and putting rights on the bus merged the movement with America's love of travel down the nation's long and lonely highways. Testing integration by sending adventurous students on long-distance bus rides with songs like those echoing in their ears was a brilliant idea, and in the end it worked. By then even white students of the purest establishment heritage had self-consciously marginalized themselves to be a part of the action; the proletarian songs helped the process.

So it was that the major event of 1961 was the freedom rides, young blacks and whites traveling together on long bus journeys through the cotton fields and red clay soil of the Deep South. Organized by the Congress of Racial Equality (CORE), soon joined by the Student Non-violent Coordinating Council (SNCC),the rides were designed to test the integration of public transportation in the South.[48] On May 4, 1961, thirteen blacks and whites together left Washington to take an integrated bus ride through the South. They encountered no trouble as they traveled down the east coast, but as they moved inland the bus they were on was bombed and burned at Anniston, Alabama. The freedom riders took another bus for Birmingham, where they were attacked by a mob. A different group, led by SNCC, now moved on to Montgomery, where they were attacked by another mob on May 20.

As the levels of violence escalated, so did calls for the federal government to intervene. The Kennedy administration, still new and already weakened by the Bay of Pigs fiasco of April 17, was by no means eager to do so, but at this point Attorney General Robert Kennedy ordered four hundred U.S. marshals to Montgomery to maintain order. On the evening of May 21, King spoke at a mass meeting in Montgomery's black First Baptist Church. An angry white crowd gathered outside and assaulted the church with bottles and bricks, as the thousand or so gathered within sang verses like, "We are not afraid, / We are not afraid, / We shall overcome some day." They had thought they were protected by the marshals, but at the end of the service congregants found themselves prevented from exiting the stifling building by members of the Alabama National Guard, allegedly also sent to keep the peace by the segregationist governor, John Patterson. After a confusing and traumatic night, punctuated by calls between Montgomery and Washington, the doors were finally opened around 4:30 A.M., and the National Guard was compelled to escort King and the freedom riders to safety.

The freedom riders were promptly joined by prestigious northern church leaders, including Henry Sloane Coffin, Jr., chaplain of Yale University, who was arrested along with many others. There is no doubt the rides were a spiritual exercise. Wyatt Walker, a freedom rider and the executive director of SCLC, said, "It's almost a religion with us. It's carried into all facets of our lives." The statement suggested a potent mixture of southern religion and Gandhi. The black demonstrators of those years were taught always to be neat, well-dressed, polite—and not afraid.

Among the riders of 1961 were twenty-seven men in clerical collars, five of them black, who tested segregation laws in Mississippi. They were Episcopal priests, sponsored by the newly formed (and controversial) Episcopal Society for Cultural and Racial Unity (ESCRU), participating in a September Prayer Pilgrimage. They met in New Orleans, then traveled by bus to various southern Episcopal parish churches to pray, thanking God for those they found integrated, and asking God's help for those still segregated. Fifteen were arrested in the Jackson, Mississippi, bus terminal; one of them, the Reverend Robert Pierson, was the son-in-law of Governor Nelson Rockefeller of New York. The fifteen got the standard freedom rider sentence of four months in jail and a $200 fine but were released on bail pending appeal so they could attend the General Convention of the Episcopal church in Detroit.[49]

An article on one of the bus-riding priests sheds light on the Prayer Pilgrimage and on the reaction it received in typical 1961 churches. The subject, the rector of a suburban Episcopal church in a border state, was not among those arrested in Jackson, but he did join some others of the party who stayed on to minister to their brethren in jail. The authors, Ellen Naylor Bouton and Thomas F. Pettegrew, surveyed his vestry and members of his parish for their reactions to their rector's participation. Only four out of sixteen vestrymen, but nearly half the parish, approved. Those opposed, on the average, were older, had lower incomes, had been in the parish longer, and had fewer children in integrated schools than supporters; women were somewhat more likely than men to be supporters.[50]

At the same time, at traditionally black Howard University, William Nelson, religion professor and one-time friend of Gandhi, gained attention for teaching the nonviolent methods of the sit-ins and the freedom rides to his students. Nonviolence, he said, is "a weapon of the strong, not of the weak. The object is to convert not by making someone else suffer, but by suffering yourself. The very sight of that suffering will draw attention to the problem. It is a way of life, a religion."[51]

Also in 1961 the Voter Education Project got underway to register voters in Mississippi under the leadership of Robert Moses, a worker with SCLC and one of the organizers of SNCC. Moses's unusual background underscores the profoundly religious underpinnings of the movement. Born in New York, he was a gifted child who, though black, attended superior, largely white high schools and colleges. After a bout of fundamentalism, he became a philosophy major at Hamilton College, taking an interest in Eastern philosophies and pacifism. He spent summers in Quaker workshops in Europe and Japan and in Japan spent some time in a Zen monastery. Moses began a Ph.D. in philosophy at Harvard but because of family tragedies was unable to complete it. At Harvard he attended lectures by Paul Tillich, the theologian on whom Martin Luther King had written his dissertation, but according to Taylor Branch was unimpressed by him.[52] He turned to activism; in Mississippi his efforts and those of his associates to register and inform poor black voters were carried out in an atmosphere of shootings and beatings.

The Year of the Colleges, 1962

Across the country, students both white and black responded to the civil rights movement's kind of idealism. By early 1962, thousands were in picket lines at the White House urging President Kennedy to advance disarmament; the freedom riders were supported not only by volunteers but in greater numbers by fund-raisings and petitions at universities across the country; UC Berkeley was already alive with student activities—though off campus—to abolish HUAC and support civil rights. But students seemed to be wary of formula ideology and more concerned with moral than strictly political issues; *Time* spoke of campus civil rights as a "Crusade" with, as the magazine put it, a "Gandhiesque color." The earlier alleged rising conservatism of campuses was, if anything, a negative by now, provoking a counterresponse more impassioned than what the rather diffident reactionaries could muster; University of Washington historian Giovanni Costigan was quoted as saying, "The tactics of the right-wingers outraged the students' sense of fair play."[53]

In October 1962, three successive *Newsweek* cover stories suggested the accelerating drumbeat of dramatic news that would characterize the Sixties: a special issue on the Space Age on October 8; a celebration of the opening of the Vatican Council on October 22; and between them, on October 15, a piece called "The Sound and the Fury" (after the novel of that title by the most famous resident of Oxford, Mississippi, William Faulkner) about the dramatic efforts necessary to enroll a black student, James Meredith, at the University of Mississippi in Oxford. Almost exactly one hundred years after General Grant's invasion of Mississippi in the fall of 1862, the city was again occupied by U.S. troops, this time to enforce a federal court order allowing Meredith to register at Old Miss. They were confronted by an angry mob, but after much violence Meredith got through.

For Martin Luther King, much of 1962 was taken up with a hard-fought campaign to integrate Albany, Georgia, a struggle that brought him jail time and ended in bitterly disappointing defeat.

The Year of the Dogs, the March, and the Bomb, 1963

In April 1963, Martin Luther King began his antisegregation campaign in Birmingham, Alabama, just after the city's notorious segregationist commissioner of public safety, Eugene ("Bull") Connor, was narrowly defeated in his run for mayor. The struggle in that industrial city, reputed to be the toughest segregation town of all, was marked by daily demonstrations and an almost total boycott of white stores by black shoppers. On Good Friday, King and fifty-three other demonstrators were arrested.

To critics who said that this demonstration was untimely, King wrote his famous "Letter from Birmingham Jail" explaining (in the title of a later book based on the letter) "why we can't wait" and outlining his philosophy of nonviolence. It was published in the *Christian Century* June 12, 1963, holding its own with reports on the death of Pope John XXIII.

The letter's eloquence defies quotation except in its entirety; the gist is that well-meaning moderates who keep deploring "direct action" such as the sit-ins and marches, urging blacks instead to "wait" and to negotiate, do not understand a people who have been waiting more than 340 years. Unjust laws, as all racist laws necessarily are, or laws unjustly applied to repress one portion of the population, can rightly be broken, and only pressure will produce results, as doleful experience has shown time and again. Poignantly describing the effects of segregation even on children, King made it clear why his people can no longer wait for "a more convenient season."

Eight days after his arrest, King posted bond and was released, ready to begin new demonstrations. These centered on the May 2 and 3 Children's Crusade, in which about a thousand blacks, mostly teenagers, marched singing in small groups to downtown Birmingham. Many arrests were made on both days, and on the second Bull Connor met the demonstrators with police dogs and fire hoses while they stood in prayer, including petitions for forgiveness of their oppressors. The pictures of dogs attacking prayerful women and children, flashed around the world on TV, horrified millions and won far more sympathy for King and his followers than for the segregationists. The religious symbols of the Sixties were being more and more strongly etched.

Birmingham's white business and political establishment was now ready for a truce. An agreement was worked out May 10, based on King's demand for desegregating public facilties, providing equal job opportunities, dropping all charges against arrested demonstrators, and setting up a biracial commission to reopen parks and other facilities closed to avoid integration. But Birmingham was not yet out of the news. The truce was shattered by the bombing of the home of King's brother and of the motel where King was staying. Blacks were enraged and ready to riot again. Because that would be playing into the hands of the segregationists, King rushed back to Birmingham from Atlanta to promote his gospel of nonviolence. It was called the Poolroom Pilgrimage, for he went everywhere he could find blacks to talk to—pool halls, barrooms, churches. With these efforts and the support of President Kennedy and the federal government, the truce was upheld. The blacks' cry of "Freedom now!" seemed realizable.

King came out of Birmingham a national hero in the eyes of the black community and to millions of impressed and guilty whites. As a speaker he drew huge crowds: 10,000 in Chicago, 25,000 in Los Angeles, 125,000 on a peaceful freedom walk in Detroit. Even more important, the Birmingham victory had moved President Kennedy from a cautious to an aggressive posture on civil rights. On June 11 the chief executive presented the most advanced civil rights legislation ever proposed, calling for voting rights, equal employment opportunities, and the end of segregation in all public places. To support it and to demonstrate the strength and unity of the civil rights community, King now called for a march on Washington for jobs and freedom. More than 200,000, including an estimated 40,000 whites, gathered on August 28, when King delivered his splendid "I Have a Dream" speech, with its prophetic biblical allusions: "I have a dream that one day, every valley shall be exalted."

The dream was not shattered, but the darkness of still-unexalted valleys was demonstrated by further tragic events in Birmingham the next month. In September, the opening of schools was marred by bitter struggles over the admission of black students to three formerly all-white schools. Once again the altercations were punctuated by bombings, demonstrations, rock throwing, and the activities of riot police. The worst event, and one that shook the nation, was the bombing of a black church on September 15. It was Sunday morning, Youth Sunday, and four girls who had been preparing to help lead the adult service were killed; scores more were injured, including women who had just been discussing "The Love That Forgives" in a Sunday school class.

On October 4, 1963, *Time* ran a story called "Waking Up to Race" about clergy in the 1963 civil rights campaign, pointing out that some one thousand took part in the march on Washington, including two Roman Catholic archbishops, ten Episcopal bishops, and fifty rabbis. During the year to date, more than two hundred clergy members had been arrested for taking part in picket lines and demonstrations, including Eugene Carson Blake; the Presbyterian leader was now far more involved in working in the streets for civil rights with a black Baptist like King, where ecumenicity was really happening, than in ecclesiastical diplomacy for mainline Protestant reunion.

The religion of the civil rights movement was in certain important ways distinct from the balance of the Sixties religion scene. Rooted in the traditions of the black church, it was not theologically adventurous like the secular or "Death of God" theologians but was biblical in language, emotional and community building in style. Unlike the Blake-Pike plan or Vatican II, it was more active on the local than the national or international institutional levels. Unlike the mysticism of the counterculture, it was more concerned with praxis along America's highways and byways than with visionary experience.

Yet, as has often been the case with the religion of American blacks, much more was going on than appeared on the surface. As far back as slavery days, biblical and religious language had been used to express this-world as well as supernatural hopes, to express yearning to cross Jordan into freedom as well as to reach heaven. Civil rights religion powerfully stimulated the secular, activist thrust of much Sixties religion by showing that religion can be a force for social as well as inward freedom, for salvation from oppression by others as well as from personal sin.

Civil rights religion introduced a couple of additional themes that would be important as the Sixties advanced. One was nonviolent resistance. Not only Robert Moses (who was to lead the 1964 Mississippi Summer) and William Nelson, but Bayard Rustin (of the Congress of Racial Equality and a co-worker with King) and other important movement figures had been influenced by Quakerism and Gandhi and had been workers for the pacifist Fellowship of Reconciliation. Like King himself, they were theologically much more liberal than the black church norm but found ways to meld their nonviolence with its deep spirituality of strength under oppression. The Berkeley free speech movement and the antiwar movement would soon quite consciously borrow these tactics.

A second theme was the importance of community. The civil rights movement learned early on that it was essential to create, define, and hold together the activist community if there was to be any hope of success; when these endeavors fizzled, as in Albany, Georgia, campaigns also failed. In Birmingham, as earlier in Montgomery, when people stayed together, they prevailed. The idea of a community with a purpose was to become important not only in other activist projects of the Sixties, but in major new concepts of the "servant church" that were emerging in both Catholic and Protestant circles in the decade. Civil rights and the black churches behind the movement showed what an activist, intentional community meant, both in suffering and in triumph, and did much to make it happen.

This leads to one final, and unfortunately more ambivalent, issue: confrontation and polarization. The civil rights movement did much to engender the Sixties mentality that saw the great issues of the day as modernist dualism redivided and raised to apocalyptic terms as good versus evil, the children of light against the children of darkness, and (no less significantly in generational terms) the righteous young—especially students, like those of sit-in and freedom ride fame—against their benighted or overcompromised elders. Undoubtedly these perceptions were justified in the case of the civil rights movement of the early Sixties. But Sixties people, like most people, were often tempted to carry their virtues and their successes to extremes, and not all disputed questions were quite so clear-cut, even in hindsight. In the end some confrontations, as we shall see, merely exposed the contradictions of modernism and impelled its transcendence by postmodernism.

Chemical Visions and Cosmic Rights

On March 28, 1960, *Time* reported, in "The Psyche in 3-D," on the psychotherapeutic use of "one of the most potent drugs known to man," lysergic acid diethylamide, LSD. Its use "in combination with orthodox psychotherapy had led to the accelerated recovery of about half the patients given doses" at the Psychiatric Institute in Beverly Hills, including Cary Grant. The drug reportedly effected powerful visions that could help the subject conceptualize family or inner disturbances, childhood fantasies, or early memories "remembered with superhuman accuracy." The value of the new remedy was that it helped the patient to see conflicts and the contents of the unconscious "projected onto the LSD screen" and "acted out before him." LSD, the article went on, cures nothing of itself, but its "apparent value lies in boosting—and accelerating—the benefits to be gained from normal psychiatry" (85)

About this same time, Alan Watts, as had Aldous Huxley before him, was experimenting—then of course legally—with psychedelic drugs. Watts took LSD on several occasions around 1960, conflating and reporting his experiences in *The Joyous Cosmology*. In the opening lines of this book he presents a thesis that was to become basic for the Sixties spiritual quest, rather a riposte to *Newsweek*'s account, in "Young Wives," of the modern woman freed from the tyranny of her body.

> Slowly it becomes clear that one of the greatest of all superstitions is the separation of the mind from the body. This does not mean that we are being forced to admit that we are *only* bodies; it means that we are forming an altogether new idea of the body. For the body considered as separate from the mind is one thing—an animated corpse. But the body considered as inseparable from the mind is another, and as yet we have no proper word for a reality which is simultaneously mental and physical."[54]

It was the drug, of course, that propelled the new mind-body realization, for it was obviously physical yet at the same time produced effects that could only be thought of in the terms with which one contemplated experiences of soul and spirit. It saw into the worlds of soul and spirit, yet saw them in things material, the folds of a garment or the tracery of a leaf.

The same summer of 1960, the summer of the sit-ins and the increasingly impassioned Catholic president debate, Timothy Leary, a Harvard psychology professor traveling in Mexico, ate six "magic mushrooms." He was sceptical; the fungi were bitter and stringy, and for Leary their smell recalled a moldy New England basement. But he consumed them, washed them down with beer, and waited for something to happen.

It did. First he burst into laughter, laughing (appropriately) at the pomposity and the "narrow arrogance" of scholars like himself, obsessed by "the impudence of the rational, the smug naïveté of words," in contrast to the "raw rich ever-changing panoramas" now flooding his brain. He gave way to delight, to awe, and finally to a realization that in the four hours of the "trip" he had explored more of his mind than in the previous fifteen years as a psychologist; he later described those hours as the "deepest religious experience" of his life. He was converted and was to remain a convert to the new sacrament from then on.

The religious dimension of the psychedelic experience was likewise the subject of the famous "Good Friday experiment" of 1962 conducted by Walter Pahnke, then a graduate student in religion and society at Harvard. The subjects were twenty divinity school students assembled in Marsh Chapel of Boston University, where they listened over loudspeakers to a religious service, consisting of organ music, solos, readings, prayers, and time for personal meditation, piped in from another part of the building. Ten of the students had been given psilocybin one and a half hours before, the other ten a placebo.

In follow-up interviews and questionnaires, those who had taken the drug in this setting reported a profound religious/mystical experience, scoring two or more times higher than the control group on such items as sense of transcendence of time and space; feelings of joy, blessedness, peace, and love; and sense of the sacred. Most also reported, six months later, persisting positive changes in attitude and behavior toward self and others.

A long-term follow-up of the experiment published in 1991, based on interviews with most of the original subjects, indicated little change in the positive attitude toward the experiment and its beneficial effect; for most it remained one of the most powerful religious experiences of their lives. At least two of the participants had subsequently become actively, and potentially dangerously, involved in the civil rights or antiwar movements; they reported that the Good Friday experience had deepened their commitment.

For them, the powerful vision of cosmic unity, of all things flowing together, forcefully indicted segregation and war. Moreover, the sense of ultimate transcendence had greatly weakened the subjects' fear of persecution and even death. As one said in the long-term follow-up, "When you get a clear vision of what [death] is and have sort of been there, and have left the self, left the body, you know, self leaving the body, or soul leaving the body, or whatever you want to call it, you would also know that marching in the Civil Rights Movement or against the Vietnam War in Washington [is less fearful]. . . . In a sense [it takes away the fear of dying] . . . because you've already been there. You know what it's about." (Once more, the politics of the Holy Ghost: it was not institutional status but visionary experience—LSD-seeded in this case—that steeled the respondent to face defeat or death in the streets.)

At the same time, the long-term follow-up revealed that, as Pahnke acknowledged, some subjects had difficult and unpleasant experiences during or after the Good Friday service, and that one, who apparently went through a "bad trip," became sufficiently distraught that he had to be given a tranquilizer, an event Pahnke chose not to mention in his report.[55]

Walter Pahnke's principal academic adviser for the experiment was the aforementioned mushroom eater Timothy Leary, soon to become famous (or notorious) as an impassioned evangelist for the world-salvific value of psychedelics, and as an evangelist with an extraordinary capacity for getting into trouble. He and Richard Alpert, both psychologists at Harvard, undertook further research on hallucinogenics. In 1961 the University Health Service made them promise not to use undergraduates as subjects in their experiments; they were fired in 1963 for violating this pledge. They continued experiments independently, though Alpert soon went to India and became Baba Ram Dass, and on his return a leading light of the mystical Sixties; in 1967 he helped establish the Lama Foundation, a universalist, mysticism-oriented spiritual center in New Mexico.

Leary, on the other hand, became the leading spokesperson of the religious drug movement. As we will see in the next chapter, he settled with a group of followers on an estate in Millbrook, New York, where in 1966 he established the League for Spiritual Discovery; in December of that year Leary was arrested; for many following years his life was mainly jails, trials, escapes, and exiles, with occasional surfacings to give much-sought interviews to the *Oracle* and other underground papers. While at Millbrook, he wrote more and more fervent treatises on the psychedelic experience as an experience of God, comparing it to the perceptions of the *Tao te ching* and the *Tibetan Book of the Dead*. He took to wearing a white robe and golden crownlike headband. As a sampler of the religio-mystical psychedelia of the early Sixties—after the pioneers but before Haight-Ashbury, as the bandwagon was beginning to roll—here are a few snippets of psychedelic reports from various subjects presented by Timothy Leary in a lecture delivered to a meeting of Lutheran psychologists in 1963:

> Mind wandering, ambulating throughout an ecstatically-lit indescribable landscape. How can there be so much light—layers and layers of light, light upon light, all is illumination.

> I became more and more conscious of vibrations—of the vibra-
> tions in my body, the harp-strings giving forth their individual tones.
> Gradually I felt myself becoming one with the Cosmic Vibration. . . . In
> this dimension there were no forms, no deities or personalities—just
> bliss.

And, in one suggesting more the awesomeness of ultimate self-
awareness and judgment:

> Two related feelings were present. One was a tremendous free-
> dom to experience, to be I. It became very important to distinguish
> between "I" and "Me," the latter being an object defined and patterns
> and structures and responsibilities—all of which had vanished—and
> the former being the subject experiencing and feeling . . . the other
> related feeling was one of isolation. The struggle to preserve my
> identity went on in loneliness; the "I" cannot be shared or buttressed.
> The "Me," structured as it is, can be shared, and is in fact what we
> mean when we talk about "myself," but once it is thus objectified it is
> no longer *I*, it has become the known rather than the knower. And
> LSD seemed to strip away the structure and to leave the knowing
> process naked—hence the enormous sense of isolation: there was no
> Me to be communicated.[56]

Other signs too hinted that the decade's new wine was about to
burst the old wineskins. In 1960 the publication of *Christian Yoga*, by
J. M. Dechanet, a Belgian Benedictine, made an extraordinary impact
in the press; this was a study, moderate and cautious by today's standards, of how Christians could benefit from the practice of certain
yogic techniques. Like Dom Aelrad Graham's *Zen Catholicism* (1963),
it helped to inaugurate an age of interreligious practice as well as
dialogue, and to mark the end of the fortress mentality of pre-Vatican
II Catholicism.[57] Also in 1960 the Zen Center of San Francisco, soon
to become the largest and most influential of such centers, and the
Unification Church ("Moonies"), began drawing Western recruits; they
had both been planted in the United States the previous year. Timothy
Leary, in *High Priest*, claimed that in 1962 there was a perceptible
shift among those interested in the spiritual meaning of the psychedelic experience from Christianity, as in the Good Friday experiment,
to the East, especially Hinduism.[58]

Vatican II

Like the Protestantism of Martin Luther King, Jr., the Catholicism
of Pope John XXIII was perceived as dramatic and innovative; the
early Sixties were one of those rare privileged spans of a few years
when individuals of more than normal stature dominated major institutions, and part of the sickness of the later Sixties lay in their being

all too soon gone. By the early years of the decade eager reporters sometimes claimed that the rotund pope, old and increasingly ill from the cancer that was to end his life, was becoming a prisoner of the curia, particularly the so-called Pentagonisti, the "Big Five" among the cardinals who headed the major Vatican departments.[59] But in fact John acted quickly and spontaneously to make changes of the sort that were important to him. In 1963, for example, he interrupted a Good Friday service to order that the reference to "perfidious Jews" be cut from the liturgy, almost as though he knew he must act fast to accomplish what had to be done before the disease killed him.

Most important of all, of course, in early 1959 he had called the General Council, the "New Pentecost" that was radically to change the face of Roman Catholicism forever, as radically as Martin Luther King's actions changed the lives of American blacks. The council was expected to deal chiefly with the relation of the church to the modern world, searching for new forms adapted to present-day needs, a broad charge that would include liturgical reform (including doing away with Latin as the general liturgical language in favor of simpler, more community-oriented services in the vernacular); updating the relation of church and state and the church's position, as we have seen, on religious freedom; and establishing greater "collegiality" between bishops and the Vatican in church administration, with augmented opportunity for discretionary actions by bishops in their own sees. There was also much hope that the council would adopt changes opening the way for ecumenical reunion.

Curialists tried to manage the council once it was a fact, hoping to limit its scope and make it little more than a ceremonial occasion, good for public relations but a paper tiger so far as threatening established ways of doing business or their established bureaucratic positions was concerned. But they found the repressed rage of the church's bishops worldwide against them too great to be contained, and they schemed without much success, at least while the council itself was in session.

John XXIII opened the first session of the council in October 1962. Meeting October 11 to December 8, it accomplished mostly organizational tasks. The 1963 session, held after the death of John XXIII, was opened by Pope Paul VI on September 29 and ran until December 4. It completed action on a document on the liturgy and accepted as bases for discussion schemata on the church, episcopacy, and ecumenism (including the religious liberty issue). For all its outward drama, the council was for participants a slow, tedious, and sometimes contentious process.

In December 1963, Pope Paul formally promulgated the first and almost only concrete accomplishment of the Vatican Council to date, a decree making sweeping liturgical changes in the Mass. It would now be said in the vernacular, except for the "canon," the actual consecration of the bread and wine (this change would come a few years later); scriptures would be read facing the congregation; and an offertory procession would bring the bread and wine from the back of the church to the altar. *Time* opined it would now be "like the Anglican or Lutheran communion services."[60]

However that may be, dramatic changes like these in the mode of worship should not be minimalized, for, to most ordinary participants, forms of worship say much more about a religion's ethos and values than does anything else. To a degreee that surprised most Catholic and non-Catholic observers alike, radical alterations in the everyday celebration of the Mass were actually occurring in the usually glacial Roman Catholic church. Decrees at this point also decentralized the church to some extent; local bishops now had the right on their own to give dispensations for mixed marriage. And the council was to continue.

The World Council of Churches in New Delhi

The early Sixties likewise saw much discussion of a Protestant counterpart to Vatican II, the World Council of Churches meeting convened for seventeen days in New Delhi, India, on November 19, 1961. This was virtually the last of such WCC meetings to win widespread public attention and unfortunately did not measure up to the Vatican Council in achievements, despite the significant Third World setting. The council was marked by the admission of new Latin American churches, and especially by the admission of the Russian Orthodox church. That action aroused a predictable outcry from the extreme Right in the United States as confirming all its worst suspicions about the World (and National) Council, and in fact there is little question that the Russian church in those years was firmly under the control of the Soviet government.

But ironically the effect of the Russian Orthodox admission was less to promote a Marxist agenda than subtly to weaken progressive initiatives in other areas on the part of the WCC by shoring up its customary domination by male and clerical representatives. Resolutions commending churches that ordained women were withdrawn after provoking heavy Anglican and Orthodox opposition, and commentators noted that subsequent to the admission of large Orthodox

Counterpoints: Tongues and Undertows

In the early Sixties the eyes of the nation and the world, if they were focused on religion at all, were likely to be on the dramas of Vatican II and the role of Protestant activists in the civil rights movement, or on the conflict between liberal Protestants and the extreme right. But there were other shows. *Time*, on December 20, 1963, published an article on "The Evangelical Undertow." It quoted Ilion T. Jones, retired professor at San Francisco Theological Seminary, as saying, "I am convinced that an 'evangelical undertow' is building up in this country and that it must be reckoned with sooner or later."

This undertow, *Time* said, is a "hard-to-map Third Stream in American Protestantism, running midway between the simplistic fundamentalism of small Christian sects, and the sophisticated faith espoused by a majority of the nation's best-known theologians and denominational leaders." It was, in other words, an emergent alternative to the standard models of American religion—both the NCC-type mainstream establishment versus the marginalized, and the hopeful Protestant-Catholic-Jew troika—and it definitely was going to be reckoned with by the 1970s and 1980s.

Time noted that such persons as Carl Henry, Billy Graham, and Cornelius van Til accept the Bible as the authoritative rule of faith and practice and attack "modern" theologians, including Karl Barth, Rudolf Bultmann, and Tillich. Yet they are culturally more advanced than many fundamentalists and are interested in intellectual dialogue with liberals rather than in denunciation only.

It seems clear that *Time* had caught on to the milieu that was to nourish the much-discussed evangelical revival of the 1970s and had pinned down what it really was: not the conversion of large numbers of people to evangelicalism so much as the coming of age of the evangelical subculture that has always existed in the United States. Like nearly everyone else in the Fifties and Sixties, people of this culture were making more money than ever before, moving to the suburbs, going to college, becoming concerned about politics and social issues. But by the Sixties some of them were no longer interested in moving "up" to a more liberal church, as they might have been in the Fifties or before; they were willing to engage their new lifestyle and concerns from an evangelical perspective and were nurturing leaders able to help them do it.

The political activism of the Christian right in the 1970s and 1980s may have roots in the fundamentalism of many of the extreme anti-Communists of the early Sixties who found themselves with the money and the political clout to operate on a national scale. Others, like Jimmy Carter or Senator Mark Hatfield, let deeply evangelical religious convictions motivate

Counterpoints: Tongues and Undertows *Continued*

more moderate or liberal political positions. In any case, a new evangelical class was beginning to appear. During the turbulent Sixties, apart from the ever-visible Billy Graham, it would largely be crowded off the front pages, and the religion pages, by more immediately newsworthy persons and events. But neo-evangelicalism was awaiting its day.

One wing of this revival was the emergence of Pentecostalism—speaking in tongues, spiritual healing, prophecy, and other gifts of the spirit—in the mainline Protestant denominations and even in the Roman Catholic church, where it is often called the charismatic movement. Though Pentacostalism has roots in the Fifties, the early Sixties saw a great upsurge of this phenomenon, typified by Rev. Dennis Bennett in the Episcopal church, mentioned earlier. Neo-Pentecostalism is a little hard to place. Just as historic Pentecostalism is not quite the same as evangelicalism or fundamentalism, so mainline and Catholic Pentecostalism cannot be completely boxed with preexistent liberalism or conservativism.

There were those who compared the fashionable mainline Pentecostalism of the early Sixties with the burgeoning interest in LSD experience. According to the psychologist of religion Francis Geddes, for example, "Both speaking in tongues and taking LSD offer a person a very deep, very profound, very soul-shaking experience. . . . Both approaches place a high priority on psychological or religious experience as an end in itself. . . . When I look an LSD convert in the eyes, I get the same look as when I look at a speaker-in-tongues—the look of 'I've got truth.' They are taking the cork out of the the stopped-up id."* Certainly palpable in the Sixties was the hunger for any experience, so long as it was intense enough, by a generation that had missed the harsh passion of the war and yearned for some moral equivalent of its own.

Most Pentecostalists were religiously conservative enough to take the New Testament and its promises of spiritual gifts as authoritative, and to believe literally in the Holy Spirit, in prayer, and in miracles. But some were socially liberal and impatient with hidebound churchly creeds and procedures. This was particularly the case in Roman Catholicism, where charismatics, including many priests and nuns, were likely to be very much *aggiornamento*, Vatican II, social activist kinds of people. Later both Catholic and Protestant neo-Pentecostalism were to become rather separatist and hidebound in their own ways, drifting toward pietistic conservatism.

*Cited in Donovan Bess, "Speaking in Tongues: The High Church Heresy," *Nation*, September 28, 1963, 173–177. Geddes went on to point to differences between the tongues and LSD experiences, and also to say that both "can be dangerous" if accepted in too uncritical, true-believer a way.

churches little movement in that direction, or toward effectively and truly independent lay voices in the council, was likely to come for years.[61]

Books

Here are some books and articles published or much discussed in the religion world of the early Sixties. Some are of lasting significance; some are named simply as indicators of the times. All helped me to get a feel for what religionists of the time who were also serious readers probably were thinking and were talking about with like-minded colleagues.

A good place to begin is Pierre Teilhard de Chardin's *Phenomenon of Man* (1959).[62] Few found this extraordinary attempt to combine science and religion totally convincing, though to many readers it was nonetheless a brilliant and provocative tour de force. Stephen Neill, reviewing the Jesuit paleontologist's dazzling account of interlocking physical, biological, and spiritual evolution from Genesis to "Point Omega" for the *Christian Century* (March 30, 1960), considered it "very stimulating" but perhaps an oversimplification; events after the emergence of "reflection" or conscious mind may not go predictably, and so to refer to *human* destiny as a continuation of "evolution" is misleading.

Yet this and the French priest's other works, most published posthumously because of church opposition, caught the world's imagination. Teilhard was the subject of countless articles and conversations on all levels in 1959 and the early Sixties. In part that was because he was a Jesuit priest as well as a scientist, which gave his vision—at once scientific, mystical, and, by his own lights, Catholic—the extra frisson of being daring and radically innovative, yet within a recognizable spiritual context. The poignant story of Teilhard's semi-exile and the suppression of his work by his church and order only added to the appeal; Teilhard virtually became a cult.

But there is also no question that Teilhard's grand concept spoke to a deep yearning of the day for a way to understand matter and life, soul and spirit, as all parts of a single organic unity. This was the same great journey on which Aldous Huxley and Alan Watts had set out, and for which the apostles of psychedelia like Timothy Leary thought they had discovered the express lane. The rising standard of living for many in the Fifties had impelled an appreciation of science and technology, even as "the bomb" raised anxiety concerning them and humankinds's future. These blessings and banes were hard to sort out, not to mention the inner malaise that many, like *Newsweek*'s "young wives," inexplicably felt amid all the abundance.

By 1960 discontent with the dualism of science and spirit, and a feeling of purposelessness or moral vacuum in the midst of plenty, had perceptibly deepened. This was a moment for which Teilhard, with his fresh kind of Catholicism and his newly humanistic kind of science, was an ideal match. Whether or not he was right in all the details, he opened a lot of windows. He was among the first—and, with John XXIII, perhaps the best—of the chanticleers of the Sixties spiritual awakening.

An interesting set of publications of around 1960 were books on Gnosticism, largely based on the Nag Hammadi texts found in Egypt just after World War II and now ready to be published in translation: the Gospel of Thomas, the Gospel of Philip, the Gospel of Truth, and others. For many these were no more and no less than standard scholarly productions. But for others the meaning of the Gnostics' often enigmatic words went beyond that. A counterculturalist once told me, ecstatically, that the Gospel of Thomas made Jesus sound like a Zen master, full of mysterious and enlightening koans—the "secret gospels" of those ancient outsiders, the Gnostics, clearly made Christianity more attractive to him than anything preached in church.

Something about Gnosticism, with its layered realms of light above this misbegotten Earth, and its oblique hints that the secret of the meaning of it all was to be discovered within—above all by the most alienated—resonated with the spiritual Sixties. The decade's nursling children of light, conceived in estrangement and weaned on LSD, tutored by Carl Jung and Aleister Crowley, thought they knew what Gnosticism was about if they were learned enough to study it, and some counterculturalists did not shrink from the old Gnostics' magic or their antinomianism. Among the books were: *The Coptic Gospel of Thomas* translated by A. Guillaumont and others (1959); Robert M. Grant's *Gnosticism and Early Christianity* (1959) and *The Secret Sayings of Jesus* (1960); and Jean Doresse's *Secret Books of the Egyptian Gnostics* (1960).[63]

Also much talked about was Nikos Kazantzakis's *Last Temptation of Christ* (1960). Fired by its author's rich and profoundly Greek imagination, unorthodox yet enigmatically reverent, *The Last Temptation* portrays Jesus' self-doubts, his hellish apparitions and his erotic dreams of Mary Magdalene, his sightings of angels "with red and blue wings," and the agony on the cross by which he finally set it all to rest. Another novel important for the Sixties was Robert A. Heinlein's *Stranger in a Strange Land* (1961), the story of a wise innocent Martian

Counterpoint: Science and the Early Sixties—
The Projectile and the Pill

The year 1960 was one of optimism and grandeur of vision among scientists that virtually approached mysticism, whether or not everyone was reassured. A president of the American Medical Association reportedly predicted that within fifty years we could become a superhuman race with perfect health, high intelligence, and a lifespan of 125 years. It was commonly believed that life, including intelligent life, pervaded the universe—as we have seen, Bishop Oxnam urged Methodist seminarians to prepare for dialogue with it, and a Russian scientist suggested the the two moons of Mars were artificial satellites like those recently launched from Earth but far larger and more sophisticated. UFO reports had an eager audience.

Like much else in the Cold War years, these developments made Americans both enthusiastic and uneasy. The Russian triumph with Sputnik in October 1957, and with the first manned space flight by Yuri Gagarin in March 1961, caused people to wonder if the U.S. flag was actually going to be the first planted on the moon and planets, and if it was not what the security consequences would be. President Kennedy acted quickly, declaring before a joint session of Congress in May 1961, "We will go to the moon," and putting the country on notice that no mission would be more exciting, or more expensive and important, than this quest to leave the first human footprint on another world. The first possible landing date was set for 1968, and the price tag would be $20 billion.

Soon enough the space race was under way, and as we have seen it was a counterpoint—one that in the end gave Americans much-needed pride and reassurance—to all else in the Sixties. Along with the grand theme of putting men on the moon, and the succession of Mercury-Atlas, Gemini-Titan, and finally Apollo-Saturn manned tests leading up to it, hardly less thrilling unmanned successes sparkled through the middle Sixties. The Mariner flights to Venus and Mars brought back photos of the clouded world and the planet of red dust unimaginable a generation before.

As above, so below—oral contraceptives, the Pill, radicalized inner space as surely as the thrusting rockets did outer. Enovid went on the market in late 1960, and within five years some 20 percent of American women of child-bearing age had taken it or another form of what the Japanese called "nobody medicine." There was much controversy, of course, about what it would mean for morals. In the Roman Catholic church, argument whirled around whether the Pill could be considered a form of "natural," and so permissible, birth control, like the rhythm method. John Rock, a

Counterpoint: Science and the Early Sixties— The Projectile and the Pill *Continued*

Catholic physician who had played a role in the development of the drug, argued strongly in its favor in the media and in *The Time Has Come* (1963). But Pope Paul VI, to the dismay of many, ruled in the negative in 1968 in the encyclical *Humanae Vitae*.

By all indications, however, American women, including Catholic women, quietly but definitely went the other way, using the Pill or other forms of birth control if they wanted to and, if Catholic, either leaving the church or remaining on their own terms. The sociologist Andrew Greeley is convinced that the Pill and *Humanae Vitae* were by far the most important reasons why, despite Vatican II and all the great expectations it raised, Catholic church attendance declined markedly in the late Sixties, and even for those who kept going to mass church authority was never again what it had been.

One can, in fact, hear arguments today that it was the Pill—not psychedelics, Vietnam, or anything else—that made the Sixties what they were. Safe oral contraception, especially before certain unpleasant side effects became well known and other sexual hazards like AIDS appeared, changed life-styles for more people more quickly than anything else, it is said. When young people learned that sex could be good, clean, innocent fun, and not the dangerous, immoral activity their elders said it was, the first and biggest generation gap was opened.

Out of it flew, as from Pandora's box, all the rest of the mistrust, the life-styles and counter-life-styles, the charges and countercharges, between the under-thirties and the over-thirties. Perhaps it is too much to say the Pill was the main thing, but the importance of oral contraception for the Sixties should not be underestimated.

It is important to realize that in the Sixties both space and the Pill were profoundly religious as well as scientific adventures. They were soul makers. Though their results have not, thus far, turned out to be quite as epochal as expected at the time, the essential thing for us to grasp now is that in the Sixties the rocket and the remedy were seen as changing human life forever, and to an unprecedented degree. We were now cosmic as well as terran beings, we would plant ourselves on many worlds; at the same time the Pill would revolutionize family life, gender roles, the meaning of morality itself. For some, this was all profoundly disturbing, for others the best news in millenia—but the expectations were there, alongside those aroused by civil rights and Vatican II.

who found himself on Earth; this book, with its study of alienation, hypocrisy, and a new community of the initiated young, a book also—and probably unintentionally—a Gnostic text, became one of the bibles of the counterculture and was even the nominal foundation of a new religion, the Church of All Worlds.[64]

I would be amiss if I did not mention the early Sixties book that awakened me from my dogmatic slumbers, the historian of religion Mircea Eliade's *Images and Symbols* (1961).[65] I read it on Okinawa, between practice assaults on beaches and parties in the officers' club, and suddenly, with his (to me) startlingly fresh phenomenological treatment of symbols of the "centre" and of ascension, of time and eternity, of knots and shells, several things fell together: my own Anglo-Catholic background; the phenomena of the Buddhist and Shinto temples I had recently seen in Japan and in the surrounding towns, with their sacred centers and symbol-laden apertures to eternity; the highly diverse religious backgrounds of the U.S. Marines to whom I ministered. I wanted more and applied to do graduate study with Eliade at the University of Chicago Divinity School when my brief naval career was over. I mention the personal aspect because I think I was not entirely atypical; history of religion programs were crowded during the Sixties.

Eliade, with Carl Jung and Joseph Campbell, were significant names in a characteristically Sixties vogue for the study of myth and symbol. It was of a piece with the psychedelic encounters people reported with gods and angels, with the interest in religion from the East or the occult traditions or Native Americans, with the presentation of myths and ancient chants in underground papers like the *Oracle*. The Sixties wanted spirituality, but they mistrusted the church on the corner; what was exotic or archaic was better, and what lay behind the most arcane symbols one could find might be best of all. In this search, history of religion as an academic discipline had a certain edge.

At the same time, some who—in spite of, or because of, all sorts of personal quests—were also interested in ministry found the French worker-priest experiment inspiring and fascinating, and the problems with which the Vatican confronted this movement distressing. The Dutch Carmelite Irenaeus Rosier, in a modest and probably long-forgotten book, *I Looked for God's Absence* (1960), presents a series of quietly moving vignettes based on his own experience as a priest, sociologist, and sometime incognito worker-priest in several of Europe's more dismal industrial settings.[66] The earnest narratives of this cleric, self-marginalized like the later round-collared ESCRU pilgrims in Mississippi, are significant as a token of the milieu out of which emerged

Vatican II and Sixties secular Christianity: a deep awareness on the part of many of the best clergy of all traditions that something was amiss; that the elite modern church, for all its transitory prestige, was not connecting with where people really lived, especially those of the working and depressed classes; and that to reach them the church would have to be shaken to its foundations, and serious reforms in liturgical and pastoral style would have to come about.

One well-known person interested in such matters was Thomas Merton. In *Disputed Questions* (1960), the Trappist concerned himself with several diverse topics: the Pasternak affair, Mt. Athos, Mt. Sinai, Christian art, the "philosophy of solitude."[67] He opens with a discussion of the Russian novelist Boris Pasternak, who had in 1958 been forced by the Soviet authorities to decline the Nobel Prize for his great work *Dr Zhivago*, and who died in May 1960. Pasternak, Merton said, "stands first of all for the great spiritual values that are under attack in our materialistic world. He stands for the freedom and nobility of the individual person, for man in the image of God, for man in whom God dwells. For Pasternak, the person is and must always remain prior to the collectivity." Such a person as Pasternak, "a genuine human being stranded in a mad world," is very dangerous to those who find their meaning instead in the collectivity, or even in being its managers.

The Pasternak essay was followed by one on Christianity and totalitarianism in which Merton asserted much the same themes; in this book the assaults on collectivity are directed mainly against Marxism, but after civil rights, Vatican II, and Vietnam, Merton would, as a "guilty bystander," voice his prophetic thrusts no less forcefully against U.S. targets. In the last essay of this 1960 book, on solitude, he lays the foundation for his later witness by developing the theme of the special position a contemplative monk like himself has as social critic: he is observant, in touch with moral and spiritual values, yet personally disinterested.

H. Richard Niebuhr brought out *Radical Monotheism and Western Culture* (1960), a much-cited work that, amid the rising incense clouds of mysticism, reasserted the fundamental premise of Western religion: a single transcendent center of value that is more than merely subjective and beside which everything without exception must be weighed and judged. Strong judgment on certain aspects of that culture was cast by one of the first of the eco-prophets, Vance Packard, who in *The Waste Makers* (1960) devastatingly described a "throwaway society" governed by "planned obsolescence"; the work followed on the heels of his no less popular attempts to blunt the cutting edge of capitalism in *The Hidden Persuaders* (1957) and *The Status Seekers* (1959).[68]

Another much-discussed volume, though curious in retrospect, was Daniel Bell's *End of Ideology* (1961).[69] The distinguished sociologist proclaimed in the subtitle of the book the exhaustion of political ideas in the Fifties, and portrayed the disillusionment of a generation of American leftist intellectuals caught between the Stalinist abuses of Soviet communism, which tempered enthusiasm for that particular working future, and the New Deal modifications of capitalism, which made the picture here at home less off-putting.

(But while it is true that ideology in the Sixties was more romantic and less doctrinaire than for the Thirties crowd, events in only a few years would prove to Bell and everyone else that ideology, or something like it, was not dead but sleeping, and in 1961 would wake up with a roar. In 1969, Bell and Irving Kristol edited *Confrontation: The Student Rebellion and the Universities*, to which Bell contributed an essay, "Columbia and the New Left," chronicling at his own school SDS-inspired strikes and protests that he clearly observed with distaste and that led to police intervention. Bell considered all this uncalled-for. He declared, no doubt correctly, that the faculty at Columbia was already generally liberal and antiwar. But "in the last two years, particularly in the student movement," "liberalism itself had come under severe attack." The New Left, he believed, was a "romantic spasm" that wanted "total" change in society but had no plan for what to do after the revolution except practice "participatory democracy"— presumably no ideology worthy of the name, and so not really a contradiction to the thesis of Bell's earlier work.)[70]

Madeleine Slade's *Spirit's Pilgrimage* (1960) was a simple, moving autobiography. The daughter of an admiral in the Royal Navy, Slade went to India and became a close associate of Mahatma Gandhi.[71] The spiritual father of Indian independence was about to become one of the unexpected heroes, ideologues if one wishes, of the Sixties; through Martin Luther King and others the nonviolent resistance tactics Gandhi developed would be the basis of civil rights and antiwar activism.

Also in 1960 Norman Cousins published *Dr. Schweitzer of Lamberéné*; the distinguished journalist had become something of an advocate of the great missionary doctor and peacemaker.[72] Gandhi and Schweitzer had been more or less equal heroes to idealists of the Fifties, but Schweitzer was never as central a figure to the Sixties as his Indian contemporary. As Third World consciousness arose on the New Left, he was criticized, probably unfairly in the context of his own era, for paternalistic attitudes toward Africans. In any case Schweitzer never presented the role model or the strategies for activity at home that Gandhi did.

A gadfly of the Sixties was the educational theorist Paul Goodman, whose *Growing Up Absurd* (1960) began the Sixties with some good questions. These bright, iconoclastic essays on many aspects of American society—schools, jobs, families, "juvenile delinquents," "hipsters," and much else—raised embarrassing queries like, Why is there so much contradiction between what we are told about America and what it is? Why is life supposed to be so easy now, and it turns out to be so hard? The Fifties were uncomfortable with such queries, and in the introduction to a 1962 collection of essays, *Utopian Essays and Practical Proposals,* Goodman complains about how often, as a speaker, he confronted in audiences the attitude that things are good enough, or at least inevitable, so don't rock the boat. "So we drift into fascism. But people don't recognize it as such, because it is the fascism of the majority."[73] Goodman then began building utopia piece by piece by addressing a number of topics large and small: banning cars from Manhattan, vocational guidance as conflict between economists and educators, youth work camps, theories of seating arrangements in theaters.

In "On the Boundary Line," in the December 7, 1960 issue of *Christian Century*, Paul Tillich addressed a theme that was to become increasingly important in theological circles, as well as in the popular mind, as the decade advanced: the relation between Christianity and other world religions. The essay was in the "How My Mind Has Changed" series, and Tillich was able to record one subtle change as the product of a recent trip to Japan and encounter with Zen. He states that Christianity in Asia must rid itself of all "Jesu-logical" (as opposed to Christo-logical) theology; it must come not as one religion among others, but as judgment and promise, pointing to the "dimension of depth" that is the essence of faith, that transcends religion and nonreligion. It is unclear whether Christianity, entering into this dialogue, points to a "dimension of depth" comparable to its own that can be found in each religion, or to a Christian dimension of depth even deeper than the deep places of the other religions; perhaps the ambivalence is intended. Tillich developed these themes further in what was to be one of his last books, *Christianity and the Encounter of the World Religions* (1963).[74] (Tillich had a way of being ambivalent; at the American Philosophical Association meeting in Chicago in May 1960, a debate focused on the topic, "Is Tillich an Atheist?")[75]

In the December 21 issue of *Christian Century*, in "Three-Pronged Synthesis," James A. Pike, the Episcopal bishop of California, also speaking to changes in himself and using as points of reference the classic three parties of Anglicanism, indicated that he was now more broad church, low church, and high church than before. But the emphasis was now on broad and low in the sense of very liberal. In unminced language that was to set medieval-sounding charges of heresy ringing, the modern bishop declared that the virgin birth was probably a "myth" and the creed was better sung than said, because people can sing things without meaning them literally more easily than they can say them.

The Catholic-Protestant dialogue that was an important early Sixties theme unfolds in *An American Dialogue* (1960) by two of its leading practicioners, Robert McAfee Brown and Gustave Weigel, S.J., with a preface by the distinguished Jewish scholar Will Herberg, author of *Protestant Catholic Jew*. Independent books by Brown and Weigel also appeared in the early Sixties. Brown's *Spirit of Protestantism* (1961) is a competent, rather conventional overview of standard Protestant themes as it delineates the centrality of grace, the authority of scripture, the sovereignty of God and the priesthood of all believers; it does, however, go out of its way to stress the need of Protestants and Roman Catholics for each other. Weigel, in *Catholic Theology in Dialogue* (1961), addresses Protestants ecumenically as he interprets Catholic thought. Employing Protestant categories so far as possible, the Jesuit found the Tillichian idiom particularly useful. We have already discussed John Courtney Murray's *We Hold These Truths* (1960).[76]

Perhaps the most-remembered religion book of these years is Gibson Winter's *Suburban Captivity of the Churches* (1961). Like Harvey Cox's *Secular City*, it is one of those few books that seem to sum up a moment in history along with an author's point of view. In the Sixties social interest was to shift from the suburbs and their baby boom families to the inner city, the arena of poverty and civil rights activism, and often of student and countercultural activities. The inner city was, in fact, frequently romanticized as though it alone was the scene of real life and real concerns. But Winter argued that in the Fifties the low-income inner city was left churchless, while the busyness of suburban churches was a sort of "Protestant penance" for this neglect. In a long review, Martin Marty evinced sympathy for Winter's argument but warned against an antisuburban bias; his sociological method, Marty contended, cannot be fair to all personal experience; there are good Christians in the suburbs as well as in the mean streets of the city's heart.[77]

Peter Berger's *Noise of Solemn Assemblies* (1961) offered even more pointed criticism of the way things were, churchwise. Berger asserted that denominational and parish systems so identified religion with place, race, and class that it was almost impossible for one to get out of those categorical boxes; the best one could do was to find salvation as an individual within one's ecclesiastical context.[78]

Karl Barth's *Evangelical Theology: An Introduction* (1963) was essentially lectures delivered at the University of Chicago Divinity School and at Princeton Theological Seminary in the spring of 1962. The visit of "the world's greatest Protestant theologian" to America that year was a much-celebrated event; in April Barth appeared on the cover of *Time,* and his lectures were packed. The lectures themselves, however, were less the evangelical textbook the title might have suggested than an elder statesman of the art ruminating on what it means to be a theologian. On these pages Barth is not so much concerned with the content of theology as with the mind of the theologian: it must be profoundly liberated in order to be open to faith, for faith can only be free, "new every morning," and to be free for faith means also to be free for doubt.[79]

There would be doubt as well as faith in the Sixties, including the well-advertised doubts and faiths of such bishops as Pike and John A. T. Robinson, author of *Honest to God* (1963). One source of their new thought was the work of the German theologian and martyr to nazism Dietrich Bonhöffer, who early declared that being a Christian today means being such as part of "mankind come of age" in a secular world. Significantly, therefore, the first major books in English on Bonhöffer appeared around the turn of the decade. There was John D. Godsey's *Theology of Dietrich Bonhoeffer* (1960), followed by *The Place of Bonhoeffer* (1962), edited by Martin Marty, with essays by such persons as Jaroslav Pelikan and Reginald Fuller. As the decade advanced we would hear much about being a Christian in, with, and for the secularized world, rather than in opposition to it, Bonhöffer's "scattered yet somehow decisive" theological explorations meaning, as Godsey put it, that secularization can no longer be a "scapegoat."[80]

No less important as a rising theological light for the Sixties was Rudolf Bultmann. His call for the "demythologizing" of Christianity to put it into the language and experience of modern secularized men and women was as basic as Bonhöffer to the programs of Pike, Robinson, and the advocates of secular Christianity. High secular theology was still a few years down the road, but John McQuarrie's *Scope of Demythologizing: Bultmann and His Critics* (1960) helped clear its path and typified the growing interest. It was also time to bring theology home: Charles S. McCoy, in "The Plight of American Theology" in *Christian Century,* contended that American theologians showed too much docile adherence to European themes and tended to talk in closed circles, especially with the "Niebuhrian renaissance" of

American theology, whose high point was the publication of *The Nature and Destiny of Man* in 1940, long since past.[81]

Theology was starting to come home in a book like William Hamilton's *New Essence of Christianity* (1961). Hamilton was to become known around 1966 as one of the Death of God theologians, but in 1961 he was content to detect a growing sense that "God has withdrawn, that he is absent, even that he is somehow dead." But beyond the Death of God, "man's place is to stand with God, in Jesus, in the midst of the world."[82]

Why the world was effectively the place of that absence was the burden of Gabriel Vahanian's *Death of God* (1961), which argued that we are in a culturally post-Christian era, an age that has no desire even to deny God, in which modern individuals refuse to bear the responsibility of questioning their own beliefs. The "revival" of the Fifties did nothing to counter this reality, for it was a revival not of faith but of religiosity and religious status seeking. In such a time, honest secularity, not religiousness, is the Christian responsibility.

A name much associated with the religious revival and religiosity of the Fifties was Norman Vincent Peale, of Marble Collegiate Church and positive-thinking fame. In his 1961 book *The Tough-Minded Optimist*, three chapter titles are "Have Prosperity and Enjoy Life," "Like Yourself—At Least Most of the Time," and "How to be Successful and Happy and What's Wrong With That?"[83]

In *This Is My God* (1959), the distinguished novelist Herman Wouk described in beautiful language and homely anecdotes the modern practice of Orthodox Judaism in a way that was to make the tradition once more attractive to many young (and older) Jews confronted with the need for roots in an increasingly pluralistic and value-free society. At about the same time, Gershom G. Scholem, in *Major Trends in Jewish Mysticism* (1941; rev. 1961), reissued in English one of the century's monumental works of scholarship and in the process laid a foundation for the rediscovery by many Jews of their mystical, especially kabbalistic, heritage. This rediscovery, as the Sixties advanced, was to be of no small value to Judaism, for it gave that faith an entry in the mystical marketplace of the counterculture as profound as any other, and better studied than some.[84]

Finally, a couple of books, though not ostensibly religous, were to be foundational to religious movements of vast importance in decades to come. These are Betty Friedan's *Feminine Mystique* (1963), the basic source of feminism in its late twentieth-century manifestation; and Rachel Carson's *Silent Spring* (1962), the wellspring of the ecological movement.[85]

100

Closing the Books

Against the world of books was the world of action, of the space race, civil rights activity, Vatican II. The two worlds had not yet fully synchronized, at least for religionists. The gnosticism and ecumenical dialogue of the study and the church assembly was only beginning to catch up with the rising tumult of the secular city outside the window. In a few years some hot titles in religion would try to close the gap. But it took one last event in November 1963 fully to convince the nation that the times were now new and ominous.

If the Fifties were a decade of baby boom births, the Sixties were a decade of deaths. On a black wall, and in sad corners of many hearts, are the thousands slain in Vietnam. The smaller but no less traumatic numbers killed at home in race riots, and in civil rights and student upheavals, live too in anguished and angry memory. Drugs and drug-related crime count their own dead.

In religion too, the Sixties were a decade of many departures: Karl Barth, Emil Brunner, Albert Schweitzer, C. S. Lewis, C. G. Jung, Martin Buber, Paul Tillich, John Courtney Murray, Thomas Merton, H. Richard Niebuhr, Harry Emerson Fosdick, Aldous Huxley, G. Bromley Oxnam, James Pike, Francis Cardinal Spellman, John XXIII. If one thinks also of the passing of Reinhold Niebuhr in 1971, it is clear that an exceptional, strong-minded, and strong-willed generation of giants who had dominated Euro-American religion and religious thought throughout a turbulent time of depression, fascism, war, Cold War, and immense change was ending. Their mantle would be a hard one to assume for a new generation, less sure of itself and less at ease as brokers of intellectual and institutional power in its different, postmodern world.

Finally, we come to the great assassinations: John F. Kennedy, Martin Luther King, Robert Kennedy. Of these, the greatest of all in its impact on national consciousness was certainly that of President Kennedy.

One can hear many arguments about what made the Sixties what they were, different from every other decade and far from normal. Drugs, the Pill, the war, the baby boom generation come of age . . . but a surprising number of people will say it was the assassination of a young president on that autumnal day in 1963. As much as anything, this assertion is a recitation of personal history. Everyone, it seems, remembers where he or she was on hearing the terrible unexpected news, and how the world seemed to stop. Games were canceled, schools and businesses shut. People stayed home quietly staring into the air.

An editorial in the *Christian Century* put it thus: "A blast from the trumpet of the Angel Gabriel announcing the end of time could hardly have affected us Americans more than did the news of the assassination of President John F. Kennedy. The unbelievable had happened. . . . Everything stood still." There was a "mood of apocalypse."[86]

This was, in a way, extraordinary. Without denigrating the horror and tragedy of the event, it may be pointed out that except for the shooting of Lincoln, the deaths of other American presidents (even the 1901 assassination of William McKinley by an anarchist—the Communist of the day) had not generated such a profound shock. Undoubtedly the "mood of apocalypse" speaks a word about the times as well as about Kennedy. Probably the Sixties would have happened more or less as they did (though one can argue how far JFK would have proceeded in Vietnam) with or without the assassination. The forces that goaded on the titanic struggles over race, that made the music and the counterculture, that set hardhats against peaceniks and fathers against sons, were already there in the emerging issues, the chemistry labs, and the demographics, like a fully formed fetus in the womb awaiting the trauma of birth. But the assassination was the birth pangs of that tempestuous child.

I think that for one to claim that the assassination started the "real" Sixties is to say that it was this event above all that forced that person to face the reality of a dark and chaotic Jungian shadow in American life, and moreover to confront the transitoriness of the rulers and societies of this world. Now things were not as they had been, times had changed and would not change back, in some way mysterious new realities had descended, and anything could happen. Oswald's shot was indeed a trumpet blast marking the end of one *kairos* and the start of a new one under Uranus, the planet of revolutionary change.

At first, that sense of change and newness enabled tasks to get done. In religion there was a mood of hope—not apocalyptic hope, but a cool, businesslike, secular-city kind of hope inspired by the successes thus far of the civil rights movement. Young people boosted this hope for the moment; they were widely said to be the best-educated generation in history and were becoming increasingly idealistic and activist, and also—like many erstwhile pulpit-bound members of the clergy—getting concerned with the practical organizational details of how to mount demonstrations and move the political process in the real world.

In a strange, cold-water way, even the trauma of the assassination gave hope. The sharp crack of that rifle said as decisively as awaking on a chilly morning that one aeon, that of all the Camelot fantasies and Communist nightmares and other-world religions and the rest of the past, was shattered and gone like night revenants when you smell the coffee and get up to a bracing shower. Now one could legitimately drydock the baroque dreamboats and get on with the day's work. After that morning in Dallas all things were possible, all things were urgent, a new generation was shocked into taking its commission now, the people of the past had let this happen and so no longer held mortmain, and the kingdom of God was what you made it to be.

Chapter 3

1964–1966:
The Years of Secular Hope

Forthwith this frame of mine was wrenched
With a woeful agony,
Which forced me to begin my tale;
And then it left me free. . . .

O Wedding-Guest! this soul hath been
Alone on a wide wide sea;
So lonely 'twas, that God himself
Scarce seemed there to be.

O sweeter than the marriage-feast,
'Tis sweeter far to me,
To walk together to the kirk
With a goodly company!
Coleridge, "The Ancient Mariner"

Opening Positions

Religion-related news stories as 1964 began swirled around three topics: sex, race, and church. More explicitly, they dealt with these engrossing issues: the "sexual revolution" now perceived to be taking place on all sides in the wake of the Pill and the advent of a new generation; the ongoing civil rights struggle, typified by Martin Luther King, Jr.'s appearance as *Time*'s Man of the Year on its January 3, 1964, cover; and the no less epochal changes taking place in the Roman Catholic church as Vatican II proceeded and thinking Catholics tried to get in step with aggiornamento on all sorts of subjects.

America in 1964 was a young person's land. The median age, about twenty-nine, was as low as it had been since the coming of modern antibiotics and lower than it would be after the Sixties had passed. Moreover, the new youth were the postwar baby boom generation, self-conscious of themselves as a new people, too massive an upward curve on the demographer's chart to be ignored, and determined to live the world their way. Like most young people in all times and places, they were doubtless more immediately aware of sex than of religion, and perhaps that is why, as church attendance declined, a man like *Playboy* publisher Hugh Hefner, the self-proclaimed spokesman for the new morality as he emitted his interminable *Playboy* philosophy in the pages of that magazine, could be quoted in *Newsweek* on January 6 as declaring that sex is the most important thing in the world. "It's obvious. Without it, we'd still be living in caves. The major civilizing force in the world is not religion, it's sex."

Many Americans lived as though that were near final truth, whether they proclaimed it in glossy magazines or not. *Time* on January 24 presented a cover story on "The Second Sexual Revolution." (The first came after World War I.) It reported surveys that showed the number of young people having sex before marriage rising markedly. The big new reality enabling this development was the oral contraceptive, the Pill, which allowed once fearful millions to live in accordance with the moral code ascribed to Ernest Hemingway: "What is moral is what you feel good after, and what is immoral is what you feel bad after." No less current was the post-Freudian idea that repression, not sex, is the great evil. With the change in practice came changes in attitude: movies, books, magazines (including *Playboy*) once widely considered pornographic were shown or on sale everywhere, and it seemed the bluestockings had, at least for the moment, retreated in disarray.

Furthermore, *Newsweek* on April 6 (and *Time* in a comparable article) noted on the big topic of early 1964, "Morals on Campus," that far more than mere hedonism and exploitation was going on. The new morality also entailed a new humanizing attitude of men and women toward each other, a détente in the war between the sexes, a "sexual democracy" in which "boys are treating girls more as persons," being now miraculously able and inclined for the first time in history to "really talk with them."

Traditional hierarchical structures and roles, in other words, were accelerating their Sixties decline in one of the key areas of hierarchical and archetypal definition, sexuality. Insofar as the new "sexual democracy" was a reality, older archetypes of what it meant to be male or female were yielding to the communitas ideal and the Peter Pan emblem of the eternal child, playfully coequal with other children, rejecting stereotyped adult roles.

Religious leaders knew they would have to deal with what Robert E. Fitch in *Christian Century* called "the sexplosion," with its attendant "orgy of antinomian open-mindedness."[1] But answers did not come easily. Even the pope was reported, on January 23, to be engaged with his church in a "wide and profound" study of the "grave" question of birth control—the study that would eventuate in the earthquake of the *Humanae Vitae* encyclical. One gets a distinct impression that religionists, though they knew something must be wrong with the new morality, had no persuasive answer at the moment to such questions as those framed straightforwardly by Peter A. Bertocci in another *Christian Century* article: "If we aren't just exploiting each other for momentary gratification, why should we not express our love sexually, especially now that foolproof precautions can be taken?" Or, "We know that our sexual intimacies are not approved by our parents, society or our churches, and we know we probably will not be married—we are not engaged—but we enjoy each other and can't for the life of us understand why anyone should object, especially now that contraceptives are really contraceptive!"[2]

Clerical writers like Fitch and Bertocci floundered about with bromides about total commitment, and love being more than the release of sexual tension. But—in those days before AIDS or the realization that countercultural sex could be as exploitative as any other uncovenanted, not to mention marital, kind—they appear unequal to the brave and very new sexual world of 1964, when the "new morality" hit public consciousness like a polar shift. What can you say to people who, though they aren't following the old rules, appear to be doing sex far more equally and lovingly than it was undoubtedly done in countless unequal and unloving marriages under the former commandments?

Some Christian moral theologians, like Joseph Fletcher in his much-discussed *Situation Ethics*, or John Robinson in certain controverted passages of *Honest to God*, came within a shadow of saying sex outside marriage was all right if it was loving, even though inside marriage was usually better; others, less sure how reliable an inner compass can be in the presence of so much magnetism, reserved judgment.[3]

Fortunately, other issues permitted the unbridled utterance of moral absolutes, at least for the sort of liberals who wrote in the *Christian Century*: the civil rights movement and, later in the year, the presidential candidacy of Barry Goldwater.

In the end, the civil rights dramas of 1964 could be seen as another flying wedge of the youth story, the new demographic reality. If the "sexplosion" represented the impatient love or hedonism of a young generation getting into its world, in large part the civil rights movement of that year embodied a corresponding idealism and capacity for passionate commitment. The Mississippi Freedom Summer of 1964, with its heroism and tragedy, would be mostly a show by college-age people. Even Martin Luther King was only thirty-four at the beginning of 1964, and most of the activists were younger still, men and women of both races whose consciousness had been shaped since the

Forties war. The year 1964, and after it 1965 and Selma, were complex combinations of concrete actions, such as voter registrations and freedom schools, whose condensed symbols of new communities with their archetypes were taking hold: the dress, hymns, interracial friendships, demonstrations, marches, and (at Selma) frontline ecumenical eucharists. Change means changing symbols.

The changes in the Roman Catholic church were also powerful symbolic/archetypal changes, both reflecting and directing the revisioned consciousness of a youthful new postwar Catholic generation. But they were, at least for Americans not involved in the process, more a backdrop to than a part of the traumatic shifting and sifting everyone felt going on around them. What was happening in Rome was not directly an answer to the new youth explosion, though it is hard to imagine it as anything other than an indirect response, in the minds of young/old John XXIII and the no less elderly council fathers, to a realization that a new age was upon us. The Vatican Council had not, after all, endorsed the new morality or dealt directly with civil rights in the United States. Nonetheless, it was a portion of what everywhere was coming to be a disturbing, or hopeful, pattern of questioning old ways of doing things and the concomitant old certainties. If after several centuries no meat on Friday can be overturned, why not—someday—no sex before marriage?

In the United States, the Catholic changes issue took form largely within the context of the Catholic-Protestant debate, so far as the general public had access to it. Thus, in a San Francisco lecture series, John Tracy Ellis, the distinguished Roman Catholic historian, argued that Catholics must face and not explain away negative aspects of their church's history, like the Inquisition, the trial of Galileo, or the oppression of non-Catholic minorities in Spain and Latin America. Robert McAfee Brown, a Protestant observer at Vatican II, urged Protestants to be open to the council's "undermining all your favorite stereotypes and caricatures of what you have always thought Roman Catholicism is. Things are happening in the Roman Catholic Church you never would have dreamed of. All the old labels, all the old tags, all the old convenient ways of 'disposing' of Roman Catholicism are now passé."[4]

Further controversy was generated by the performances in English of Rolf Hochuther's play, *The Deputy* (*Der Stellvertreter*), which accused the late Pope Pius XII of excessive neutrality in not raising his voice in protest against atrocities toward Jews and others by Nazi Germany, crimes he knew were taking place. A *Newsweek* article began: "In his catalog of human failings, Dante reserves a special place for those who, in moments of great moral crisis, maintain their neutrality."[5] Others, including prominent Catholic ecclesiastics, were prepared to defend the pontiff's record, contending that his speaking out in moral outrage would have meant only more suffering for Jews and Catholics alike. Rome did better, they said, by holding its tongue but helping victims of the European horror as best it could, including interceding on occasion with Axis officers still occasionally able to respond to the vicar of Christ. The debate may never finally be resolved, but fairly early in an activist decade it was a significant one. The points of contention were not entirely irrelevant to those being raised in connection with civil rights and Vietnam.

The New Youth

But dominating 1964 was youth. For better or worse, these young people would become the makers of postmodern America. As we have noted, the Sixties began amidst buoyant idealism and optimism. It was widely believed that a new wartime and postwar generation, under the leadership of a youthful president, would tackle the nation's problems in fresh and bold ways. The New Frontier, despite some hitches, did get off to a promising start, especially on the level of potent symbols. There were the early successes of the civil rights movement and the first astronauts in space, together with pledges of a moon landing within the decade. Stable economic expansion and widespread prosperity suggested that penury was past.

It was a time of innumerable developments great and small that changed the way Americans lived and, at the time, seemed to almost everyone to herald a more rational, efficient, and prosperous America than ever before. The three brief Kennedy years alone saw the creation or vast expansion of zip codes, interstates, direct long-distance dialing, space exploration, jet airliners, lasers, and federal commitment to civil rights, not to mention the advent of the Pill and LSD and a rate of economic growth rising from 2 percent to 6 percent a year.

The hopeful, expansive spirit was particularly felt by the young, now beginning to reach college with none of their parents' memories of depression and war. Stirred by the new president's challenges, thousands of them joined such agencies as the Peace Corps and Volunteers in Service to America (VISTA). Millions more entered colleges, often the first in their families to do so. The number of young persons between the ages of eighteen and twenty-four increased from 16.2 million in 1960 to 24.4 million in 1970, and the proportion of them attending college went up from 22.3 percent in 1960 to 35.2

percent in 1970. The nation's monetary support kept up with them: annual national investment in higher education rose from $2.2 billion in 1950 to $5.6 billion in 1960 and $23.4 billion by 1970.[6]

The young generally sensed in the early Sixties what a new and privileged class they were. They not only were exposed to a wider variety of political, cultural, philosophical, and religious perspectives than most youth before them, they also acquired a sense that they could choose freely among those options, and no one could say them nay. They could make this new world their world, make it work any way they wanted it to—and for a while they did, with a characteristically youthful combination of hedonism and idealism. They were strongly for egalitarianism, tolerance, and individualism, and for liberalism in regard to gender roles, civil liberties, sexual attitudes, and divorce.

America in 1964 was indeed—in the eyes of both young and adult observers—a land of hope and glory, a view soon to be exalted in the radical, secular theology of the day. Never, we were repeatedly told, have there been more promising youth, never have they been better educated in an exponentially expanding system of colleges and universities. Never have the prospects for future growth and progress, including the conquest of other worlds in outer space, been more open-ended.

Time's cover story for January 29, 1965, reflected the 1964 situation, viewing Sixties teenagers as warrants that America was "on the fringe of a Golden Era." They were, first of all, more numerous and more sophisticated than ever before. "Young kids all over the U.S. are pulling down the entry age to teendom," even as an unprecedentedly prosperous society was pushing up the average age of school leaving. The growth rate of the teenage population was four times that of the U.S. average; 24 million people were now aged thirteen to nineteen, one-eighth of the nation. "In no society in all history have more teenagers gone to school and stayed there through such advanced ages." In the United States in 1900 only 13 percent of those aged fourteen to seventeen were students; in 1940 it was 73 percent; 95 percent were in high school in 1964–1965, and more than half of those would enter college. Gazing into the ever-brightening educational future, *Time* was able to report that "experienced trend-watchers forecast that by 1980 the ordinary U.S. student will not leave the classroom till he is 20 or 21."[7]

Nor were these demographic prodigies a cause for anything but optimism about education and the golden era to come. Lee DuBridge, president of CalTech, was quoted as saying, "There is no question that

today's teenager coming to one of the major colleges is better educated
and more seriously motivated than ever before." That happy finding
was attributed to vast improvements in high school teaching methods,
curriculum, and equipment made possible by the postwar affluent
society. Even the burden of added numbers, *Time* said, "rather than
forcing down academic standards, has raised them." Test scores were
improving among all those millions. Indeed, Ellsworth Tompkins, secretary of the National Educational Association's thirty thousand sec-
ondary school principals, held that "over the past seven or eight years
we have experienced in the schools the most important developments
since the establishment of public education" (56).

Furthermore, *Time* commented, "the most startling part of the
change may be that the classic conflict between parents and children
is letting up." In the present fortunate world of prosperity and education, no "big rebellion scene" was necessary "in order to prove you're
an individual" (56). That was partly because parents were no longer
prepared to exercise the old-fashioned type of authority, and also
because teenagers, finding haven in their immense numbers, were
simply making for themseves a separate culture. Their garb was beginning to go mod, and their music was the Beatles and Joan Baez.

High schoolers, in contrast to some college students, were reportedly nonpolitical in 1964–1965, though there was reference to a teenager in San Francisco devoted to liberal causes who wanted to "join
the sit-ins at Berkeley" but whose mother wouldn't let her. And the
article does mention "Negro" teenagers, whose world was rather different, and some of whom said they "just wanted a chance to talk"
with their white counterparts.[8]

As we shall see, the golden youth of 1964, or rather a significant
few of them, were that summer to become the dedicated and danger-
courting activists of Freedom Summer in Mississippi and the frontline
troops in the Berkeley wars that commenced that fall. Many of the
former came back from the Deep South disillusioned, angered, and
determined to push ahead. At Berkeley these veterans wanted to set
up tables on campus to recruit students for civil rights activities. They
were denied permission on the grounds of university regulations. This
led to the free speech movement, and to social cleavages that would
soon define Vietnam activism and the counterculture.

Mississippi Freedom Summer

The period from 1964 to 1966 was a time of testing and turning for
the civil rights movement. The years of Mississippi and Selma, 1964

and 1965, were the last two of the movement's five great years, the Martin Luther King years of idealism, the successful practice of non-violence, and major legislative victories. Though it was not always apparent at the time, they were years of irreversible change in both law and public opinion, of the formal dismantling of Jim Crow and securing minimal legal rights for all Americans of color. They were also years of marked civil rights polarization and violence. And by the beginning of 1966, it was clear that a new phase of the struggle, with new names and new attitudes, was on the way.

But let us take the story as it unfolds. Although 1963 was the year of Washington and Alabama—the Birmingham dramas—Mississippi was not forgotten. In the spring, Medger Evers, leader of Mississippi's chapter of the National Association for the Advancement of Colored People (NAACP), was shot as he got out of his car. His brother Charles was brought down from Chicago to take his place but proved to be less effective than Medger had been.

Partly to fill this void, SNCC stepped up its Mississippi activity, particularly to spearhead a group called COFO (Council of Federated Organizations). COFO included SNCC, other civil rights organizations, and indirect sponsorship by the National Council of Churches, though most of its funding and administrative talent was from SNCC. It had been founded in 1961 after freedom riders had been beaten and jailed in Jackson and McComb, Mississippi. This collective was therefore used to Mississippian confrontations and ready for more. It was dominated by young radicals, as SNCC increasingly was.

Because of SNCC's growing presence, and because Mississippi was generally regarded as the toughest of all segregationist, white supremacy states, the attention of activitists eager for challenge and final victory turned in that direction. If Mississippi could be turned around, Jim Crow would surely be on his deathbed. The summer of 1964 was to be the Mississippi Summer. The summer project, staffed by student volunteers, was headed by Robert Moses, then twenty-nine, the black with a Quakerish and FOR pacifist background and a Harvard M.A. in philosophy introduced in the last chapter.

An early sign that liberal northern churches would be in the lead in making it happen was the Hattiesburg Ministers Project sponsored by the NCC. The small Mississippi city of Hattiesburg had an abysmal record on black voter registration. Federal court injunctions to provide equal access to registration to citizens of both races had been ignored. The Ministers Project commenced on January 22 with a Freedom Day demonstration. Fifty-two ministers from across the country joined SNCC representatives and more than a hundred local blacks on a picket line outside the Forrest County courthouse in Hattiesburg to protest the county's refusal to register blacks on the same basis as whites.[9]

Also by January 1964, COFO was prepared to try to register Mississippi blacks across the state to vote in large numbers. In March, the NCC board approved a budget of $250,000 for a Mississippi Delta Project beginning in September to combat poverty and racial tension in fifteen Mississippi Delta counties, including food distribution, literacy centers, and community leadership development. The NCC in turned asked the World Council of Churches for 40 percent of the funds, with the remark that, though U.S. Christians had money enough, "our psychological and spiritual unwillingness to face the full seriousness of the crisis means we cannot do it alone."[10] This was the Delta Ministry that was to continue working among blacks in Mississippi, as a sort of Freedom Summer afterglow, for some twenty years after 1964.

Then came the 1964 young people. The National Council of Churches, as part of its relationship with COFO, had also invested much energy and resources in setting up an orientation program for summer civil rights workers in Mississippi on the campus of the Western College for Women in Oxford, Ohio. The two-week-long sessions in mid-June brought up full-time civil rights workers from Mississippi and elsewhere in the South, including such major figures as Bayard Rustin, James Lawson, and Aaron Henry, to brief the volunteers, though the program was staffed chiefly by SNCC veterans. The week was, by all accounts, a hard, fast-paced, intense, transformative experience, like an initiation; in Doug McAdam's words, "the beginning of an intensely stressful, yet exhilarating, confrontation with traditional conceptions of America, community, politics, morality, sexuality, and, above all else, themselves." The Oxford, Ohio, week clearly brought a kind of "ecstasy," combining disorientation and liberation, that comes from "stepping outside" normal patterns of thought and life and that creates new intentional communities well oriented toward seeing themselves as children of light in a darkling world. Over it all was the growing realization that this was no college game, but a real-life adventure fraught with real danger and opportunity.[11]

According to Stephen C. Rose, the students at Oxford were "neither irresponsible, fanatic, nor immature." If one spirit dominated them, it was the ideal of the Peace Corps—Freedom Summer was a domestic mission on that order. Whatever was lacking in sophistication, Rose felt, was more than made up for by a sense of participation in what Paul Tillich called the *kairos*, the "moment of God's activity in history."[12] They may have been at times naive and argumentative, and they may have expected too much too soon. But they were also brave and dedicated, and neither white nor black Mississippi—nor America as a whole—would be the same after Freedom Summer.

Throughout that summer about a thousand enthusiastic young volunteers filtered southward to a mixed reception. Most of the thirty-two principal summer project centers had three separate components. First was voter registration, the centerpiece; because the Mississippi Democratic party was closed to blacks, the registration effort entailed the setting up of a Mississippi Freedom Democratic party (MFDP). Second, freedom schools offered remedial education and guidance in leadership and contemporary issues for blacks. Third, community centers provided health and welfare services oriented toward the black community. Demonstrations were also held in front of companies that discriminated against blacks in hiring and pay.

As they set up freedom schools and registration centers, the volunteers encountered from blacks both enthusiastic gratitude and the frustrating passivity of a people long bound by fear, poverty, and limited horizons, though in general registration figures for voters and in the freedom schools were even higher than hoped for. In Hattiesburg, more than six hundred blacks attended freedom schools, and more than four thousand were registered in the Freedom Democratic party. From whites the response ranged from violent rage to studied indifference, with a few exceptions. The violence end of the scale produced about fifteen murders thought to be related to the civil rights campaign, as well as the burning of at least as many black churches. It was a summer of fear in Mississippi, fear on all sides, and a sense of violence possible at any moment.

Of the deaths, by far the best known were those of three civil rights workers—two white New Yorkers, Andrew Goodman and Michael Schwerner, and one black Mississippian, James Chaney. They disappeared on June 21—just as the training session for the second group back in Ohio was ending—after being released from a Philadelphia, Mississippi, jail where they had been held for a few hours on a speeding charge.

Stephen C. Rose was at the training school in Oxford when news of the disappearances came in. Immediately, he reported, about half the students and staff workers joined in a voluntary service of worship. The strains of "We Are Climbing Jacob's Ladder" were followed by those of the freedom movement's anthem, "We Shall Overcome." Sally Belfrage, a participant, reports that "then a thin girl in shorts was talking to us from the stage: Rita Schwerner, the wife of one of the three. She paced as she spoke, her eyes distraught and her face quite white, but in a voice that was even and disciplined," telling the assembly to wire their members of Congress, get action, "to identify with the three, to be prepared, irrevocably, to give one's life."[13]

The bodies would be found by the FBI on August 4 in a recently built earthen dam some five miles southeast of Philadelphia in Nashoba County, Mississippi. According to the FBI autopsies, the three had been shot, and Cheney, the black, had also been subjected to "inhuman beatings." But a county coroner's jury reported on August 25 that it had been unable to determine the cause of death of any of the victims. No state indictments were ever brought in the case. On December 4, the FBI arrested nineteen men on federal charges of conspiracy to deprive the murdered men of their civil rights, but the charges were dismissed December 12 by a U.S. commissioner in Meridian, on grounds that the evidence was hearsay. After much legal maneuvering and delay, seven defendants in this case were finally convicted of the federal civil rights charges on October 20, 1967, and given sentences ranging from four to ten years in December.[14]

The voter registration project sent a black Mississippi Freedom Democractic party delegation to the 1964 Democratic National Convention in Atlantic City. With much publicity and nationwide support, it challenged the white Mississippi delegation. The Freedom delegation was led by Fannie Lou Hamer, a Mississippi black woman of indomitable character, whose example, speaking, and singing led hundreds of thousands of black Mississippians to register and vote. Later, after a futile race for Congress against an entrenched incumbent, she was asked why she bothered; she replied, "All my life I've been sick and tired. Now I'm sick and tired of being sick and tired."[15] Hamer was a woman of simple and deep religious faith—like that of many others in the black church wing of the civil rights movement, her theology appeared at an opposite pole from that of secular theology, or of pacifist liberals like King, Lawson, or Moses, but it arrived at the same practical ends. She said, "We are fighting in Mississippi for the common democracy. Men and women and children are dying. All because of liberty. Jesus died to make me holy. Let us fight to see me free. Cause we're movin' on, movin' on."[16]

In the end, however, the Freedom delegates failed before the steamroller political tactics of Lyndon Johnson and his supporters, determined to keep the southern vote. In a so-called compromise, the MFDP had to be content with two at-large delegates. This fiasco did much to weaken SNCC, and on a larger scale to weaken the willingness of SNCC workers and their radicalized white student volunteers to trust or work within the system. The theme of the human against the system was much enhanced, with subsequent results from Berkeley to the Pentagon, and the upshot was a corresponding spotlighting of the contradictions of modernism; they were now on public display and shown to be hardly less conspicuous than its promises.

None of this, however, mitigated the spiritual dimensions of the Freedom Summer experience. McAdam found, in interviews some twenty-five years later with 348 veterans of the adventure, that it was overwhelmingly remembered as a, or the, decisive event in the person's life, the sort of thing that divides a life into "before" and "after." It shaped social, political, and philosophical awareness; for some it was also a time of first sexual freedom (not excluding interracial sex); for some it was the first time they had lived away from home or school and dressed in blue jeans.

Some were profoundly motivated by religion, some by Old Left secular-radical passions. Some found the experience spiritually deepening; others were religiously disillusioned, finding at least the conventional religion of their past inadequate to what they confronted daily around them and within themselves in Mississippi. But, all in all, the glory and terror of Mississippi in 1964 was a fiery anvil on which was forged the mid-Sixties alliance of the New Left, comprised in large part of young people like those who had the Freedom Summer experience seared into their awareness, and new styles of ministry and religious consciousness now stirring within the churches. It had begun with the commitment of the National Council of Churches to COFO and the Delta Ministry (though the latter was soon independent in funding).[17] It was to go much farther, in matters both of race and war.

The next stage was unveiled elsewhere during that long tense summer. More than a hundred race riots occurred in cities large and small across the country. Against that backdrop, and that of a presidential election year, a comprehensive civil rights bill that banned discrimination in voting, jobs, and public accommodations was furiously debated, definitively passed on June 29, and signed by President Johnson on July 2. Churches were substantially involved in this process.

Religious leaders and seminarians kept up a conspicuous religious presence—that is, an orchestration of symbols and definition of communities—on behalf of civil rights in the nation's capital that summer until the bill passed. Services were offered daily at the Lutheran Church of the Reformation on Capitol Hill. A demonstration, sponsored by the NCC's Commission on Race and Religion, occurred at the Supreme Court on the tenth anniversary of the decision outlawing segregation in public schools; demonstrators then processed to the Senate gallery. In early May the vigil keepers were visited by leaders of three faiths: John Bennett of Union Theological Seminary, George H. Dunne of the Jesuit Georgetown University, and Bernard Mandelbaum of Jewish Theological Seminary all stood with them for a time. The religious community was, in other words, defined in new ways in relation to issues other than the traditional ecclesiological structures, hierarchies giving way to symbols of equality within a children of light alliance on an issue of equality.

Most mainline religious periodicals maintained a steady drumbeat of editorial support for civil rights legislation. Even *Christianity Today*, the more conservative national evangelical counterpart to the liberal *Christian Century*, produced an editorial on May 8 commending the pending civil rights legislation and pronouncing the matter a moral issue. Its stance was oddly muted, though, by a murky argument that even though equal rights were an "inescapable outcome of the Gospel," to say that the call for such rights is "itself the Gospel" may "come perilously close to the Christian heresy of proclaiming 'another gospel.'" So, readers were admonished, "let not a stand for civil justice and participation in demonstrations be confused with the gospel through which alone men are redeemed by faith." And juxtaposed with this warning was another editorial castigating professors of the "secular meaning of the Gospel," especially Paul van Buren.

On July 3, a day after the bill was finally passed and signed, *Christianity Today* published "One Nation, Under God," by George W. Long, an Edinburgh-educated Presbyterian minister in Tupelo, Mississippi. Very cautiously this clergyman affirmed that, under Romans 13 ("Everyone must submit himself to the governing authorities. . . . The authorities that exist have been established by God"), we must recognize federal law as superior to state law. But in the midst of Mississippi Summer the writer said nothing about civil rights, much less race, or about racist murders and burning churches, though he referred circumspectly to "civil affairs."

The 1964 Religion Issue

No sooner had the civil rights bill of 1964 been passed than the conservative senator from Arizona, Barry Goldwater, who had voted against the legislation, was nominated for the presidency by the Republican National Convention. The candidate who proclaimed that "extremism in the defense of liberty is no vice . . . moderation in the pursuit of justice is no virtue" was seen by many to court, and to attract, a kind of support that could only be compared to religious extremism. At least as perceived by its opponents, the Goldwater juggernaut gave credence to the view that Sixties politics meant politics as a branch of shamanism if not of demonology, as well as a battlegound for the growing class and regional cleavages previously mentioned in connection with McCarthyism and extreme anticommunism.

The GOP convention in San Francisco was marked by uncharacteristic hooting and shouting down of more moderate challengers to its anointed one. As early as July 1, 1964, the *Christian Century* editorialized, "Goldwater? No!"—"not so much because he is a conservative . . . as because he is an ideologist," by which it clearly meant a charismatic manipulator of rhetorical symbols evoking paradises and perditions, rather than a person of real ideas or even ideologies in the philosophical sense.[18]

Thus, twice burned—by McCarthyism and by its aftershocks in the anti-Communist crusades of the early Sixties—liberals were understandably wary of what Hubert H. Humphrey, writing in the *Christian Century* of September 23, called "the G.O.P. 'Jihad.'" The Democratic vice-presidential candidate was not alone in comparing his opponents to participants in a holy war. In an editorial of October 7, "The 1964 Religious Issue," the same periodical described the faithful at Goldwater rallies as ardently devoted disciples, displaying "mannerisms and attitudes which most people bring to religion." It was like a "cultic following," and this "devotion to Goldwater is 'the religious issue' of 1964," as was John F. Kennedy's Catholicism in 1960. But in 1964 the religion issue "reaches much deeper than such matters of person and policy" as a candidate's personal religious affiliation or stand on federal aid to parochial schools; it was rather a question of "a nationalism which is adhered to with a sense of total justification and ultimate concern." It entailed a claim that America can be "omnipotent and omniscient," possessing weapons that could end human history, and can thereby "confront any nation with military ultimatums." In Goldwaterism, it was claimed, "such an America is clearly advertised as being a worthy object of human devotion and utter reverence," and this was nothing other than idolatry.[19]

In the July 8 issue of *Christian Century*, seven moral theologians, including James M. Gustafson, Robert E. Fitch, J. Robert Nelson, and Paul Ramsey, answered the query "Goldwater Yes or No?" All replied in the negative, though with varying nuances. On September 2, the activist lay theologian William Stringfellow discussed "God, Guilt and Goldwater," and after the nation's eventual repudiation of the Arizona Republican in November, the *Christian Century* was able to commend the vote as vindicating the churches' loyalty "to One who transcends church and state" and their refusal to become "fawning lackeys of parties and factions."[20]

Of course many conservatives, and other citizens who for various reasons were not enamored of the Johnson administration, believed that fawning partisan lackeys were just what the anti-Goldwater liberal churches were becoming as the Sixties advanced. This year, 1964, marked the first time the *Christian Century* had openly made an election endorsement. So, on the anti-Goldwater side of course, did *Christianity and Crisis,* the *United Church Herald,* and several Roman Catholic publications, as well as an unprecedented number of individual theologians and religious leaders, including Paul Tillich and Rabbi Erwin Herman of the Union of American Hebrew Congregations. In late October, eighty Methodist ministers and seminarians demonstrated with signs and singing in front of Republican headquarters in Kansas City, Missouri. The protest was initially against the GOP's selling John Stormer's 1964 book *None Dare Call It Treason,* which attacked alleged leftism in the churches in language mainstream Protestants considered untruthful and offensive.[21]

This year was also the first that many churches, and state and local councils of churches, made comparable overt statements of electoral support or opposition. Opposition was expressed not only to Goldwater, but also to Alabama governor George Wallace's Democratic primary effort. Though the way had perhaps been prepared by the 1960 religion issue debate, in 1964 observers saw churches and other religious bodies more deeply engaged than was usual not only in national moral issues but also politically. Previously, American religion might have been involved in single-issue moral/political campaigns, like abolition and prohibition. But now some religionists seemed to be concerned with the details of legislation on a wide range of topics and with the thought processes—and symbolic meaning—of candidates in a way that appeared to be new.

This demons-and-deliverance politics was strange and disturbing to many, as numerous agonized letters to the editor in the *Christian Century* and other religious organs indicated. At the time I was interim pastor in an Episcopal church in Gary, Indiana, and chose to read from the pulpit a declaration by the Indiana Council of Churches opposing George Wallace in that state's primary election. The depth of support and criticism this reading produced was a gauge of the mid-Sixties power of the religion issue—and of the desire not to have a religion issue. But religion, or quasi-religious dimensions of reality appearing even in the secular sphere, would not go away.

Instead, the world seemed given to devilish extremes. In the first week of August 1964 Harlem and Jersey City were enflamed by racial violence, the bodies of the three civil rights workers were found in the earthen dam in Mississippi, and U.S. planes attacked North Vietnamese bases in retaliation for the alleged Tonkin Gulf assault. On the angelic side, Ranger 7 took close-up moon photographs revealing craters only three feet wide. A little later, on August 24, the full Roman Catholic Mass was celebrated in English for the first time in the United States, at a liturgical conference in St. Louis. Also a first was the singing of Protestant hymns at the beginning and end of this service. In late October, on the eve of the "extremism" election, Martin Luther King was awarded the Nobel Peace Prize.

Selma

If, for the civil rights movement, 1964 was the Mississippi Summer, in 1965 the center of attention was back in Alabama. It was the year of Selma. Selma brought south a new wave of highly visible nonviolent troops—clerical activists, some of them prominent, as well as students. Like Mississippi, Selma produced its three martyrs; and Martin Luther King, just back from receiving the Nobel Peace Prize in Oslo, was again the central figure, now one of worldwide fame and importance.

Selma began with the year 1965. On January 2 King told a rally in the Alabama town that a new voter registration drive would be launched there.

On January 15 the United States sued Alabama for making voter registration too difficult. On January 18, King took a room at a formerly segregated hotel in Selma and was assaulted by a segregationist. As the drive got under way, in early February thousands of blacks were arrested as they demonstrated against voter registration requirements, and on February 10 Alabama officials attacked black protesters at Selma with nightsticks and electric cattle prods. That confrontation was followed by another in early March, when tear gas and clubs were employed by the state.

By then the nation was aroused. On March 9 King led a civil rights march of some fifteen hundred blacks, joined by many white clergy from elsewhere. The procession was blocked by state troopers. On the night after King ordered his followers to return "and complete our fight in the courts," The Reverend James J. Reeb, a white Unitarian minister from Boston, ate in a dingy café in the black area of Selma with two other white Unitarian ministers. As the three were walking away, they were assaulted by a group of whites who taunted and mauled them. One took a vicious swing at Reeb with a club three or four feet long. He died from the blow twenty-four hours later. Four suspects were arrested for murder.

The day before Reeb was bludgeoned to death, King had sent out a call to supporters to join him on an ultimate Selma voting rights march, a procession from that town to the state capital in Montgomery, some fifty miles distant. As *Newsweek* put it, "Like the lame to Lourdes they came—bishops, rabbis, ministers, priests, and nuns—several thousands in all, sensing somehow that God was stirring the waters in Selma, Ala." The visiting clergy stayed in a two-block "compound" in Selma's black neighborhood. Here the conclave of religious persons united by a common mission became, in the words of one Presbyterian, "the greatest ecumenical conference in history, perhaps." There was a working out of "joint theology and spontaneous liturgy. One Episcopal communion service was held in a Negro Baptist Church with borrowed Roman Catholic vestments and vessels and common bread instead of wafers. Jews and Christians joined in freedom hymns, litanies of freedom chants, ecumenical vigils, and fasts and processions to the police barricades and back."[22]

The Rt. Rev. C. Kilmer Myers, Episcopal suffragan bishop of Michigan, put the mood accurately when he said, "In a real sense, the American Negro, in his travail, is causing the rebirth of the white church." To be sure, there were those, like William Stringfellow, to warn that "the danger in Selma is the possible reversion to a simplistic social gospel" (78).

So it had been in the church arguments, pro and con, on Mississippi and Goldwater the year before. Now the positions seemed even more firmly staked out, reinforced for the growing number of participating Roman Catholic priests, nuns, and others by the now-emerging post–Vatican II spirit. Clearly, the strong denominationalism of modern religion, its bureaucratic national organization paralleling that of the unitary modern state, was rather suddenly "not relevant," in the jargon of the Sixties, and giving way rapidly to something else.

The march left Selma on March 21 and arrived at the state capitol in Montgomery on March 25. Though subordinates handled the details, Martin Luther King walked at the head of the virtually liturgical procession like a prophet or canonized saint. His opposite, George Wallace, esconced in the capitol, watched the Old South's nemesis and the twenty-five thousand behind him through binoculars. Later the same day a rights worker from Michigan, Viola Gregg Liuzzo, was murdered as she was driving some marchers back to Selma. The governor refused to meet the suppliants face-to-face until March 20, though he brusquely received their petition through an aide.

Then on May 11 and 12, a number of religious leaders maintained a silent vigil at the Pentagon to protest the Johnson administration's escalation of the Vietnam War. The irony was that only a year before a similar vigil at the Lincoln Memorial and the Supreme Court had supported the same administration's civil rights bill. In a real sense the Selma march, in the context of Washington's voting rights suit against Alabama, was also pro-administration. But the world was turning.

On August 20, an Episcopal seminarian, Jonathon Daniels, who had elected to stay on in Selma to work, was fatally shot by a deputy sheriff in Hayneville, Alabama. A Roman Catholic priest, Richard R. Morrison, was critically injured in the same incident.

A few things had changed since the Mississippi Summer a year before. Suspects in the Alabama civil rights murders were first brought to trial in state courts, though they were acquitted in trials that were widely regarded as travesties of justice. In December 1966, however, a federal jury convicted Liuzzo's killer of conspiracy to deprive Liuzzo of her civil rights. (As noted earlier, some federal convictions on the same charges would finally be obtained in 1967 for the brutal Mississippi killings of 1964.) The Voting Rights Act of 1965 was passed in direct response to Selma and further racial violence, including the riots in the Watts district of Los Angeles in August 1965. Old-style segregation and discrimination were clearly dying, with few mourners. By Janury 2, 1966, a *Christian Century* editorial entitled "Will Success Spoil Civil Rights?" would appear. (To be sure, on December 28, 1966, an article by Margaret Halsey in the same periodical, titled "Integration Has Failed," would cite the rise of black separatisim, "Black Pride," "Black Power," Black Panthers, and the insistence of new black leaders, like "young Stokely Carmichael of SNCC," that they did not need white liberals.)[23]

There would be little more important civil rights legislation or activism, wanted or not, from those same white liberals. By August 1965, President Johnson was forced to state that much of his vaunted Great Society program, including its centerpiece War on Poverty, would have to be deferred until the escalating Vietnam War was over. And religious and other protest energies, aroused by civil rights, were shifting to that Asian target.

The Secular City

One of the most famous magazine covers of the decade was that of *Time*'s Good Friday issue, April 8, 1966. Set against solid funereal black, large gray letters asked the ominous question, "Is God Dead?" The article was quite a respectable survey of contemporary theology in the context of the secularization assumed to be gripping the world, and it treated of much more than the small but often sensationalized group of thinkers known as the Death of God theologians. But it was the nihilism of the magazine's face that launched a thousand sermons that Easter Sunday, and that captured the spiritual anxiety of a year increasingly pulled between hope and dread.[24]

The "God is dead" talk was only the radical fringe of a secular theology or secular Christianity movement that had been gathering steam since the beginning of the Sixties. The basic point was to make a distinction between religion and a life of faith, that is, the Christian life in an authentic sense. The premise was that for modern individuals, traditional religion, Christian or otherwise, with all its doctrines, mythologies, pious feelings, and esoteric rites, was no longer accessible.

Secular theology has deep roots in the great intellectual and social forces that forged twentieth-century experience: Freudianism, the Marxist critique of religion, the poets and philosophers (Shelley, Blake, Hegel, Feuerbach) of the romantic era who so expanded the divine within humanity and history as to crowd out heaven, and the Age of Reason's earlier reduction of heaven to the *deus otiosus* of deism.[25] But the immediate suspects in the death, or incapacitation, of God are twofold: secularization theory, and the traumas of the Second World War.

Peter Berger has defined secularization as "the process by which sectors of society and culture are removed from the domination of religious institutions and symbols," and to this he posits a subjective corollary, the "secularization of consciousness."[26] The notion is commonplace that, compared to the Middle Ages or some other premodern era, the hand of religion has progressively been loosed from such major sectors of society as the state, education, art, and economics, and correspondingly from subjective consciousness as a major instrument of self-knowing and decision making. It has been an assumption as well as a product of such modernity-making projects as those of the Enlightenment, of Hegel and Marx, or of Freud and the fathers of sociology, Auguste Comte, Emile Durkheim, and Max Weber.

Fundamental to their approach, and to that of countless lesser lights in the fabrication of modernity, was the belief that religion could be subjected to some higher and more universal modern interpretation; that its myths and rites can be rewritten in the broader, more abstract languages of history, sociology, or psychology. But if religion can be interpreted, in whole or in part, by more general analyses, that religion is then dethroned as absolute monarch and subjected to a higher law. In Durkheimian parlance, if the real though unacknowledged object of religion is society itself, then particularistic religious knowledge can be replaced by sociological knowledge and must be when the latter arrives on the scene; and so with the higher, because more universal, laws of historicism or psychoanalysis.

The reality of secularization remains a controverted issue. While it is patent that the role of religion has in some ways changed over the centuries in both public and personal life, it has not proved as easy as at first thought to say conclusively that in sum there is less religion now than fifty, a hundred, or a thousand years ago, and that this amount is continuing to decrease at a steady rate. Anyone familiar with the Evangelicalism and Pentecostalism burgeoning around the world, with the Islamic revival, or with the quasi-magical world of the New Age could not easily conclude that the decline of faith or the banishment of the supernatural is an obvious contemporary reality.

Yet, for some, secularization is one of those things "everyone knows" to be true, and they are likely to look at a nonbeliever in the hypothesis as one would a flat-earther. For secularists, it is a confirming doctrine; for many churchpeople a hardly less necessary modern version of the perennial religious myth that the past was more pious than the present. But to doubters of secularization theory it seems obvious that, at best, by the late twentieth century the process has gotten seriously behind schedule, and one may wonder if a theory that requires so many qualifications and epicycles to make it fit the facts is not a sociological version of Ptolemaic astronomy.

In any case, the secularization hypothesis—as a quintessential part of modernism—was still taken very seriously by liberal thinkers in the Sixties, and out of it came secular theology with all its energies and blindspots. In the end, perhaps the Sixties marked the apex and nemesis of secularization theory as of secular theology. In that decade, it became increasingly obvious that the concepts involved a difficult conflict between what "everyone knows" and what "everyone can see." By every rubric of secularist common sense, as science and affluence advanced, religion ought to have declined, yet it was quite evident that this was not happening as predicted and furthermore that, insofar as it did, new and stranger forms of religion—for example, Timothy Leary's—were arising to take its place.

As I see it, Sixties secularization thought and its religious concomitants were actually the last phases of modernism, in the sense of a unified worldview that presumes to explain the world from a privileged academic position. But the Sixties also saw the first great breakthrough of postmodern radical pluralism, in religion above all, as it ripped modernism's seamless robe apart from within.

World War II as a proximate cause of secular theology is not quite as easy to articulate as the march of social science secularization theory, yet seems no less important. Neo-orthodoxy, beginning with Karl Barth's thunderous *Römerbrief* (1919), was a clear response to World War I. The Swiss theologian dramatically set the horrors of that conflict against liberalism's largely immanent God and easy confidence in human goodness. In contrast the God of the new theology was Wholly Other. He presented himself to humans only in his "straight down" Word, proclaimed out of the Scriptures, which overrode all human natural religion, feeling, or morality. To the voice of this terrible and righteous God one could respond only with faith or rejection; there was no hope to be placed in argument or equivocation or aestheticized "religion."[27]

But the stark horrors of the next war, beside which even those of 1914–1918 almost seemed moderate, set a new generation to wondering whether a God could be in charge at all. If the theologian who rode the wake of the first war was Barth, he of the second was Bonhöffer. That martyr to the Nazi gallows wrote, "We are proceeding toward a time of no religion at all," when a "mankind come of age" will need to be Christian without religion.[28]

In his *Letters and Papers from Prison*, first published in English in 1953, Dietrich Bonhöffer spoke of the messianic role of the church to suffer with a nonreligious world.[29] The church of Christ must not engage itself in religion as a province set apart from the world, thereby providing easy escapism—"cheap grace." But as a "religionless Christianity" the Christian community should instead be a church that responds to the world by existing for others under the paradigm of Jesus as the representative of all those it serves. In him what is done for others—feeding the hungry, clothing the naked, visiting those in prison—is secretly done for Jesus in the midst of such a secular world. And those who are therein secular Christians are no more and no less than human. They claim no special, peculiar wisdom or authority. The ethical choices they make are human, not "churchly," as was Bonhöffer's decision to join the conspiracy against Hitler.

Certainly this breakthrough on the part of Bonhöffer and his followers into religionless religion and secular Christianity was catalyzed by the exigencies of the war, above all in confronting the evil represented by a Hitler. The old pieties and the mouthing of old dogmas hardly seemed enough when, in a new world of action and evil, the real calls were political not churchly.

But it is important to note that Barth is in the background of secular theology, however paradoxically, and in fact most of the significant secular theologians had Barthian training. What they did was simply accept and double Barth's view that the world is secular, widening the famous gulf of "Otherness" between world and God to the point where God is only a very remote star in its sky or has disappeared over its horizon. The war presented horrendous problems of theodicy, of justifying the ways of a God supposedly sovereign over Earth. How does a believer in a God who attends even to the fall of a sparrow explain the apparent indifference of the same God to the murder of innocent millions, above all the Holocaust of six million of Europe's Jews? The young Jewish theologian Richard Rubenstein, in his important 1966 book *After Auschwitz*, found faith in the traditional God of Israel no longer possible after such a disconfirming event.

Then there was the happy side of the new secular world. The war and its successful ending accelerated the sense many people felt that we were now in a new age that entailed, along with new duties and perhaps even a new kind of religion, the prospect of new freedoms and new joys. This was the world of which the new youth and education optimism of around 1964 and 1965 briefly seemed to be a fulfillment.

Other theological influences obtained to create secular and Death of God theology besides secularization theory, Bonhöffer, and World War II, though to my mind less important ones than those. Rudolf Bultmann's "demythologizing" of Scripture implied that its truths transcended its temporal language and Paul Tillich, with his talk of God as the "Ground of Being" and the incarnation as Jesus' "transparency" to it, provided new language some found congenial to modern experience. The historian of religion Mircea Eliade, who spoke of religion in such terms as the symbolic creation of sacred space and time, clarified the meaning of religion to set over against religionless Christianity.

Albert Schweitzer, in writing as early as 1906 of the quest of the historical Jesus, helped radical believers to see their way through the "Christ of faith" to a "Jesus of history" who was actually a better model for the spare, secularized, and religionless "man for others" the times called for than the former. That Jesus was found not in "sacred space" amid gilt and between candlesticks, but in the suffering, like those Africans to whom Schweitzer ministered. Yet, in the end, it was Bonhöffer who most set the radical theological tone of the Sixties.

A word should also be said about Marshall McLuhan, the Canadian media philosopher who was among the most discussed of Sixties intellectuals. Although not a theologian, he influenced some of them and moreover embodied a mood and spirit that help us understand the radical theologians and vice versa—epigrammatic, worldly, deconstructionist, believing more in the importance of technology as a culture artifact than anything in particular that is done by technology.

McLuhan made all sorts of extreme and forgettable statements and was nonetheless adulated by his admirers. The blurb on one of his books called him "the most important thinker since Newton, Darwin, Freud, Einstein, and Pavlov"; few would now probably so describe him.[30] But his main point, in a time of rapidly changing communications technologies, was important: that the medium is the message. The fact that a message between, say, London and Chicago comes by telephone rather than written letter, or by TV rather than radio, says more about the cultural, and even religious, difference between the world of Sixties people and that of their Victorian great-aunts or Twenties uncles than anything contained in their perhaps banal communications.

This idea certainly plugged into what the secular theologians and the Vatican II church fathers alike were trying to articulate. It was a new world, and in this world the church needs to learn anew *how* to say things as well as what to say. New liturgies with lots of lay participation, civil rights marches and the Delta Ministry—all practices that projected instant images rather than linear words—spoke what was new better than could a pile of books.[31] If religion deals in archetypes, it was again a matter of how to clarify archetypes into condensed symbols that would work in the dramas now being enacted.

Turning then to Sixties theologians themselves, a few were widely discussed in the popular as well as professional media and, though regarded as "radical" and "secular," were not quite in the Death of God camp. Generally they were concerned to translate a Bonhöffer/Tillich type of Christian perspective into lay language, together with a fillip of the "new morality." Interestingly, the most talked-about of these writers were nearly all Anglicans or Episcopalians. (Perhaps that has to do with the special role of that church in American, and English, consciousness—Unitarians and other liberal "nonconformist" Protestants had been saying broadly comparable things for years without creating the Sixties stir of these sons of Canterbury.)

The person who got it all started, so far as popular awareness of the new theology was concerned, was the Anglican bishop of Woolwich,

England, John A. T. Robinson, author of the bestselling *Honest to God* (1963). In this short, readable book the bishop speaks of the difficulty of believing the traditional Christian creed today. He tries to rework conventional doctrinal language, occasionally using flip caricatures of traditional views that some critics found irritating. Jesus Christ is not some "superhuman" being, coming to earth as though a visitor in a spaceship to "save" humankind from sin "in the way that a man might put his finger into a glass of water to rescue a struggling insect." He is instead simply "the man for others," a man whose life and death thoroughly reveal "the ultimate, unconditional love of God."[32]

All the rest, such as the image of Jesus as "God the Son," is in the realm of "myth." Myth, the bishop of Woolwich assures us, has a "legitimate, and indeed profoundly important, place," but that place is to unveil significance, not truth plain and simple—and for Robinson the supernaturalist view of Jesus destroys the profoundest reality of Jesus' life: that it displays a human being who lived unreservedly in and for others, out of a "union-in-love with the Ground of our being."

For God is not to be experienced as a supernatural being "up there," but as depth, the "ground of our being" "in there," and prayer is "openness to the ground of our being." This simple but deep Christian life can be shared by all who move into the orbit of Jesus and can present itself today as a life of "worldly holiness" motivated by service and love, not by legalistic morality. Robinson's little book sparked a furious debate, from countless letters to editors to reviews and essays pro and con, assembled in *The Honest to God Debate* edited by David L. Edwards (1964).[33]

Many of the same points were presented on the American side of the Atlantic by the Episcopal bishop of California, James A. Pike, in *A Time for Christian Candor* (1964). Here Pike, a friend, colleague, and in a real sense disciple of Bishop Robinson, distinguished plainly between what he regarded as the "essential" of Christianity (belief in a providential God revealing himself normatively in Jesus Christ) and the "packaging" (the doctrinal and other ways in which that is expressed). The latter included much that some Christians would consider essential: literal interpretations of Scripture, special forms of ecclesiastical authority, creeds, specific moral injunctions, cultic traditions, supernaturalistic theological and christological formulations, and even the Trinity.[34]

Bishop Pike called not for atheism but for a minimalist Christianity of "more belief, fewer beliefs," hoping to save the Gospel by pruning it of such excrescences as the Trinity and the Virgin Birth, leaving God to be only the loving personal ground of existence and Jesus "the all-out acting out of the being of God who is the Whole Ground of all being." The loquacious San Francisco prelate was criticized by many for hastiness and lack of intellectual weight as he dealt summarily with some of the most venerable and meticulously argued components of the Christian tradition. But it cannot be denied that he spoke with candor in a time when foundations seemed to be shaking. And at least he got people talking. The Reverend John Krumm, then rector of the Church of the Ascension, New York, was quoted in *Time*'s cover story on Pike as saying, "It's been a long time since the doctrine of the Trinity was cocktail party conversation, but now it is."[35]

The story of Bishop Pike is an interesting, if tragic, icon of Sixties religion. Born in Oklahoma City in 1913, Pike was raised by his widowed mother there and in Hollywood, California, as a devout Roman Catholic. He began college at the Jesuit University of Santa Clara with the intention of entering the priesthood but rebelled against the church, became agnostic, and left, eventually to receive law degrees from the University of Southern California and Yale. In time rescinding his agnosticism though not his antipathy toward his natal church, he became an Episcopalian in 1940 in the midst of a short but successful legal career. After wartime service as a navy legal officer combined with theological study, Pike was ordained an Episcopal priest in 1946.

By 1952 the brilliant young clerical star had become dean of the Cathedral of St. John the Divine in New York. From that prominent base his lively ministry, TV shows, books, and hard-hitting, often topical sermons, all reflecting both an exuberant personality and what he was later to call "smooth orthodoxy," attracted crowds and much attention. (A 1958 *Reader's Digest* article called him the "Joyful Dean," no doubt in contrast to the "Gloomy Dean," William Inge of St Paul's, London.) An Episcopal throne was obviously next in line, and in 1958 Pike became bishop coadjutor of California, succeeding to the position of diocesan the following year.[36]

Once in California, the new bishop almost immediately aroused controversy for his outspoken liberal stands on social issues such as civil rights, on controversial church topics like the ordination of women, and, increasingly, on matters of theology, as we have seen with the Blake-Pike proposals for Christian union, the Catholic president debate, and the school prayer issue. His December 1960 article in the *Christian Century,* already mentioned, "Three-Pronged Synthesis," openly expressed doubts for the first time about the literal truth of the Trinity, the Virgin Birth, and Christ as the only way to salvation. As books—not to mention sermons—followed the articles, charges of heresy were formally lodged against him by groups of conservative Episcopal priests and bishops. Pike was censured by that church's House of Bishops in 1966, although, despite his demand for a formal heresy trial, none was conducted. The confrontation was one from which the Episcopal church shrank. But the same year, Pike resigned as bishop of California to become a fellow at the Center for the Study of Democratic Institutions in Santa Barbara, California.[37]

During the California years Pike's personal life was no less difficult than his public career. In 1964 he ended some twelve years of problem drinking by joining Alcoholics Anonymous. Around the same time he commenced an affair with a woman, apparently supporting her with diocesan discretionary funds; it ended with her suicide in 1967. In 1966 Pike's son had committed suicide. In 1967 Pike was divorced by his wife of twenty-five years, and the same year his daughter attempted suicide.

Amid all this he took solace in spiritualism, believing that he had contacted his dead son through a medium; this was recounted in his book *The Other Side* (1968).[38] In 1968 he married Diane Kennedy, who had helped him with that book. In 1969 he announced his intention to leave the institutional church and set out on "an unencumbered journey into an open future," and to establish a Foundation for Religious Transition to assist others in a like journey beyond institutionalism.

His own earthly pilgrimage, however, was now near an unexpectedly abrupt end. At Santa Barbara he had become interested in the Dead Sea Scrolls, and in the summer of 1969 he and his wife made a trip to Israel to study the site of the Qumran community. There he became lost and stranded in the Judean desert. Pike was found dead by a search party some five days after his wife reported him missing and was buried on September 8, 1969, in Jaffa, Israel.[39]

Like the religious decade, the splendid and sad career of the bishop of California had begun in 1960 with outspoken engagement in the civil rights and Catholic president debates. With many companions he then moved into joyous radical theology to celebrate the hopeful new world wrought by the Sixties. He next underwent domestic strife and turmoil—the inner equivalent, perhaps, of the mid-Sixties riots and protests—and with a thousand counterculturists and their allies became increasingly alienated in a way that led both to occultism and personal disestablishmentarianism. Finally, like not a few others, he ended the decade amid conflicting winds of bitterness and personal renewal, and with sudden death.

Joseph Fletcher's *Situation Ethics: The New Morality* (1966) also drew attention and scandal. Fletcher, then a professor at Episcopal

Theological School in Cambridge, Massachusetts, argued for morality based not on predetermined objective or internalized law, but on an ascertaining of the requirements of love in the particular situation. It was, in other words, an intentionalist and consequentialist ethic in which the important thing was less the act than the intention of the actor, and the goodness of the consequences so far as she or he could honestly assess them.

Fletcher opened with a story. A friend of his had arrived in St. Louis just as a presidential campaign was ending. His taxi driver remarked that he, his father, and his grandfather had always been straight-ticket Republicans. "Ah," said Fletcher's friend, "then I take it you voted for Senator So-and-so." "No," replied the driver, "there are times when a man has to push his principles aside and do the right thing." Fletcher concluded that this St. Louis cabdriver is his book's hero. *Situation Ethics* aroused passionate debate in the Sixties and produced a debate book, *The Situation Ethics Debate* (1968), just as had *Honest to God*.[40] Fletcher was, naturally, accused in it of "the most unstable and absurd relativism" (by John Lachs, 242) and worse but made a strong case in his reply that he was simply stating openly and without obfuscation what had long been the real Christian stance on issues ranging from marriage (it is in principle indissoluble, but there are situations open to divorce) to war (it is evil, but there are situations where "love" permits a "just war," 263).

The Englishman Ronald Gregor Smith's *Secular Christianity* (1966) is a more academic book but has been influential.[41] Smith sees faith in Christ as an act of the will that does not, of itself, prove God or depend on any metaphysics or philosophy. It is not to be confused with "religion." Yet it is secular Christianity because it affirms Christ, known through the spirit within, as a presence in the world standing with worldly humanity as we wend our way through the vicissitudes of history. Though not always or easily seen, Christ has been with humanity through the Christian centuries, often in disguise, yet he is able to receive the faith of those who have eyes to see: "Secular Christianity means the dialectical expression of the presence of the Spirit [not of the simple presence or simple absence of God] which is the way of Christ in the world, in forms which can be neither objectively distinguished nor enumerated. . . . [It is] a theology of a pilgrim journey which makes its own map as it goes." The "historical reality [of Christ] cannot be pinned down," but "the form of Christ in the world is . . . *the* historical Reality. It is the prolepsis of the End" (204).

The secular city was canonized as the place of vital Christianity in Gibson Winter, *The New Creation as Metropolis* (1963).[42] Here the author of *The Suburban Captivity of the Churches*, another Episcopalian, set himself the positive task of defining ministry in the emerging metropolis, the now and future context of essential ministry. "The word 'metropolis,'" he said, "identifies this new situation of God's people in the world. Metropolis is the form of the new society." Seldom has the "secular hope" of those years, the consummation of modernism, been defined more stunningly:

> Metropolis is the mother city, the nurturing totality of interdependent regions and municipalities where children may find a climate conducive to growth, where education may enrich life as well as capacities, where men and women may have opportunity to participate as members and receive their rewards, and where advantages may be distributed with equity. Metropolis is the realization of unity of life out of the conflicting factions which now plague metropolitan areas. . . . Metropolis is the human society which different groups subvert and which all groups need for their well-being. Metropolis is the power of the New Mankind refracted through human history. (1–3)

In a church ministering to the city in this spirit, endeavoring to bring about this pseudo-secular kingdom of God and call forth the pseudo-eschatological new mankind, Winter said, individual piety subverts the gospel in an emerging metropolis, but true piety emerges in the engagement of the Church with the world. Here the servant church, primarily lay and oriented toward servanthood in the structures of public life, will find its true mission. But it cannot find this mission without giving up its traditional structures and their false security.

Donald L. Benedict, who reviewed this book for the *Christian Century*, August 14, 1963, concluded by remarking, "Out of concern for their emotional stability, I refrain from recommending this book to pastors and church executives." We can now, however, receive *The New Creation as Metropolis* as an early- to mid-Sixties image of what the church ought to be in a time of urbanization, or more precisely of ecclesiastical discovery that the country was already urbanized, and of still unsullied modern secular (or rather secular and covertly religious) hope.

But in a class by itself is Harvey Cox's *Secular City*, the supreme icon of this spiritual moment.[43] This book sold nearly a million copies in all languages and editions, a modern record for a serious work of theology.

No one else quite got the hopeful, secular-as-sacred spirit of the early- to mid-Sixties city like Harvey Cox. It was, first of all, a city of young men, like Yeats's Byzantium, and his book is a young book. Cox was in his thirties, like most of the radical new theologians. They saw a splendid new world arising around them and wanted to be among the elohim present at its creation. When did this new world come into being? When "modern secular man" knew that the way the world is seen is not a sacred given, but is socially and historically conditioned. Thus, "secular man's values have been deconsecrated, shorn of any claim to ultimate or final significance" (31). But this is not a bad thing, even from the point of view of religion.

Cox opens his work by saying that "secularization is the liberation of man from religious and metaphysical tutelage, the turning of his attention away from other worlds and toward this one." The secular world is, he says, in the words of the German theologian Friedrich Gogarten, "the legitimate consequence of the impact of biblical faith on history" (217). The age of the secular city is, then, Bonhöffer's age of "no religion at all," and that is not a bad thing, but rather the proper end product of biblical faith (241–242).

Cox's equivalent of Winter's Metropolis is Technopolis, the love-child of secularization and urbanization. Technopolis amounted to the promise of paradise, an eschatology-in-process, the kingdom of God under construction, the rising habitat of the saints. Though Cox was not so foolish as to hold that the New Jerusalem had already descended in the skyscraper shapes of the modern metropolis, he saw definite signs that the new city of the Sixties was reaching toward heaven in more ways than one.

Some of the most provocative passages of *The Secular City* argue that precisely those features of urban life most decried by romantics, traditionalists, and moralists—including not a few religionists—are in fact those in which the city most foretells the kingdom. Urban anonymity, for example, can be celebrated as offering a freedom in which there is no distinction of persons. Urban mobility is no more than a key characteristic of Yahweh, the God of the Hebrew scriptures, who led his people from one place to another and, unlike the Baalim, was linked to no one spot. The city does not require "I-Thou" relationships, but only "I-you" recognitions. In it one can find, like a modern balm in Gilead, liberation from *Angst*, that great hoarded treasure of the lately fashionable existentialists. But now, Cox says, *Angst* is a feeling "increasingly irrelevant to the ethos of the new epoch" (80–81).[44]

Such breezy confidence grated on some readers, as was doubtless expected. But more importantly the book said the right word at the right time. Numerous readers found it put into language something they had felt but been unable to express: that our new urbanized civilization somehow *is* different and is not all bad and has some kind of novel spiritual meaning. Scriptures written in an era of camels, shepherds, and kings have to be reoriented for a time when the working images in most people's lives are more likely to involve cars, corporations, and congresses. And the rethinking has to affirm that the metropolis *is* Jerusalem as well as Babylon, Salem as well as Sodom, a place of liberation as well as alienation. This Harvey Cox did for the *Playboy* generation, getting something of the Gospel in edgewise, showing the city's denizens they were doing the Word even if not aware of it. (The book contains a critical discussion of *Playboy*, calling it not lewd but "anti-sexual," which led Cox into a lengthy debate with the magazine's publisher.)

And to be sure, Jesus Christ, no doubt anonymous, wearing blue jeans and an old sweater, could certainly be a citizen of such a city. He might well like the ambience. But the Savior would now save his people as they went about their secular lives, on the streets and in schools, in the slums and city halls; Jesus would only seek or be sought through humanistic action in the world. And, in his memory, the need was now for an avant-garde church that would make visible the emergent secular city (144). It would proclaim to the oppressed the power that is already theirs and would be a "cultural exorcist" (149), driving out the fantasies and "superstitions" that keep us from living positively in the real, and secular, world. At the same time, Cox in *The Secular City* and elsewhere distances himself from the Death of God theologians, holding to a concept of God as God of history, always moving ahead, "free and hidden."

When *The Secular City* came out I was a graduate student in Chicago. The Windy City was then as now a good way this side of paradise, rife with crime, riven by race, riddled with ethnic enclaves, and still in the grip of the Daley machine. Yet I can recall walking the icy streets of that metropolis in this magical book's glow, thinking that, despite all appearances, this place was real, was holy, was the future, was where real life had now to be lived. With the help of a new spirit one felt blowing in the wind, together with a new kind of church and President Johnson's Great Society programs, this hard brick-and-asphalt city was where we were going to build Jerusalem. Then the culture changed, the enchantment of world disenchantment wore off, and I thought of some other aspects of religion that Cox (as he freely admitted later, as in his 1969 *The Feast of Fools*) had left out. But the vision of *The Secular City* has had an enduring life of its own; in 1990 the book was to receive the rare honor of a twenty-fifth anniversary edition, with a new preface by the author.[45]

Camelot Rising

The image of King Arthur's Camelot, and other venues of romantic neo-medievalism, haunted the Sixties and were in silent dialectic with the secular city and the new creation as Metropolis. The wildly successful Lerner-Loewe musical *Camelot* opened December 3, 1960, just after the election of John F. Kennedy. The new president himself greatly enjoyed it and often referred to his White House and administration as Camelot. After Dallas, it seemed right to refer to the thousand days of the Kennedy administration by the same title. Like the court of Arthur and Guinevere, of Lancelot and Galahad, theirs was a palace of people bright but flawed, beautiful but marked for tragedy and death.

Then came *The Hobbit* by J.R.R. Tolkien, together with his mighty three-volume heroic-age fantasy set in a fairyland, mythical Middle Earth, *The Lord of the Rings*. The American paperback editions appeared in 1965, the same year as *The Secular City*. Tolkien immediately became a campus cult figure, as sales zoomed to unprecedented heights for mythopoeic fiction of this kind. In 1966 Ballantine's paperback of *The Hobbit* led the mass-paperback market with 700,000 copies in print. The first volume of the trilogy, *The Fellowship of the Ring*, was second with 581,000 copies. But Middle Earth and the secular city were each top of their class; Cox's work faced the fantasies off fairly by making it to the peak of the trade-paperback market the same year, with 300,000 copies.[46]

Tolkien, a heretofore obscure Oxford medievalist known chiefly for his conservative Catholic and romantic High Tory views, was—at least on the surface—at an opposite pole on almost every imaginable issue from the Baptist radical theologian with whom he shared unexpected fame and fortune that mid-Sixties year. One could imagine the radical traditionalist who wrote *The Lord of the Rings* and the ostensibly radical modernist of *The Secular City* agreeing on very little, whether in religion or politics or manner of life. (In regard to the last, the Britisher's notorious distaste for international travel and cuisine—indeed, for anything un-English or untraditional—was much at odds with his trans-Atlantic colleague's enthusiastic descriptions of round-the-world expeditions wherein, at least from the vantage point of international airports, he saw the secular city springing up on all sides.) Yet both writers are necessary to a full understanding of the Sixties.

Tolkien presented us an entire world (and hardly a secular one), Middle Earth, full of magic, elves, orcs, dwarves, and hobbits as well as wizards and warrior-heroes. His was a full-blown romantic-medieval world of chivalry and hierarchy, a European conservative's paradise of true kings, dashing swordsmen, jolly peasants, and faithful retainers, with faerie and magic added in, and evil dark enough to contour sharply the mythic splendor of the good. In this alternative reality one could immerse oneself deeply—as many did with perfervid devotion (there were Tolkien clubs, journals, and costume festivals, even elvish language classes)—forgetting Vietnam and the burning streets while waiting for the eschaton to arrive, whether as Technopolis or Camelot.

As though to augment Tolkienism, the recently translated novels of the German neoromantic Hermann Hesse, such as *Siddhartha*, *Damien*, *Steppenwolf*, and above all *The Journey to the East,* also rose on the charts in 1965 and 1966 as the counterculture set in. Except in *Siddhartha*, set in ancient India, Hesse characteristically portrayed outsiders who lived in drab modern cities in late Wilhelmine or Weimar Germany and yearned for something else. That Otherness usually seemed not so much undiscovered as once discovered and then half-forgotten, lost like the colors of a long-ago dream or the world before the War. Its *Sehnsucht*-laden devotees found ways to make excursions from their dismal boardinghouses and cold streets to seek it out in the fantasies of Steppenwolf's magical mystical theater, or in the eyes of the strange wise-child Damien. Or, in *Journey*, they went on pilgrimage to the League's marvelous land of sunrise origins, superimposed on an outer world of scarred World War I veterans and train schedules; in the League's land, past and present could be interchanged, and one could walk from the medieval Europe of romance to the Asia of Kundalini and the Princess Fatima.[47]

What was going on here? First, the Sixties were a neoromantic era. The fundamental point of romanticism, as I see it, is the exaltation of imagination over reason and its restraints—imagination in the strong Renaissance sense of images, based on important ideas, formed by the mind within the mind and inseparably associated with equally exalted emotions. For the romantic, imagination fueled by feeling expands consciousness and moral power, while mere reason, like mere facticity, reduces them to pedestrian levels. Needless to say, romantics are in some deep natural sense religious, even if, as for Shelley or Nietzsche, their transcendence may be found in the liberating exaltations of atheism.

And so for all their vaunted secularity, surely Winter's Metropolis and Cox's Technopolis are profoundly romantic constructs in this sense, and therein lay their power to move people to vision and action. No theology was ever more romantic than the Sixties' Death of God.

But if an ideal future secular city is a romantic construct, with its alabaster cities and I-you brotherhood, so is an idealized past of misty castles and romantic love and knightly deeds on the field of honor. So are Camelot, Middle Earth, and the Hessian East of half-forgotten wisdom and wonder. The genie of romanticism, once released, can go either way, so long as he can offer a shining alternative to the dusty present. The neo-medieval cover on the paperback of Theodore Roszak's *Making of a Counter Culture* (1969) says it all. Here is a diffuse, impressionistic study of three young men, slim and sensitive as troubadours, in tight-fitting "mod" pants reminiscent of courtier hose and what look like doublets of a vaguely medieval cut, and one crowned with something silvery that could be either hippie long hair or the helm of a questing knight.

I suspect Tolkien and Hesse also appealed because they offered striking models for some of the emergent Sixties themes mentioned in chapter 1. All these novels embody a conflict between light and darkness, often generational, and moreover construed as a struggle between the romantic and a mechanized, impersonal system. In *The Lord of the Rings* the combat was between the regimented, machine-like slave society of Mordor and the heroic few who were friends of elves and of starlight; in *The Journey to the East* it lay between the League, with its love of legend and its reverence for old churches, and the world typified by railroads and rainy streets.

These works, in other words, established boundaries marked out by brave and unmistakable flags, and the battle lines were all too familiar. Here were "turned on" but ostensibly weak rebels in their pilgrim bands, and there the system or establishment. There was the gray modern world—now suddenly turned seamyside up, Mordor instead of Technopolis—and here, pulled in out of the deeps of space and time, a magical mystical mysterious alternative.

The Death of God

Then there are the Death of God theologians themselves.

It seems to me that the fundamental difference between the secular theologians just presented and the Death of God theologians to follow lies in the role of history. The secular theologians certainly saw the historical process, particularly "secularization," as immensely important to human consciousness, and therefore crucial to the human understanding of God; one can only effectively understand God and the Christian faith in a way congruous with one's moment in history, which is now moving past religion in its the traditional form. But the concept of God, however attenuated, in the merely secular theologians was nonetheless ultimately Platonic; God is that reality which is itself unchanging, the ground of being, though the world may change, and with it the thought forms by which we apprehend God. Cox, when assuming his prophetic, biblical theologian role, does sometimes severely criticize the notion of God as a metaphysical being, changeless and eternal, while he affirms divine reality. But, at least to my mind, the inherent difficulty in yoking ontological realism to historicism (while also avoiding something like Hegelianism) makes him hard to follow here.

On the other hand, the real Death of God theologians took history to an absolute and apocalyptic point, where they could speak of God himself being subject to history. Like Hegel they saw God as Absolute Spirit molded and shaped by history, and like Nietzsche they saw God die in historical time. Thomas J. J. Altizer put all this most clearly and dramatically, but the others also seemed tacitly to make history an a priori to God, rather than the other way around, and in this way they were Christian—Christianity being the most historical of the religions in the sense that, even in traditional incarnational thought, God can be born and die in historical time. In this respect the Death of God theology was an appropriate, perhaps necessary, concomitant of the Sixties as a moment of radical apocalyptic awareness.

We have already mentioned Gabriel Vahanian, who was a radical Barthian, and less a Death of God theologian than a commentator on the death of the God of culture, and he saw that as not a bad thing if it meant getting rid of the kind of religion that kills the spirit. The three others most cited are Paul M. van Buren, Thomas J. J. Altizer, and William Hamilton.

Paul van Buren, then professor at the Episcopal Seminary in Austin, Texas, published *The Secular Meaning of the Gospel* in 1963. Though a bit ahead of the label *Death of God* as a cult term, this lucid but serious work honestly tried to do theology without a doctrine of God, even avoiding such substitutes as "ground of being" or "transcendence." Instead, van Buren takes to heart Bonhöffer's demand for nonreligious Christian language. Turning to the British language analysts for equipment, he finds a vocabulary in which Christianity is just a particular "blik," or way of seeing the world and setting forth a corresponding mode of action. But the life, death, and resurrection of Jesus are crucially important to the structuring of that "blik."[48] (The October 2, 1963, *Christian Century* review by William Hamilton of *The Secular Meaning of the Gospel* is entitled "There Is No God and Jesus Is His Son.")

Thomas J. J. Altizer was the most serious, consistent, and extreme of the Death of God theologians. Altizer places the movement firmly in the radical European spiritual/philosophical tradition of Hegel, Blake, and Nietzsche, affirming with Nietzsche, and implicitly with the others, that God has died in our world, in our time. Many would agree but assume that of course such words must be taken metaphorically. But Altizer, in such works as *The Gospel of Christian Atheism* (1966), proclaimed as good news that in fact the ancient Deity is quite literally dead, having become totally immanent in Jesus.[49] The unimaginably happy tidings, offering joy sharper than any grief at the loss, are that thereby, in Jesus' death, humankind is now set free from all the transcendent norms, judgments, guilts, and resentments by which the old Heavenly Father's presence had poisoned human life, and can instead enter into a secular promised land of hope and freedom.

To be sure, in Altizer's dense, abstraction-laden prose, no concessions to everyday application are allowed, and as Harvey Cox once complained, "there is not a humorous line in his books." Yet Altizer must be permitted his role as the mystical visionary of the movement. He maintains the intellectual passion of an old-fashioned German philosophy student—the sort one envisions holding forth over a beer in old Heidelberg, eyes dancing, his talk a torrent of ideas, books, movements, schools, surging toward the most excitingly extreme Hegelian or Nietzschean position. He seems willing to live out his life as a prophet now seldom heard but entrusted with the most exciting news since creation, news embedded in the gospel itself but misunderstood until our own day and still understood by very few.

In Altizer's books the philosophers who truly laid down preparations for the Sixties gospel of God's death were not those Greeks like Plato and Aristotle, nor even (as for some more recent academic theologians) the likes of Kant or the Schelling whom Tillich revered. Looking at Jesus on the cross, Altizer points instead to Blake, glad to be free of old Urizen and Nobodaddy, and Nietzsche's Zarathustra declaiming in all his holy pagan joy as he comes down from the clear air of the mountain that God is dead, and we have killed him. But Jesus lives, because he was one of us and we are still here. And in the last analysis the death of God can only be a Christian thing, for it is only in Christian theology that history is taken seriously enough to bear such an apocalypse, or that gods ever live and die—like God in Christ—in real time and space.

Another tone, sometimes the humorous tone for which Harvey Cox looked to Altizer in vain, is given to Death of God theology in

William Hamilton's work. If for Altizer the radical gospel conveys a message of ponderous importance, Hamilton makes it a green light for the lightness and wit of a liberated soul. A good entry is his wonderful period piece "The New Optimism: From Prufrock to Ringo."[50]

First Hamilton limns the factors producing the new theological mood of optimism by showcasing them against their gloomy, but now thankfully passé, opposites: neo-orthodoxy, hot war, Cold War, existentialist anxiety. The most striking aspect of neo-orthodoxy was its doctrine of human nature: Reinhold Niebuhr's *Moral Man and Immoral Society* (1932) was a product of the depression, his *The Nature and Destiny of Man* (1941–1943) of war—little wonder their melancholy portrayals of sin and human helplessness.[51] The Fifties, the heyday of American neo-orthodoxy, were also a time of Cold War tensions and, for intellectuals, the inward reflex of world *Angst* in the form of endless self-analysis; the age of Stalin and McCarthy was also the era of anxiety, existentialism, I and Thou, psychoanalysis, and obsessive dissections of Hawthorne and Melville in literary reviews.

But now in the Sixties a new spirit is in the land. "Neo-orthodoxy now doesn't work," and "pessimism doesn't persuade any more," Hamilton writes. The old age, he says for the fun of it, ended on January 4, 1965, when T. S. Eliot, whose Prufrock was its embodiment, died, and President Johnson delivered a State of the Union message calling for us to "enter the world of the Twentieth Century" and "accept revolutionary change." We were as of that date no longer Eliot's "hollow men," but a generation ready to accept the secular challenge and start building the Great Society without any more fussy, neurotic introspection (160).

Hamilton saw the new optimism at work in three areas. First, in the social sciences, writers like McLuhan and Kenneth Boulding made clear we were in a new *postcivilization* era (Boulding's term) so far as communication and world orientation were concerned.[52] Second, in arts such as music there were people like John Cage and the Beatles. They were experimental, unshackled by past structures or sentiment or *Angst*—they just made music. In them we realize that the Sixties "may well be the time for play, celebration, delight, and for hope" (163–164).

And third is the civil rights movement. Indeed, in documenting the overall cultural swing toward optimism, Hamilton calls the spirit of the civil rights movement "my most decisive piece of evidence." "That there is a gaiety, an absence of alienation, a vigorous and contagious hope at the center of this movement is obvious and this optimism is the main source of its hold on the conscience of America, particularly young America." One can experience it by singing the songs of the cause, above all "We Shall Overcome" (164).

Hamilton ends this remarkable essay with these thoughts: "This is not an optimism of grace, but a worldly optimism I am defending. . . . [It is] a cause and a consequence of the basic theological experience we today call the death of God" (169).

An interesting feature of the death of God discussion was the eschatological role that the United States played as the principal locus of the new revelation/realization. Perhaps this is related to the special meaning of America as a nation fraught with destiny, whether as best or worst in the world, already depicted as a major Cold War, Sixties theme. (But in this, as in their radically historicist theology, the Death of God prophets were really at the end rather than the beginning of a cycle, for all too soon, with Vietnam mixed into the stew, talk that sounded like American messianism would leave a bad taste in many mouths.)

Thus Thomas Altizer believed that America had a theological mission and was drawn to Blake's mystical vision of America as the place where the apocalyptic freedom of the Christian will finally be experienced. America's mission for both seers was to reject the past and make a new world where the totally free, untrammeled human being could sing with the sons of morning for the first time since the prisonhouse of civilization closed round—a Sixties vision not limited to the Death of God theologians but echoed in the counterculture's primitivism and exaltation of the Native American.

Cox's Technopolis, clearly thus far best realized in America though universal, is a comparable vision, even if it sings a more scientific, less poetic utopia than Altizer's. So also are such William Hamiltonian sayings as "the death of tragedy [that which makes for the much-despised *Angst*] is due to the death of the Christian God," a God who slipped away first and foremost in America, on that cold day early in January 1965 when an American expatriate poet died and an American president spoke.[53]

So Altizer, in "America and the Future of Theology," can say that "as Americans, our past is simply an extension of a horizontal present . . . the American who is in quest of a deeper form of existence must look toward the future."[54] And Hamilton, in "Thursday's Child," writes that America

is the place that has travelled farthest along the road from the cloister to the world that Luther and the Reformation mapped out. We are the most profane, the most banal, the most utterly worldly of places. Western Europe is positively numinous with divine substance compared to us, and even the Communist world has a kind of spiritual substance and vitality that we are said to lack. . . . [If] the American theologian . . . is fated to be a man without a sense of past or future, then it follows that the theologian today and tomorrow is a man without faith, without hope, with only the present, with only love to guide him.[55]

On the face of it, these would appear to be among the most awesomely misguided statements ever made by a significant writer. By any social scientific criteria—church attendance, poll responses on beliefs and attitudes, even the political importance of religious values in free elections—the United States is, and was in the 1960s, far more religious than most of Western Europe had been for a long time. Nor was its anticommunism any less pseudospiritual than the Communist world's communism was quasi-religious.

And, admittedly, the failure of the secular and Death of God theologians to read their cultural milieu aright, despite their professed high sensitivity to popular culture, does much to explain the short tenure of their success. Had they turned the superlatives around and worked out of arguments that America is more religious, even in a conventional sense, and more profoundly shaped and influenced by religious history—even that it is more sacred and, at least to its citizens, more numinous—than any other place this side of India, they would have come nearer the mark and better prophesied the rest of the twentieth century.

But of course those statements are extreme too, and it is crucial to understand what it meant to these theologians to call America empty of religion. For it is true, as we have seen, that America does have a different kind of religion than the Old World, and did as far back as the Great Awakening and the frontier. It may be a nation with the soul of a church, but souls are invisible compared to coronations and cathedrals. Altizer is no doubt working toward something when he speaks of America's special theological mission—a people with a mission, like the ancient Israelites on their way out of Egypt, has to be spiritually prepared yet clear of any particular spirituality, so as to make the promised land a place clean and empty, ready to receive the new.

The trouble is that America, with its high sense of national purpose and of having an "errand to the world," had already taken unto itself a surfeit of theological missions, from Peace Corps to Pentecostalism, and the Death of God apocalypse could only take its place in line. And it may have been its linkage to the God of history, rather than its proclamation of an American tabula rasa, that ironically put the death of God in the modernist past rather than in the postmodern future and so sealed its own death.[56]

The problem with the God of history is the key point in the work of Richard Rubenstein. Though a part of the Death of God dialogue, *After Auschwitz* (1966) reflects a more cautious, not to say pessimistic, view of history than one finds in Altizer or Hamilton.[57] Rubenstein found it difficult to believe in God after Auschwitz (as others were to find it hard to believe in the death of God and its concomitant secularized, Americanized urban paradise after Vietnam), but that was because the Jewish theologian discovered the historical experience represented by that dread city all too real. He did not believe, as did the radical Death of God theologians, that history and all its tears can be negated. Like Jews generally, he bears the past with him and does not think we have the capacity—or the right—to let go of the sufferings of those who have gone before.

As opposed to Hamilton, Rubenstein holds that to give up the "tragic sense of life" would only diminish, not liberate, humans; and "unlike Dr. Altizer," he states, "I cannot rejoice in the death of God. If I am a death of God theologian, it is with a cry of anguish" (204). For if the Death of God theologians have any God left, it is the God of history—meaning, in the view of their late modernism, a progressive to radical revolutionary God—and if that God is found anywhere it is as the Messiah, who as Jesus Christ appeared in historical time. But this is just what Rubenstein rejects. After Auschwitz the God of history is the God he most cannot believe in. "If there is a God of history, he is the ultimate author of Auschwitz. I am willing to believe in God the Holy Nothingness who is our source and our final destiny, but never again in a God of history" (263).

Here Rubenstein had a finger on the significance of the Death of God theology: it was the last, and most frantic, religious outburst of modernism, with its progressivist/historicist view of revelation in history, or through history as divine self-realization. Now in desperation modernism transfigures history into apocalypse and divine self-destruction.

In this and subsequent works Rubenstein tried to find replacement spiritualities in nature and mysticism, but the looming void in the place of heaven left by that cynosure of all evil, Auschwitz, refused to go away. For others, too, it appeared that God could not coexist in the same universe with that abomination. And if God is gone, then men and women, ready or not, will have to be the adults and make the decisions. And do so without the help of the old God's religion.

The Birth of Satan, Krishna, the Powers of the Air, and Others

But if God with a capital *G* had died, other gods were born. On Walpurgisnacht 1966 (May Day eve; in Germany, a traditional day for the gathering of witches) Anton LaVey announced the formation of the Church of Satan in his black San Francisco manor. LaVey achieved no little notoriety for his venture through such means as the association of the actress Jayne Mansfield with the church, the bit part he played (as the devil) in the movie *Rosemary's Baby*, and the black masses he celebrated on the bodies of nude women as altars. But his message, communicated in such books as *The Satanic Bible*, was serious: the conventional God is a tyrant who only wants humans to inhibit and repress themselves, while the promethean Satan represents healthy self-indulgence and freedom.

In late 1965, A. C. Swami Bhaktivedanta Prabhupada (1896–1977) arrived in New York from India virtually penniless but filled, he believed, with a spiritual mission to carry devotion to Krishna to the world. He began by simply chanting and radiating the love of Krishna in drab Lower East Side locations, moving to San Francisco a year later. Rarely have time and ministry so well coincided. The romantic, fanciful, almost psychedelic heavens of Krishna's Hindu paradises, the simple, fervent bhakti music and practices, their transformative power—better, devotees said, than the drug experience—and the "pure" communitarian life-style all appealed to the emerging counterculture, especially to those who had been through chemical drugs and were now ready for a nondrug high. The Hare Krishna movement became part of the new culture.

To get an impression of how Hare Krishna was received in the counterculture world of 1966, look at one of the earliest journalistic notices it received, a story from the *East Village Other*, on October 15, 1966. After observing that one of Swami Bhaktivedanta's disciples was the poet Allen Ginsburg, that paper presented a confession about the movement's practice from another new disciple: "I started chanting to myself, like the Swami said, when I was walking down the street . . . suddenly everything started looking so beautiful, the kids, the old men and women . . . even the creeps looked beautiful . . . to say nothing of the trees and flowers. It was like I'd taken a dozen doses of LSD. But I knew there was a difference. There's no coming down from this. I can always do this, anytime, anywhere. It's always with you."

"Everybody's trying to get high and stay there," another young devotee stated. "Everybody's looking for an exalted state of consciousness, a way to flip out and stay out. But there's something bringing you back to the old miserable routine. Not in this. This has a snowballing effect. You can chant your way right into eternity."[58]

Another early disciple, a one-time literature instructor at a midwestern university, related that after he began chanting, he "began to notice that the buildings, the people, and the sky all looked very beautiful . . . he sound of the Supreme Lord of the Universe was passing through my body, coming upon me like a beautiful exhilarating song that had somehow been dormant, choked in me for centuries."[59]

Krishna Consciousness posters and handouts of the same period, like many other testimonials, compared the drug high to the even greater Krishna high, to the latter's advantage. One flyer said "STAY HIGH FOREVER. No More Coming Down. Practice Krishna Consciousness. Expand your consciousness by practicing the TRANSCENDENTAL SOUND VIBRATION." Then, echoing Timothy Leary's famous triple admonition: "TURN ON . . . TUNE IN . . . DROP OUT."

Perhaps the ultimate high of that era was the night Swami Bhaktivedanta, after transferring to San Francisco in January 1967, attended a "Mantra-Rock Dance" thronged with hippies at the famous Avalon Ballroom. Accompanied by conch shells, drums, and a multimedia light show featuring slides of Krishna, with Timothy Leary and Allen Ginsberg onstage with him, the Swami led thousands of counterculture youth, many no doubt already high, in the Hare Krishna chant.

By 1970 the emphasis had changed. ISKCON (the International Society for Krishna Consciousness) literature now spoke less of highs, more of love and community. But that throws all the more into relief the relation of the early movement to the mid-Sixties yearning for powerful subjective states that could equal the drug experience but did not share its already apparent drawbacks.[60]

And as more American bombs fell on Vietnam, powers of the air appeared over Michigan as well. The spring of 1966 was the UFO spring. Like satanism and orientalism, UFO reports had been around for some time. But something about 1965–1966, as American society unknowingly prepared for its plunge into the explosive year 1967, made them multiply. Thus, on March 20, 1966, eighty-seven women students and a civil defense director at Hillsdale College in Michigan (a college well-known, incidentally, as a conservative bastion), saw a glowing object hover over a swampy area a few hundred yards from their dormitory. In hypnotic terror and fascination, they watched the object for four hours.

On two subsequent days, the alien intruder was reported over other sites in the region. The accounts, carried in newspapers nation-wide, sparked tremendous interest. An expert retained by the air force, the astronomer J. Allen Hynek, suggested the aerial mystery might be "swamp gas." This explanation provoked widespread ridicule, expressed through innumerable cartoons and jokes. There were calls, even in some of the mainstream media, for more open-mindedness toward UFO reports, and suggestions that something was being covered up.[61]

Perhaps the impatient response to Hynek's deflating explanation was a sign of the times. Might it be related to the yearning for signs and wonders so evident in the counterculture and to growing public scepticism, on the other hand, toward official communiqués like those coming out of Vietnam? (Hynek may have been sceptical himself of his prosaic observation, for the astronomer was later to became a full-time science-oriented but by no means debunking UFO investigator.)

Also in 1966, an African American festival called Kwanzaa, observed for seven days commencing December 26, was designed by Maulana (Ron) Karenga, an activist and scholar in Los Angeles. Though employing many traditional symbols, such as colored candlesticks and corn stalks, and the exchange of gifts, Kwanzaa is neither a black Christmas nor an ancient African holiday, but a part of the black consciousness movement that came to fruition in the Sixties. It has become remarkably popular, expressing something apart from black Christianity, black Islam, or black power.

And other movements were in the wings in 1966 too—Nichiren Shoshu, Scientology, the Unification Church, transcendental meditation—ready for the great burst of speed 1967 would give them.

The Servant Church

And what about response to secular theology and the death of God down in the church's pastoral trenches? First the positive returns. The "servant church" concept sums it up, and that was the title of a significant cover story in *Time*'s Christmas 1964 issue. This piece rather breathlessly but comprehensively brought together a great many new things that were going on in the ecclesiastical world, in notions of the church and in styles of ministry. Both Vatican II and the National Council of Churches' involvement with COFO in the Freedom Summer were manifestatons of these changes. This article catches the mood of late 1964, after the civil rights bill victory and the traumas of Mississippi, amid the hopeful urban renewal and secular city enthusiasms, with what was going on in Rome as exhilarating background.

145

Something radical, exciting, dangerous, but beautiful was happening in religous life, it seemed—nothing less than, in the words of a parallel *Newsweek* article, "a second Reformation."[62]

Fashions in theology come and go but are likely to have only a limited impact on ordinary worshippers until they begin seriously and visibly to affect how the Sunday morning service is done, and what they read about the church in the Monday morning headlines. This happened in the Sixties, as it did in the earlier Reformation of the sixteenth century. Worshippers arrived to find altars pulled away from the sanctuary wall to become freestanding centers of worship in the round. Once-staid services were enlivened by guitars, dance, and dialogue instead of sermons. And when they picked up the papers, these same bemused churchgoers were likely to see clergy in protest marches and church councils passing resolutions on pending legislation. All this was in the name of a church that was to be no longer a paternalistic authority figure but a ministering agent of change and hope. This church liked to think of itself as servant rather than magister, not just to the people who comprised it, but through them to the whole community.

To some, of course, the servant church seemed more of an unruly clerk with ideas above his station and outside his competence than servant. And, to be sure, many rocketing new ecclesiastical notions quickly burned out or fell to earth on stony ground. But not much remained the same either, and it was an adventurous and intense time to be in the church. Why was this?

The Sixties Reformation was based, first of all, on the idea of secularization. As we have seen, the new theology that went with it was also founded on the notion that midcentury people were secular in a way they had not been before, and that the church itself in its traditional role was rapidly losing ground. The *Time* article quoted without question the French Catholic demographer Adrian Bouffard's projection that by the year 2000 only 20 percent of the earth's population would be Christian, compared with 35 percent in 1900. It pointed to declining rates of growth in the mainline denominations in the United States; to falling church attendance in Europe; to the way the church under communism has been forced "back to the catacombs"; and to threats even to the rapidly growing churches of Africa and Asia from resurgent indigenous faiths and militant nationalism that painted Christianity as "white man's religion."

In the 1990s the situation does not look quite so dire for the church's cause. As incredible as it might have seemed to many then, at the time of writing it appears to have been communism, far more than Christianity, that has succumbed to the acids of modernity, or rather of postmodernity. As we have seen, no doubt even the concept of secularization, in the years 1964–1966 one of those things that "everyone knows," could and perhaps should have been subjected to a searching cross-examination. As early as 1967, the sardonic Catholic writer James Hitchcock observed that, while his church was changing its liturgy from a dead language to the vernacular in an attempt to keep up with the times, young people seemed eager to chant in Sanskrit.

But it is necessary to color a given situation in dark hues if one is going to motivate something as earthshaking as a reformation. While it is easy to make light of its excesses, the Sixties Reformation did open church windows and rearrange furniture, leaving behind lighter, airier, and more commodious cathedrals where one could laugh or talk activist strategies, living and enjoying religion without falling into hushed, stained-glass tones.

In any case, what was really crucial to the Sixties church was not theoretical arguments over secularization but the rather sudden realization that the world around it was powerful, important, changing, and capable of more change in interaction with values important to religion. (Why this awareness hit home as a call to a new kind of church in the early Sixties is not an entirely easy question to answer; I have presented some possibilities in the preceding discussion of secular theology.) It was in the world, not in sermons and symbols only, that the godfearing must handle serpents and rescue the perishing. And, wielding Peter's two swords, they must do so with the wisdom of the world, when necessary: in the demonstration, the strike, the lobbies and chambers of capitols, as activists did in the civil rights movement. There was talk of "worldly holiness" and "holy worldliness."

That religion should not be Sunday-only has, of course, long been a staple of piety. What distinguished the Sixties case was that, first, the church's weekday holiness was to be not only individualistic but corporate. It was not only to be charitable but to agitate for radical change in structures as well as in personal lives.

Second, if the weekday was to be holier, Sunday was to be more worldly, and so were holy persons. The clerical avatars of the new church were widely seen, as they were meant to be seen, smoking, drinking, and wearing Levis even during Sunday service. This was intended to say symbolically that, far from being icons of rigid rectitude in the old-fashioned sense, they were exemplars of Bonhöffer's inward and unostentatiously "constitutive Christian" who was in the world as a servant, not an angel, and who was no different and no better than anyone else except in his or her desire to be of help.

A good example of the new clergy was the Episcopal priest Malcolm Boyd, who was on the Sixties frontlines in most of the key places. He was in Mississippi in 1964, served as a university chaplain (in the Sixties, definitely a frontline religious role), and was an antiwar activist. Much later he came out of the closet as gay. His 1965 book of prayers, *Are You Running With Me, Jesus?* says much about the new churchly spirit.[63]

In short passages that are really more sermon/meditations than petitions, Boyd runs with Jesus far past the theological themes of Cranmer's Prayer Book. He notifies the Lord instead about old people waiting for death in ugly red buildings, about burned-out teachers, about homosexual bars, and about the faces of those he saw in Mississippi. There are meditations on films from *Citizen Kane* to *La Strada*. What gets Boyd praying is the sight of something very, very deep in this anguished world that hides yet also hints at the glory or the cross. And then this streetcorner priest tells Jesus about it in language as close to secular pain and as far from classical orisons as one can get and still ostensibly be talking to the Savior. *Are You Running* is a powerful and effective Sixties classic.

Then there is the Sixties theme of reaction against the Christianity of the Fifties, often characterized as worship of an American deity ("the God of your choice") as chummy and indulgent as that generation's parents were supposed to have been toward their overly gratified children. At the same time, if paradoxically, it was a reaction against the God of neo-orthodoxy, considered excessively remote for American needs, too preoccupied with inner existential *Angst* and with his own unimaginable Otherness. Against all this, the God of the servant church was definitively immanent, in and of the world. This worldly-wise Deity, rather than high and lifted up, was down in the world and one with the church when it truly acted as what it was meant to be, the People of God.

The church as People of God was a Vatican II idea, voiced by Hans Küng, the great Catholic theologian from the University of Tübingen, but it also influenced Protestants of the era. The concept emphasizes that the church is equally the laity and the clergy. The clergy are not hierarchical leaders but themselves servants of the servant church. Since the laity are the bulk of the church, it can meet wherever they are: in homes, in the workplace, in the fields, as well as in Gothic settings; and in its eucharists it can use everyday bread and wine as well as anything fancier.

How was all this expressed? Worship emphasized community symbols over hierarchical layerings. (In the Episcopal church of my childhood, the richly vested priest—to me a remote and awesome figure—prayed facing the altar with his back to the congregation, because, it was said, he was speaking not to the people but to God on their behalf. After the mid-Sixties, however, the idea was that priests, perhaps more simply attired, spoke the words of eucharistic supplication over a now freestanding holy table into the faces of the people, for God was in their midst and could, so to speak, overhear. So was the communal emphasized over the sacerdotal character of the church.) Laypeople increasingly took part in services, reading, giving communion, assuming many other roles than that of taking up the collection.

Yet, ironically, at least at first the changes seemed to reclericalize the church, and this did not escape the many critics of reform. Inevitably it was the professionals who devised and promoted most of the often traumatic rearrangements. Some worshippers might have sympathized with the words of that archetypal layperson, C. S. Lewis: "Novelty may fix our attention not even on the Service, but on the celebrant. You know what I mean. Try as one may to exclude it, the question 'what on earth is he up to now?' will intrude. It lays one's devotion to waste . . . I can make do with almost any kind of service whatever, if only it will stay put."[64]

But the implication that a service was primarily intended to provide a convenient occasion for private devotion was, of course, anathema to progressive liturgists. Changes in patterns of worship are generally stressful, and those who introduce them can seem pushy. In the Sixties there were those who were pushed up to new levels of spiritual life, pushed sideways into more congenial settings, and pushed out of church altogether.

For the new spirit meant a new kind of church, more concerned with activist service to the world than with the inner life or in-group fellowship. No doubt it brought in some things that had been neglected and neglected some legitimate traditional areas of religious concern—though the new people would have responded that the best spiritual life has always been found in selfless service rather than in introspection or narrow communities. The church—or perhaps one should say certain cutting-edge, high-visibility churches—began acting like small, tightly knit fellowships of the children of light set in the midst of a dark world, rather than like William Whyte's easygoing, inclusive United Protestant Church set in Fifties suburbia. In a word, as observers pointed out, these new-style congregations—often cream-of-the-cream mainline in background—acted like sects rather than like the old-style church.

149

The difference was sometimes one of tone, not the sort of thing institutional or theological historians of religon frequently mention, but obvious to those who were there. Youthful clerics used expressions like "Jesus is neat" or at their best uttered streetwise topical prayers like Malcolm Boyd's. Jazz and rock masses drew hordes of young people. Church interiors were swept and garnished with bright pop-art banners, and Victorian stained glass and dark wainscoting were downplayed. The sermons were sometimes dialogues, the congregation encouraged to talk back with their own insights.

Within Protestantism, the servant church mood was nowhere better expressed than in the magazine *Renewal,* sponsored jointly by the Chicago and New York City missionary societies, and until late 1966 edited by one of the most articulate spokespersons for the new kind of ministry, Stephen C. Rose. Leafing through the mid-Sixties issues is an evocative experience. They are full of gritty black-and-white photos of urban slums, Vietnam horrors, pinched and soulful African American or Third World faces—and of hard-hitting articles on corresponding topics, from Mississippi to Chicago politics to the war to calls for radical ecclesiastical renewal.

Critics sometimes alleged that the outspoken prophets of the Sixties within and without the church were merely destructive, without a clear affirmative agenda. But in a February 1966 manifesto, "The Grass Roots Church," Rose spelled out the basics of a radical renewal program. Its foundation is the postmodern idea that denominationalism is obsolete. The church has three functions, none of which is related to denomination: "Chaplaincy," or the proclamation of biblical insights to the human situation; "Teaching," the integration of biblical insights into the realities of today's world; and "Abandonment," the rather unusual word used for the church's ministry to the world outside the church. To accomplish these ends Rose called for cooperative, ecumenical ministries in local churches, the reform of theological seminaries to train specialized ministers who would be part of such teams, and the decentralization of denominations so that "denominational dollars" would go to local renewal needs rather than to national or maintenance programs. Here was clearly a postmodern alternative to something like COCU.

Liturgy was not a conspicuous concern of *Renewal,* as it might have been for Catholic or Episcopal servant church revitalization. But the passion for cutting centralized bureaucracy and putting the church to use on the local level was as evident in *Renewal* as it was at Vatican II.

The lack of theological engagement in *Renewal*, and perhaps even more the lack of any evident interest in what is known as spirituality, may have represented a more serious one-sidedness. For there were other alternative churches waiting in the wings, some of them heavily engaged with the slums, the Vietnams, and the liturgies of the mind.

The Acid Church

For those ceremonies of the soul, let us return to the story of Timothy Leary and LSD. In the last chapter we left the defrocked Harvard professor traveling the world attempting to find a base of operations for the new chemical consciousness. He was thrown out of three countries. Then, in an example of the marvelous luck that often seemed to parallel his cosmic-scale disasters, for her own tax purposes a New York heiress offered Leary the use of an estate located in Millbrook, sixty miles north of the New York City. In September 1963 Leary, some students, and his movement, then technically called the International Federation for Internal Freedom (IFIF), moved in.

Timothy Leary established at Millbrook the Camelot of the psychedelic age. The unused Dutchess County mansion was a vast, dark, lonely Charles Addams kind of manor, a Victorian extravaganza of turrets, porches, and fretted woodwork set amid acres of pines. The labyrinthine sixty-four-room interior, creaking but rich in frayed red carpeting, drafty corridors, and frail elderly furniture, bloomed with mandalas, occult sigils, and paradisiacal visions.

But in its brief years of glory under Leary and his acolytes, those approaching its welcoming lights could well feel that, in Jay Stevens's memorable language, "they have stumbled across a fairytale castle, entering a timeless dimension where the gap between psychedelic time and real time doesn't exist."[65] (One always imagines Millbrook at night, a roaring blaze in the great central fireplace and one of its famous midnight banquets under way within, and above its towers scattered stars and a cloud-crossed waning moon.) Leary liked to compare this paradise to Castalia, the technological monastery in Hermann Hesse's visionary Nobel Prize–winning novel, *The Glass-Bead Game* or *Magister Ludi*. Indeed, IFIF was renamed Castalia in 1964.

Millbrook has been described variously: as a monastery or ashram, as a research institute in psychotropic drugs, and also as a commune, a school, and, as Stevens put it, "a house party of unparalleled dimensions" (208). Like alchemists of old, Castalia's new priesthood converted one of the tower rooms into a laboratory, with gold ceilings and images of Shiva and the Buddha, where disciples could engage in "ontological adventures" leading in the end, Leary hoped, to the complete mapping of the Other World. The visitor might also sample Sufi dancing, *I Ching* readings, and concerts of electronic music. Nearly everyone of importance to the new consciousness came around—R. D. Laing, Alan Watts, the jazz legend Charlie Mingus.

Millbrook's fabled weekend parties, which included upscale drugs and sex as well as conviviality in the Catskills, were the places to be seen and to talk about among the City's[66] fashionable avant-garde crowd. Summer schools introduced numerous students to the new mysticism. Serious work got done too. The quasi-scholarly journal *Psychedelic Review* was published, and *The Psychedelic Experience* came out, a new turned-on version of the Tibetan Book of the Dead, first fruits of IFIF's mapping of the other world.[67]

It could not last, of course. Late in 1965 Leary, with characteristic carelessness, got himself arrested on a marijuana possession charge in Laredo, Texas, on his way into Mexico. Despite much publicity, much support from New York "names," and a defense that included the introduction of Hindu and other witnesses to claim that psychedelic drugs had a legitimate religious use and so Leary's prosecution was a First Amendment violation, the south Texas jury was not impressed. Leary was convicted in March 1966 and sentenced to thirty years. He appealed and returned to Millbrook, but trouble was gathering for him back in New York too, as clamor for the outlawing of psychedelics rose across the nation.

The mansion was becoming increasingly unpopular with the neighbors. In April, at their instigation, it was raided by local sheriff's deputies led by a Dutchess County assistant district attorney named G. Gordon Liddy, later of Watergate fame. Despite a diligent search, the deputies could find nothing illegal. Nonetheless, the community was given to understand that when psychedelics were outlawed, Castalia would be kept under close surveillance. By the end of 1966 the prohibition was in effect virtually everywhere in the United States.

Leary, increasingly playing a cat-and-mouse game with the police, was finally evicted from Millbrook by the owners in February 1968 and set out to live half in hiding, half in the glow of the publicity he loved. Counterculture buttons appeared saying "Leary Is God." He went to California, the center of the new faith of which he was widely considered—and certainly considered himself—the pope if not the God. In place of IFIF and Castalia he founded the League for Spiritual Discovery—LSD. For a while his luck held. In 1969 the Texas conviction was finally thrown out by the Supreme Court on the grounds that the state's marijuana law was unclear. But in March 1970 he was convicted in California after a Laguna Beach bust, denied bail, and sent to a minimum security prison in San Luis Obispo, where he remained for several years.

Timothy Leary and the psychedelic revolution were not well regarded by the political wing of the Sixties, particularly in the early, civil rights years.[68] In the summer of 1964, Castalia and Mississippi coexisted in the same Republic but might have been in alternative universes for all the correspondence they had. Leary's indifference to the political and social crisis was inexcusable to COFO activists, while to the new ontological Columbuses earth-plane political struggles appeared superficial. Yet in a couple of years, on the streets of Berkeley and San Francisco particularly, the twain would meet, though warily.

In any case, the historian of Sixties religion can in no wise leave Leary and psychedelia on the sidelines. Though Castalia was hardly a church or monastery, it was a spiritual collegium by intention, and its experiments were odysseys into unknown, God- and Circe-infested waters. Psychedelia generally was rebellion and adventure on no small scale, and it took the combined powers of the church, state, media, and scientific establishments to quash it.

Whatever wisdom chemical trips may hold was wisdom for which those power worlds were not ready in the 1960s and are not yet ready. In the end, that particular kind of laboratory-generated wisdom or folly was more feared even than civil rights, the antiwar movement, or the servant church and was more firmly exorcised by all the reigning priesthoods. Though many were called, the *kairos* was not right, and argonauts of consciousness like Leary became not a new priesthood but the designated devils of an era.

The antidrug reaction is all too understandable given the doleful scenes of exploitation, crime, and disease widespread drug use brought to city streets and counterculture communes. But abuse by overeager teenagers hardly proves the visions of the best psychedelic mystics to have no spiritual or cognitive worth. Yet any kind of research using psychedelics became politically impossible to undertake or fund, even privately. Data in Watts and Huxley and the *Psychedelic Review*, or gathered from Castalia or the Good Friday experiment in those few years between 1954 (the year of Huxley's *Doors of Perception)* and delegalization in 1966, remain fascinating but confusing. What researchers could accumulate and analyze in that brief span is insufficient to permit final conclusions about the geography, meaning, or worth of psychedelia's inner worlds. Instead, ontological exploration met a police barricade before it could much more than leave base camp. Until it can set out again, one range of the potentially knowable remains forbidden knowledge.

The Council Closes

During the heyday of Leary's acid church at Castalia, on another continent the last two sessions of the Vatican Council were held in the autumns of 1964 and 1965. The great conclave was concluded at about 1:45 P.M. December 8, 1965, with the words of Pope Paul VI to the assembled bishops: "In the name of our Lord Jesus Christ, depart in peace." Peace the prelates may have felt in their hearts, despite the need to pack and make their way to Rome's chaotic stations and airports. But there were doubtless other feelings as well: exhilaration at having been a part of four years whose impact on the future life of the church could be, and widely was, compared with such immense watersheds as the Constantinian or Reformation eras; uncertainty as to how it would all work out.

Here are some of the major fruits of the council. The decree "On the Church" was called by Bishop James V. Casey of Lincoln, Nebraska, "the mother of the other decrees." It proclaimed the collegial principle that the bishops share power with the pope in guiding the church and interpreting divine revelation. The document "On the Pastoral Office of Bishops" thus called for a synod of bishops to assist the pontiff and urged modernization of the curia. "On the Apostolate of the Laity" went beyond the hierarchy to emphasize that the whole church, not its ordained leadership alone, is the "People of God"; it repudiated clericalism to urge the laity to take initiative in implementing the faith within the complex structures of modern life.

That point was also made in the great document "On the Church in the Modern World," which dealt with such problems as atheism, poverty, nuclear war, and parenthood. The council fathers were firm in their opposition to the nuclear terror threatening the world. They affirmed the relation to God as the foundation of human fulfillment and dignity, while finding value in culture and science and placing all of history under the judgment and mercy of God. The spirit was quite at odds with that of the famous (or infamous) Syllabus of Errors of a century earlier, in which Pius IX condemned the modern world with a broad brush and denied that the Roman church could or should reconcile itself to it.

At the same time, the document's schema on birth control seemed to straddle that very sensitive issue, calling conjugal love equal to procreation among the purposes of marriage, yet also asking Catholics to remain "submissive toward the church's teaching office" in the matter of artificial birth control while appearing to leave the door open to change in its future teaching on this issue. (That door was, however, firmly closed in 1968 with the encyclical *Humanae Vitae*, which denied change and which was to many progressive Catholics a disillusioning first and greatest in a series of curial underminings of the spirit of Vatican II.)

"On Divine Revelation" reaffirmed the importance of scripture, acknowledging that the church is always in need of judgment and renewal by biblical standards. By implication, this document condemned the self-assured "triumphalism" of which many accused the preconciliar church, and put in its place a more Christlike ideal of servanthood. It also affirmed responsible biblical scholarship and saw no barrier to Catholic scholars cooperating with Protestant colleagues. "On the Church's Relation to Non-Christian Religions" expressed respect and a desire to dialogue with the world's other faiths, while denying collective Jewish guilt for the crucifixion of Christ.

In the same spirit, the important decree "On Religious Liberty," largely drafted by John Courtney Murray, ended the Counter-Reformation and Constantinian eras in church-state relations. Rejecting the principle that "error has no rights" and the legitimacy of any state coercion in religion, thereby reversing many centuries of Catholic history, the council asserted that no one can be compelled to act against conscience, except for the minimal demands of public order; that the right of dissent must be respected; and that the church must spread its message by its own spiritual means and without the dubious help of the secular arm.

Probably for many Roman Catholics, the decree that most forcefully told them that a new era had come to their church was "On Liturgy," for it produced sweeping changes in public worship that were visible Sunday after Sunday. As a result of this early fruit of the council, in a series of steps beginning with the late 1964 translation of most of the Mass into the vernacular, followed by the late 1967 rendering of the Canon, the most sacred part, into the common tongue and the 1970 issuance of new and simplified liturgies, the old hieratic Latin Mass with its gestures and genuflections was gone. In its place was a new, much-simplified rite in everyday speech, with laypeople often taking significant parts in its communal celebration. Far more than conciliar words alone, this experience bespoke the fresh emphasis on the laity, the Bible (scriptural lessons were now read aloud in clear speech), and in a mysterious way the whole new open, nonintimidating, servanthood concept of the church.

Hardly less important was what the council experience said about the nature of the church. First, there was the important role of the *periti*, or theological consultants brought to assist the council prelates. Typically these were theology professors of liberal bent, like John

Courtney Murray or Hans Küng of the University of Tübingen. These experts were undoubtedly decisive for the unexpectedly radical extent to which the council carried its reforms. It was they who effectively countered the curialists' and conservatives' alleged intention to make the meeting essentially a showpiece that they would control from behind the scenes, and that would be much stronger on rhetoric than real change.

The American Methodist observer Albert C. Outler commented that "this is the first council since Nicaea where the decisive balance was tipped by theology professors. . . . This council of 2,400 men was led to form honest convictions on the progressive side—and without any real leadership in the American sense of the word. In every instance it was the professors who tipped it. Most bishops didn't know the answers. But they knew administration, and one point of administration is to ask if you don't know."[69]

Vietnam and the Churches

We cannot here rehearse the whole long and messy story of U.S. involvement in Vietnam, but a little background information may be of help. The first U.S. military person to be killed in Vietnam's midcentury wars was Lt. Col. A. Peter Dewey of the Office of Strategic Services (OSS), shot by the anticolonialist Viet Minh while driving an unmarked jeep near Saigon's airport on September 26, 1945. This was only a few weeks after Japan's surrender marked the end of its wartime occupation of Indochina, and less than three weeks before France began trying to reconquer Vietnam, its former colony. In that project France received considerable U.S. aid. The French withdrew after the military catastrophe of Dienbienphu in 1954, leaving North Vietnam to the largely Communist Viet Minh under Ho Chi Minh, and South Vietnam under Paris's disastrous surrogate, Ngo Dinh Diem.

Diem, a Catholic and protégé of Cardinal Spellman, refused to hold a promised 1956 national election, though he did subsequently conduct one in the south, receiving 98.8 percent of the vote. But despite this remarkable show of support—augmented by massive U.S. aid, including nine hundred military advisers by 1960—Diem continued to lose territory to the Vietcong, as the North Vietnam–supported guerrillas in the south were called.

Between 1961 and 1963, under President Kennedy, 16,000 more U.S. military personnel arrived in Vietnam, of whom 109 died. New counterinsurgency methods were tried, including open fire zones, "strategic hamlets," and air "training missions" for the south's bombar-

diers. But Diem remained ineffectual, persecuting Buddhist dissidents—
leading some monks to undertake self-immolation as a protest tactic—
while failing to prosecute the war effectively or to undertake reforms
urged by the Americans.

In 1963 the United States was visited by Madame Nhu, also a
Catholic and the wife of Diem's brother, who was chief of South
Vietnam's secret police. The exotically beautiful Nhu, often called the
Dragon Lady, accompanied by her no-less-stunning teenage daughter,
attracted much attention as she lectured on U.S. Catholic campuses
and elsewhere. But, given as she was to confiding in asides that, for
example, she enjoyed the Buddhist "barbecues," Nhu won little new
support for the family regime. Then, on Novemer 2, 1963, while she
was still in the United States, her husband and Diem were assassinated in a coup endorsed by the administration of John F. Kennedy—
whose own assassination, ironically, was only three weeks away.

Thereafter, even as U.S. buildup and involvement grew, the government in Saigon was essentially a series of coups and juntas until
stabilized under Air Vice Marshall Nguyen Cao Ky in June 1965. The
presidency of General Nguyen Van Thieu (with Ky as vice-president)
followed an election in September 1967 widely denounced as fraudu-
lent. These regimes, though dictatorial and repressive, proved no better able than their predecessors to deal with the Communist threat.

They were nonetheless assisted by an unceasing escalation of U.S.
aid and presence. There was the questionable naval engagement in
August 1964 that produced the Tonkin Gulf Resolution in Congress
allowing all necessary U.S. military measures, the bombing of North
Vietnam ordered by President Johnson in February 1965, the increase
of U.S. forces in Vietnam to 75,000 in July, 1965, and to nearly 200,000
by the end of that year.

In early 1968, when the number reached 510,000, the Tet offensive convinced many that a military victory was impossible, U.S. public opinion was decisively turning against the war, and Johnson
announced his decision not to run for reelection. He then rejected
General William Westmoreland's call for another 206,000 U.S. soldiers (the peak U.S. commitment would be 543,000 troops in April
1969). Johnson instead restricted bombing in the north and initiated
negotiations with Hanoi; these commenced in Paris on May 13, 1968.
Thereafter, under Johnson, Nixon, and, at the very end, Ford, the
agony of Vietnam continued through a long winding-down process of
off-and-on bombings, gradual U.S. withdrawals, "Vietnamization," interminable negotiations that never stopped the fighting for long, and
finally the fall of Saigon on April 30, 1975. The United States had

suffered nearly 50,000 combat deaths, and it received over 165,000 Vietnamese refugees.

In 1964 little antiwar activity had yet appeared in the United States. Even the Gulf of Tonkin did not arouse much public interest; most ordinary Americans did not know where the Tonkin Gulf, or for that matter Vietnam, was, and the attention of both the general public and activists was focused instead on the burning domestic issue, civil rights. Not quite at hand was the day when civil rights abuses and the war were seen as parts of a continuum bespeaking deepseated malaise all through American society, and protest energies generated by one cause were readily transferred to the other.

The small but seasoned pacifist community, largely Quakers and other "peace church" members, together with such committed and fairly radical (though not as radical as later) groups as the Catholic Workers, the Fellowship of Reconciliation, and the War Resisters League, was far more concerned with civil rights and with U.S.-Soviet disarmament, especially nuclear. (No matter which side of the debate one was on, "the Bomb" was the big peace issue in those years.)

True, one sign at a traditional Hiroshima Day peace and disarmament rally in New York on August 6, 1964, read "United States Troops Belong in Mississippi, Not Vietnam," and also in early August, Robert Moses of SNCC compared shooting in Mississippi with Vietnam at a memorial service for the three civil rights workers killed near Philadelphia, Mississippi, but most activists even on the Left had not made this connection yet. The first regular antiwar protest began October 3, 1964. Twelve people, sponsored by traditional pacifist groups including those just mentioned, began a vigil; it was to be held every Saturday in Times Square until the war ended.[70] Insofar as the war was an issue in the 1964 presidential election campaign, Barry Goldwater's "extremist" calls for total victory and the use of field nuclear weapons in Vietnam enabled Johnson to appear the moderate.

The seeds of something else were planted at the very end of 1964, at a meeting of the Students for a Democratic Society in New York on December 29. The SDS, founded under that name in 1960 and aided by an initial grant from the United Auto Workers, was a descendant of a youth organization of the League for Industrial Democracy, a respectable Old Left, labor-oriented, anti-Communist group. The SDS, however, by the mid-Sixties had become the most important focal organization of the New Left, brought into that role in large part by its early and consistent antiwar activity. In the process, SDS was torn by bitter debates over "inclusiveness" and the exclusion of Communist and Communist-sympathizing groups from its demonstrations and other projects; the debate was, however, less about principle than public relations.

The antiwar project began on that cold New York winter night. An eloquent longtime speaker for the Left, I. F. Stone, called passionately for opposition to the war, and as a result the SDS decided to organize a march on Washington the next Easter weekend, April 17, 1965, to protest it, in conscious imitation of King's epic triumph in the same city in 1963.

By then interest in the new threat from Southeast Asia had swelled considerably on campuses and in peace groups. The Johnson administration had helped by ordering air strikes over North Vietnam up to the Twentieth Parallel, in response to a Vietcong attack on a U.S. air base at Pleiku in which several Americans were killed. (April 4, 1965, a full-page ad protesting the bombing appeared in the *New York Times* signed by twenty-five hundred priests, rabbis, and ministers.) The first antiwar teach-in was conducted on March 24 at the University of Michigan; others followed. The April 17 SDS march on Washington attracted no fewer than twenty thousand (any groups considered dangerously Red, like the DuBois Clubs, had been excluded), and speakers included A. J. Muste, the grand old man of American pacifism; Senator Ernest Gruening of Alaska, who with Wayne Morse was the main antiwar voice in Congress; Robert Moses from SNCC; I. F. Stone; and Paul Potter, the twenty-two-year-old head of the SDS. Also on the platform were Joan Baez and Judy Collins, who sang, and a SNCC trio, the Freedom Voices, who rendered "We Shall Overcome," thus clearly connecting this movement with the other one.

On May 11 and 12 an Interreligious Committee on Vietnam, John Bennett of Union Theological Seminary, Martin Luther King, and Daniel Corrigan, the Episcopal bishop of New York, sponsored a silent vigil at the Pentagon, stating it was "appalled by the human tragedy and suffering involved in the struggle in Vietnam."[71] Late in July and August the Committee for Nonviolent Action (founded in 1957 to organize antinuclear projects, such as sailing ships into Pacific testing zones) set up marches in New York and pickets at the White House, followed by an "invasion" of the halls of Congress to demand a declaration for peace. A. J. Muste and Robert Moses were among the organizers. SDS helped bring people in, and the numbers were in the thousands rather than the hundreds as originally anticipated; more than 350 were arrested. One public activity in New York had been the burning of draft cards by young men; the only tangible legislative result of the Washington fracas was a law making the "willful destruction" of a draft card an offense calling for five years in prison.

The religious connection of this 1965 activism is as apparent as its link to civil rights; at this point that link was clearest by far with the radical pacificist, "peace church" strand in American religious life. A. J. Muste, for example, was a powerful force both behind and in front of the scenes. Born in Holland in 1885, he was brought to the United States as a child. He had been ordained in the Dutch Reformed church, but as his theology grew more liberal he became a Congregationalist minister and then a Quaker, after being forced because of his pacifism to leave the Massachusetts church of which he was pastor during World War I. He worked as a labor organizer between the wars, was a Marxist for a time, but returned to Christian pacifism during the Thirties. From 1940 until 1953 he was executive secretary of the Fellowship of Reconciliation, a leading interdenominational religious pacifist organization. As we have seen, FOR was an original spiritual home of such Gandhian early civil rights activists as Bayard Rustin, James Lawson, Robert Moses, and James Farmer. Martin Luther King, a great admirer of Muste, had joined it in the early Fifties.

Muste was himself no less committed to civil rights than to pacifism and had been a founding member of CORE in 1942 with James Farmer, then race relations secretary of FOR. One could fairly say that the civil rights movement of the first half of the Sixties, the days of the sit-ins, the freedom riders, the march on Washington and the Mississippi Summer, was the Quakerish Muste/FOR movement, founded on the FOR kind of nonviolent activism and dominated by Muste disciples like those just named. The movement in the second half of the decade, by contrast, brought to the fore men like Bobby Seale or Stokely Carmichael of the Black Panther party, a generation younger than most of the FOR group, educated in the ghetto rather than the divinity school, and with no particular commitment to nonviolence.

In the Fifties and early Sixties Muste had been an often lonely participant in acts of civil disobedience against nuclear testing—including one in Red Square. He had few illusions about communism and criticized militarism and totalitarianism within the Soviet bloc as acerbically as he did militarism and McCarthyism at home. His writings from the early Fifties, when he was at the top of his form and in deference to nothing but his inner light, in retrospect read like rare expressions of sanity in a mad time. Would-be radicals of less than half his years were drawn to this senior bearer of the light; one said that Muste was "a devastating reminder to young pacifists of what a real radical is."[72] I can remember hearing Muste speak in the Fifties; he was tall and lean, characteristically in a rumpled and threadbare suit, and there was about his glittering eyes something that, like the ancient mariner's, held one as tightly as did the startling reasonableness of the pacifist case as he presented it. He died on February 11, 1967, in the midst of his last struggle, for peace in Vietnam.

It was not until fall 1965 that large-scale church and campus antiwar activity really got in gear. That spring radical activists of the mainline Protestant churches were busy at Selma, and their Roman Catholic counterparts were still preoccupied with the conciliar dramas and corresponding far-reaching internal reforms transpiring in their church. But those ecclesiastical transformations would soon enough release powerful fresh Catholic energies for antiwar work; Selma and Vietnam would be the first beneficiaries of a style of social-political protest activism, unprecedented in Roman Catholicism but unleashed by the spirit of the council. Selma, as we have seen, was more than another civil rights march; it was a new discovery about the church and society, even as in the Roman church the new wine of individual initiative and social activitism could no longer be entirely corked in authoritarian bottles.

That fall, large Vietnam Days were held in New York and on campuses again—this time up to ten thousand participated at Berkeley beginning October 25. Demonstrators from Berkeley temporarily stopped troop trains, and in a scene reminiscent of Selma, police stopped fourteen thousand marchers as they tried to cross the city line from Berkeley to Oakland to picket the Oakland Army Supply Depot. By now the protests were making headlines and newsmagazine covers.

A November 1 *Newsweek* article gave decidedly mixed reviews, claiming—rightly at this point—that the movement was unrepresentative of American public opinion as a whole. The piece stressed alleged extreme leftist ties in its leadership and called attention to the bearded and "unwashed" appearance of some of the demonstrators. But the *Newsweek* writers also saw the demonstrations as reflecting the vague but profound uneasiness of many less vocal Americans about a war that seemed to keep getting bigger than anyone intended, as well as more brutal—with its napalming of villages—more costly, and more divisive than they liked. Strident antidemonstrators were also present, with heckling, eggs, and red paint, and so was a surprising hysteria in Congress, even on the part of liberals, about "draft-dodging," "Communist influence," and "treason." Some observers anticipated a new "McCarthyism." President Johnson himself made caustic comments about the demonstrators, while Attorney General Nicholas Katzenbach and FBI Director J. Edgar Hoover claimed Communist involvement and called for investigations.[73]

According to a far more sensitive *Newsweek* article two weeks later on developing religious opposition to the war, it was actually these remarks "that convinced many moderate clergymen that the right of dissent was under attack" and pushed them into the opposition. The opening paragraphs of this piece are worth quoting:

> One of the more obvious ironies of religious history is the ease with which most Christian churches, despite their theoretical commitment to peace and universal brotherhood, have repeatedly baptized the aims of their own national governments in time of war. The exceptions—the German Protestant martyrs who formed the "confessing church" in opposition to Hitler, the Roman Catholic French priests who went to jail rather than support the war in Algeria—only prove the rule: it is much easier for organized religion to condemn the enemy as totally evil or join in uncritical support of national policy than to attempt those onerous judgments that may find one's own country guilty of immorality.
>
> In the last few weeks, however, the stepped-up U.S. role in Vietnam—and the vocal protests of U.S. students—have jarred the consciences of influential clergymen. More and more they are voicing concern—and in some cases, outright dissent—over the Administration's policies in Southeast Asia.[74]

The distinguished rabbi Abraham Heschel put it this way:

> For many years, I felt that the Federal government had all the facts and was competent to make the necessary decisions. But in the last few weeks I have changed my mind completely. I have previously thought that we were waging war reluctantly, with sadness at killing so many people. I realize that we are doing it now with pride in our military efficiency. (78)

The upshot was the formation of an ad hoc group, Clergy Concerned About Vietnam, which in New York in October brought together about a hundred clergy, largely mainstream liberals, and began holding news conferences and seminars. As we have seen, it included such persons as John Bennett, Robert McAfee Brown, the Catholic lay philosopher Michael Novak, the Lutheran pastor Richard Neuhaus, the Jesuit Daniel Berrigan, Yale chaplain Henry Sloane Coffin, and Rabbi Heschel. Martin Luther King indicated his support, despite widespread concern that it would only weaken his civil rights position. Reinhold Niebuhr, Harvey Cox, and many others would soon be with them, either as formal members or sympathizers. The following May this group became Clergy and Laity Concerned About Vietnam (CALCAV).[75]

CALCAV would be the heart of religious opposition to the war. Though its members did not represent the rank and file of either clergy or laity across the country, they included some of religion's most vocal, articulate, and respected leaders. It is clear that many rabbis and churchpeople had been shaken out of dogmatic slumbers regarding religion and society by civil rights, student protests, and the arrogant-seeming unresponsiveness of the administration. Many had demonstrated on behalf of that administration in 1964, or at least against Goldwater, in what liberal religionists saw as a presidential race involving unusually profound moral issues, and in which the *Christian Century* had endorsed a specific candidate for the first time. They had passionately supported the government's Great Society anti-poverty programs and its civil rights and voting rights bills. They had cheered when it sent FBI agents and troops to Mississippi and Alabama only months earlier. Now, suddenly (or so it seemed when the war finally got their full attention), it was an administration as ready to napalm children as to put them in Head Start centers, as ready to support corrupt and illiberal governments in Southeast Asia as to confront them in the American South—and the switch, or internal contradiction, was crazy-making.

Undoubtedly it pushed some over the edge into total alienation, or to the passion of a Norman R. Morrison, a thirty-two-year-old American Quaker who doused himself with kerosene and burned himself to death on November 2, 1965, in front of the Pentagon, his body charred and melted like the victims of napalm or those anti-Diem Buddhist monks who had immolated themselves in Vietnam; he was made much of as a hero in Hanoi.[76]

The collective schizophrenia that built up in 1965 is well reflected in the popular music of the latter part of that year, as the days darkened both literally and figuratively. In August 1965 a song written by a nineteen year old, P. F. Sloan, and sung by snarly-voiced Barry McGuire, "Eve of Destruction," hit the top of the charts only five weeks after its release. As Todd Gitlin reports in *The Sixties: Years of Hope, Days of Rage*, there had never been anything like it before, either in its rapid rise or the apocalyptic message of its lyrics as they broke into the heretofore upbeat world of pop music. Back in the more hopeful world of 1964, hits had included bouncy tunes like the Beach Boys' "California Girl" and the Beatles' "A Hard Day's Night." Even Bob Dylan's hit, the sensual and disturbing and possibly drug-related "Mr. Tambourine Man," popular earlier in 1965, struck a different note. But in "Eve of Destruction" comes rough and raw reference to the "hate" in Red China and Selma, war and bodies floating even in the Jordan River, and lines suggesting that youth too young to vote are being taught to kill and declaring that such a pass must mean we are on the brink of catastrophe. The song was denounced, and stations refused to play it—but its strident, bitter, and unprecedentedly topical lines were heard.

Then, as though in retort, a different rhythm rose to the top of the charts: "Ballad of the Green Berets," sung by another Barry, Staff Sergeant Barry Sadler. Its virile lines and march tempo extolled the fighting men and even made many listeners feel good about the war. (In the fall of 1965, a Chicago station held a "Battle of the Barrys"; on a certain day listeners were invited to call in to cast a ballot for the song they preferred: Barry McGuire's "Eve of Destruction" or Barry Sadler's "Green Berets." The Berets won—reportedly by a single vote out of thousands.)[77]

To antiwar religionists, John C. Bennett's *Foreign Policy in Christian Perspective* (1966) was an important statement.[78] Starting with a basically Niebuhrian position holding that "all nations live under the providence, the judgment and the love of God," that all states, like all persons, have known both sin and righteousness and therefore none are uniquely favored or damned, the object of a foreign policy informed both by Christian realism and Christian love would be not absolute victory but reconciliation. The church should be an agent of this reconciliation. On the other hand, the United States in the Cold War has tended to become as rigidly and intensely ideological as its opponents, eschewing reconciliation in favor of pursuing elusive total triumph, a prime example being Vietnam.

This contention was not without its questioners. Harold E. Fey, a contributing editor to the *Christian Century* and by no means a hardline hawk, asked in a review of Bennett's book if the author were not in fact applying his strictures inconsistently, passing over the resistance to reconciliation and acts of aggression of the Communist nations more lightly than those of his own country. He therefore, Fey charged, called on the United States to abandon its commitment to Vietnam unilaterally; Fey was not ready yet to do so.[79]

The prominent social ethicist Paul Ramsey presented a dissenting view in the *Christian Century*, "Vietnam: Dissent on Dissent." This proponent of "realism" contended that negotiation now would only fulfill the Vietcong aims and would amount to simply surrendering South Vietnam to communism.[80]

Even if public opinion, dominated by traditional patriotism and Cold War attitudes instilled throughout the Fifties, was still uneasy with the antiwar movement, religious and other intellectuals were increasingly coming out on the "anti" side in 1966. Awareness was growing that Washington had frequently concealed facts and real policies on Vietnam, professing to be seeking negotiations while spurning overtures from the enemy and calling for more bombing.

The upshot was a plain loss of faith, and an unwillingness to believe anything from people who had lied too often. In the spring of 1966 Reinhold Niebuhr, long a Cold War liberal, concluded that the U.S. government was not truly interested in seeking a political resolution of Vietnam and said, "For the first time I fear I am ashamed of our beloved nation." In September 1966, Richard Fernandez, executive secretary of the rapidly growing CALCAV, wrote, "Six months ago most of us would have said that some very good men in Washington had made some very bad mistakes from which they should try to extricate themselves as soon as possible. Today it seems that this kind of judgment is both out of date and inaccurate."[81] Washington too was becoming more desperate to justify itself.

The antiwar demonstrations of 1966 were not reassuring to those hoping for national trust and unity, any more than was the inexorable bombing and "escalation." By that year demonstrations drew thousands in the major northeast and west coast cities, and by now they were spewing out nasty chants ("Hey, hey, LBJ, how many kids you kill today?") and displaying symbols like skulls, coffins, and ghoulish military figures. The smoke of burning draft cards rose from some of them.

It seemed that change, if it came, would now have to come from the battlefield, or from the streets, or from a change in the hearts of those in the seats of power. And as the grim year of 1966 closed, none of those appeared likely prospects. The religious opposition to the war was certainly an outgrowth of modernist religion's confidence about its role in society and the importance of its stands on social issues, just as was its growing role in civil rights a year or two earlier. Yet even as Selma somehow changed the nature of the church's self-perception and overnight dated the kinds of denominational beliefs and structures that had produced that first wave of activist clergy and laity, so did Vietnam. Under these pressures the old church expanded and extended itself to the point where it was ready to undergo metamorphosis. The next wave would be something else.

Books

In addition to those already mentioned in connection with secularism and the Death of God, here are some books relevant to religion that people were reading and talking about between 1964 and 1966.

Pride of place must go to Martin Luther King's *Why We Can't Wait*

Counterpoint: Captain Kirk and the Cold War

The TV series *Star Trek* premiered on September 8, 1966, and continued until 1969. The series has had many exfoliations. There have been cartoons, a "Second Generation" TV drama series, and several films, the latest (at the time of writing, VI) quite obviously reflecting the end of the Cold War in the Nineties. A not insignificant collection of dramas based on *Star Trek* and its characters have been composed by fans, predominantly women.[*]

Yet perhaps few observers have noted the extent to which Captain Kirk, Science Officer Spock, Medical Officer "Bones" McCoy, and the rest of the starship *Enterprise* crew articulated Sixties themes, including those with spiritual overtones, while idealizing them. In retrospect this science fiction epic emerges as one of the most revealing popular culture documentations of American social and political attitudes in the Sixties. Its humane, clean-cut, uniformed heroes of the twenty-third century seemed, for the Sixties, right at the interface between the conflicting archetypal dreams of the decade's own Right and Left. The *Enterprise* company was a little bit Green Berets, a little bit Peace Corps, a little bit Merry Pranksters, a little bit freedom riders. Surprisingly, out of this conundrum the show managed to image some quite positive values and visions, Sixties but not radical Sixties, Cold War but with a heart, civil rights but with the right people still at the top. Thus *Star Trek* promoted the ideal of racial equality at home, and the equally important "pay any price" ideal for freedom abroad (as defined by those at home).

Rick Worland, in "Captain Kirk: Cold Warrior," points out that this perennially popular mythos was originally shown during the greatest escalation of the Vietnam War, 1966–1969. The crew of the *Enterprise* was multiethnic yet distinctly Anglo-American in command and character, just as were the forces in Vietnam. During the second season, a "United Federation of Planets" was presented as a "Free World" in opposition to the swarthy, autocratic Klingons. Two ideologically contrasting superpowers were thus set against each other, and in their all-out struggle each used propaganda, ploys, proxies, sabotage, and as a last resort military action— preferably in primitive locations far removed from the home bases of either power.[**]

The Romulans also came into action against the Federation. They were like the Chinese, or perhaps the World War II Japanese, of an ancient and ornate but unfathomable culture given to enigmatic, Daoistic philosophies of war and suicidal concepts of honor. They were related (through the Vulcans, Spock's people) to the "good guys," but by some tragic flaw in history came to be ranged against them.

Counterpoint: Captain Kirk and the Cold War *Continued*

Nonetheless, the Klingons were the major threat to the Federation and its ostensibly democratic values, and it was with them that the Federation troops chiefly clashed on Third World planets, between their R and R's in exotic, sensuous, but exceedingly tricky places. So it was that on February 2, 1968, *Star Trek* offered "A Private Little War," clearly a Vietnam allegory—ironically two days into the Tet offensive. Other Sixties topics occurred as well. In "The Way to Eden" the *Enterprise* crew encountered "space hippies," a band of twenty-third-century counterculture youths, led by a "Dr Sevrin" who seems to have been based on Timothy Leary. He, with his disciples/slaves, is in search of a legendary paradise, Eden, and has jettisoned scientific research and values for the sake of this passionate quest. This fanatic pied piper and his vacuous following are by no means presented sympathetically, yet they clearly stamp the series with the years of its provenance.

At the same time, the continuing popularity of *Star Trek* indicates that this culture vehicle transcends the Sixties or, perhaps better, packages the more enduring of its values for the ages. As I have indicated, the immense cultural importance of space and space exploration was a Sixties theme. So was the great idea that certain human, democratic values were worth fighting for, but in the right way and by the right people. The *Enterprise* exemplified the latter better than many exemplars of the same ideal on the ground, and the contrast was not overlooked by many of *Star Trek*'s largely youthful fans. When, as in "Amok Time," *Star Trek* made allusion to the dangers of altered states of consciousness and their chemical agents, the tone was always illustrative, never preachy or punitive.

In short, *Star Trek* was the Sixties—warts, Cold War, drugs and all, yes, but as it could or should have been in better hands and in some better universe, maybe that of the twenty-third century.

*Camille Bacon-Smith, "Spock among the Women," *New York Times Book Review*, November 16, 1986.
**Journal of Popular Film & Television* 16 (Fall 1988): 109–117.

(1964). This little volume, which contains King's powerful Birmingham Jail letter, reiterates the great nonviolent tactician's case that any time is a good time for ending oppression—so why not now? He rejects tokenism and separatism (like that advocated by the Black Muslims), being prepared to settle for nothing less than the full integration of blacks into the mainstream of American life, with all the rights and privileges held by anyone. King's ideal was a nation entirely color-blind, where character alone counted and persons of all hues could work, eat, and play together, the society he had envisioned in his great "I Have a Dream" speech.[82] And it would be achieved not by arms but by moral force.

But other African Americans were beginning to express other views more and more openly. They did not want, they said, to share the white man's dream but to fulfill their own apart from his: separatism. They did not believe that dream would be attained merely by trusting to his goodwill. They called for revolution, violent if need be. In two words: Black Power. Some of them had been formed by a very different sort of black experience than King's parsonage: the streets, crime, drugs, prison. Some of them professed other religions or ideologies than King's pacifist Christianity: Islam, Native African, Marxism, nihilism.

As we have seen, 1965 was the hinge year for this transformation of the black movement. In 1964 the Civil Rights Act and the Voting Rights Act of 1965, and some degree of tacit shift in public opinion even in the South, were set to make a difference. Though it may not have been completely evident at the time, King's dream was already on an irreversible course toward fulfillment, at least on the level of law and the overt dismantling of Jim Crow. But by now something had been aroused in the black community that was not content to ride out the rest of the journey on automatic pilot. A new, younger generation of blacks felt a rage, a militancy, a comradeship with Third World revolution everywhere, and a cultural assertiveness—"black pride," "Black is beautiful"—that demanded to be heard, whether "Whitey" liked it or not. The likes of King, Forman, and Farmer decreased, and they of the new generation increased.

Berkeley was as usual at the cutting edge when, in 1966, the concept of black power began to sweep through the nation's black communities. The word *Negro* went out, and with it went the sort of politesse the civil rights movement had manifested thus far. Blacks were no longer the polite, neatly dressed young men and women of the sit-ins and freedom rides. They were now angry and proud, sporting Afros and dashikis, with no use for white liberals or for the Quakerish, pacifist type of leadership the movement had so far enjoyed. The heretofore oppressed were now ready for men like Stokeley Carmichael, who had succeeded James Forman and King-style nonviolence in SNCC in 1966, and who visited Berkeley several times in those years.

The first and greatest voice of this shift was that of Malcolm X. Born Malcolm Little, he had rejected the "slave" surname in favor of an anonymous X. Two books of his were published in 1965, after his assassination on February 21 of that year. In *The Autobiography of Malcolm X*, written with the assistance of Alex Haley, we find that, like King, Malcolm X was the son of a Baptist minister. But the resemblance ends there. X's father had worked with Marcus Garvey's Back to Africa movement, which brought the family to the unwelcome attention of the Ku Klux Klan in Omaha in 1925 while Malcolm was still in his mother's womb; their house in Lansing, Michigan, where they subsequently moved, was burned, apparently by whites. On top of that his father, despite his ministerial status, was violent and abusive; he died violently when Malcolm was only six. His fair-skinned mother was the product of a white man's rape of a black woman, and that unpunished crime was further reflected in the reddish tinge to Malcolm's hair.

After his father's death, Malcolm's single-parent family fell into desperate depression-era poverty, and Malcolm grew up with limited education (though better than average for blacks of that period) and drifted into crime, pimping, rackets, and jail—experiences through which he lost whatever illusions he might have had about the whites who were in the seats of the mighty, and for whom blacks were chiefly vehicles for the acting out of sexual and power fantasies.

He was exposed to the Black Muslims and was promptly converted, accepting Elijah Muhammad's contentions that whites were devils and blacks' only salvation was in separation from them. But the autobiography climaxes with Malcolm X's pilgrimage to Mecca. The Hajj was an overwhelming experience for the American black of deprived background. Not only was he an honored guest of King Faisal of Saudi Arabia, enjoying all the lavish hospitality of which that monarch was capable, but he was also profoundly impressed by the equality in Mecca of all the many races that comprised the House of Islam. Thereafter Malcolm muted the racist and antiwhite themes of his message and moved decisively toward orthodox Islam and away from the peculiar separatist views of the Black Muslims. (That shift of emphasis was also taken up by Elijah Muhammad's son Wallace [Warith Deen Muhammad], who suceeded his father as head of the movement upon the latter's death in 1972.)[83]

Malcolm's revolutionary zeal did not diminish, however, judging from his posthumous *Malcom X Speaks*. During his trip to Mecca, Malcolm had also traveled to Africa, where he had been entertained by revolutionary Chinese and Cuban embassies and been patronized by the more radical governments of that ex-colonial continent. The speeches of this volume, almost all from the last year of his life, seem to go out of their way to be provocative from the revolutionary perspective, perhaps exaggeratedly so. Here he admires the Mau-Mau and a nine-year-old Chinese girl he had seen pictured pulling the trigger on her kneeling father, an alleged counterrevolutionary. Malcolm rejoices that after such measures there are few "Uncle Tom Chinamen" left.[84]

He was no less dubious of nonviolence in his own country. An interview in the *Young Socialist* quoted in the book had him commending the Mississippi Summer attempts to register voters in the South, "because the only real power a poor man in this country has is the power of the ballot." As for those doing the registration, "I don't believe sending them in and telling them to be nonviolent was intelligent. I go along with the effort toward registration, but I think they should be permitted to use whatever means at their disposal to defend themselves from the attacks of the Klan, the White Citizens Council and other groups." As for white liberals: "When a white man comes to me and tells me how liberal he is, the first thing I want to know, is he a nonviolent liberal, or the other kind. I don't go for any nonviolent white liberals. If you are for me and my problems—when I say me, I mean *us*, our people—then you have to be willing to do as old John Brown did. And if you're not of the John Brown school of liberals, we'll get you later—later" (224).

On this Malcolm X was clearly at an opposite pole from Martin Luther King and the nonviolent tactics that (unlike Malcolm's violence) were put into practice on a large scale and shown to produce results. King said in *Why We Can't Wait* that nonviolent action was a way in which "the Negro" could "divest himself of passivity without arraying himself in vindictive force" (36). "Acceptance of nonviolent direct action was a proof of a certain sophistication on the part of the Negro masses; for it showed that they dared to break with the old, ingrained concepts of our society . . . there is something in the American ethos that responds to the strength of moral force" (37). Lines were drawn pretty sharply between that two views of how to reply to oppression.

Another take on the Sixties is presented in Timothy Leary, Ralph Metzner, and Richard Alpert, *The Psychedelic Experience* (1964), produced as we have seen in the Millbrook years. This exotic volume is a presentation of the LSD trip in terms of the language of the famous Tibetan Book of the Dead (*Bardo Thodol*), that guided tour of the afterdeath "Bardo" state where various peaceful and wrathful deities are encountered in all their mind-shattering transcendence, and from out of which one can finally reach enlightenment or return to rebirth in this gray-light world. In large part as interpreted by Leary and his coauthors, the Book of the Dead became one of the bibles of the acid counterculture, and especially of its mystical, orientalizing wing.

Other kinds of spiritual experimentation continued as well. Consider Morton Kelsey, *Tongue Speaking: An Experiment in Spiritual Experience* (1964). This is an intelligent and sympathetic account of a phenomenon that, in the Sixties, impacted numerous mainline Protestant and Catholic churches, as though in critical parallelism to the window opening of aggiornamento and counterculture. The author, an Episcopal priest, offers many firsthand accounts of this Sixties "latter rain." It is, Kelsey maintains, a sign of spiritual renewal to set alongside the others of the decade, one that opens access to the realms of dreams, visions, and the subsconscious. But Kelsey, a noted Jungian psychologist of religion, often interprets these realms more in the terms of the Swiss master than those of the fundamentalism embraced by many of the practicioners.[85]

Also published in 1964 was the posthumous *Markings* of Dag Hammerskjöld, distinguished Swedish diplomat, secretary-general of the United Nations, and—unknown to most—interior mystic in the midst of a busy and active life.[86] These personal aphorisms and haikulike poems, Christian in their love of God and sacrifice, Confucian in their this-worldly social imperatives, Daoist in submission to the flow of events, greatly appealed to the mid-Sixties. Perhaps it was the almost convergence of their austere rhetoric with secular theology as they displayed the undogmatic spirituality of a man wholly given to worldly action. Perhaps it was the way these spare but lucid lines seemed almost countercultural as they harmonized mysticism Eastern and Western. One of the more unforgettable aphorisms: "Do not seek death. Death will find you. But seek the road which makes death a fulfillment" (159). Hammerskjöld (1905–1961) died in an air crash in Northern Rhodesia en route to negotiate a cease-fire between United Nations and Katanga forces in the Congo.

Robert McAfee Brown's *Observer in Rome* (1964) is a delightful account of the second (1963) session of the Vatican Council, at which Brown—already cited in connection with his Protestant-Catholic ecumenical labors—was a Protestant observer. Though it deals with just one session, and the author's bias toward the liberal faction within the conclave under observation is unconcealed, few books capture the personalities, the flavor, and the issues of those often-exciting (and often-tedious) autumnal days in Rome so well and so compactly. There is a tribute at the end to Brown's sometime coauthor, Gustave Weigel, SJ, whose death in January 1964 deprived the church and the world of a preeminent ecumenist and interpreter of the council on the Catholic side.[87]

On the level of substantial theology, apart from those works solidly within the secular or Death of God camps, there is the Whiteheadian or "process" theologian Schubert Ogden's *Reality of God & Other Essays* (1966). This is a book very much within the context of the great religious-theological issue of the day, the existence of God himself. Ogden avoids the fetishes of both the Christian atheists and the traditional theists. He speaks of God as "creative becoming," the one reality related to everything, eminently social and temporal, expressing his unconditionedness through continuous creation manifested in a universe of continuous change, and cocreating with creative entities like us humans. God is therefore secular but not limited to secularity or anything else. In a chapter chiefly referring to Sartre, "The Strange Witness of Unbelief," Ogden declares that the implicit values of secular humanism itself point to a larger dimension to human life than it can contain, and elsewhere shows that death bears witness to the presence in life of more than secular meaning.[88]

The world's most famous Trappist monk, Thomas Merton, was very much a religious presence in these years. He was last mentioned in connection with his *Disputed Questions* (1960), with its essays on the value of solitude and the eulogizing of Boris Pasternak as a man who stood against a totalitarian system. Merton was to undergo a remarkable transformation in the Sixties from the deep-thinking and deep-praying but ultimately proper American Catholic of his Forties and Fifties books. Works like *The Seven Story Mountain* (1948), *Seeds of Contemplation* (1949), *The Waters of Siloe* (1949), *Ascent to Truth* (1951), and the like were very much a part of the Fifties undercurrent, cited in chapter 2, of interest in the world's contemplative traditions through bringing them back more or less whole as a visible, present alternative to the world of modernity. The generally uncritical celebration of conventional monastic asceticism in *The Waters of Siloe*, and the rich but deeply personal rather than social spirituality of *Seeds of Contemplation*, are excellent examples of the period.[89]

The very titles of many of Merton's mid-Sixties books tell of a whole new perspective: *Seeds of Destruction* (1964), *Gandhi on Non-Violence* (1965), *The Way of Chuang Tzu* (1965), *Conjectures of a Guilty Bystander* (1966), *Mystics and Zen Masters* (1967), *Faith and Violence* (1968), *Zen and the Birds of Appetite* (1968). Here is a revolutionized monk highly aware, even if from the sidelines (he became a hermit in 1965), of a world of social upheaval, of injustice and the need for action, and also filled with a fabulous East-West pluralism of spiritual options.[90]

The new Sixties outlook on the world said that the past had to be accessible on an equal level with modernity but in itself was not enough, and that moreover interior contemplation was not enough. Spirituality should also be the spirituality of social action, and even sacred revolution was not unthinkable. These powerful aromas reached, like Vatican II, into one of the the most enclosed cloisters to sensitize, and call to action, a Trappist monk already in touch with the most subtle currents of the inner life.

The German expatriot philosopher Herbert Marcuse enjoyed a short but splendid Sixties reign as a guru of the counterculture's protest against the "punchcard" society and was thought to be a covert apostle of revolution. In *One-Dimensional Man* (1964) he made a major part of his case. Here Marcuse argues that the technologizing of society has made it one-dimensional. By this he means that a technological society is essentially totalitarian, for it renders free speech, popular sovereignty, and everything else but the technological imperatives meaningless on the real issues of how our lives are lived. Such freedoms as we think we have are no more than sops; far more than we know, the nature of an industrial society and its human and material requirements condition nearly all serious aspects of our existence. Further, it virtually demands war and exploitation to keep itself going.[91]

Technology has coopted most of us to its vision of the world and made us its willing servants. "The people," "previously the ferment of social change, have 'moved up' to become the cement of social cohesion" (256). There is thus a conservative popular base. But outside it are still real outcasts and outsiders—people of other colors, the exploited, the unemployed. They reveal that the technological takeover is not complete, perhaps never can be since it seems to require people in such roles, as well as in the better parts played by its more compliant and privileged servants. These underclasses at home and abroad therefore offer some hope for breaking the system, though the process of change they would employ would not be a pleasant one.

And in such a world, in which "rationality" means nuclear arms and technological totalism, the irrational becomes rational—art, imagination, or internal exile can become a wedge, if only for the preservation of one's own sanity. Here is where the counterculture, dropouts in the service of sanity and potential revolutionaries, saw themselves scripted into Marcuse's bleak scenario. (The academic rabble-rouser of San Diego eventually exasperated his would-be disciples, however, by continually insisting, whatever they said, that it was not *quite* what he meant. The local American Legion chapter nonetheless tried, without success, to get him fired from his professorship at the University of California campus in that city, and he received personal threats that at one point required he go into hiding.)

Nonviolent activists and inactive revolutionaries, nonmystical theologians and a mystical diplomat, tongue speaking in the Episcopal church and raised voices in the baroque halls of St. Peter's—so was the mix on the bookshelves of the years of secular hope.

In other media besides books, the autumn of 1966 witnessed the close of the Vatican Council and the birth of the *San Francisco Oracle*. Those first pastel pages included the flowery protest against the delegalization of psychedelic drugs mentioned in chapter 1 (October 1966) and an interview with Timothy Leary (December 16, 1966).

Death of the Church, Death of Tradition, Death of the Mind, Death of God

We have observed that, in the mid-Sixties, the former "suburban captivity" Protestant church and "triumphalist" Roman Catholic church were widely declared to be dead or dying, to general rejoicing, replaced by a leaner, humbler, more activist "People of God" servant church.

On April 22, 1966, *Time* published an essay, "On Tradition, or What Is Left of It." The editors noted that puritanism and all conventional sexual morality is gone or is "giving way." At weddings (when they still have them), couples now insist on writing their own marriage service, or at least varying the hallowed music. Moreover, "art has gone beyond all limits," and privacy is a "lost Eden." Tradition, in the sense of any kind of time-honored conventions that set norms for contemporary behavior, was dead.

In the fall of 1966, Timothy Leary, as an "Impresario Religioso," mounted a drama called *The Death of the Mind*. The program announced "a psychedelic celebration, presented by the League for Spiritual Discovery, at the Village Theatre, Manhattan, $3. (No Smoking)."

THE CAST
The Guide—Dr Timothy Leary
Harry—Dr Ralph Metzner"

This popular performance was said to relive one minute of LSD. Harry, under that influence, plunges into the "green viscera of the body," hears the guide say "All girls are yours" (a line from the magical mystery play in Hermann Hesse's *Steppenwolf*), picks one, then hears "It's time to play the game of death." So Harry strangles her as a hangman dangles a noose, and then he vaporizes into "the galaxy of the senses," all to the accompaniment of strange and strong electronic music.[92]

And then came the Death of God game, and 1966 was the year of the Deity's most public obsequies. And, perhaps all too soon, the death of the Death of God, for the Death of God was to be apocalypse, and an apocalypse is supposed to mean the end of history as we know it, followed only by a New Heaven and Earth, in this case the secular city as New Jerusalem. But, despite the efforts of Timothy Leary to fabricate paradise in his alchemical/ontological laboratories, instead of the twelve jeweled gates of the heavenly city coming down to earth, a long dark cloud the shape of Vietnam hung over the western horizon, and history marched sullenly on.

The years of secular hope were, then, years of many deaths. They were seasons of ideological deaths, even as human corpses of frail flesh were piling up in Vietnam, and the burning inner cities together with the Mississippi piney woods were numbering their dead. Yet they were also years of religious hope. New life forms were stirring among those dry bones. Something must always die before something else can live. The deaths, the years seemed to say, were on schedule. It remained to see if the next *annus domini* would bring in a secular religion paradise or some stranger, less expected avatar of the sacred.

Chapter 4

1967:
The Year of the Avatars

The many men, so beautiful!
And they all dead did lie:
And a thousand thousand slimy things
Lived on; and so did I. . . .

Beyond the shadow of the ship,
I watched the water-snakes:
They moved in tracks of shining white,
And when they reared, the elfish light
Fell off in hoary flakes.

Within the shadow of the ship
I watched their rich attire:
Blue, glossy green, and velvet black,
They coiled and swam; and every track
Was a flash of golden fire

O happy living things! no tongue
Their beauty might declare:
A spring of love gushed from my heart,
And I blessed them unaware.
Coleridge, "The Ancient Mariner"

Descents and Embodiments

In Hindu mythology, an avatar is the "descent" of a deity to Earth and the world of men and women, wherein the god takes visible form, whether human or animal or some mix of both. More broadly speaking, an avatar may refer to the embodiment in concrete reality of an abstract idea. Avatars are embodiments of archetypes plus soul.

The year 1967 was not one in which clear-cut, easily isolated events happened, and it is not as easy to chronicle religously as certain other years. There were no "religion issue" elections as in 1960 or 1964, no programmatic civil rights events as in every year from 1960 to 1965, no deaths of God. Nonetheless 1967 was a hinge year, a time of epochal turning for American religion. That smoldering year was when modern civil religion turned decisively to radical pluralism; when those very late fruits of the modern spirit in religion, the Death of God and Vatican II, became overripe, and new seeds germinated.

So in 1967 fresh avatars came down to augment the wearying older teams. It was the year new gods commenced feeling their way across America, when Krishna Consciousness and transcendental meditation, Nichiren Shoshu and witchcraft, hit their stride as articulations of a spiritual counterculture. No less, it was the year when the bubbling, curdling, and now congealing distillates of the Sixties took defined, tangible, avatarlike shape.

Who were those embodiments among us of divine ideas whose times had come?

First, the new youth. *Time*'s January 6, 1967, Man of the Year cover story honored the "Man and Woman under 25." This "Now Generation," the newsmagazine confidently stated, is nearly half the population and will soon be the majority in charge. They have the best education in history, with 40 percent of them having been in college, and, though scattered from Vietnam (by now home to nearly half a million of America's male youth) to New England, they are developing their own culture. Those in colleges and universities were turning away from subjects like science and technology to fields like urban planning and the humanities. ("Last year nearly a third of engineering openings in the U.S. went unfilled.") In January, youth in the aggregate was still perceived as socially and religiously uncommitted and skeptical. But the article acknowledged that, while "activists" were only "at best 5% of this cohort," a significant and growing number were troubled by Vietnam. They had also largely "exorcised sexual inhibitions," and 20 percent were estimated to have taken drugs, though the periodical felt constrained to state that their usage was chiefly to "ease the weight" of living, not for "spiritual" purposes.[1]

By the time 1967 was over this collective avatar would loom in, with, and over America as a huge volatile mass ready to go critical, alive with the dangerous beauty of its rainbow colors. Indeed, the "youthquake" increasingly saw itself in avatar terms, though of course those "twenty-five and under" ranged immensely in their degree of participation in a new culture. As counterculture journals like the *Oracle* interpreted the arriving people, they were saviors attuned to new saving values, the Love Generation, heralds of the Aquarian Age, and among them the drugs, dress, and rock music that so terrified certain elders were sacraments and flags of identity. The overall avatar was personified in the visible, specific avatars of new faiths, Krishna, the Maharishi, UFO believers, the Beatles. Other teenagers were not ashamed to be "grunts" in Vietnam or even Young Republicans.

Another descent, a rough beast of an avatar even more menacing in its fair beauty, was the breakthrough of hard, alienating truth. Thus *Ramparts*, in the blockbuster March 1967 issue that contained the seminal article "The Social History of the Hippies," to be cited later, presented Sol Stern's "NSA and CIA," exposing covert funding of the National Student Association by the Central Intelligence Agency, especially in connection with its international programs. The article created a tremendous furor, almost unimaginable in a far more cynical post-Vietnam, post-Watergate, post-IranContra, post-Iraqgate, post-Cold War generation.

Time felt compelled to reply with a cover story, "The CIA and the Students," in its February 24 issue. (The *Ramparts* March issue had hit the newsstands in mid-February.) This article amounted to an apologia for the CIA, though it acknowledged the grave mistrust that had been aroused. While noting that a CIA agent's typical afternoon might be spent clandestinely transmitting information, paying an informer, or "arranging a revolution," as in Iran in 1953 or Guatemala in 1954, the story ends with paeans to the agency as only a well-regulated arm of the U.S. government—"It does not, and cannot, manipulate American policies. It can only serve them."[2]

Undoubtedly, that closing line reflected the staunch cold war values of the magazine's founder, Henry Luce, and in fact that issue might be said to have been the great but opinionated journalist's epitaph, for he died only four days after its appearance, on February 28, 1967.[3]

The unfortunate CIA story was paced by another of *Time*'s classic religion pieces, an Easter-season cover story on Martin Luther (March 24), commemorating the 450th anniversary of the ninety-five theses. This essay quoted the church historian Wilhelm Pauck to the effect that "one could characterize the spirit of our epoch as pre-Reformation. The old order is in a process of dissolution, but there is also a great positive religious expectancy"; this was augmented by word from Michael Novak that, although there is need for a new Reformation, "the Luthers today are not in the established church"—"the impulse for reformation today is in the New Left."[4]

Undeterred, *Ramparts* continued its crusade in its April issue with an article called "Three Tales of the CIA" and a cover portrait of an anonymous ex-member, his face obscured by text: "When I joined the 'Company' I expected to be involved in a battle of wits between professionals and the opposition. It wasn't until they taught me to kill civilians and to recruit foreign students to spy on their own country that I realized what the CIA was all about. Of course I had to quit."

This dirty-truth avatar was rough and restless, ready to take on the establishment represented by Washington, Vietnam, and the ghost of Henry Luce.[5]

It quickly expanded and metamorphosed into the general antiwar avatar. The antiwar movement went in 1967 from argument and protest to a new avatar community that fully came into its own in the great Pentagon demonstrations and draft card burnings of October, when it was clear that what separated Americans was deeper than what united them. And the antiwar, counterculture, and youth communities were coalescing—though of course far from unanimously—on one side of that divide. Before the grim stony walls of the Department of Defense's central keep some shouted slogans and waved signs, others chanted mantras and did magic, but they were as one in antipathy toward an edifice they saw as alien to the values of their lives.

So did the cities seem alien to numerous American blacks that summer. The glorious King years of freedom rides, civil rights marches, and nonviolent victories were history, and a new avatar was descending: black power. Malcolm X, Stokely Carmichael, and the Black Panthers were among its personae. The new mood was for blacks to make and take what was theirs as their own, and to assert their own cultural identity, rejecting the sort of integration that to them meant becoming white, and without the unwanted help of whites. It also meant a burgeoning sympathy for Third World "anti-imperialist" revolutionaries, an appropriation of that rhetoric for the American situation, and an assertion of the right to use violent means "if necessary."

The Black Panthers went about conspicuously and provocatively armed. While black power cannot be directly blamed for the urban riots of the summer of 1967, both stemmed from the same cause: a frustrated realization on the part of blacks in the northern cities, especially restless youth, that the great victories against Jim Crow in the South had not changed their situation very much. They wanted to get someone's attention, and they had a lot of rage to express. Another chasm opened, and fresh, powerful black archetypes arose: the proud, blunt-talking paladin with a "natural," the clear-eyed revolutionary cradling a weapon, fire gods protesting and purifying a corrupt city.

New religious archetypes marched with the new black power archetypes. The predominant old archetype was the nonviolent Christian image, represented by King and associates of his like Lawson and Moses; it was an image drawing much substance from the black church heritage. Courageous Kingly Christian nonviolence had been strikingly successful, but now there was a sense that its potential had been exhausted. Three other icons arose to supplement or replace it: the militant, black-power Christian image represented by Albert Cleague with his "Black Madonna" and "Black Messiah" figures; the Muslim archetype, represented by Malcolm X; and the revival of traditional African religious themes, represented by Ron Karenga and others attempting to recover to African Americans motifs from Yoruba, Dogon, and other cultures in the ancient homeland.

New archetypes with a new avatar possibly hidden among them also danced through the Roman Catholic church in its second post–Vatican II year. New liturgies, new roles for priest and laity, the "new nuns" with their modish new habits and assertive manner—all were the very stuff of archetypal change and as such almost too much for the consciousness of some, both those who wanted more and those who yearned for less.

For reaction also was building. Avatars have their antiavatars, as Christ his Antichrist. Middle America, the Silent Majority, and Catholic traditionalists were opening their eyes and beginning to stretch themselves awake.

And the lunar landing program continued. In April eight possible landing sites were selected to be studied for final decisions. Several satellites were put up. In October the Soviets landed Venera 4 on Venus. Here was another kind of avatar, an avatar in reverse, man (all astronauts then were male) going into the heavens rather than waiting for the gods to descend. (Even this program was not without the tragic dimension that seemed to attend every Sixties deed of monumental hubris. On January 27, 1967, a flash fire killed three astronauts in their spacecraft at Cape Kennedy: Virgil Grissom, Edward White, and Roger Chaffee. It had been a presumably safe trial ground-exercise for the moon run; the tragedy took place not in outer space but two hundred feet off the ground. Grissom had been one of the original seven Mercury astronauts in the 1961 "man-in-a-can" days of pioneer space flight and was a leading candidate to be the first human to set foot on the moon.)

1967 as a Year of Soul

Avatars as embodiments of ultimately religious realities require response on the same level—shall we say on the level of soul. So it was in 1967. Even in the case of the most contrived-seeming image making, in the Sixties there was always the possibility of something religious hovering around the contrivance. Perhaps that was because, for the Sixties, image making was soul making too, at least as James Hillman understands the term. That archetypal psychologist made an important distinction between spirit and soul, as does St. Paul in distinguishing *pneuma* and *psyche*. Spirit governs the realm of religious sensibility, art, and especially ideas; it is otherworldly, seeking to dwell on "peaks," and it can be idealistic, literalistic, and "after ultimates."[6]

Hillman values spirit highly, yet his unique contribution lies in the rich understanding he gives the concept of soul. Soul has to do with the "inside meaning" of human behavior as it is "suffered and experienced." Words associated with soul include "heart, life, warmth, humanness, personality, individuality, intentionality, essence, innermost, purpose, emotion, quality, virtue, morality, sin, wisdom, death, God. A soul is said to be 'troubled,' 'old,' 'disembodied,' 'immortal,' 'lost,' 'innocent,' 'inspired.' Eyes are said to be 'soulful,' for eyes are 'the mirror of the soul,' but one can be 'soulless' by showing no mercy." There is much more in the same vein, including reference to the concept of multiple souls in many primal religions, but this will suffice to illustrate the Hillmanian relating of soul to the profoundest and most meaning-laden reaches of human experience.

I suggest that 1967 was above all not so much a time of spirit as of soul, and no less religious for that. Revelatory of this perhaps was the use of the term *soul* by African Americans to refer to the things and the feel of their culture; one heard of soul food and soul music. The decade was an era when, for many, events were "soul-sized," involving the greatest depths they were capable of plumbing. Images and symbols, even actions, tried to reveal the soul dimension of what they were about and so may in a broad sense be considered religious.

Certainly this was true of the New Left, Michael Novak's putative Luthers for the reformations of our day. An excellent 1967 *Time* essay on "The New Radicals" says as much, in a rather backhanded way, by quoting Daniel Bell to the effect that, "at best, the New Left is all heart. At worst, it is no mind." "Heart" is very much a soul term in Hillman's vocabulary, though possibly, when the sociologist Michael Harrington is then cited as calling the New Leftists "mystical militants," the phrase could imply a tenderness for the "literalistic" and "single-minded" in one corner of their leftward soul that allowed for an opening toward spirit.[7]

But the positive visions of the New Left had the richness and texture of soul; they were utopian, and their utopias seemed almost postmodernistically medieval—wanting to repeal "bigness" and even the industrial revolution, they yearned for the small, self-contained idyllic villages of such nineteenth-century visionaries as Charles Fourier and Robert Owen—"New Harmony computerized," the article puts it. They dreamed of "'the totally beautiful society,' with smogless air, unpolluted rivers, swift and clean public transportation and, in the phrase of Atlanta lawyer Howard Moore, 'airlines carrying the people all over the country to the great museums.'" "In a broad sense, the movement is not political but religious," *Time* declared. "'We want to create a world in which love is more possible,' says an S.D.S. leader, Carl Oglesby. For all their rant and naivete, the New Radicals can sound strongly appealing." Surely that appeal goes hand in hand with their appeal to the emotions and images that articulate the deeps of soul, where life is really experienced and suffered, and where joy first wells up.

That idea was expressed in this article in another, more ambiguous way by a sympathetic historian of the New Left, Jack Newfield, as he compared the New Left Students for a Democratic Society (SDS) to the Marxist Old Left DuBois Club: "DuBois members are just not hung-up by the same things S.D.S.ers are. They don't make embarrassing speeches about how we must love each other. They are not viscerally outraged by the moral deceits of society in the way S.D.S. members are; they are not in total rebellion. The key difference is that the DuBois Club members don't hate their fathers; S.D.S.ers do."

"Spiritual" radicals, one might say, are given to rigorous analysis, single-minded commitment, and some suspicion of the visionary, aesthetic, and sensual except as it is well subordinated to commitment; the "soulful" radical instead is open to a rampant pluralism of vision and experience, deriving passion from the poetic harmonization at some deep level of a horizon full of radical visions, medieval moods, and inner apocalypses. The Old Left people, like Marx and Lenin, were ascetics of the spirit; the New Leftists were ensouled instead, more inspired by such soulfully romantic Americans as Thoreau, Emerson, and Whitman than by the Europeans.

Images, Archetypes, and Their Clarification

The clarification of archetypes as well as the descent of avatars culminated in 1967, and of course the two were much the same thing. This clarification marked a decisive shift to archetypes suggestive of postmodernism. During a spring and summer of hate and love, the modernist mainstream broke into halves of equal weight, postmodern and "rump" modern, and finally splintered into flakes of scattered light.

William Hamilton, as noted in the last chapter, suggested "for the fun of it" that the old era of *Angst* ended, and the new one of secular

Counterpoint: Old Souls in New Vestments

The year 1967 was not a landmark for the founding of new religious movements in the institutional sense; it was too much a time of ferment before crystallization. Some, as we have seen, were already in place: Nichiren Shoshu, Zen, Scientology, the Church of Satan, Krishna Consciousness, the Unification church. These groups reportedly enjoyed remarkable growth in that year and the three or four years following. Others, from Tibetan Buddhism to "Jesus movement" sects, were not to take name and form until the very end of the Sixties, when they in effect became agents of what Steven Tipton described in his *Getting Saved from the Sixties* as bodies that perpetuated certain Sixties spiritual and communal values while setting dikes against the decade's chaos.*

Some significant counterculture religion happened in 1967, however. The greatest publicity probably went to the Maharishi Mahesh Yogi of transcendental meditation, who exuberantly toured the United States—giggle, hair, flowers, and all—and briefly numbered the Beatles among his disciples. Photogenic, charismatic, mystical, claiming an ancient Indian lineage, he and his movement, despite charges of commercialism, were one product of 1967's search for condensed symbol and soulful substance conjoined.

Also in that year two small but prototypical neopagan groups were established, Feraferia and the Church of All Worlds. Their very existence seemed to bespeak a new wide-ranging spiritual freedom and a new vision of human spiritual relationships with nature and the imagination. Feraferia was the product of the rich spiritual creativity of Fred Adams of Los Angeles. As early as 1956, while he was a student of art and anthropology at Los Angeles City College, he experienced a sudden sense of the "mysterium tremendum" in feminine form. Dazzled and overcome yet powerfully changed, he realized that "the feminine is a priori." From then on he devoted himself to the feminine sacred, gradually developing a series of elaborate festivals and rituals for the goddess, aided by such writers as Robert Graves, J. J. Bachofen, and Mircea Eliade. Between 1957 and 1959 Adams lived in a multifamily commune with a group interested in the same ideals; they worshipped at an outdoor altar dedicated to the "Maiden Goddess of Wildness" and made some use of psychedelic drugs, then legal.

But it was in 1967 that the name Feraferia, "Nature Celebration," came to the religion's founder, as did its symbol, a trident with sun and crescent moon superimposed. A banner bearing this insignia was first unfurled at a great love-in in Los Angeles's Elysian Park on the vernal equinox of that year.

Continued

Counterpoint: Old Souls in New Vestments *Continued*

Those drawn to Feraferia found themselves participating, nude, in pagan rites offering such poetic and evocative chants as these for Beltane. Facing west at the gates of an outdoor "henge" or shrine, the leader would intone: "Moon Door, Moon Door, Door of Alder, bound with Willow, open now, revealing night, and fiery stars, and silver moon, and demiurgic dark." And facing east: "Sun Door, Sun Door, Oaken Door, bedecked with holly, open now, revealing day, and azure airs, and golden sun, and archetypal light." And, as all raise their arms in invocation: "Antheides and the Great Fays of the East, Dawn, and Spring, join us now in the Faerie Ring between Worlds. Through the portal between Moon and Stars, return into your Earth Abodes from the far Faerieland of Stars."

Other prayers are offered, such as this to the Great Goddess in her Maiden form: "Oh Holy Maiden of the kindling quick and merging mist and mazing echo: The Innocent Bounty of the trees bares your Faerie Flesh and Wildness, Wonder, Magic, Mirth, and Love. . . . Your beauty seals our bridal with all Life. The dance of your green pulse unfolds all bodies from earth's fragrant form. Evoe Kore!"**

The Church of All Worlds, incorporated in 1967, was the offspring of discussions begun in 1961 by Tim Zell and Lance Christie, then both students at Westminster College in Missouri, of Robert Heinlein's novel *Stranger in a Strange Land*. As we have already noted, this was one of the great paradigmatic works of fiction for Sixties youth. Zell and Christie determined to go beyond talk to establish "Nests" like those in the novel where people could become "Water Brothers," greet one another with "Thou art God," and "grok" or intuit the fullness of something or someone completely from within. The movement officially commenced on April 7, 1962, when Zell and Christie shared water and formed a water brotherhood called Atl, incorporated as the Church of All Worlds in 1968.

This body published a magazine called *Green Egg*, which became a major voice of the pagan wing of the counterculture and was especially interested in deep ecology or ecospirituality. The Church of All World's adherents were mostly radical pantheists and perhaps the first ecofeminists; they identified the Earth with the Goddess and saw to it that she was worshipped by priestesses as well as priests. The mostly under-thirty members of its dozen or so Nests advanced through nine circles of increasing awareness named after the nine planets. (After a period of abeyance in the late Seventies and early Eighties, the Church of All Worlds has been reconstituted on a less structured basis, and the *Green Egg* is again published)

Although various forms of pantheism and nature mysticism go at least

---

Counterpoint: Old Souls in New Vestments *Continued*

as far back in America as transcendentalism and Walt Whitman, insofar as these movements incarnated them in definite religious symbols and rites they were something new in 1967, indicative of an archetypal seismic shift toward the sacred feminine, now boldly named the Goddess. Sacred nature was identified with that Goddess, rituals were innovative rather than antique, associated with the values of the emergent counterculture.

New Eastern movements, a phenomenon considered quintessentially counterculture-Sixties by some observers, also hit the scene. Here are a couple of less well-known examples. Awareness of the miracle-working new avatar in India, Satya Sai Baba, began in 1967 with a series of lectures by his chief American disciple, the white-haired yoga teacher of Russian birth who called herself Indra Devi; soon there were groups, prayer and meditation meetings, lights and incense, and pilgrimages.

About the same year another Russian immigrant, Neville Pemchekov-Warwick, started Kailas Shugendo in San Francisco. It was an esoteric Buddhist group in the mountaineering Tibetan and Japanese yamabushi tradition. Its energetic young members, colorfully garbed, went into the mountains to do such practices as fire walking, meditating under cold waterfalls, and the spectacular *goma* or fire ritual of Buddhist esotericism.

(I once watched them do the *goma*, amid much smoke and sparks as well as heavy incense, chanting sutras at a rapid clip as they threw stick after stick cut with a ritual sword into a small firepit situated in a tiny city apartment—probably in violation of every conceivable fire ordinance—and the master waved his hands through the flame in mystic mudras.)

*Steven Tipton, *Getting Saved from the Sixties*
**Based on the account in Robert Ellwood, *Religious and Spiritual Groups in Modern America* (Englewood Cliffs, N.J.: Prentice-Hall, 1973), 194–200, and my interviews with Fred Adams.

---

hope commenced, on January 4, 1965. That was the day T. S. Eliot died, whose Prufrock embodied the old, and the day an American president gave a State of the Union address advocating a this-worldly Great Society. In the same spirit, I suggest that the modern age in America died, and the new postmodern era was born, in July 1967.

In that month Carl Sandburg died, a poet whose vision and anger so expressed America's modern dreams and frustrations in the Thirties and Forties. Also, on July 7, well into the Summer of Love, *Time* (now without Henry Luce) produced its famous cover story on the new counterculture. Within the week *Newsweek* unveiled a grimmer account of the increasingly visceral antiwar agitation, by now rending the heart and reins of the body politic. And toward the end of that month Henry Ford's Detroit—the manufacturing metropolis that so much epitomized what the modern meant to America—was burning and bleeding from the worst riots thus far of the century. Of the modern only Vietnam (which had by now swallowed up the Great Society), the aftermath of Vatican II, and the lunar landing program remained. But by July 1967 Vietnam was no more than a huge lingering problem left behind by modernist overconfidence, Vatican II looked like a modern/postmodern muddle spuming malaise in its wake, and compared to the issues here below space seemed increasingly more escapist than futurist.

Images are appropriate vehicles for understanding 1967, for the year was a golden age of images. In that period the longstanding hegemony of books and their linear mode of communication began to break down. Alongside the black-and-white information transmitted by the printed page, fiery picture images burst in the brain like artillery shells blasted out from the evening news and the street corner: harrowing scenes from the "living room war," the great rallies and demonstrations, the unearthly art and disturbing garb of the counterculture. The Sixties were the first generation of nurslings of that great mother of images, television, and the conscious or unconscious clarification of the images or archetypes governing one's life—in religion, politics, life-style—was a major preoccupation. One might expect image construction to be a major task of a time of transition from one world to another.

The clarification of archetypes characteristically begins with polarization. Polarization, of course, requires and enacts a definition of that which it is polarized against. It hardly needs to be reiterated that 1967 was a year of polarization. Conversely, polarization can be a catalyst, igniting the need to clarify one's personal archetypes. The background decades to the Sixties embraced such archetypal polarization in the Second World War, the Cold War, and finally the passions of the civil rights movement. When one experiences polarization on all sides, one assumes appropriate roles for oneself, clarifying oneself as the embodiment of a distinct archetype, seeing the world as an arena for comprehensive definition and heroic conquest.

Clarified Images in a Wartime Spring and a Summer of Love

Some slices of 1967 life may indicate the interplay of image, role, gesture, and soul-sized issues of which I am speaking.

The summer of 1967, the "Summer of Love" and hardly less the summer of hate, was in some respects the epitome of the Sixties. The polarities and possibilities of the decade, not least in its spiritual dimensions, were in full display, without the earnest tentativeness of its earlier expression or the "clotted glory" of some of the later.

On one side, let us take as an example General William E. Westmoreland's visit to Washington in early May, when the commander of forces in Vietnam addressed a joint session of Congress. He was brought home by President Johnson to shore up support for the faltering Southeast Asian cause. The grave, erect product of the Citadel and West Point was imposing in his crisply pressed uniform with four shiny stars as he spoke of the enemy's resilience and brutality. "He believes in force and his intensification of violence is limited only by his resources and not by any moral inhibitions." But he ended on an encouraging note: "Backed at home by resolve, confidence, patience, determination and continued support, we will prevail in Vietnam over Communist aggression."[8]

Westmoreland then neatly, dramatically saluted the rumpled civilian figures of Vice-President Hubert Humphrey and Speaker of the House John McCormick who shared the rostrum with him. A day or two later, speaking to a group of Associated Press reporters in New York, he criticized dissenters and "recent unpatriotic acts at home." "The enemy," he intoned, "believes that he can win politically that which he cannot accomplish militarily" (32). The dissenters, including such senators as George McGovern, Mark Hatfield, and Frank Church, in an increasingly emotional atmosphere reacted angrily to the implication that by questioning administration policy they were acting unpatriotically or supporting "the enemy." Yet to the extent that their argument was with a uniform rather than with a man, it was the more difficult; that put it on the level of archetype, and of someone's soul.

For the Sixties were, as much as anything, a decade of uniforms— or, if one wishes, antiuniforms on the counterculture side, which were nonetheless uniforms—and uniforms were perceived as souls made visible. That is because it was the decade of commitments at soul level. And a uniform also, of course, raises the emotional level of any debate by putting it on the plane of inward commitments, of faith against faith, rather than on that of President Johnson's favorite

187

biblical passage, "Come, let us reason together." It furthermore makes the caricatures of opponents all the more telling—the absurdly bespangled "General Waste-More-Land" who became a staple of anti-war rallies.

Only a couple of months after Westmoreland's visit—which in the end did little to enhance support for the administration—*Time* magazine published its famous July 7, 1967, cover story on the hippies and the counterculture, and *Newsweek* its July 10 special issue on the Vietnam War and American life. The former described an emergent and uniformed new culture that sought to orient its subjectivity by entirely different stars, including "peace," "love," and psychedelic vision.[9]

Symbols rough and raw were the stock-in-trade of the American debate described by *Newsweek* in its special issue, especially in the commentary on writers and artists and the war. Norman Mailer named a new novel *Why Are We in Vietnam?* even though it was about a bear hunt in Alaska, explaining that "I wanted that question to reverberate through the book." Susan Sontag said of her *Death Kit,* "It wasn't my intention to talk about the war, but I couldn't keep it out." The dying protagonist "turns on the television in his hotel room and what does he see?"[10]

These statements are mild, *Newsweek* reported, compared to the explosive shock techniques of visual artists. From them appeared such unsubtle satires as smashed dolls, the Statue of Liberty upraising a bomb instead of a torch, and Peter Saul's war-comics-style painting, "I Torture Commie Virgins," displaying a Green Beret captain riding a jet, ready to strafe a bound Vietnamese girl (86).

The *Newsweek* issue further describes the "fear and anger" on campus, not only in connection with campus protests against the war—only then beginning to become widespread—but more particularly at how the draft sharpened the issue in colleges and universities. As students and professors were well aware, grades and graduate admissions could quite literally be life-or-death matters for males, a student deferment or a trip to 'Nam. This situation was heartily resented by most of those placed in such an unaccustomed and unacademic bind and undoubtedly did more than even the most horrendous graphics of napalm bombing or savaged peasants to build campus opposition.

Knowledge Holders and the Holy Ghost

The section on campus fear and anger in the July 10 *Newsweek* special issue ended on a curious note. "The war," the newsmagazine reported, "has not notably increased the demand for the relative handful of academicians with a background in Vietnamese affairs . . . and the prestige of Far Eastern specialists has not been greatly enhanced." An explanation was offered by Malcolm Kerr, chair of the political science department at UCLA: students "are not particularly deferential to faculty members with greater expertise in the matter who support the government. They seem to feel this is the kind of issue that is beyond politics . . . and take open exception to people who are better informed. Many of our graduate students no longer trust the experts" (87–88).

This item, though presented in 1967 almost as an aside, is rather astounding and quite revelatory. The issue of the war was "beyond politics" and no less beyond the expertise of "experts." Certainly it would be a sorry world if only an expert in the relevant discipline could ever make a moral judgment on a life-or-death issue. In all periods, ordinary people, because they must, have made moral judgments unaided in the context of their own lives and sometimes have determinedly and rightly sought to impose them on governments and society at large. Often they have proved in hindsight more right than the contemporary experts. Abolitionists, labor organizers, and feminists who were a generation ahead of the economists and gynecologists of the day come to mind.

Nevertheless, the 1967 disdain of experts is telling. It bespeaks the kind of time many felt it was, a day of the committed rather than the experts, an hour for mystic militants more than scientific utopians, for the politics of the Holy Ghost rather than of the art of compromise. The knowledge elite, who should have been talking freely and independently if knowledge truly is moral authority as well as power, were perceived as either coopted or retreating into the maze of the specialist. That left the public arena to others—those wearing uniforms, of whatever sort, rather than carrying books. And it bespoke the modern world of universal knowledge, to which the expert is priest, giving some ground to postmodern subjectivism.

Even more curious was the relative quietude and ambivalence of the churches in the situation, caught between their modern and postmodern roles, as described in the July 10 *Newsweek* article. Retrospectives have tended to suggest that the churches and synagogues, or at least the religious leadership, stood rank on rank in prophetic protest against the bloodshed across the sea, but that is not how it looked in the Summer of Love.

Certainly there were those who did. *Newsweek* cites several CALCAV stalwarts in opposition. There was the venerable Reinhold Niebuhr, earlier accounted rather hawkish, first against fascists and then against Communists. His 1952 book, *The Irony of American History*, was virtually a bible of those who took very seriously the nation's responsibility to oppose communism even when the struggles required "Christian realists" to use distasteful means.[11] But in fact he was a profoundly moral voice subservient to no party label. Also mentioned were John C. Bennett (president of Union Theological Seminary), the Jesuit Daniel Berrigan, and the distinguished rabbi Abraham Heschel. The Catholic philosopher Michael Novak (more recently notable as an outspoken neoconservative) and the Protestant Robert McAfee Brown are reported to have written a 128-page handboook, "Vietnam: Crisis of Conscience," for Clergy and Laity Concerned About Vietnam. The recent adherence of Martin Luther King to religious antiwar activism is also cited.

Nonetheless, the article overall suggests a mixed picture. The antiwar clergy were said to be having no great success in making an impact at the level of the local congregation. On the other side, Cardinal Spellman, after visiting the war zone, had proclaimed the conflict a "war for civilization" and its combatants "solders of Christ." Though their language might be more measured than the cardinal's, academic moral theologians no less respectable than those in the antiwar group, such as Paul Ramsey and David Little, were on hand to say that "war can be a moral means of insuring peace" and to refuse to condemn this war as totally immoral.

Perhaps most significant of all, though, was the muddle this article discovered at the pastoral levels of church and synagogue. "It's a terrible thing," admitted the Reverend G. R. Wheatcroft, rector of St. Francis Episcopal Church in Houston, "but we don't know what to say." And the Methodist bishop of Georgia confessed, "The position of our church is that we live in a very imperfect world. The church kind of prays about it and hopes by faith we won't get involved next time." Quentin L. Quade, professor at the Jesuit Marquette University, could only say, "The prophetic voice which presumes to know in advance what the U.S. should do has no place in Vietnam discussions." Churches were beginning to draw up position papers, characteristically composed by social concerns boards distinctly more liberal than the church at large, and were anticipating a long hot summer as these pronouncements hit the local level.

As most ecclesiastics dithered and academic experts were ignored, lay voices filled the void, especially on the Left. The loudest protesters, like the most ambitious makers of the new culture, were conspicuously noninstitutional, people "out of nowhere." They were graduate students at Columbia or Berkeley, dropouts in Haight-Ashbury, messiahs of new religions, plus a few mavericks in church hierarchies or on Capitol Hill. Otherwise, the establishment could only become, often incongruously for the leftover Roosevelt-Truman liberals still dominant in Washington, the right wing of the moment; or had to try, like some churchpeople and educators, to identify with the New Left and the new culture, however awkward it felt; or simply appear, in a key word of the times, "irrelevant."

Thomas A. Langford, writing in the *Christian Century* on February 8, 1967, commented that, "partly because of the ineffective witness of the church, today's student places too much hope in the university and inevitably is disillusioned."[12] Students were saying that they wanted to meet their professors as persons, they wanted education to be more personal and at the same time more communal and, in a word, *relevant*. Exactly how all this would be achieved was often not clear, and the vagueness of the word *relevant* especially made it beloved of satirists. Yet the discontent and yearning for something else was obviously real, suggesting that some kind of rearranging was going on at the deeper levels of the collegiate personality structure. One kind of person was therefore set against another for a few years, and out of the frustrations of that struggle came a do-it-yourself mood in politics and religion.

This was clear very early in the Sixties in the context of the civil rights movement, when, as we saw in an earlier chapter, crisis at Vanderbilt University and the formation of an independent civil rights activist group within the Episcopal church spotlighted committed individuals, often obscure and of no great status, against a backdrop of institutional fuzziness.

Venerable but compromised institutions, then, left the field to others whose vision was single and who spoke as persons with authority, not as scribes, though that authority might have come only from the the Holy Spirit within or the power of soul rather than via canonical empowerment. Because they had no other visible means of legitimation, these persons had to make it for themselves, in the manner of shamans.

Although hardly unprecedented in American history, in the Sixties context these shamans/performers, from William Coffin to Abbie Hoffman, were avatars of a postmodern religious consciousness ready and willing to work within the context of radical pluralism. They may have yearned for consensus, but like such prototypes as John Brown or Susan B. Anthony, they would rather be right than mainstream. Like them but perhaps even more so, they expressed their differentness by prophetic signs rather than words of sweet reason. Rather than abridge their principles they were prepared to see the country divided and riddled with symbols, as it had been before by slavery versus abolitionism or male hegemony versus feminism. The new wizards were persons who clearly believed with Nietzsche in *Ecce Homo* that "a sedentary life is the real sin against the Holy Ghost."

The Essence of the Counterculture

More than for anything else, 1967 will leave its mark in history as the heyday of the celebrated counterculture of San Francisco's Haight-Ashbury district and similar colonies in other cities, together with a scattering of rural communes. But not everything is clear about the background and real nature of the rock, acid, and paisley life-style that burst forth so unexpectedly in late 1966.

Opinions vary even as to its defining characteristics. Indeed, in many respects it was less counter than caricature of mainstream America. As was often pointed out, its pot and psychedelia were the equivalents of tobacco and alcohol, its regulation paisley, beads, and boots a play on the establishment's three-piece suits. Still, some new cultural focus was at work too.

Some say it was rock music, especially as embodied in the lyrics and style of the Beatles or the Grateful Dead, that really ignited the counterculture. That is where Charles Perry, a former *Rolling Stone* editor, starts in *The Haight-Ashbury: A History* (1984) though he ends the book with a capable discussion of other themes: the motifs of self-discovery, exploration of psychic "wild territory," and semiconscious fear of the "straight" world.[13]

The celebrated counterculture participant/observer and acid messiah Timothy Leary, in his reminiscences, *Flashbacks* (1985) understandably perceived the psychedelic drug experience to be the touchstone of the new consciousness.

Theodore Roszak, in *The Making of a Counter Culture* (1969) viewed antitechnology as the deep theme. The devotees of the new age were rising up in resistance to the regimentation and dehumanization they saw in the world made by standard brands, multinational corporations, and computer printouts. The counterculture's postmodern mysticism and new tribalism were not so much ends in themselves as human-scale counterpoints to the world of the machine.[14]

Walter Truett Anderson, in his engaging history of the Esalen center on California's Big Sur coast, *The Upstart Spring: Esalen and the American Awakening* (1983), stresses the importance of the "human potentials" movement of which Esalen was the Vatican in those years. The freedom and new consciousness celebrated in the 1960s, he contends, were stimulated by an upwardly revised view of the human self as full of potential for radical self-expression and life construction limned by such Esalen gurus as Abraham Maslow of humanistic psychology and Fritz Perls of gestalt therapy and applied by the center's influential and controversial techniques.[15]

It is easy, in writing about Haight-Ashbury and other colorful sites of the famous hippie counterculture during its brief golden age, to fall into impressionism. Indeed, impressionism may be about as well as one can do. The counterculture was a tapestry threaded out of thousands upon thousands of personal narratives, some happy, some sad, some triumphant, and some disastrous. They cannot all be told, nor all about any of them; one can only be selective.

I will focus specifically on the acid-dropping hippies, who were generally considered the counterculture's most visible manifestation, and who were a cultural-religious phenomenon worth attention in their own right. Like much in the background of this culture, the evolution of the words *hip*—to be "with it"—and *hippie* is not entirely certain but is thought to derive from the Forties and Fifties jazz terms *hep* and *hepcat* and to have been much popularized by the March 1967 *Ramparts* article by Warren Hinckle, "The Social History of the Hippies."[16]

Apart from the natural appeal of the city on the bay with its long bohemian and Beat tradition, Ken Kesey, author of *One Flew over the Cuckoo's Nest* and the subject of Tom Wolfe's classic on the counterculture, *The Electric Kool-Aid Acid Test,* probably did more than anyone else to popularize the movement.[17]

Kesey had been turned on to acid as early as 1960 in a Veterans Administration hospital experiment. In the summer of 1964 he, with his gang known as the Merry Pranksters, traveled about the country in an old Day-Glo-ornamented bus, driven by the Kerouac-era Beat hero Neal Cassady. Like apostles, wherever they went they practiced and disseminated the psychedelic gospel. By the fall of 1965, Kesey and companions were back in the San Francisco area, promoting LSD through a series of public events called Acid Tests, in which, according to Hinckle, Kesey gave "earnest psychedelic talks" and "handed LSD around like the Eucharist." Though the first distribution was at a Unitarian conference at Big Sur in August of 1965, by the time the Acid Tests reached the city, the substance (still legal) was introduced to thousands of seekers in an atmosphere of costumes, pulsating lights, weird high-decibel musical sounds, and strange talk. The movement was accelerated by a series of dances put on in such legendary San

Francisco ballrooms as the Fillmore and Avalon, largely by impressario Bill Graham. These events were complete with light shows and rock music produced by groups with names (the Grateful Dead, Quicksilver Messenger Service, Jefferson Airplane) that sounded like the bizarre wordplay inspirations that come to the very high.

The movement coalesced in San Francisco, centering in the celebrated Haight-Ashbury district, throughout 1966. In Hinckle's words, "Hippies are many things, but most prominently the bearded and beaded inhabitants of the Haight-Ashbury, a little psychedelic city-state edging Golden Gate Park," possessing a "daily street-fair atmosphere" enlivened by "upward of 15,000 unbonded girls and boys interacting in a tribal, love-seeking, free-swinging, acid-based type of society."

The "Hashbury," then a pleasant neighborhood of Victorian homes accessible to the park and to the De Young Museum with its stunning Indian and Tibetan collections, was a traditional student district. Soon it acquired a Psychedelic Shop and related businesses. By summer of that year it became known as a place where the LSD talked about by people like Timothy Leary and Ken Kesey was easily available, and where a community interested in the new vision of life that acid implied was gathering.

By September 1966, when Leary began his "Death of the Mind" show in New York and announced the formation of the League for Spiritual Discovery, recruits were moving in almost daily, and the cultural artifacts of the new vision, from mystical art to windchimes, were appearing everywhere. But acid was the real definer of the new culture, and an extraordinarily appropriate guardian of the gates it was. The chemical could usher one into a pluralistic postmodern world fueled by soul, symbol, subculture, and the Holy Spirit—and then push the psychic adventurer into an inner space of self-validating visions and archetypes.

In the fall of 1966 a series of events brought the community together and staked out its position against the world. In September the urban riots hit San Francisco in the form of an insurrection in the Hunter's Point ghetto. One youth was shot by police, and his death was metamorphosed into an opening wedge of the Aquarian Age. The troops who were then moved in were greeted not only by angry natives but also by the more disconcerting apparition of long-haired, often acid-primed visitors from Haight-Ashbury exhorting them to "make love, not war."

At the same time, the *San Francisco Oracle* appeared, to give the community a voice and journalistic identity (the first issue is dated

September 20, 1966). It immediately offered a platform to such potent figures as Tim Leary and Ken Kesey and took up causes like the rights of Native Americans and protesting police busts of allegedly obscene books and plays.

On October 6 LSD became illegal in California, and the counter-culture's response took the form of a great Love Pageant Rally, at which the new people danced and sang and offered flowers to their tormentors. This event gave the defiant culture new self-conscious cohesion as well as news value. So we read in the *Oracle* that on October 6, 1966, a "celebration" was held in Panhandle Park opposing the "legislative repression of chemical mysticism":

> The Panhandle packed with Beautiful People ecstatically costumed and handing out flowers to friends and FBI agents. Dancing on the greensward to the Grateful Dead's electronic music. What sort of world is this? Whose world is this?
>
> Gaggle of real estate dealers on their way back from a convention at Masonic Hall (where Ronald Reagan assured them that their real estate was really real) crossing the Panhandle, come upon this fantastic congregation. And in broad daylight, too! Flutes and finger cymbals, tinkle and toot, and all that long hair, short skirts, and laughter. You don't see a circus like this every day.[18]

As for the tricksters and ritual clowns,

> Ken Kesey's fabled bus is there; splashed yellow, green, blue, brown, and purple. Colors of the raggle-taggle gay gang inside it, on top of it, all around it. Six hundred to a thousand young souls . . . dancing with brave banners waving. . . .
>
> . . . poor righteous citizens were absolutely helpless on the periphery of the crowd of beards and beads and Crazy Jane hats bobbing madly in the afternoon sunshine.
>
> The FBI agent held his flowers behind his back, and a handful of real estate men standing near him all stared at their shoes when a slim girl approached them with a juicy slice of watermelon. They were terrified that she intended to offer them a bite. "Don't be afraid," she said sweetly.
>
> Young Beautifuls, young beggars and mummers, dancers and singers, laughing boys and girls—soon to be outlawed—that afternoon lay down their gentle message, loud and clear. LOVE.
>
> For a few hours on October Sixth, they had their world their way.[19]

But 1967 was the golden year of the hippie, flower child counter-culture. Perhaps it was only helped, at least in its California heartland, when Ronald Reagan was sworn in (allegedly at an astrologically auspicious hour) as governor in January. The conservative former actor's presence in Sacramento, along with the outlawing of psychedelics, drew the cultural lines hard and fast. But the new cartography was assisted even more by demographics. *Time* declared 1967 the "Year of Youth," and, although what was happening in the "Hashbury" was not what was suggested by the earnest, clean-cut students on the New Year's cover, events quickly overtook that image. As early as January 14 the "Human Be-in," also known as "A Gathering of the Tribes," brought tens of thousands to Golden Gate Park to hear music; listen to talks and chants by such figures as Gary Snyder, Allen Ginsberg, and Jerry Rubin; to admire one another's fantasic costumes; and to get stoned. Again, the gathering was tremendously photogenic and garnered great media attention, and the rush was on.

Personal appearance was definitely a statement. The colorful illustrations that accompanied *Time*'s July 7, 1967, cover story, "Youth: The Hippies," reveal a panorama of hues and cuts but make evident that one could hardly mistake the flowers and paisleys, the boots and beads, of hippie-type garb for anything else, even if a precise definition defies language. One picture featured a young woman in only a flowered bikini and the kaleidoscopic body paints of the new tribe. As the caption solemnly informed doubtlessly astounded readers, "At 'love-ins' . . . college kids wear exotic garb and decorate themselves to look like the moving, multihued objects that fill the visions of psychedelia."

(The year was also a golden age of pins and bumperstickers with messages like "Burn Pot Not People," "Kill a Commie for Christ," "Jesus Was a Dropout," "God Is a Teeny-Bopper," and many more.)[20]

According to a sociological study made by Lewis Yablonsky in 1967, full-time hippies across the country numbered perhaps 200,000, together with another 200,000 part-time "plastic," "Clark Kent," or "teenybopper" cohorts. Of the full-timers, this sociologist estimated that 10–15 percent were "high priests," philosophers, and guides to the new culture, the remainder being "novices." Many were "true seekers," but some 20 percent of both full- and part-time hippies he believed to be severely disturbed individuals.[21]

Over 70 percent, according to Yablonsky, were from the middle to upper segments of American society—then overwhelmingly white—so as persons who had deliberately "dropped out," their relationship to the marginal life was very different from that of blacks. Like all tightly knit, self-defining communities, hippies used a distinctive argot: words like "bag," "bummer," "cool," "far out," "out of sight," "rap," "square," "stoned" (367–368).

The hippie subculture quickly divided into two wings, town and country. The former continued residence in the Hashbury and similar enclaves. But a growing segment of the movement, increasingly seeing themselves as forerunners of a new civilization that would reconstruct human life from the ground up, took dropping out to mean finding an appropriate setting for an entirely new way of life. According to Timothy Miller, the first commune with a "hip spirit" was Tolstoy Farm in Washington State, founded in 1963. Two years later came Drop City in Colorado, and the anarchic and archetypal Morning Star Ranch outside Sebastopol, California. Many more arose in 1967, perhaps a thousand, with over ten thousand members by the end of the decade. Miller states that communes were widely believed in the hippie culture to be derived from the spirit of rock festivals, at which a short-lived but intense communal feeling was often achieved.[22]

They were no doubt also inspired by the Diggers, a remarkable Haight-Ashbury organization that mounted anarchist street theater and handed out leaflets ("The Death of Money and the Birth of Free"), gave out free stew every afternoon at 4:00 P.M. for a year, ran a Free Store ("It's Free Because It's Yours"), and burned dollar bills. On the surface the Diggers, named after the seventeenth-century English radical redistributionists, might seem to be Robin Hoods, or even the most naive of all the flower children. But the leaders of the movement, like Peter Berg, were serious anarchists who were older than the average on the street. They saw an entrée for their beliefs in the counterculture; they "liberated" or recycled what they could and got what money they needed from wealthy patrons of the counterculture like Owsley Stanley, early entrepreneur of legal LSD. But a new commune in new territory would be the ideal place to show what the counterculture thought of money and the sharing of goods.

The communes also reflected new ideas about sex and family life. Some, though certainly not all, took them as places to experiment with nudity, sexual freedom, and group marriage and child rearing. The reporter Rasa Gustaitis has presented an unforgettable account of a casual commune deep in wild country behind Gorda, California, in which the leading couple was planning a wedding in a tree. They planned marriages to each other whenever they felt like it (weddings that sometimes happened and sometimes didn't), though never legally, because the perpetual groom insisted of his eternal bride that he "didn't want to buy her off the state."[23]

What exactly was the essence, if there was one, of the counterculture? It was, of course, chiefly a youth phenomenon. At the time much was made of alienation, of a generation gap impelled by a youth culture with a heavy antiestablishment theme. But the counterculture also had a positive philosophy, discussed by Yablonsky in terms of such concepts as the importance of love, of communalism, experience, exploration.[24]

It would certainly be possible to discuss the counterculture in Freudian language. On one level it was all about libido or, not to put too fine a point on it, sex. Or it was the same thing through the surrogate orgasm of drugs. The stress on free love and orgy in the communities of the new society, the skimpy and colorful costumery, the dances with their rather explicit courtship ritual overtones, the music with its heavy beat, all more than hinted at Norman O. Brown's "polymorphous perversity." The libido whose repressions and sublimations had, according to Freud, made civilization possible seemed now dangerously near the surface. The July 7, 1967, *Time* article on the hippies spoke of them as "the Freudian proletariat," whatever exactly that meant. It also cited the well-known literary critic Northrop Frye to the effect that the new utopians were inheritors of the "outlawed and furtive social ideal known as the 'Land of Cockaigne,' the fairyland where all desires can be instantly gratified," which sounds a good deal like the Freudian primal paradise.[25]

Yet the new culture also had a Jungian side. It loved the mythical, the archaic, the spiritually exotic and adventurous, and it was not content merely to reduce them to Freudian categories of interpretation. The *Oracle* presented a centerfold of the heart sutra, with a mysterious winged nude woman apparently representing *prajna*, or wisdom, in the center of the sutra, in its April 1967 issue. To find a Freudian meaning in this apparition would have been possible, but the mystical maiden was surely also in the great tradition of identifying deep spiritual wisdom with a feminine anima or *sophia* personification of the cosmic matrix. On the surface, the counterculture wanted not merely to explain but to experience all conceivable states of consciousness, ancient and modern, erotic and mystical, and perchance to make them initiatory waystations toward the emergence of the Jungian *puer aeternus*, the deathless marvelous child within us all.

To do so it would need power, the Adlerian motif, so clearly manifested in the powers of the weak exhibited by the counterculture: the power to shock, to disrupt, and above all the power of youth to suggest they will joyously outlive their offended elders. And there was the Timothy Leary motif of gaining the knowledge that is power through psychedelic/metaphysical exploration, with a hint that what was being excavated was not just intrapsychic libidinal stuff, but the real inner fretwork of the objective universe.

Finally, there is a way in which the Sixties counterculture or youth culture can be considered normal, not requiring any special psychological explanation. In other times and places, not as obsessed as the America of the time professed to be with the nuclear family, it was quite natural, indeed expected, for young people to drop out, spending months in initiatory lodges, forming warrior bands, setting out on mystical or military quests and crusades, or (like many in the nineteenth century) leaving home and hearth for the frontier or the colonies to build new societies with as much idealism and hardship as any Sixties communard.

The response of the conventional religious community to the hippies was uneasy. Many could see the clear parallels to such venerated dropouts as the Buddha and his disciples, the early Christians, Francis of Assisi and the first Franciscans. Lest they be among those who failed to honor new prophets in their own time and place, sensitive religionists were understandably cautious about casting stones. Yet alongside the love, peace, and spiritual questing, beside the gurus and the communes, were the drugs and promiscuity, with their attendant crime and disease, that had to be dealt with as well before the new saints could be fully canonized. Martin E. Marty was quoted in the July 7 *Time* article as saying the hippies are more than just "creative misfits," for they reveal "the exhaustion of a tradition: Western, production-directed, problem-solving, goal-oriented and compulsive in its way of thinking" ("The Hippies," 19).

Harvey Cox, writing in 1967, saw the hippies in a way many counterculturists saw themselves (they loved referring to Thoreau and Walt Whitman), as part of a highly traditional form of American spirituality:

> Hippieness represents a secular version of the historic American quest for a faith that warms the heart, and religion one can experience deeply and feel intensely. The love-ins are our 20th Century equivalent of the 19th Century Methodist camp meetings—with the same kind of fervor and the same thirst for a God who speaks through emotion and not through anagrams of doctrine. Of course, the Gospel that is preached differs somewhat in content, but then, content was never that important for the revivalist—it was the spirit that counted.[26]

Yet these reactions, sympathetic in tone though they may have been, were not wholehearted endorsements. Marty may have shared the hippies' critique of a culture at the end of its modern tether but not necessarily their answers; Cox, as we have seen, was not himself merely a nineteenth-century Methodist.

And there were mixed pastoral signals toward the hippies as well. All Saints Episcopal Church in the Haight-Ashbury established, in

virtually unused parish hall facilities, a twenty-four-hour-a-day counseling center, clinics, a legal aid center, and a dispensary for food and
information on shelter for the hippie community, under the energetic
leadership of the rector, Leon Harris. Unfortunately this activity, similar to that of other area churches, brought the pastor into conflict with
several prominent parish families, including the senior warden. They
objected to the unaccustomed scene of a church full of bearded, allegedly unwashed and promiscuous denizens of the neighborhood. But
Harris vowed to make up the loss in revenue from his own less than
princely salary and served on.[27]

War and Antiwar

As in so much else, 1967 represented a crucial turning point in
the antiwar movement, especially in its spiritual dimension. In that
year many heretofore concerned but indecisive clergy were finally
driven toward critical, and increasingly alienated, stances toward the
war. Clergy and Laity Concerned About Vietnam (CALCAV) discovered it had a growing if reluctant army of supporters in grassroots
churches and synagogues across the country.

Even in midsummer, as we have seen, there was much dithering,
but by the time of the culminating 1967 antiwar event, the Pentagon
march in October, lines were drawn in countless clerical minds and
through numerous churches across the nation. Not all clergy or religionists, of course, were antiwar, but it is probably fair to say that by
year's end the bulk of mainstream religious leadership and articulate
opinion was. This concern took several forms. First, one notices a
sharper, more confident response to the criticism that the clergy were
undemocratic and unpatriotic in opposing the war. Richard John
Neuhaus argued that dissidents worked within the American tradition, claiming that the vast majority of relgious liberals kept faith in
democratic institutions. Robert McAfee Brown said that "to insist that
criticism is unpatriotic is already to have started down the path to
totalitarianism, and to have forgotten that the right of public expression and the right of dissent are among the most honorable modes of
democatic expression."[28]

But protest as they might their democratic legitimacy, critics like
those of CALCAV were frustrated that their moral arguments were
ignored by policymakers, and that they were at best treated to conde-
scending lectures by such powers that be as consented to meet with
them. That frustration led them toward a second sharp new emphasis:
increased support for draft resistance and civil disobedience. Not until

Counterpoint: Sergeant Pepper

Warren Hinckle wrote that J.R.R. Tolkien's *Lord of the Rings*, which as we have noted shared 1966 paperback bestsellerdom with Harvey Cox's very different *Secular City*, was "absolutely the favorite book of every hippie."* But in 1967 the favorite music group, if not of every hippie (some of whom preferred the Grateful Dead or even the Doors), at least of young people generally, was the Beatles.

The reason for the exceptional popularity of these four attractive young men of working-class Liverpool background is, like so many cultural phenomena of the mid-Sixties, not entirely easy to plumb. The music, at least when they first became widely known in 1963, was not that distinguished. But the Beatles grew and changed with the advancing decade, keeping just enough ahead to seem in the vanguard, not so far as to lose anyone. By 1965 they were dressing mod and wearing their hair longer. By 1967 the Beatles were experimenting with Indian sounds, their lyrics included words with discreetly mystical and psychedelic overtones, and for a time they followed Maharishi Mahesh Yogi of transcendental meditation. "Sgt. Pepper" of that year, for example, contains "Lucy in the Sky with Diamonds," and, as though to hint at realities of countercultural sociology, "She's Leaving Home," "A Little Help from My Friends," and "Within You! Without You!"—the last, played to a sitarlike twang, suggests an almost Vedantic perception that it is behind a "wall of illusion" that we hide ourselves and cut off love; the song then preaches the need to realize that the ability to change is also "all within yourself."

Many of the songs also sailed in the following year in *Yellow Submarine*, the Beatles' feature-length cartoon movie and a major Sixties cultural monument. It commences with an attack on Pepperland, a rather Edwardian (or mod) paradise, by the Blue Meanies. To save it, the Beatles and an old-fashioned sea captain travel in a yellow submarine through regions of psychedelic-seeming terror and rapture, culminating in scenes set to "Lucy in the Sky with Diamonds." They encounter No-where (Know-where?) Man, a donnish academic who at first seems impossibly conceited and irrelevant, but who in the end saves the day by transforming the Blue Meanies into flowers. Like much of the Beatles' work, *Yellow Submarine* dived deeper than its frothy surface motion at first indicated.

*Warren Hinckle, "Social History of the Hippies," *Ramparts* (March 1967): 25.

Counterpoint: Dark Shadows and People in the Shadows

The last chapter anatomized *Star Trek* as an ambivalent Sixties relic, reflecting both the Cold War and the pacifist idealism of the era. Another TV series from the same period, which attracted (and still holds) almost as many fans but which otherwise is less well known, is *Dark Shadows*. An ABC daily half-hour soap opera screened from 1966 to 1971, *Dark Shadows* reached a daytime audience of mainly women and children and probably for this reason never reached the cultural monument status its outer-space counterpart achieved. But probably for the same reason, the chronicle of the Collins family (the principals of *Dark Shadows)* was apparently able to do and be things about which prime time TV had to be circumspect.

The Collinses in this epic were a clan involved in everything that made up the Sixties spiritual counterculture. They did astrology, the Tarot cards, witchcraft, the *I Ching*. The show featured supernatural characters: witches, werewolves, and a family vampire called Barnabas Collins. It often employed time-travel motifs, in which favorite characters would travel back to various historical epochs—medieval, Egyptian, and the like—often supported by others in the company in appropriate period-dress roles. The show shamelessly appropriated themes from such gothic classics as *Frankenstein* and *The Turn of the Screw*.

The occult baddies were merely fun, but one serious heavy who frequently turned up was Reverend Trask, a puritanical clergyman cast as a witch-hunter and hypocritical sermonizer in several eras. His part laid out the show's ideology, and it is not surprising that the series engendered a substantial backlash from fundamentalist Christians. A considerable ephemera of articles and tracts labeled *Dark Shadows* "Satan's favorite TV show," the jibe bolstered by cartoons of the Old Deluder himself relaxing in front of a big screen watching it.

Indeed, one may wonder how *Dark Shadows*, together with other shows of that era like *Bewitched* and *Jeanie* that treated witchcraft in a light and sympathetic way, held huge followings against such clerical opposition. Perhaps even these daytime comedies would not have made it after the religious Right had risen to the fullness of its power. But in the Sixties conservative religion was mentally marginalized, at least in the minds who held rein on the media. They had seen the impact of censors and codes do nothing but wither since the Fifties, and the occult become no more than popular culture in the Sixties.

But it may also be that, as a midday show, *Dark Shadows* could get by with more counterculturalism than would have been the case on prime time. For this reason its supernaturalism and time travel appear in retrospect more important cultural signs than they seemed in the Sixties.

Counterpoint: Dark Shadows and People in the Shadows *Continued*

The eternal dream of travel in time, for example, enjoyed a revival in the Sixties, no doubt as part of the transcendence of the ordinary structures of existence offered by drugs and mysticism, and as a spin-off of the fantasy dress and life-styles of the Hashbury and the trips festivals. In the counterculture's universe, limits were not the objective structures of space and time but in the mind. The same theme obtained in such popular novels as Hermann Hesse's *Journey to the East*, whose protagonists found themselves jumping between the modern and medieval worlds as easily as they wandered about middle Europe and, in imagination, ventured toward the sunrise lands of the exotic East.

Dark Shadows no doubt also appealed because of its enactment of archetypal images. As we have noted, the Sixties were particularly a time of the clarification of archetypes, so a strong response was to be expected to stories that manifested, in magical form, fundamental archetypes: candles and shadows, the wise old woman ("witch"), the maiden goddess. Lara Parker, a major actress on *Dark Shadows*, later wrote: "But it was years after I had been on the show, when I read Joseph Campbell's book, *The Power of Myth*, that I realized why these stories were so potent. We have heard them before. . . . We recognize them, or remember them from some unconscious source in our souls. And we respond to them with reverence and wonder. They are deeply moral, and at the same time, profoundly in touch with human frailties."*

The prevalence of witches and werewolves in *Dark Shadows* also reflected a widespread worldview emerging in reaction against the rationalism thought to characterize the establishment and to be a main gearbox of its control mechanism. In this other frame the world was not rational but magical mystery theater. Time and space were a silver screen on which anything could happen in interaction with someone's mind, like a dream or a dreamlike movie from the brain of a mad genius of a director.

It was all part of postmodern neoromantic subjectivism. If witches or werewolves, time travel or horoscopes, can be thought, they have some kind of reality, so let them be. The werewolf world—so long as it remained subjective reality—was far more interesting than such depressing outerworld fantasies as those of Middle America or the Pentagon. And compared to the outer world, an inner space populated by witches and werewolves was far more amenable to control by women, the young, the marginal, the dropouts in relation to the establishment in charge of official reality.

*Lara Parker, "Out of Angelique's Shadow," in *The Dark Shadows Companion: 25th Anniversary Collection*, ed. Kathryn Leigh Scott (Los Angeles: Pomegranate, 1990), 17.

1967 did draft resistance become an organized movement. But on October 25, 1967, just after the Pentagon march, CALCAV released a "Statement of Conscience and Conscription" signed by eighteen members of the clergy, including Brown, Coffin, Heschel, Neuhaus, Cox, Daniel Berrigan, and Martin Marty, urging conscientious, nonviolent resistance and affirming the right of selective conscientious objection to participation in war. Noting that civil disobedience can be a form of religious obedience, the statement said, "We hereby publicly counsel all who in conscience cannot today serve in the armed forces to refuse such service by non-violent means . . . in the sight of the law we are now as guilty as they."[29]

The study of Tolstoy, Thoreau, Gandhi, and of course Martin Luther King was in the air. I recall seeing a table with smiling students distributing such pacifist material even on a campus in conservative Arizona. By early 1968, Coffin was advocating massive civil disobedience, proposing that male seminarians and young clergy give up their draft exemptions and declare themselves conscientious objectors, and urging older clergy publicly to support draft resistance and subject themselves to the penalties of their actions.[30]

Third, in 1967 the antiwar movement increasingly aligned itself with the civil rights movement, which had already displayed so dramatically the power of nonviolent resistance. That natural marriage was much aided by the open adherence of King to the antiwar cause beginning in late February 1967. On February 25, King told a conference on Vietnam organized by the *Nation* magazine in Beverly Hills that "the promises of the Great Society have been shot down on the battlefield of Vietnam." A month later he declared to an Easter peace rally in Chicago that the war was "blasphemy against all that America stands for," and five days later at an SCLC convention in Louisville he asserted that civil disobedience might be called for in arousing the conscience of the nation against the hated war.[31]

But King's major antiwar pronouncement was a speech given in Riverside Church in New York April 4, exactly a year before he was assassinated, entitled "A Time to Break Silence." In this powerful address the civil rights leader recommended a boycott of the war through conscientious objection and presented a five-point plan for disengagement from it, including a bombing halt and unilateral cease-fire. In answer to those who argued that he should stay with civil rights, he declared that his Nobel Prize for Peace was not only an award, but also a commission, and one that took him to work for peace everywhere, "beyond national allegiances." But opposition to the war was also work for the good of America, for "if America's soul becomes totally poisoned, part of the autopsy must read Vietnam." As a leader advocating nonviolence in response to oppression at home, he said, "I knew I could never again raise my voice against the violence of the oppressed in the ghettos without having first spoken clearly to the greatest purveyor of violence in the world today—my own government." In this struggle he wished to challenge young men "with the alternative of conscientious objection." The ultimate of this tumult of conscience would be not only ending the war, but, he prayed, a "revolution of values" that would declare "eternal hostility to poverty, racism, and militarism." All the foes against which King had so valiantly fought by peaceful means were, in the last analysis, one enemy, and in scoring against any one of them all would be weakened.[32]

Other of King's companions in the already legendary civil rights marches were with him now as well. The Reverend James Bevel of SCLC was a major organizer of the great April 15, 1967, Spring Mobilization to End the War in Vietnam. Marches held simultaneously in New York and San Francisco were quite successful, despite behind-the-scenes disputes over whether groups identified as Communist, or planning to carry the Viet Cong flag, should be allowed to participate. (Both were permitted. But the "Mobe" did not permit draft card burning on its podium, though some seventy young men set cards aflame offstage.) Like King, Bevel was a great preacher in the black church tradition. Asked if the Mobilization was Left, Bevel responded, "We're going to get left of Karl Marx and left of Lenin. We're going to get way out there, up on that cross with Jesus."[33]

And major moral support for the resistance came from stories of virtual crucifixions taking place in Vietnam. Nothing aroused the anger of activists, and in many cases converted the indifferent to that role, than the use of napalm B, a petroleum jelly that burned at a thousand degrees Fahrenheit and stuck to whatever it hit, including human flesh. It was used to destroy the Viet Cong in their trenches and tunnels, but is also spread horrible suffering and death indiscriminately among civilians. "It's a terror weapon," one air force pilot who frequently dropped the chemical from as low as fifty feet was reported to have said. And, he added, "People have this thing about being burned to death." Those who survived, including women and children, were frequently hideously disfigured; the diabolical substance burned hot enough to melt and grotesquely remold human flesh. Extremely unpleasant pictures of these fruits of U.S. action reached the underground press, and by January 1967 such a mainstream periodical as the *Ladies' Home Journal*. Protesters began particularly to target the Dow Chemical Company, which manufactured napalm.[34]

Another light on religion and the war: on September 4, 1967, the first U.S. military chaplain to die in combat in Vietnam was killed in circumstances of considerable heroism. He was Vincent R. Capodanno, a Roman Catholic priest. Born in 1929 in Staten Island, Capodanno had attended Maryknoll seminaries, then served as a missionary in Taiwan and Hong Kong from 1958 to 1965. As the war accelerated he became, at his own request, a navy chaplain and was assigned to a marine unit. By all accounts he deeply loved his marines and shared their life in the field. On his last day Father Capodanno made his way through fire to join a besieged platoon on a hill. There he went among the wounded and dying, attending to the physical and spiritual needs of at least six desperate young men. He saved the life of a lance corporal radio operator, lifting him out of the line of fire at risk to his own life. Then, under fire, the chaplain began to bandage the leg of a hospital corpsman who was in danger of bleeding to death. He had taken him in his arms and put his own body between the wounded man and enemy bullets when he was himself hit and killed.

According to a chaplain-historian, Capodanno wanted to be with his "grunts" more than anything else; just the day before his death he had written to his commanding officer to the effect that he wished voluntarily to give up his upcoming holiday leave in order to spend Christmas and New Year's with them in Vietnam.[35]

But the September 8 issue of *Time*, on the newsstands the week of Capodanno's death, had as its centerpiece, in a story on growing discontent with the war, a picture of Bishop C. Kilmer Myers (now Episcopal bishop of California, Pike's successor) lighting a peace torch. The newsmagazine noted that "in no other American war has there been such an absence of hatred for the enemy"—and, it might have added, such visceral hatred *for* the war, not to mention its advocates and perpetrators, on the part of a growing "peace" minority. *Time* did say that "antiwar groups finally feel that they have tapped a rich lode of pacifism in the U.S. public."[36]

The Resistance, founded in the San Francisco Bay area early in 1967, stood for firm opposition to the war and the draft, uniting those who refused to cooperate with it in any way. By fall, it had the support of religious leaders like Myers, and Resistance-sponsored events of turning in or burning draft cards took place in eighteen cities on October 16, and in thirty places on December 4.

A participant described a typical Resistance scene: "It was a beautiful, sunny day on October 16th on the Boston Common, thousands of miles away from the jungles and paddies of Vietnam, where men and women and children were dying at that very moment. I walked around with a sign, 'They Are Our Brothers Whom We Kill,' watching between 4,000 and 5,000 people assemble for the ceremonies known as The Resistance. . . . An attractive, blonde woman . . . carried a sign, 'LBJ Killed My Son.'" After speeches, and some heckling, the resisters wound their way around the Common to the historic Arlington Street Unitarian church, where a moving service included an offer by the Reverend William Sloane Coffin, chaplain of Yale, on behalf of a number of clergy for churches and synagogues to provide sanctuary to draft resisters. Bread was broken together in communion. Then young men were invited to come to the altar to turn in their draft cards, or to burn them in the flame of an altar candle. About 260 responded. The services ended with a minute of silence for war victims, a hymn, and the playing of the church's mighty carillon chimes.[37]

The Resistance rites were followed on October 21 by the climactic antiwar event of 1967, the march on the Pentagon in Washington. Headlines and newsmagazine covers reported the historic event in declaration-of-war-size type like *Time*'s "Protest! Protest! Protest! A Week of Antiwar Demonstrations!"

This was the culminating week of the movement's transition from protest to resistance. The day began with a rally at the Lincoln Memorial attracting roughly a hundred thousand people, of whom some thirty thousand then marched across the Arlington Memorial Bridge to another rally near the Pentagon itself. The event was generally peaceful, but that evening more radical contingents from the rallies tried to storm the building; this gesture ended in thrown bottles and eggs, and a number of arrests. Others tried to stay peacefully on the scene as the cold night approached.

Certain counterculturists, led by the up-and-coming radical harlequin Abbie Hoffman, attempted to magically levitate the Defense Department building; several hundred more dissidents remained to burn draft cards and otherwise continue the protest. After midnight, when the permit to assemble expired, more arrests ended the vigils of those who refused to leave peacefully; in all, 683 were taken into custody.

The Pentagon demonstration is strongly evoked in Norman Mailer's classic Sixties novel, *The Armies of the Night*. This tale begins with an account of a drunken speech by the writer, not known for moderation with the bottle, and ends with a prayerlike meditation called "The Metaphor Delivered," as profoundly spiritual as it seems out of character. Few will read this book without experiencing something as pungent, powerful, flawed, gut wrenching, and unforgettable as the era it epitomizes.[38] The historian of the Sixties William L. O'Neill considers the author of this work something of a prophet without honor: "If a fool, he was a holy fool. Even his enemies, and they were legion, sensed the power in him. If given a choice, he was not the prophet Americans would have asked for in those years. But he was what they got, and they were lucky to have him—though rarely grateful."[39]

Mailer describes the magical attempt to levitate and exorcise the Pentagon as an "almost Shakespearean" drama, perpetrated by figures in love beads and leather, on whom bells, "sandals, blossoms, and little steel-rimmed spectacles abounded." It began with

> a permit requested by a hippie leader named Abbie Hoffman to encircle the Pentagon with twelve hundred men in order to form a ring of exorcism sufficiently powerful to raise the Pentagon three hundred feet. In the air the Pentagon would then, went the presumption, turn orange and vibrate until all evil emissions had fled this levitation. At that point the war in Vietnam would end.
>
> The General Services Administrator who ruled on the permit consented to let an attempt be made to raise the building ten feet, but he could not go so far as to allow the encirclement. Of course, exorcism without encirclement was like culinary art without a fire—no one could properly expect a meal. Nonetheless the exorcism would proceed.[40]

A mimeographed sheet of paper had been circulated with a legend "something like this:"

> October 21, 1967, Washington, D.C., U.S.A., Planet Earth
> We Freemen, of all colors of the spectrum, in the name of God, Ra, Jehovah, Anubis, Osiris, Tlaloc, Quetzalcoatl, Thoth, Ptah, Allah, Krishna, Chango, Chimeke, Chukwu, Olisa-Bulu-Uwa, Imales, Orisasu, Odudua, Kali, Shiva-Shakra, Great Spirit, Dionysus, Yahweh, Thor, Bacchus, Isis, Jesus Christ, Maitreya, Buddha, Rama do exorcise and cast out the EVIL which has walled and captured the pentacle of power and perverted its use to the need of the total machine and its child the hydrogen bomb and has suffered the people of the planet earth, the American people and creatures of the mountains, woods, streams, and oceans grievous mental and physical torture and the constant torment of the imminent threat of utter destruction.
> We are demanding that the pentacle of power once again be used to serve the interests of GOD manifest in the world as man. We are embarking on a motion which is millenial in scope. Let this day, October 21, 1967, mark the beginning of suprapolitics.
> By the act of reading this paper you are engaged in the Holy Ritual of Exorcism. To further participate focus your thought on the

casting out of evil through the grace of GOD which is all. . . . A billion stars in a billion galaxies of space and time is the form of your power, and limitless is your name. (121)

Despite much ululating and chanting, and words of command in the names of countless gods, the Pentagon stood solidly on the ground. Yet the rite helped make some sociological, if not magical, statements.

October 21 defined the antiwar movement at this point in two ways. First, it made clear that movement activists in large numbers had gone beyond discussion, argument, or even protest; they were ready for all-out confrontation and defiance. The majority had not committed and probably would not commit serious civil disobedience, but the point was that their sympathies were plainly with those who found the courage to do so, and their faith in the government nil. A very deep divide, therefore, split American society.

Second, this movement was not connected to party politics. It was rather in the lineage of those other great moral-social movements of the American past that worked outside the compromised partisan politics of their day but in the end were to achieve greater social and political change than normal politics were capable of and finally tended to be coopted ex post facto by some party: abolition, temperance, the women's suffrage movement. (Though the antiwar movement had sympathizers in Congress on both sides of the aisle, administration Democrats were, after all, the war party, and many Republicans if anything even more hawkish.) It is therefore appropriate to speak of antiwar activism as a spiritual rather than political movement, one based in moral and religious values or their secular equivalents, not in pragmatic considerations or partisan advantage—the politics of the Holy Ghost or of Isis, Kali, and the rest, whatever spirits are beyond the fringe of conventional America and of workaday compromise.

Yet crusades do not generally persuade everyone, and the antiwar movement by the end of 1967 had still not convincingly turned the nation around, even though support for the war was perceptibly falling late in the year. Antiwar activists, still widely portrayed as scruffy scofflaws, were not popular either. The movement itself, however, had decisively turned and was not turning back. It now saw itself as a dissident community, with its saints and martyrs; its initiation rites (protests and at best civil disobedience, including the sacrament of draft card burning); and its sacred history complete with the Spring Mobe Exodus and the Jericho experience at the Pentagon. It was a new avatar in the world, and its troubled and troubling mission was not over.

Catholicism after the Council

The year 1967 was only the second full year after the great Vatican Council and was the year the full English Mass and other fruits of the council went into effect at the parish level. As we have seen, in late 1964 the vernacular Mass was introduced, except for the canon (the long eucharistic prayer that is its heart). Then, in 1965, the "last gospel" and other extraneous prayers and devotions were eliminated. In June 1967 appproval was given in principle for a vernacular canon by the Vatican, and new simplified directives for celebrating Mass were issued. Finally, on October 22, 1967, simultaneously with the sorcery before the Pentagon, the entire Mass including the canon was first said in English in parishes throughout the English-speaking world.

Sad to say, the spirit of American Roman Catholicism in 1967 does not seem to have been as upbeat as these rather spectacular changes might have suggested. Pain was still felt by those for whom any change in something as intimate as one's way of worship was bound to be painful. Others, for whom the changes fell far short of hopes and dreams, remained disappointed. There was the inevitable morning-after letdown following an event as momentous as the Vatican Council, when one is forced to realize that in spite of everything the millenium has not yet come, and life must still go on in the gray everyday world.

And the grayness of that world, shot through with occasional apocalyptic fire and smoke, was brought home all too forcefully by the continuing horror and bitterness out of Vietnam, together with the smoldering summer riots in Detroit, Newark, and elsewhere. That is not to mention the emergent counterculture spirituality, with its beads and Sanskrit chants and Hindu gods, which made some wonder if a Mass in plain English was too little and too late, if not a move in the wrong direction.

But then all revolutions produce two kinds of discontent. Some rebels, once engaged, can hardly accept even a successful conclusion of the upheaval but need to sustain the excitement, to go further and further. And as they go they find that, after the world they had known has turned upside-down, they are open to more radical hopes and doubts than they had ever entertained before. Sometimes, not stopping, they altogether pass out of the institution they had at first revolutionized. Others are pushed into more adamant, even schismatic, conservatism. They are those frightened rather than exhilarated by upheaval and the unfamiliarly profound hopes and doubts revolution stirs up to the surface.

The year started off badly for informed Catholics when Charles

Davis, "England's most notable young Catholic theologian," renounced both the priesthood and the Catholic church. Davis had embodied the spirit of Vatican II and Catholic reform, had been *peritus* (theological adviser) to Britain's Cardinal Heenan at the council, and was editor of the prestigious *Clergy Review*, using this professional journal as a forum for modernization. Now Davis said he no longer believed in papal infallibility or in the church as the institutional voice of Christ on Earth. Davis's departure, amid so many trials and changes, made for a crisis of confidence in the Catholic church that some compared to what Anglicans had experienced a hundred years before when John Henry Newman left their communion for the one Davis was now quitting.

That was only the beginning. Before the year was out, the press and airwaves would be full of restless nuns, James Kavanaugh's *A Modern Priest Looks at His Outdated Church*, and more leavings.[41]

At the other pole, Catholic traditionalists, wishing to preserve the Latin Mass, were gathering under Fr. Gommar A. DePauw, who had served as a canon law expert at Vatican II but who, on December 31, 1964, issued a manifesto opposing its innovations. DePauw's activities, centered in Westbury on Long Island, included a magazine and Sunday masses in the old style which drew hundreds of faithful weekly. (Among other traditionalist groups are the Society of St. Pius X, founded by Archbishop Marcel Lefebvre in 1970, which spread to the United States within a few years; and the controversial, allegedly cultlike Tridentine Latin Rite Church established in Coeur d'Alene, Idaho, in 1968.)[42]

The sort of next-day muddles and decisions the post–Vatican II church had to contend with were epitomized early in 1967 by tension over the council's decree number twenty-two, on missionary activity. This edict called for profound adaptation of the liturgy to the "genius and dispositions of each culture." That principle sounded fine when applied to work among "natives" somewhere out in the mission field but became problematic in the context of post-Christian Euro-American culture. In the wake of the conciliar openness, all sorts of liturgical experiments had been talked about and tried: kitchen masses, jazz masses, calypso masses, and more. But on January 4 the Congregation of Rites and the Commission for the Application of Vatican II's Constitution on the Sacred Liturgy solemnly forbade the use of music of "a totally profane and worldy character" and spokesmen mentioned with distaste "almost incredible" liturgical celebrations reported as "news items." "Pope Forbids Jazz Masses," the news headlines now said, though jazz had not been specifically mentioned.[43]

Perhaps the issue was not entirely unrelated to the problematic of a later article on adaptation written by a real missionary in Africa, who pointed out that because Africa itself was changing, tradition was not what it was; to "go native" could well mean simply to appear outdated and irrelevant.[44] Comparable agonizing pieces appeared all over the Catholic press on celibacy, liturgy, dress, nuns, collegiality, and trust, and on rules for students at Catholic colleges. Despite all the confusion, a *Newsweek* poll of Catholics published March 20 found a solid majority in favor of the Vatican II changes.[45]

Pope Paul sent out peculiar signals from the Vatican, seeming to favor fairly rigorist positions on sexual and family matters, but positioning himself more to the left on others. Papal pronouncements in 1967 spoke against divorce and contraception, and in favor of continuing priestly celibacy. But a March encyclical supported land expropriation by and for the poor when required by the common good, the pontiff appeared ecumenical by praying in an Eastern Orthodox church in Constantinople and later with the patriarch of that communion in Rome, and he called on President Johnson to continue the Tet truce ceasefire in Vietnam.

But though none other than their pope had appealed for an extension of the holiday truce, in the tense American political atmosphere not one U.S. bishop publicly supported him. In a widely reported and widely criticized (especially overseas) 1966 Christmas Eve sermon, Cardinal Spellman had called Vietnam a "war for civilization" in which "less than victory was inconceivable." But dissent from the war was building in the more liberal Catholic press and among the more liberal clergy, even in New York. As early as January 17 Spellman would find his own St. Patrick's Cathedral the site of antiwar demonstrations—a scene that infuriated him and would indeed have been "inconceivable" a decade before, in the heyday of his power and glory. By fall the conservative old autocrat was more than a little bewildered by a world and church very different from those he had once manipulated so well. Then on December 2, following a brief illness and before he could make still another planned Christmas visit to Vietnam in support of his beloved troops and the war for civilization, Francis Cardinal Spellman died.

Also dead, by and large, was the kind of Catholic surety the New York cardinal epitomized. The trouble was that, by 1967, surety was becoming elusive on the renewal side as well. A March article in *Commonweal* put the discouraging situation straightforwardly. Daniel Callahan wrote, "For a time, especially during the years of the council, spirits were high, enthusiasm was the order of the day. Much of this seems to be disappearing, despite the gradual achievement of just those new goals which originally inspired the enthusiasm."[46]

Why so? Callahan's perception was that even the achievement of desirable "new goals" in a religious institution entails heavy costs in the necessary sacrifice of other legitimate religious needs: for established kinds of religious experience, for a stable liturgy, for clear-cut moral norms. The reforms had to come, Callahan conceded, but even "progressive" priests were discovering they were being implemented in ways that too often showed failure to understand the psychology or sociology of religion.

Yet heavy pressure weighed in from the progressive side too. Later in the year, a "Commonweal Symposium" brought together an assortment of Catholic students, seminarians, and other young people. Predictably, it being the fall of 1967, they were full of guilt for "what the Church and America have done" yet felt they couldn't just withdraw from either institution. They were "extremely idealistic" and said they expected "this old and very ancient institution, the Church, to be just as idealistic as we are."[47]

At the very end of the year, much publicity about the "new nuns" appeared, much of it centered around the great confrontation between the sisters of the Immaculate Heart of Mary in Los Angeles and their eighty-one-year-old archconservative archbishop, Cardinal McIntyre, a Spellman protégé. *Newsweek* offered a December 25 cover story featuring Sister Corita Kent, superior of this order. Half the cover showed her in starched wimple, high headdress, and floor-sweeping black skirts; the other half presents her as an up-to-date coiffeured and sensibly dressed "new nun."

Dress was only an outward-sign issue; more to the heart of the new religious mentality was the desire of orders of sisters to exercise far more control than before over internal governance, including assignments and educaton as well as garb. But the sisters and the cardinal had arrived at an impasse over dress, contracts, and the right of the order to release nuns for academic training and in general to run its own affairs. When McIntyre declined to approve many of the order's proposed changes, Immaculate Heart of Mary threatened to withdraw two hundred nuns from Los Angeles Catholic schools. In the end, as we shall see, this order dissolved and restructured itself as a lay fellowship of individually contracting teachers and closed its main college rather than submit to demands it felt were unbearable.

It was possible to look at the traumas of postconciliar Catholicism not just as discouraging tensions but as tokens of a new sort of vitality. An article in the Jesuit periodical *America* by Philip Gleason spoke of a "New Romanticism," citing Peter Drucker's characterizing the undergraduates of the day as "the Romantic Generation," J. M. Cameron's speaking of the "querulous romanticism" of many young liberal Catholics, and even Marshall McLuhan's "highly romantic" preference for murkiness over "clear prose."[48]

Evidence of parallels to the celebrated romanticism of early-nineteenth-century enthusiasts began with "trivialities," as Gleason unfortunately calls them, such as the "Ossian-Frodo parallel"—the love of epic quasi-medieval fantasy by the voguish youth of both centuries. He suggests the parallel use of drugs by the earlier opium eaters and the latter-day acid droppers; the similarities in the bohemian culture of the two sets, both flaunting sexual freedom and provocative dress; the corresponding vogues for "the primitive," "the mythic," and "the archaic" in the eras of both Byron and Gary Snyder; and parallels between the current use of the word *perception* and what the earlier romantics meant by *imagination*. Politically, romanticism loved both "organic" community and colorful diversity—at once foreshadowing communalism, fascism, and anarchism—and all these had their echoes in the 1960s.

In connection with the modernism-postmodernism theme, the role of the earlier romanticism is provocative and ambivalent. Though in itself individualistic, "spiritual," and often backward looking, it provided a powerful impetus for many of the ideals that made the modern. Its celebration of change over stability became progress and finally eventuated in largely materialistic and technological models of well-being. Too often the organic community for which it yearned ended as a bureaucratic unitary state sanctified by a few nationalistic sacraments meant to manifest the loyalty of "the people," but in practice chauvinist if not totalitarian. And its love of diversity was generally sentimentalized into a few odd folk customs that did not seriously threaten progress or union.

Yet romanticism can hardly be condemned for all its abuses, some of which are no less the fault of covert classicism rationalizing the romantic's dreams. More to the point, romanticism contains a rare power of historical self-correction, for its abuses are so much the opposite of what it intends as to call forth a new generation of romantics to undo the corruption of the last. That, in effect, was what happened in the Sixties. Though often stalled in neutral between its forward and reverse gears, the Sixties were aware of the difficulty, and in religion (as in politics) it is clear that something of the original romantic vision—and even more romantic feeling as antidote to jaded modernism—was what they wanted to recover.

Finally, 1967 was an interesting year for Catholic publications. Here are a few of that year's crop of important books.

Karl Rahner was one of the best-known Catholic theologians of the Vatican Council era. His *Belief Today* is a simple collection of theological meditations, starting from everyday life. Reflections are offered on the spiritual dimensions of work, laughter, sleeping, and eating, all as potential loci of "common grace." We are all priests, affirms this book clearly intended chiefly for a lay audience. For us, moreover, a simple faith based on a few clues to transcendence is best, since God is utterly beyond our concepts anyway. All we need are a few bridges coming out of intellectual integrity; but *"intellectual integrity requires that one summon the courage necessary to spiritual decision."*[49]

In *The Christian of the Future*, Rahner tackled somewhat trickier material, though with the same lucid simplicity as his other 1967 volume. This work is a collection of essays on the post–Vatican II situation in the church. The key example is "The Church's Limits." Here Rahner warns against "Clerical Triumphalists and Lay Defeatists," both obstructionists in his scope. The triumphalists say the church should have "all the answers" and proclaim them in season and out; the defeatists no less vehemently declare that the church *should* have the answers and give up on it because it obviously does not. Both forget that the church and the church's ministry are not necessarily the same thing; often the church's real "answers" to the world's wounds are not given in doctrinaire words so much as in the quiet, sometimes wordless, ministries of its lay priests.[50]

At the same time, much remained to be done in redefining the ecclesiastical tradition for such a world. This was a task undertaken in Hans Küng's mighty work, *The Church*. More than any other single book, this volume and its predecessor, *Structures of the Church* (1962, English 1964), influenced and then articulated the Vatican II concept of the church, especially in its radically new departures, and hardly less the dramatically fresh servant-church ideas of thinking Protestants.[51]

For Küng, the church is an "eschatological community" of salvation based on the kingdom of God, of which the resurrection of Jesus is a sign. But the kingdom of God is a purely religious reign, not a "religio-political theocracy." It is called to the selfless service of humanity, "of its enemies and the world," and is future oriented (p. 99). The church has three keynotes: (1) It is the People of God, thereby continuing the role of ancient Judaism as a historical entity and, ideally, a unity within history; (2) it is a Creation of the Spirit and as such also manifests a new freedom and continuing charismatic gifts as did the early church; (3) it is the Body of Christ, which members enter through baptism and are further united with in the Lord's Supper and so is also an organic, quasi-biological as well as historical and spiritual reality.

Küng emphasized, within this kind of a church, the priesthood of all believers and the role of ecclesiastical office as ministry. Bishops are "overseers" (*episkopoi*), not originally monarchical in function. The Petrine office (that of the pope) is also a ministry; the bishop of Rome is not "head" but pastor of the whole Church and so its servant. To underscore this new perception, Küng pointed out, Vatican II in effect replaced the language of the Council of Trent (1545–1563), which had used nonbiblical terms like "hierarchy" for the ranks of bishops, priests, and deacons said to have been established by divine ordinance. The Vatican II vocabulary embraced more modest, egalitarian-sounding expressions like "ecclesiastical ministries" instead. Küng did not shrink from saying that the Tridentine decrees, in their original context directed primarily against the Protestant reformation, "cannot be regarded as binding definitions where they concern questions which are being put differently today in the light of completely different problems" (418–419).

Hans Küng described the new church—or better, the new way of viewing the old church—very impressively. Some, however, were not impressed; like Charles Davis they found that light from newly opened windows only enabled them to see more clearly the abuses that were still there. In 1967, the year postconciliar realities good and bad sank in, debate about what had really happened in Rome, whether it went too far or not far enough, rose high and began to drive some of the best as well as the worst out of the new church altogether. (Among those who wanted more was a Chicago group that called itself Vatican $2^1/_2$.)

A popular writer who that year expressed the negative, critical side of the intra-Catholic debate furiously well was James Kavanaugh, who published two much-discussed articles in popular magazines, and a book, *A Modern Priest Looks at His Outdated Church*.[52] Kavanaugh, ordained in 1954, relates how for nine years he outwardly gave out the "party line" in the old-fashioned church but felt more and more inward anger at the needless suffering he saw caused by rigid, legalistic policies regarding such issues as marriage, celibacy, the church's teaching role, and political involvement, and above all by the twisted priorities of a religion "obsessed with sex." (Critics pointed out that Kavanaugh himself, at least, was clearly preoccupied with that topic; fully three-quarters of his examples of misguided teaching have to do with it.) He increasingly disbelieved what he was saying and finally, amid the upheavals of the Vatican II years, exploded in this powerful, relentless book. Part autobiography as Kavanaugh describes his Catholic upbringing and priestly formation, part polemic, part visionary when the author evokes a new and healthier Catholicism, *A Modern Priest* may be one-sided, but one does not doubt that its finely wrought rage spoke the burden of many hearts. This racy, fast-paced mix of story and sermon is impossible to ignore or, indeed, to lay down. (The author soon left the priesthood and married.)

Vincent Yzermans edited *American Participation in the Second Vatican Council*, the verbatim "interventions" or statements entered into conciliar debates by American bishops. Cardinal Spellman presented 131 interventions, more than any other American; they were generally brief and circumspect, and usually on the side of conservative cautions, especially in regard to the substitution of the vernacular for Latin and other liturgical innovations. In his heart the archbishop of New York had little faith in the council and yearned for the days of Pius XII, but so long as he and the other Americans were there in Rome, he strove, though with diminishing effectiveness, to maintain his position as the "titular leader of the American hierarchy."[53] Spellman knew as well as anyone that the succession of John XXIII, and above all the coming of the council, marked the end in his lifetime of the sort of conservative, authoritarian, and stridently anti-Communist church in which he had flourished in the Fifties.

Most of the other prominent American prelates were less enamored of an ecclesiastical world now clearly passing away. Yzermans notes of the statements of Albert Cardinal Meyers of Chicago, a thoughtful progressive: "It did really not matter much to him who liked or disliked what he would say. Once he was convinced, under the assurance of the Spirit as he saw it, he was absolutely fearless." But this cardinal's interventions were respectfully received "because they were from the very depths of his own soul." Still another image was presented by Archbishop John J. Krol of Philadelphia, a workmanlike member of the assembly and its English-speaking undersecretary, and in Yzermans's view perhaps "the most effective as well as the busiest American at the Council" (9).

Rosemary Ruether, in *The Church against Itself*, presents the perspective of a radical woman theologian of Roman Catholic background. In this first of a long series of books, Ruether discusses Catholic, reformation, and radical reform polities but finds none of them adequate in their present crystallized forms. The church, she avers, is essentially a "happening," new every moment, catalyzed in the breaking and sharing of bread. Ideally, it is scattered, gathered, and ecumenical—a diaspora—formed where two or three are gathered together, and embracing all those who so gather in the name of Christ. Its ministry is "encounter," created where it is performed, and its function is at once "image-making and image-breaking." This ideal church, both post-Catholic and post-Protestant, is the eschatological community of the saints set against the historical churches unwilling to be made new. But there were those in the Sixties who tried to make not a few red-brick inner city or Main Street American churches, Old First or Old Sacred Heart, into such communities of futuristic saints, with varied results.[54]

In the year's harvest of books there was also evidence of weariness of a world and church continually being made new, and of the process itself becoming a banality. In Peter Riga's *Church and Revolution* one detects odd hints of both revolutionary ardor and revolutionary burnout. One here reads crisis and at the same time the clichés of a crisis by now gone on so long as to become itself almost drab normalcy.

In the preface, Riga's indictment reads:

> The Church and Revolution is an attempt to confront in a meaningful way the crucially important task facing the Church today: to proclaim the good news of Jesus to a world in ferment, in revolution. Never in recorded history have events moved with the pace they have during our lifetime. Today men stand on the threshold of a new era in human history. . . . Throughout the whole world the 'revolution of rising expectations' is in full swing, and the prospects offered to the human race by twentieth-century technological breakthroughs stagger the imagination. The age-old problems . . . remain. . . . The Church must be in the vanguard.[55]

Note the cascade of cliches: "meaningful way . . . crucially important task . . . world in ferment . . . stand on the threshold of a new era . . . Church in the vanguard." And note also the characteristic Sixties assumption that the present moment was absolutely unique, and a hinge of history. To those inside that decade it was as certain as sunrise that theirs was a time of unparalleled revolutionary change and unprecedented technological prospects. Right or wrong, and probably it was some of both, the significant point is that these awesome tenets were not so much proven as simply repeated and taken for granted.

It is no doubt unfair to pick on Fr. Riga's book in this way, for it is generally an admirable exposition of the great modern papal social encyclicals. The author was a stalwart of Clergy and Laity Concerned About Vietnam. I do so simply because it is an example at hand of printable 1967 on a level that needs to be represented: one a little below the stellar, yet not falling into the broken ranks of the discouraged or bitter, by a soldier in the trenches still holding to the revolutionary, renewal faith when its new words no longer taste fresh.

Race after the Victory

The year 1967 would be remembered as the long, hot summer as well as the Summer of Love. By fall, two images were likely to hold the foreground in the minds of most people: Summer of Love hippies and burning, riot-torn cities.

Riots began in May on southern black campuses, on the tenth at Jackson State College in Mississippi, and on the sixteenth at Texas Southern University, where a white policeman was killed. In June racial violence reached Boston; Buffalo; Cairo, Illinois, and Syracuse, New York. Between July 12 and July 17 twenty-six people were killed during a second season of violence and destruction in Newark. The most destructive of all the riots was in Detroit, from July 23 to July 30. It started with a raid on a black speakeasy and ended with nine days of fire and looting, 42 dead, 386 injured, and $44 million worth of property damage. But these were only the worst of more than a hundred racial disturbances in cities large and small.

What was the response of the religion community to these tragedies? In the *Christian Century* in August, John M. Gessell wrote, "What is required is a dramatic act committing the national and local power-structures to a massive eradication of the despair that issues in riots."[56]

The Jesuit periodical *America* for August 12, 1967, was a special issue on the topic, the cover blazing with red flames and the words, "Riots and Revolution: From Boston 1770 to Detroit 1967." Most of the words were sound but, again, all too predictable and in the event all too ineffectual. Fred M. Henley did offer an unusual historical perspective in his "Boston 1770," pointing to parallels between ghetto frustration and the frustration that brought on the American Revolution. "The mere removal of a tax on tea, or the marching off of two regiments [half the garrison, an offer made by the British governor of Massachusetts to Samuel Adams to placate the colonists], would not do. The same may be said today of our present racial difficulties. It is not simply a matter of tearing down a slum building or providing more recreational facilities."[57]

It was rather a matter of lack of trust, lack of a sense of power, and a feeling of angry, vulnerable isolation on the part of the oppressed;

Counterpoint: The Peasant of the Garonne

Le Paysan de la Garonne by the great Neo-Thomist philosopher Jacques Maritain was the bestselling nonfiction work in France in January 1967, and although not yet available in English it was much discussed that year in American Catholic periodicals.* The author was eighty-five the same year, and in certain respects this is an old man's book, rambling, full of opinions and reminiscences.

But what an old man! Maritain was widely recognized as a leading philosophical architect of the liberal Catholicism that underlay Vatican II; as the chief intellectual influence on the reigning pope, Paul VI; indeed as the ideal modern Catholic, at once devout, cultured, humane, intelligent—and, as he put it, an "inveterate layman." Further, the book made clear that the octogenarian's razor-sharp mind and stylistic scalpel had by no means grown dull with the years. That made it all the more painful for Maritain's many admirers to see him now appear to turn against the values of the new Catholicism.

The old convert and churchly philosopher was at the time a semihermit at a monastery near the Garonne River in rural France—hence the book's title. While rejoicing in many of the positive achievements of Vatican II, especially in its affirmation of religious liberty, he saw in the church around him immense losses in respect to objective truth and the contemplative life. Compared to the relativism now abroad, which saw all descriptive expressions of the faith as little more than helpful myths, the notorious modernism of Pius X's day was only "hay fever." And how much was lost for truly contemplative souls in the modern insistence that those present at Mass must actively participate in the liturgy, rather than use the sacrament as an occasion for simple adoration. Further, there was too much emphasis on controversial ethical, especially sexual, issues. In all this, the "old layman" insisted, lay real danger of a "complete temporalization of Christianity."

The fundamental point for Maritain was the objective, and therefore timeless, nature of Christian truth and of the objective validity of the words in which it is deposited. The bedrock verbal and ideological affirmations of the faith may be minimal and are not quite to be idolized or made the occasions of witch hunts (as they were by his onetime adversaries, the "Integralists"). But, as opposed to the other extreme, that of the modern pan-mythologizers, the vital core of the objective faith is irreducible and not to be chipped down or turned into putty.

Thus, in his critique of his celebrated contemporary Pierre Teilhard de Chardin, Maritain is satisfied to declare of the great Jesuit paleontologist's speculations about human destiny that "the Teilhardian theology is one

---

Counterpoint: The Peasant of the Garonne *Continued*

more Christian gnosis, and like all the gnoses from Marcion to our days, it is 'theology fiction,'" in analogy to "science fiction." Teilhard, the peasant of the Garonne avers, was a good poet but a bad philosopher, who would have spared the church a lot of trouble had he just proclaimed his theories as no more than literary excursions.

Liberal Catholic theologians understandably reacted with pained indignation to Maritain, feeling betrayed by their mentor. Some felt he simply could not understand the philosophical and theological language of an era different from that of his heyday. Here, it seemed, was a voice from a past that had once been the future—not an inept conundrum in a year in which many futures were becoming pasts.

*Jacques Maritain, *The Peasant of the Garonne* (New York: Holt, Rinehart and Winston, 1968), 56, 119. See also Robert A. Graham, "Jacques Maritain on Aggiornamento," *America*, March 11, 1967, 348–349, and James Collins, "Martitain Asks Some Questions," *America,* January 13, 1968, 29–30.

the police presence in the ghetto areas was compared not only to British troops in Massachusetts but also to Russian troops in Hungary at the time of the freedom fighter uprising there ten years before. When police, who are supposed to protect and serve a community as its public servants, are perceived instead as an army of occupation, there's bound to be trouble.

"The Rising Tide of Violence," an editorial in the evangelical *Christianity Today* for August 18, likewise perceived that the problem was as much one of spiritual as of material poverty. Some riots, it pointed out, took place in relatively prosperous and well-integrated black communities, and ones to which considerable government funds had been directed. The answer was not in more government programs, nor in calls for more of the same by "large denominations" that "seem content to pass resolutions about the problems of the slums and to let the government carry on the battle from there." Indeed, "on the local level, many pulpits have been doling out a monotonous endorsement of social-gospel legislation for so long that the man in the pew has lost all sense of personal responsibility." Nor was the solution blaming the black ghetto dwellers who are also the victims, but rather for "the two-thirds of the American people who belong to churches [to] assume a personal obligation in regard to national problems," making themselves "the salt of the earth."[58]

One can certainly sympathize with a call for personal involvement by religious people. But this editorial may not have given a completely fair picture of the role of clerical liberals or of the "large denominations." Perhaps some preachers had been excessively devoted to "monotonous" social gospeling, but the background to the Detroit riots lay in the defeat, not the success, of the social gospel. Several major political battles had taken place in that city between 1964 and 1966 over open housing and the appropriation by Wayne State University of predominately black residential land. Though those struggles were led by members of the black middle class and supported by many liberal white ministers and laypeople, the black leaders lost to the white power structure, with the inevitable result of alienation and bitterness.[59]

Nor were the mainline churches inactive during the disturbances, content merely to pass resolutions. More than eighty volunteers worked with the Interfaith Emergency Center to collect and distribute food and necessities, and to provide other urgent services (such as expediting welfare checks and locating missing persons) to those whose lives were disrupted by the riots; its leadership was chiefly Episcopal and United Church of Christ clergy.[60]

As for resolutions, the General Board of the National Council of the Churches of Christ passed one in Atlanta in September 1967 called "The Crisis in the Nation." This text declared that the disasters may have been the judgment of God and blamed them on white racism. It pointed out that the churches, "identified as they generally are with the dominant affluent majority of the land, can scarcely claim to lead the way to reconciliation" but need first to "confess with humility our part in the common guilt." Far from calling for more programs by outside agencies, the document denigrated the ways in which, "in the past, some of us assumed that we knew what was best for others— usually without consulting them—and we have tried to do things *for* people. Thereby they were deprived of what was needed most: participation in the determining of their own destiny. This kind of helping has been denounced as paternalism and 'welfare colonialism' by those who were supposedly its beneficiaries." Christians cannot, however, use such understandable sentiments as excuses for withdrawing and doing nothing. Instead, through vocal support and taking part in coalitions, they must find ways of helping that are not harmful or self-deluding.[61]

The board directed that 10 percent of its capital funds be used in ghetto community programs, to be planned and directed by representatives of those communities. Similar commitments of substantial amounts of money, without strings, to black groups and communities were generously proposed and often acted upon by all the large main-stream denominations.[62]

The General Convention of the Episcopal church in September 1967, for example, debated a wide-ranging proposal advanced by the presiding bishop: a million-dollar-a-year plan to aid "organizations of black people, in programs under their control, to gain economic and political power." "Skilled personnel assistance" was also offered. The total proposed budget for programs and grants directly related to the urban and racial crises for the coming three years came to $6 million, of which $2 million was granted by the Episcopal Church Women from their venerable United Thank Offering.[63]

In the debate, amendments were offered that would have restricted the choice of organizations that could receive these funds. There was uneasiness over church money going to groups not under church control, especially those that might employ radical rhetoric or condone the use of violence. The programs passed easily, however. Several bishops reported that such activities were bringing new life and vitality to their jurisdictions. Almost unnoticed was the way in which, for the moment, this debate had eclipsed the bitter partisan battles between "high church" and "low church" factions that had long characterized the General Convention. Nor was it remarked that, for all their well-meaning, servant-church attitudes, and despite brave efforts at local empowerment, the Episcopalians' urban programs still maintained the outlook of a modern institution—national, bureaucratic, money manipulating—in a rapidly changing, pluralizing, fragmenting world. Unbeknownst to the convention, in the strange new postmodern religious world dawning over 1967's fire and smoke, they and all their kind would decline precipitously in both influence and membership.

But bitter partisanship, indeed the prerevolutionary mentality of which Henley spoke, was far from banished, though it may have attached itself to new issues. A 1967 statement by the United Presbyterian Commission on Religion and Race minced no words:

> Nothing has better exposed the deterioration of the recognized civil rights groups and the ineffectiveness of the old coalition between the white liberal establishment and middle class black leaders than the riots of this summer.
>
> The civil rights movement as we knew it before Watts is no longer in existence. The old leaders like [Roy] Wilkins, King and [Whitney] Young still continue to speak for a certain segment of the Negro community and still maintain contact with Washington and with their white counterparts. But they no longer have the influence in the black community that they had at the time of the March on Washington or during the struggle for the Civil Rights Act of 1964.

> Their leadership in the ghettos of the cities has been successfully
> challenged . . . by young militants under 30 years of age who . . . speak
> and act in the mood of the people who have gained the least from the
> civil rights movement and the war on poverty.
> That mood is one of anger and hate; its mode is the knife, the
> gun and the Molotov cocktail.[64]

Speaking of the covert violence against the black poor, with which
they live continuously, this remarkable statement went on:

> This is why the people indigenous to the ghetto show no great contri-
> tion about the violence of the summer. Several reporters have noted
> the "carnival atmosphere." Urban poverty does violence to people.
> "Paying back" those unseen white people who keep you in that con-
> dition is a celebration. A time of laughter and deep satisfaction—like
> a Fourth of July picnic with plenty of fried chicken and beer.

This was the mood that gave rise to the expression "black power"
and birthed the Black Panther movement (which provided, if not
chicken and beer, at least hot breakfasts as well as the glamor of
potential violence). And the "now" spokespersons for black power
declaimed in a revolutionary mode.

Some were ready for revolution of some kind, whether even the
most radical whites were ready for it or not. *Black Power: The Politics
of Liberation in America* (1967) by Stokely Carmichael and Charles V.
Hamilton was an important statement of the new rhetoric on race.
(The May 29 *Newsweek* article on the May 1967 riots at Houston's
Texas Southern University, which Stokely Carmichael had visited the
month before, was entitled "The Stokely Generation.") The radical,
Black Panther authors of *Black Power* called on their readers to face
statements that "most whites and some black people would prefer not
to hear": that American racism is not a matter of easily changed attitudes but of a system, in which "white liberals" are just as much
participants as other whites, that will only yield to revolutionary
change. Carmichael and Hamilton did not want "integration," a matter
of "middle-class goals, articulated primarily by a small group of Ne-
groes with middle-class aspirations or status," which only "become
meaningless show-pieces for a conscience-soothed white society."[65]

They wanted instead self-determination for blacks: "We blacks
must respond in our own way, on our own terms, in a manner which
fits our temperaments. The definitions of ourselves, the roles we pursue, the goals we seek are *our* responsibility" (ix). In articulating this
stance, they found much to admire in the words of Frederick Douglass
more than a hundred years before: "Power concedes nothing without
demand . . . the limits of tyrants are prescribed by the endurance of

those whom they oppress" (x). But above all else they drew from the Third World revolutionary movements, especially as articulated by Frantz Fanon in *The Wretched of the Earth*, as he called on the new societies just liberated from European colonialism not to imitate Europe but to "start a new history of Man."[66]

Carmichael and Hamilton perceived the U.S. situation as colonial and so related directly to the anti-imperialism of Fanon. Their point is that colonial subjects have political decisions made for them even if by indirect rule, as in parts of the colonial world. This, the authors believed, was the case in the United States when "co-opted" black leaders backed integrationist reforms that essentially kept the white colonialist plantation workable. In contrast, they pointed to the then-recent Lowndes County, Alabama, election when the Black Panther symbol was first used.

For better or worse, for all the bold rhetoric, defiance on a revolutionary scale was hardly possible for a population constituting a 10 percent minority in the United States, any more than such revolutionary language worked as a long-term anodyne for the poverty-wracked nations of the ex-colonial world. But for a few years black power and Third World solidarity were rallying cries for minority emotions aroused but hardly assuaged by the far more successful pacifist parades of the King years. Carmichael's and Hamilton's book supplies the words and the sentences behind those cries and offers a glimpse into why they were so forcefully appealing.

It was this appeal, and not the (in retrospect) more idealistic and genteel call of King and the Freedom Summer people, that confronted confessions of guilt and programmatic solutions like those of the Presbyterians and Episcopalians. The world had pivoted almost too much for them. Yet perhaps the Presbyterian statement, in a characteristic 1967 way, was also overwrought, overdramatizing the appeal of nihilists and revolutionaries. Needless to say, just as the great majority of whites were neither rednecks nor counterculturalists, so the majority of blacks were not Uncle Toms, nor committed Kingites, nor Black Panthers.

But in 1967 a great many people of both races were confused and anxious, sensing themselves trying to live ordinary lives as hurricane winds whirled around them, pulled this way and that not so much by real change—of which there was much less in 1967 than in the first half of the decade—than by the velocity of the rhetoric and a whole cyclone of symbols: urban destruction as a sign, a counterculture with its beards and new gods hinting at apocalypse in the wings, more radical/revolutionary subsects than in St. Petersburg in 1913 prophesying the eve of destruction. It was not so much substantive change as a change in the barometric pressure, and as one ominous expression of the times had it, "You don't have to be a weatherman to know which way the wind is blowing."

Books

By 1967, it was beginning to dawn on average Americans—with a sense of shock—that not only was there crisis at home but that Americans were not liked in many overseas places either. Thomas B. Morgan wrote *Among the Anti-Americans: Why They Don't Like Us* (1967), based on nineteen weeks spent in other countries, to explain why. He summed it up in the introduction. The reasons "include our race crisis and the war in Vietnam, the memory of McCarthyism and the unforgettable assassination of John F. Kennedy, the workings of the Central Intelligence Agency and the tragic inadequacy of our global economic policies. Above all, virtually the whole world seemed to have had about enough of what was once a good thing: our post-war interventionism." In the chapters based on his experience among the masses in various countries—Brazil, Japan, Indonesia, Kenya, Egypt, France—Morgan found responses less sharply political than those complaints might suggest, except among intellectuals, but no less telling: ordinary citizens of other nations saw too many billboards for American products such as Coke and found the Americans among them too self-righteous and preachy, altogether too obsessed with communism. Such attitudes could only breed jealousy and resentment.[67]

The Vietnamese Buddhist monk Nhat-Hanh was a one-man peace movement. His 1967 book, *Vietnam: Lotus in a Sea of Fire,* was introduced by Thomas Merton, himself by then a trenchant and radical peacenik much concerned that American Catholics, just emerging from the era of Cardinal Spellman-style anticommunism, hear his Asian monastic colleague's words, discomfitting as they might be. Nhat-Hanh strove to explain forcefully the position of Vietnam's Buddhists, including those monks who had immolated themselves. He related why the traditionally Buddhist Vietnamese saw themselves caught as if in a vise between Catholicism and communism. Both were outside forces aligned with outside interests: Catholicism with French colonialism and churchly "triumphalism," communism with an alien ideology. Nhat-Hanh no less angrily opposed U.S. troops and escalation, portraying the American allies as intruders with no sensitivity to Vietnamese culture. Left alone, he contended, the Vietnamese people could settle their own affairs, for even in the Vietcong front the majority were not Communist ideologues but patriots fighting against outside control. As hard as it may be for Americans to accept, the monk contended, they must realize they are not welcome in Vietnam, and their Vietnamese sycophants not respected.[68] Publication of Nhat-Hanh's hard-hitting volume coincided with disillusionment about Vietnam on many grounds; it was read, and it had its impact.

Jurgen Moltmann's *Theology of Hope* appeared in English translation in 1967. Seeking to discard "transcendental subjectivity" in both God and humankind in favor of a theology of the world and its structures, this work differed from the conventional secular theology of the day in its emphasis on the radical rediscovery of Christian eschatology.[69] Although the 1967 timing of the American version may have been coincidental, one thinks of the general move in this year toward refinding the sacred, even the reenchantment of the world, in new and odd places. One thinks also of the New Left's revolutionary apocalyptic and the counterculture's simultaneous discovery of radical Aquarian Age eschatological thought.

Dean Peerman edited *Frontine Theology* (1967), a collection of short essays originally published in the *Christian Century*'s "How I Am Making Up My Mind" series, by the leading radical to moderate theological names. A comparable volume was *The Religious Situation, 1968* (1968), from articles presumably written in 1967. Its essays were more wide-ranging and worldwide than Peerman's, however, covering such topics as secularization, the Christian-Marxist dialogue, religon and culture, and even churches and taxation, some in a topical and some in a more general and theoretical manner that seems to lack focus.[70]

The sociologist Thomas Luckmann, in *The Invisible Religion* (1967), argued that any ideological and social construction of reality can be labeled religion, if by its making humans show their transcendence over their purely biological nature. Science as a world system is thus as much religion as Catholicism. By this reckoning all societies however secular have a covert religion, and the more widely accepted such a religion is the more it is taken for granted, and so the more it is invisible.[71] The book may be considered important as a 1967 publication because of the way it pried open a cognitive space for postmodernist criticism of modernist universal truth systems like science.

One controversial figure in 1967 was Adam Clayton Powell (1908–1972), ordained Baptist minister and long the leading black member of Congress. He represented Harlem, where he was also pastor of the Abyssinian Baptist Church. Powell was an early civil rights crusader, both in the pulpit and in the corridors of power. In 1960 he became chair of the House Committee on Education and Labor, from which position he helped pilot through Congress major Kennedy/Johnson administration aid-to-education and antipoverty bills.

Though adulated in Harlem, Powell was not well liked by many of his colleagues in Washington. His absenteeism and his hedonistic private life, not to mention an early-Sixties defamation suit brought by a constituent (which Powell lost but refused to pay), were considered scandalous. On top of this, in early 1967 he was accused of misappropriation of public funds. A vote of the House censured him and denied him his seat. He and his supporters, of course, alleged racism, and Powell, now at odds with his fellow Democrats, lent his support vocally to the black power movement. (Much of Powell's behavior was irresponsible and inexcusable, but one does wonder if a white member of the congressional club would have been treated as harshly.) Powell was reelected by a seven-to-one margin in a special election in 1967 but still not seated; although he was finally allowed to return to the House in 1969, he never regained his committee chair and was narrowly defeated in the 1970 primary. In 1967 he published a book of short, lively but rather conventional sermons, *Keep the Faith, Baby.*[72]

Then there are two books from the real frontlines by Stephen E. Rose, editor of *Renewal. The Grass Roots Church* (1966) places itself with an epigraph by Bonhöffer and an introduction by Harvey Cox. The volume expounds *Renewal*'s already mentioned "Manifesto for Protestant Renewal." In his prefatory piece, Cox lauds Rose's willingness to work as a radical within the institution, saying there is a need for renewal but also for organization, which the church provides, and attacking "pseudoradical" critics of all institutions. He cites the Mississippi Delta Ministry as a manifestation of Rose's supreme ideal.[73]

But Rose starts off radical: "It is no longer possible for Protestantism to survive in its present form" (3). Denominationalism is obsolete, with all its time- and money-wasting works. The church, or perhaps rather churchpeople, need instead to fight for social justice, to be radically ecumenical, especially on the local community level, and to practice "abandonment," the giving up of present locations and structures in order better to give oneself to others. At the same time, Rose also calls for the renewal of the traditional functions of the church—the nurturing of community, the teaching of faith, the pastoral and preaching ministries—but obviously in renewal ways that lead churchpeople to express their faith ecumenically in the social justice struggle.

That 1966 book was, by our paradigm, a "years of secular hope" book. Rose's next work, *Alarms and Visions: Church and the American Crisis* (1967), consisting of essays from *Renewal* magazine, has about it more of a 1967 sense of crisis, of living in a society on the edge. Between these two books we sense a move from progressive eschatology to apocalypse, from hope for renewal to dread of destruction. In the first chapter, "Toward Ecumenopolis," Rose already sees Cox's *Secular City* as too sanguine. But the struggle must be continued. "Agitating Jesus" portrays Jesus as an agitator because of his refusal of all responsibilties that might entail a conflict of interest with his revolutionary role, his identification with the suffering, his outspokenness, and his underdog role. Yet Rose was not wholly convinced that revolution would come or, if it did, that it would be entirely good. The last piece, a remarkable dialogue with himself entitled "On the Possibility of Revolution in America," sorts out radical dreams and doubts with great honesty, clarity, and even humor.[74]

William Styron's *Confessions of Nat Turner: A Novel*, is a powerful fictionalized interpretation of the life of the black slave preacher who Styron said led the only sustained and effective American slave revolt, that in Tidewater Virginia in 1831. The book appeared as a remarkable counterpoint to the mid-Sixties transfigurations of the civil rights movement from pacifism to black power. Styron laid bare the brutalization of both races engendered by the evil institution of slavery, and—with considerable contemporary relevance—showed the malignancy of the distorted stereotype each had of the other. He makes the hatred of whites and the violence to which Nat was goaded all too understandable; at the same time he shows its futility against the overwhelming power of the dominant race—intellectual, legal, and at the most basic level, physical, that is, whose hands held the whips and the guns. All too relevant. So also was the moral, though Nat could grasp it only through the mysterious but fair words of scripture that ran through his head the morning of his execution: *Surely I come quickly. Amen. Even so come Lord Jesus . . . The bright and morning star.*[75]

An Endnote on Theology in 1967

What was 1967 like on the deeper levels of religion? Although theology is not the same as religion, perhaps a glance at what was going on in that discipline will afford some clues. First, 1967 was widely said to be a year of the decline of secular and Death of God theology.

In that year Thomas Altizer published *The New Apocalypse*,

celebrating, in the words of the subtitle, "The Radical Christian Vision of William Blake." Altizer's thesis was "that William Blake is the most original prophet and seer in the history of Christendom," one of whom the world, or at least the theological world, has thus far shown itself neither ready nor worthy. Alitzer's Blake was, of course, a Death of God Christian, a celebrant of Christ while dismissing the tiresome, tyrannical old Father-God, Urizen, or Nobodaddy. But there was more to it than that.[76]

"Blake was the first Christian seer since the author of the book of Revelation to insist that human redemption is inseparable from the total transformation of the natural world" (10). Therefore Blake opposed the usual Western dualism of humanity and nature, and the idea of an autonomous nature apart from humanity, saying in the *Marriage of Heaven and Hell,* "Where man is not, nature is barren." It is not nature but humanity that is conditioned and enslaved by needless laws. Free the human microcosm, and all nature reverts to its former glory, for, Altizer says, "the universe is but a mask of man; its 'infinity' testifies to man's original and eternal state; the barrier that separates nature from man is but a sign of man's present alienation" (11).

Along with this stunning perception went Blake's "passionate refusal of any distinction between body and soul," and his choice of sexual imagery as the language most truly reflecting the mystery of life in the Godhead or, better, his seeing "the very reality of sex as the deepest epiphany of the Divine Man." And in *The Marriage of Heaven and Hell* Blake declared that "Energy is Eternal Delight," Altizer notes (19).

Critics quibbled over whether Altizer was rightly reading Blake, or just using him as a platform from which to make his own statement. But theology is seldom limited to original intent. What Altizer did with Blake is what constructive theologians always do with their texts, whether biblical, patristic, reformation, or—as in this case—poetic. The significant achievement is to make a theologian's theology contemporary, even as textual critics try to put it in its life situation.

In this respect *The New Apocalypse* becomes brilliantly luminous as a 1967 book. It touches on numerous themes of the new countercultural romanticism and links them to the old romanticism of which Blake was at least an associate member and to the occult tradition (Gnosticism, the kabbala, Swedenborg) where Blake went to school.

Those romantic-occult themes were all important to 1967 countercultural voices, as a glance at the *Oracle* will reveal—the subjective creation of reality, nature, the positive affirmation of sexuality as spiritual, the coming new heaven and earth. Now Altizer shows that these splendid new visions of humanity are put more radically by radical Christians than by anyone else.

This radical theologian implicitly makes clear that the fantasias of 1967 are continuous with the late secular theology and Death of God, but under a different sun. Last year the new people exalted in the gritty but sternly hopeful black-and-white realism of the secular city, and their prophets were in the streets. In 1967, the same year the Beatles sang about a "girl with kaleidoscope eyes," we are given the kaleidescope colors of an apocalypse, and the augur is less an activist than the Blakean visionary poet who sees beyond the years.

The year 1967 also produced a burst of theological interest in the meaning of the years that measure historical time. Wolfhart Pannenberg of Mainz University, in Germany, was a young theologian getting a lot of attention. In dispute with Barth, Bultmann, and others, Pannenberg emphasized that God's revelation cannot be so "demythologized" or made a matter of pure faith as to be pushed outside the boundaries of history. It is, rather, in history that God reveals himself, whether to ancient Israel at the Red Sea or, for Christians, in the coming of God in Christ. History is the horizon of Christian theology. All theological questions and answers are meaningful only within the framework of the history of God dealing with humanity, and history is moving toward a still-hidden future foreshadowed in Jesus Christ.

Although Pannenberg insisted that the Resurrection, properly understood, was a historical event, he came under attack from conservatives for saying that the Virgin Birth was probably a myth. He received sniper fire on the other flank from secular theologians like William Hamilton, who accused him of reviving the "outdated" concept of God as extraneous controller of the universe and human affairs.

But whether in agreement or disagreement, Pannenberg, like Altizer, had people talking about the religious meaning of time and history. On one level, that was probably the real religious issue in 1967. History was very much a present reality.

The great ideas generated by nineteenth-century historicism—progress and secularization—were both taken for granted as explanations of why we are who and what we are today. Yet they were not working well. They had to be either speeded up to apocalyptic, sanctified, or spaced out to eternity. The oppressiveness of living in mere stifling historical time, in what Mircea Eliade called the "terror of history," was very much behind all the old ways to rocket out of history that were being rediscovered and ignited in 1967: mysticism (whether chemical, carnal, or traditional-spiritual), apocalypticism, revolution, crusading, or plain dropping out into some new variation on the monastery or the commune as a city on the edge of the world.

For us, the important point is that, at a time of rapid historical change, Pannenberg showed that events could be seen religiously as history with sacred meaning—*heilsgeschichte*—as well as escalating into apocalyptic, or requiring the radical surgery of the mystic and the ascetic.

Then there were those concerned with the history going on at the time and prepared to read—and write—it as a scenario by God. Nowhere was the literary hand of God more evident than in the compelling saga of the civil rights movement, now only two or three years past the Egypt-and-Exodus-scale events of Mississippi, Birmingham, and Selma. One of the most interesting books in that sort of theology, a pioneer work in what would come to be called black theology or liberation theology, was *The Politics of God* by Joseph Washington (1967).[77]

Washington's view of the world images on a small scale the dilemmas of progressivism and secularization theory. As a black writer, he is naturally concerned first to look at the situation of his own community, which he sees changed but not necessarily improved in all ways. He perceives the world becoming more "rational," that is, prepared to view matters in scientific (i.e., objectifying and universalizing) categories. Science has disqualified whatever rational bases there were once thought to be for racial inequality or discrimination, such as claims of genetic differences in intelligence or behavior patterns. In its cool light, all human beings are essentially the same and, so to speak, interchangeable. A decline in outmoded "rational" racism has indeed come about.

Well and good, according to Washington, but the upshot has only been a rise in "irrational" racism as humans have nonetheless formed communities of inclusion and exclusion, not least churches, on the basis not of science but of feelings and admittedly nonrational preferences. To be guided by feeling and free choice as well as cold reason is a privilege of being human; it humanizes and can be enriching. But often these racial preferences are founded on stereotypes, such as those of the black as fun-loving half child or as half-savage threat, which come from not knowing the other as real humans, to be neither idealized nor demonized.

Here blacks have an important role, Washington believes. It is their job to be in the middle, as the suffering servant, as a humanizing factor between the dehuman rational and the stereotyping irrational, helping others to make choices that truly humanize rather than diminish both parties. The profoundly human black understanding of the Bible, and the black spiritual together with the life of the black church, provide resources of inestimable richness.

Washington's book suggested another way out of the spiritual crisis of the collapse of progressivism from those of Altizer, Pannenberg, or the countercultural dropouts, and one that was to become increasingly important to one wing of late-twentieth-century religion: the liberationist proclamation of the redemptive role of poor, oppressed, and marginalized people.

For Washington, religion was not so much the way of the visionary looking beyond time or of the theological historicist looking up and down all of human time, but of the suffering redeemer right in the middle of time. This person, as a member of a group in the middle, knows time will neither stop nor self-destruct, and that nothing in it is self-contained. She or he will row down the middle channel of that mighty river for a few miles, singing loudly enough for the other boats to hear, striving to bring them all into closer formation.

In 1967, then, theology was constrained finally to look straight into the eyes of a kaleidoscope world that was more than a residue of metaphysics, or a natural product of progress and secularization. Theology was not yet focused, but it was looking. It knew now it could neither canonize the secular nor reinvent the metaphysical. Some third way had to be located. Perhaps it was to be found in radical visions upstage from history, or in God *and* history, or in a people of God *in* history.

Judaism in the Later Sixties

The American Jewish community participated conspicuously in the Fifties religion "boom," the simultaneous move to the suburbs, and the postwar emphasis on "tolerance," "goodwill," and assimilation of the nation's diverse ethnic groups into an idealized middle-class homogeneity. Indeed, these trends probably meant more to Jews than to most other affected groups. Prewar Jews had been particularly urbanized and subject to "restrictions" in housing, employment, university admissions, and social life. Only nonwhites had been forced to endure as much blatant prejudice, not to mention cruel humor, as they.

As we have noted in connection with country club admissions, some of these changes were slow to come, and some discrimination lasted into the Sixties. But a marked opening in attitude toward Jews on the part of most of the non-Jewish population after 1945 made those years especially rich in change both physical and psychic, as Jews moved in large numbers out of cramped inner cities to expansive new suburbs and contemplated careers with fewer hidden barriers.

Indeed, as though in compensation for past wrongs, and above all for the horrors of Hitler's Holocaust, Jews could often sense a distinctly positive appreciation of them and their heritage by many in gentile America. Enthusiasm for the new state of Israel was widespread and enshrined in popular movies like *Exodus*, Jewish writers like Herman Wouk and Saul Bellow were much read, and expressions of the old-fashioned anti-Semitism, once a staple of everything from radio demogoguery to jokes and slang, were usually not acceptable anywhere outside the lunatic-fringe Right.

(I can recall that the casual anti-Semitic slurs I had heard all of my young life rather abruptly ceased about 1944 and 1945, as the full meaning of the Final Solution was revealed. Thereafter gentiles widely regarded Jews with a strange mixture of guilt and awe, guilt for all the secret sins we knew did not pertain to Nazis alone, awe at the sufferings this people had undergone. The way the state of Israel appeared, in these eventful times, as a miraculous recompense only enhanced the near supernatural mystery in which the Jew was clothed in those years.)

The talk was now of brotherhood, tolerance, goodwill, and dialogue. The new spirit was embodied in February's Brotherhood Week, and in 1962 the book *An American Dialogue* (1960) by Gustave Weigel and Robert McAfee Brown, with an introduction by the Jewish Will Herberg of *Protestant, Catholic, Jew* (1956) fame, won a Brotherhood Week prize.

But by the end of the Sixties, although there was less discrimation against Jews (and Catholics, not to mention Americans of color) than at the outset of the decade, Brotherhood Week was little regarded. Dialogue and interfaith activity, like the National Council of Churches type of ecumenicity, declined in the Sixties. How tolerance changed from rather tepid but high prestige ceremonies in the Fifties to Sixties struggle and came out the other side bloodied but unbowed, and the various ways in which that saga affected American Jews, is a key story of the decade.

To begin with, Jews participated in disproportionate numbers in the civil rights movement, in the counterculture, and in antiwar activity. Although percentages obviously involve subjective assessments of how participation in such fluctuating causes is defined, 30% or so, as compared to just 5% of the population then Jewish, would probably not be misleading. Not a few prominent voices in all these activities, from Allen Ginsberg to the Yippies Abbie Hoffman and Jerry Rubin, were of Jewish background. This participation certainly had roots in longstanding Jewish commitment to social justice, based in turn on Jewish experience of pogroms and persecutions. Even after arriving in the United States, Jews knew firsthand the lot of unempowered immigrants, and what discrimination from the Anglo-Protestant establishment could mean. Theirs was a proud heritage of activity in the labor movement and in the campaigns for reform and civil liberties of the Old Left.

But the deepest roots of Jewish activism undoubtedly lay in the long Jewish tradition of being a people set apart, always a little different, and so able to appreciate and flourish in the role of the marginalized, the cheerful iconoclast, or the outsider with a message. Over against formal or informal universalisms, whether of church or state, Judaism has a way of saying, "Yes, but . . ." If anyone is a stranger in some grand human scheme, the Jewish experience says, it is not truly complete or truly human, whether it is an ostensibly universal religion or a perfect society. If it is a religion of mystical oneness or of a particular plan for salvation, or a social order based on a single monolithic ideology or ethnic identity, and it leaves out Jews as such, Jews rightly say, "Yes, but . . ." We Jews are here, Judaism seems to say, as perennial outsiders to show that human reality is always larger than any map one can make, and the last word has not yet been said.

235

Thus the relative assimilationism embraced by American Judaism in the Fifties and early Sixties was something of an anomaly, though not without predecedent. Being so accepted and so successful, at least on the surface, was both welcome and disturbing to many Jews. Not a few wondered how real this new situation was, how long it would last, and what the cost would be to Jewish identity, questions to which the Sixties would give mixed and sometimes unexpected answers. Further, was there not something important about the Jewish witness that called one instead to be somewhat marginalized, to have the clear-eyed outsider's angle of vision and to identify with the weak and oppressed? Perhaps that is why so many Jewish young people rushed eagerly to the dissident, self-marginalizing yet idealistic roles that became available in the Sixties. In Jewish families as in others the upshot was often the famous generation gap and stormy living-room scenes, but also there were reservoirs of understanding; the anxiety of many parents was based on knowing all too well what it meant to be *involuntarily* marginalized.

Uneasy rumblings arose from Judaism in response to the secular and Death of God theology of the mid-Sixties. That Christian phenomenon permitted much opportunity for Jews to say, "Yes, but . . ." A great deal of the terrain, new to Christians, was familiar to Jews: the this-worldly emphasis on salvation in and through history, the secular city apotheosis of urban life, for liberal Jews the downplaying of the personal God, were congenial themes up to a point. But secularism as a religious system evoked anew an edgy sense that we've seen it all before, and it leaves us out.

Eugene B. Borowitz, writing in *Judaism*, was pained on reading *The Secular City* by Harvey Cox's continual attacks on tribalism and legalism, standard objects of Christian polemic but which understandably remind Jews of polemic against them. Borowitz granted that "much that Cox says about tribalism is in accord with the universalism implicit in Jewish particularism," but as for legalism, "Cox may be anxious to avoid the difficulties of Roman Catholicism, Protestant fundamentalism and proliferating denominations, but where in this world is there, can there be, a city without law?"[1]

More telling, however, is his critique of Thomas Altizer and the liberating Death of God in history. Here Borowitz echoed Richard Rubenstein's comments in *After Auschwitz*, cited earlier. History as the arena of divine revelation and action is very important to Judaism, but to absolutize it, to subordinate individual humanity and even God totally to history, cries out for the Jewish "Yes, but . . ."

Borowitz says that Altizer may be right about the cultural situation, "but what shall a sensitive human being, much less a Jew, say of this boundless affirmation of whatever history brings? How can one not recoil in horror from what twentieth-century history has brought." "It is difficult to believe Altizer means what he says theologically since it necessitates a complete suspension if not negation of the ethical" (87).

Borowitz concludes by asking "what secularization has made it so difficult for us to know: where do we find God in the historical process? In the admission of Red China to the U.N.? In an unconditional cease-fire in Viet Nam? In supporting civilian review boards for the police? In busing children to school? If transcendence is so critical to man, why spend so much energy finding a secular style to speak to him within a profane context?" (93–94).

An important set of questions, and questions to which the Christian secular theologians too often gave only sweeping or enigmatic answers. Over the centuries Jews had frequently felt compelled to say, "Yes, but . . ." to Christian otherworldly salvationism; now that the Christian penchant for universal dogma had shifted to the opposite pole of making all things secular, a different caveat was called for from Judaism.

A complementary note was sounded by Nathan Rotenstreich in "Secularism and Religion in Israel," an article in *Judaism* that made more general remarks on secularity and religion than the title might suggest. "God has not died," Rotenstreich declares. "Nietzsche missed the mark when he proclaimed the death of God. His shafts misfired for many reasons, but for our immediate purpose it suffices to note that he celebrated the death of God as saving mankind by relieving men of responsibility toward God. But without responsibility, salvation cannot be accomplished. . . . Judaism represents man as essentially a responsible creature . . . capable of understand and obeying commandments."[2]

For Jewish experience in the Sixties, as well as for the American Sixties generally, 1967 was a hinge year. But it was so in a very special sense for Jews. The Six-Day War in June indelibly marked American Jewish experience and sense of identity from then on out, in a degree comparable to, but different from, the searing of American consciousness generally by Vietnam.

Thus Vietnam was not the only conflict to stir American feelings in 1967. This was also the year when, with lightning speed and apparent ease, Israel defeated a coalition of much more populous Arab neighbors to secure its safety and acquire occupied territories that have troubled its existence ever since. In Israel a wild euphoria prevailed.

"I can't believe it, I can't believe it" was reportedly on everyone's lips. The Old City of Jerusalem was now Israeli forever, it seemed, as was the Golan Heights, from which Syrian guns had shelled Jewish settlements in the valleys below for years. The Six-Day War lasted from June 5 through June 10 and stood in painful contrast to America's ponderous and apparently interminable effort in Southeast Asia.

All this had a remarkable impact on American Jewish consciousness. Pride in being Jewish soared; posters of the dashing commander Moshe Dayan garbed as Superman sold in the tens of thousands. For American Jews this conflict involving Israel had quite a different aura from Vietnam. According to an article by Arthur Hertzberg in *Commentary*, "The mood of the American Jewish community underwent an abrupt, radical, and possibly permanent change. In general, the immediate reaction of American Jewry to the crisis was far more intense and widespread than anyone could have foreseen." Many Jews were themselves surprised at how deeply they felt Israel's crisis and triumph as they lived through it. Hertzberg wryly noted that "it is ingrained in the American Jewish soul that the correct response to a danger is to give money," and in the period between the closing of the Gulf of Aqaba by the Egyptian leader Gamal Abdel Nasser on May 25 and the Israeli victory of June 10, more than $100 million was realized by the Israel Emergency Fund of the United Jewish Appeal.[3]

More than money was involved, however. Lucy Dawidowicz observed that the impact of the war on young Jews was intense. Accustomed to the atmosphere and ideology of the anti-Vietnam War movement otherwise so pervasive in mid-1967, many "were perplexed and dismayed that the events did not conform to their political notions. . . . Views on pacifism, civil disobedience, resistance to government, and the inherent evil of military might were suddenly questioned. Unlike the confrontation in Vietnam, this was a just war, a war of self-defense against the threat of military genocide."[4]

One young Jewish woman, Nancy Weber, expressed the transformation poignantly in the *Village Voice*:

> I think it must have been this way for many of my generation, that the Israeli-Arab collision was a moment of truth. For the first time in my grown-up life, I really understood what an enemy was. For the first time, I knew what it was to be us against the killers.
>
> Us. Two weeks ago, Israel was they; now Israel is we. I will not intellectualize. I will not say that it is only because Israel was in the right during this brief war as I never felt my own country to be in the wars of my own life-time. I will not intellectualize it; I am Jewish; and the we has to do with more or less than the brotherhood of man, the bond of the good; it is a Jewish we. Something happened. I will

never again be able to talk about how Judaism is only a religion, and isn't it too bad that there has to be such a thing as a Jewish state. I will never again say as I said two years ago: Yes, I feel sympathetic with Israel, but I would feel the same way if France were involved in this kind of crisis. I will never kid myself that we are only the things we choose to be. Roots count.

And I will never again claim to be a pacifist; I will never again say that if I had been an adult during World War II I might have been for non-intervention, or, if a man, been a conscientious objector. I have lost the purity of the un-tested, and when someday my children are very pure with me about how there is no reason for us not to buy a Porsche, I will argue with them the way my parents have had to argue with me: impurely, from the heart.

I was walking along the street listening to a transistor radio when I first heard that the Israelis, the Jews, had reached the Wailing Wall and with guns slung over their shoulders were praying there. No one was watching me, but I wept anyway. Sometimes even the tear-glands know more than the mind.[5]

To grasp the full depths of the significance of the stunning Israeli victory for Jews, it is necessary to recall centuries of politically impotent ghetto existence, centuries of Jews savagely caricatured as weak and cringing, centuries of persecutions and pogroms culminating in the Nazi Holocaust when Jews seemed unable effectively to fight back.

Many pacifistic Jews like Nancy Weber, though appalled by Vietnam, could not help but see their spiritual homeland's relatively "clean" desert triumphs in a very different light from the dirty jungle war on the other side of Asia. Although Jews were disproportionately represented in that antiwar movement (there was even a button that said, "You Don't Have To Be Jewish To Oppose The Vietnam War"), polls found that 99% of American Jews supported Israel's position in its war.

Indeed, in the eyes of a writer like Jacob Neusner, the 1967 victory served to complete the sacred meaning of the Holocaust—to make it part, but now only part, of a "Judaism of Holocaust and Redemption" that has become a "public, civil religion of American Jews."

The extermination of European Jewry could become the Holocaust only on 9 June when, in the aftermath of a remarkable victory, the State of Israel celebrated the return of the people of Israel to the ancient wall of the Temple of Jerusalem. On that day the extermination of European Jewry attained the—if not happy, at least viable—ending that served to transform events into a myth, and to endow a symbol with a single, ineluctable meaning.[6]

The more complicated response of American Christians contributed to the Jewish sense of abandonment by the world that only added to the feeling that, up to victory, the events of Spring 1967 were like the Holocaust *redivivus*. After the war, polls showed that 41 percent of Americans generally felt more sympathy for Israel, 1 percent for the Arabs, and another 40 percent had no strong feelings either way. But most did not want the United States involved, although at the time the Six-Day affair undoubtedly strengthened overall positive American attitudes toward Israel. Conservative American Christians were on the Jewish state's side at least in part because of their association of it with biblical prophecy; they also were inclined to divide the world into good and bad and heartily approved of Judaism's anti-Fascist past and anti-Communist—or at least anti the Communist bloc's Arab clients—present.

Some liberal Christians also could be found backing Israel. The press reported that such leaders as Reinhold Niebuhr, Martin Luther King, and John Bennett—all outspoken Vietnam doves—were counted in. The Committee for a Sane Nuclear Policy (SANE) postponed a Washington rally scheduled for the same day as a pro-Israel Washington rally sponsored by the National Conference of Christians and Jews and major Jewish organizations.

However, the *Christian Century* took an ambivalent position and claimed that, though Edwin Espy, executive secretary of the National Council of Churches, spoke at the June 8 rally for Israel in Washington, his address was incorrectly taken to imply complete NCC support for the Jewish state's militancy. In an "ironic development," the *Century* said, before he could get to the more moderate and even-handed parts of his speech, Espy was drowned out by excitement over news of the United Arab Republic's acceptance of the United Nation's cease-fire demands. The most pro-Israel portions of his remarks were thereby taken for the whole.[7]

Some lines from the uncompleted portion of the speech by Edwin Espy of the National Council of Churches, as subsequently published in the *Christian Century* article, read:

> Our hearts are filled with compassion and concern for the people of Israel and of all the Middle East. Our identification is not of course exclusively with any one community, one belligerent, or one set of national aspirations. . . . Had we been invited to attend a corresponding meeting of the Arab community in the United States we would have been bound by our principles to bring the identical message— the plea for peace with justice and freedom which we derive from our Judeo-Christian heritage. (804)

On the same day, June 8, the National Conference of Catholic Bishops issued a rather noncommittal statement deploring the war and designating June 11 a day of special prayer for peace. Various NCC and other Protestant resolutions, and articles by mainstream Protestants in religious and national journals, tended to be cautious, supporting the U.N. positions, professing to recognize rights and wrongs on both sides, and taking the long view of what would make for peace. They generally granted Israel's position in the immediate cause of the war—the right of access to the Gulf of Aqaba and the Suez Canal by all nations. But they typically contended that Israel's retention of occupied territories and its annexation of the whole of Jerusalem would not prove helpful to peace in the end, and they also held that Israel must accept substantial responsibility for the plight of Palestinian refugees.

Such perhaps well-meaning but distanced sentiments, displaying a cool evenhandedness that hardly fit the Jewish mood of the hour, raised the hackles of Jews and of Israel's stronger Christian supporters. To them, far more important than the long view was their firm conviction that a genocidal holocaust before the end of June would have been the fate of Israel's Jews had they lost the brief war, and that only putting Israel in a better strategic position would keep the horror from happening in the future. Some spoke of a "silence in the churches" like that of the Nazi era.[8]

Such perceptions of Christian sentiment as these did harm to Jewish-Christian relations. Goodwill and brotherhood would not for a long time be what they had once been. Many Jewish leaders, generalizing under the pressures of that superheated summer, began to speak as though Christians had no real concern for Israel's survival, and their excessively qualified response to Israel's hour of desperate crisis only confirmed Judaism's deepest suspicions.

Rabbi Balfour Brickner, director of the Commission on Interfaith Activities of the Central Conference of American Rabbis, charged that the "organized Church" seemed to regard the Middle East crisis as only a "political issue," though "the survival of the Jewish people" was far more than that. Lucy Dawidowicz voiced the opinion that the reason the NCC was "so unfeeling with regard to Israel's survival and so carping in its criticism of Israel" was that a number of churches had "vested interests" in the area and a pro-Arab bias based on many years of missionary activity in Arab lands.[9]

Some Christian leaders reponded angrily to such charges. Msgr. George G. Higgins, secretary to the Commission for Catholic-Jewish Relations of the Bishops' Committee for Ecumenical and Interreligious Affairs, alleged that the rabbis' "criticism of the Catholic Church in the United States, whether they realize it or not, is a form of ecumenical or interreligious blackmail." Henry P. Van Dusen, past president of Union Theological Seminary, wrote in the *New York Times* of July 7 that "All persons who seek to view the Middle East problem with honesty and objectivity stand aghast at Israel's onslaught, the most violent, ruthless (and successful) aggression since Hitler's blitzkrieg across Western Europe in the summer of 1940, aiming not at victory but at annihilation"—a breathtakingly insensitive comparison hardly likely to improve the situation, and one that drew condemnation from Christian as well as Jewish readers.[10] In response to this and other Christian critics of Israel, A. Roy and Alice L. Eckhardt wrote in the *Christian Century*, "Whenever original Israel is assailed, certain suppressed, macabre elements in the Christian soul are stirred to sympathy with the assailants. It is difficult to account in any other way for the vehemence and mendacity of some of the current Christian attacks upon Israel."[11]

But for many Jews, the shock of what they viewed as Christian indifference ranked only a little behind the positive impact of the sudden and surprising victory. Some felt there was no more point in Christian-Jewish dialogue; others thought the inadequacy of Christian understanding of the religious meaning of Israel, particularly Jerusalem, to Jews called for intensified dialogue. But the prevailing mood, though sometimes publicly understated, was one of a combined new Jewish confidence in themselves and disillusionment with the outside world that made for a fresh look at the Jewish heritage and community as self-sustaining. As the previously cited remarks of Jacob Neusner may have suggested, 1967 brought a renewal of Jewish interest in the Holocaust, which now seemed to parallel the crisis Israel went through that spring before the Six Days, and which seemed finally redeemed by the arrival of Israeli troops at the temple wall in Jerusalem. Holocaust memorials and commemorations sprang up through the Jewish world and Holocaust studies multiplied after 1967, to achieve what has been called a Jewish "civil religion" of Holocaust and redemption, the latter in the form of the victorious state of Israel. Israel's triumph finally made the unimaginable horror of the Nazi years meaningful.

What then of Sixties Jews in the New Left as these paradigms shifted? Concomitant with the Six-Day War, and partially but not entirely related to it, were other forces that intersected at several angles with the New Left (and counterculture) agenda: the beginnings of tragic alienation between Jewish and African Americans, the beginnings of Jewish feminism, the rediscovery of Jewish traditionalism and mysticism.

Christians, Jews, and secularists who identified with the New Left, including its sympathy for Third World revolution, were swayed, or in some cases simpy confused, by the anti-Israel statements of such of its heroes as Fidel Castro, Ho Chi Minh, Nasser himself, many African statesmen, and black power leaders like Stokely Carmichael of SNCC at home. Not for the the first or last time, the puzzle as to whether the state of Israel is liberationist model or bane was acutely presented. Some Jews became, perhaps for the first time, critical of the Left; a smaller number highly committed to radicalism became all the more alienated from mainstream Judaism.

The pain was not seldom intense, both for leftist Jews and for others in the Jewish community. Marshall Sklare, for example, claimed that most New Left Jews were East Europeans rather than "old-line German Jews" in background and added, "That an American Christian might support the Arab cause is understandable to many Jews; that a Jew of East European origin could do so is inexplicable."[12] Yet it happened.

An article by Michael P. Lerner, "Jewish New Leftism at Berkeley," reflected the bitter conflict the New Left had by now created in Jewish life: conflict between traditional forms of Jewish identity and traditional Jewish support for liberal, liberationist ideals; tension between Israeli and Third World concerns—all made more acute by the violent swings of the Sixties, by civil rights, Vietnam, and the Six-Day War. The Berkeley New Left Jews, Lerner stated, were both sufficiently disdainful of general American culture that they opposed Jewish assimilation, and sufficiently mistrustful of the U.S. government that they condemned Zionists as "out-and-out tools of the U.S. State Department."[13]

Despite the Six-Day War and New Left crises, the concern of Jewish theological students over Vietnam was maintained and capable of producing profound moral debate. In March 1969 a student at the Jewish Theological Seminary of America in New York refused to accept induction. A number of other students signed a letter of support for him at the time of his arraignment, stating that they affirmed his "right to refuse to be forced to kill" and that they would spend a special day in prayer and study as an expression of this solidarity. One further wrote:

> The night before was one of the most momentous for many of us. . . . For a rabbinical student to sign a petition for a protest that will take place on Seminary grounds is no simple matter. For many of us it was a night of soul-searching. Will we risk ourselves in the support of a fellow Jew? Can we support his right to refuse to be forced to kill? Do we concede and encourage a Jew to live up to his conscience

even though we will support a milhemet mitzvah, i.e. a war enjoined by the Torah? In the three years that I have lived in the Seminary dormitory I had not witnessed such serious grappling with such a basic human issue. Still, by 1 a.m. over half the dormitory residents had signed, with many to follow the next morning.[14]

Despite the qualification, it is clear that even after June 1967 for many Jews the issue of pacifism was by no means a simple one, and willingness to stand with the moral outsider remained.

But it must be recognized that, while probably most Jews, especially the young, changed attitudes on some matters amid the turmoil of the Sixties, not all were thoroughly "radicalized"; many found ways to nuance responses and to distinguish between theory and practice. A 1969–1971 survey of young and adult Reform Jews found that for them the generation gap lay mainly in the areas of affirming social activism and rejecting Jewish exclusivism by the young. The latter were much more likely than their elders to approve of intermarriage and to believe that rabbis should take a stand on social issues. They thought being versed in Jewish history and culture, and attending weekly services, was less important than did adults. But the actions of the younger cohort were likely to be more moderate than their attitudes; for example, while accepting intermarriage, many also said they themselves were not likely to marry outside Judaism. The gap was perhaps more attudinal and ideological than behavioral in many cases.[15]

In a 1967 article, "The Rabbi on Campus," Richard J. Israel, chaplain to Jewish students at Yale, remarked that the "only religious rebellion" he encountered was students rebelling *toward* tradition and away from the "oppressive religious conventionalism of their parents."[16]

Indeed, after the pivotal year 1967 came a period of Jewish revival: of pride in Jewish ethnic identity and interest in study of it. The Holocaust itself recovered as a field of inquiry, for reasons already suggested, and Orthodoxy underwent something of a renaissance. There was fresh inquiry into connections between Judaism and the new spirituality of the counterculture, showcased in an upsurge of interest in Jewish mysticism, kabbala, and such Jewish communitarian ways of life as in the Israeli kibbutzim.

These concerns may have had roots in the considerable Jewish participation in the counterculture, but they embraced the discovery that Judaism itself was a counterculture of very long standing, with its own mystical and magical strands as potent as any imported from Tibet or conjured up in the Haight-Ashbury. Judaism, because of things that started around 1967, emerged from the Sixties more spiritual (for some), more confident, and yet also more traditionalist and wary of complete assimilation, than before.

None of this was without conflict and pain. I recall that once in those years I was asked to speak at a conference of Reform rabbis as a last-minute replacement for a distinguished philosopher of Jewish background who had become ill. The topic was the appeal of Eastern and esoteric spirituality for the young and was certainly related to the concern of these rabbis over the number of young people who were leaving their temples to explore other pastures. Though not Jewish myself, I tried to show what dimensions of human spirituality were widely perceived, at least, as better met by these alternatives than by conventional Western religion, and to suggest there were resources in Jewish mysticism, kabbalistic and hasidic, that might be recovered to answer to them as well as do the more exotic imports. I found some acceptance, but also sharp resistance from rabbis who strongly associated liberal, modernist Reform Judaism with the sort of ethical, scientific humanism to which any kabbalism or mysticism is automatically categorized as medieval, superstitious, and unhealthy.

Some change was on the way, however, as Judaism (like Christianity) moved toward the level playing field of the postmodernist world in the Sixties. One token of this is a 1969 book by a Reform rabbi, Herbert Weiner, *9¹/₂ Mystics: The Kabbala Today*.[17] This work, which has long been a personal favorite of mine, details in appealing narrative the author's exploration of the intricate and partly esoteric world of Jewish mysticism, including its manifestations in New York and Israel in the Sixties. Writing as a curious insider/outsider (he was himself the half-mystic), Weiner built on the labors of such monumental scholars and spiritual figures as Gershom Scholem, Martin Buber, and Rabbi Isaac Kook. He made the mysteries of the kabbalistic tree and the hasidic dance come alive for a new generation of Jews who had already been shaken out of old presuppositions by the Six-Day War and, many of them, the psychedelic revolution. Weiner happened to be in Jerusalem studying mysticism at the moment of the Six-Day War. He ends *9¹/₂ Mystics* with an account of the conflict and triumph from his perspective, and also with a discussion of the provocative ideas left him by an encounter with Timothy Leary.

Along with the post-1967 Jewish euphoria and reconsideration came a gradual and quiet, but eventually important, withdrawal by many Jews from the radical political and cultural frontlines of the Sixties. One result was growing estrangement, despite considerable support for the civil rights movement by Jews, between Jews and blacks as the Sixties advanced and positions became more polarized.[18]

All this required a fair amount of rethinking of Jewish life at the practical as well as the theoretical level. This is reflected in an interesting 1969 article by Richard N. Levy, "The Reform Synagogue: Plight and Possibility." Levy begins by noting that "the American Reform Synagogue is in trouble. It has generally defaulted on all three of its traditional functions—as a house of prayer (Bet Tefilah); as a house of study (Bet Midrash), and as a house of meeting (Bet Knesset)." Few Reform synagogues could be found where these are major projects, Levy contended, beyond the minimal concerns of Sabbath services and the occasional social affair. They have failed for their largely middle-class constituency, and even more for the majority of Jewish intellectuals, whether students or adults, who take their Jewishness seriously but want to explore it in a creative way with like-minded others.[19]

Levy called for a different sort of synagogue, in which worship could be experimental and linked creatively with study. He suggested that prayers could be interrupted for dialogue on their meaning, and paintings and sculptures by members of the group could be employed to help interpret texts under discussion. It all sounds remarkably like the new worship and liturgical experiments then going on in Christian churches. As for community meetings, he argues that this function could also be creative and combined with traditional Jewish social concerns. There could be coffeehouses, peace programs, sessions to meet neighborhood needs, plans made to "infiltrate" the environs to find out what they are. As it is, Jewish protests against the Vietnam War seem to be limited mainly to sermons and committees, with no action on the community level.

A response to concerns of this sort was the Chavurat movement, a Judaism of small, informal groups of Jewish seekers emphasizing the need of each to find and follow an individual spiritual path, while valuing the opportunity to meet to share knowledge and experience. A small minority of Chavurat members live communally, but the sense of being a part of a community of shared lives as well as ideas is important. Although there were earlier attempts, and similar groups in Reconstructionist Judaism, Chavurat Shalom, established in Massachusetts in 1968 by several young rabbis and a number of graduate students attending Boston area universities, became a model. Bernard Reisman writes that "they came together as dissidents, alienated from the prevalent practices of their society. They felt estranged from American society, as exemplified by the Vietnam war and mass culture, and from the Jewish community, as exemplified by what they considered to be its inauthentic, bureaucratic institutions."[20] But this important, characteristically Sixties response did not solve all the problems of Judaism's place in a changing land.

Milton Himmelfarb, in a *Commentary* article, "Relevance in the Synagogue," pointed to such Christian phenomena as "the far-out nuns and priests, the new-morality and secular city theologians, the community activism of the mainline Protestant denominations, the traditional peace and service activities of the Quakers," and acknowledged that "in image, at least, and probably also to some extent in deed, the synagogue is substantially to the rear of the churches in these matters." But Himmelfarb pointed out one important relevant fact: the society in which this activity was taking place, while secular and subject to thorough separation of church and state, was also a Christian society.[21] And it was becoming increasingly clear to Jews that their role in it, even—or especially—in the midst of the Sixties turmoil, was not, could not, should not be the same as that of Christian churches. For example, what about the question of identification?

Levy, in connection with social action, had also discussed the Jewish identity problem in regard to black nationalism. The desire of Jews to advance the cause of blacks is frustrated by a sort of structural alienation. We are not black, he says, we are not poor, we are not even Christian; we often feel totally estranged from those we would help.[22]

Race was a serious matter of Jewish concern in the late Sixties. Many Jews, like Levy, felt frustrated and unappreciated in connection with their important role in the civil rights movement; at the same time, they could not help but wonder how far it, and especially the new black militancy, really served Jewish interests. In the northern cities, blacks were moving into areas Jews had often just left for the suburbs, but where they continued to operate as landlords and shopkeepers. This relationship was bound to incite tension, and anti-Semitic rhetoric could be heard in the black community. Some blacks wanted a scapegoat for their continuing problems, and the choice of Jews for that role by a few was no doubt abetted by the new black militancy and its ideological links to Third World circles in which the Palestinian cause was perceived as liberationist. Yet, although strains arose, the major black-Jewish confrontation many feared never occurred.[23]

Nonetheless, the situation seemed to many Jews to call for a reassessment of traditional attitudes and alignments. Earl Raab, in an article in *Commentary* that attracted considerable attention, "The Black Revolution and the Jewish Question," called for an "inward turning" in the Jewish community, and a new understanding that in a pluralistic society it is entirely appropriate for each community, on the political level, to look after its own interests. The old half-joking question,

"Is it good for the Jews?" can properly be asked seriously by Jews in connection with several important current questions, including black militancy and the situation of Jews in the Soviet Union, as they evaluate their relationship to them. Brotherhood, dialogue, and goodwill, hallmarks of what Raab calls the "Golden Age" that set in just after World War II, have their place, but only in the context of a sober understanding of power and the interests of one's own group.[24] The journal *Commentary* came to be a leading voice for this reassessment, as somewhat later the journal *Tikkun* advocated a continuation of a liberal, Sixties-type peace-and-social-justice Jewish agenda.

All in all, the changes that American Judaism underwent between 1960 and 1970, though perhaps less traumatic than those experienced by Roman Catholicism, were probably on the same scale as those Protestantism underwent. But they were different changes. Protestant churches tended to lose something of traditional ethnic and denominational identities, picturing themselves either as parts—ideally as servants—of a larger society, or as collections of spiritually questing individuals. Jews, on the other hand, came out of the Sixties often more ready to affirm an ethnic and cultic identity that had been there all along. But in a broader sense that development was part of something else that had been happening in American society: rejection of the premature melting-pot leveling of the brotherhood era, and realignment of that society into a more complex and radical pluralism than had been known before. The new complexity is reflected in innumerable details, from corporate cultures to new religious movements to ethnic power. In this mosaic Jews were an important and distinctive light.[25]

Chapter 5

1968–1970:
The Bitter Years

But some there are who deem themselves most free
When they within this gross and visible sphere
Chain down the winged thought, scoffing ascent,
Proud in their meanness . . .
Others, more wild
With complex interests weaving human fates,
Evolve the process of eternal good

And what if some rebellious, o'er dark realms
Arrogate power? yet these train up to God,
And on the rude eye, unconfirmed for day,
Flash meteor-lights better than total gloom.
Coleridge, "The Destiny of Nations"

Opening Vistas

The year 1968 was marked by the traumatic assassinations of Martin Luther King and Robert Kennedy. It was the year of dreadful events at the Democratic convention in Chicago, and of the ultimate election victory of Richard Nixon. With 1969 came hope of national reconciliation under Nixon, then profound disillusionment as his rhetoric and that of his vice-president, Spiro Agnew, turned bitter and taunting against the antiwar "radicals," and the year ended with huge moratorium demonstrations against the war. This was also the year of the moon landing, seen as a triumph of Middle American values, and of Woodstock, that last quasi-legitimating festival of the youth counterculture. The 1969–1970 academic year was marked by unprecedented campus demonstrations and takeovers, mostly over antiwar and black power issues. The first half of 1970 meant more divisiveness, culminating in the late April Cambodian "incursion," the Kent State and Jackson State shootings of student protesters, and the tremendous May demonstrations, which seemed to exhaust the Sixties spirit and gave way to the more inward, disillusioned mood of the Watergate decade.

By 1968, then, one world was well-nigh dead, another struggling to be born. It was not a time of revolution. But the specter of revolution haunted the nation, unrealistic as that hope or fear may have been, though the "revolutionary situation" some detected was only the surface symptom of crisis and break in another kind of fever. Yet the patient was in serious condition, no doubt about it. With no world in place, 1968–1969 was a time between dreams, so a time of horizonless vision.

A wedge-moment of unblinkered perception can be exhilarating, but it also lets slip the terror of seeing even a single shard of reality bare, without myth or science or world to put it in. As a *Christian Century* editorial on the occasion of Robert F. Kennedy's assassination put it, "Future generations may stand in awe of how much the citizens of the 1960s were able to absorb as they passed through a shift of epochs, daily benumbed and battered by signs too magnificent to comprehend or too terrifying to forget."[1]

Indeed, few mortals can long endure so much light. The pressure is on to fit another world, any world, into the slots of the firmament as soon as possible. The revolutionary spirit of the late Sixties itself was probably the product of a somber realization that the Sixties dream was in extreme jeopardy and would only be realized by such bravado means—and that without revolution, counterreformation was likely to set in.

Yet because of this rare opening, events in the late Sixties took on a dramatic, mythological quality. The Johnsonian abdication, the assassinations and other disasters, the festive pilgrimage comedy of Woodstock, the great Armageddon gathering of all the protest tribes in fall and spring, the abrupt ending of the enchantment—all had the wondrous overtones of the Shakespearean stage, or even of a Last Days scenario over which the Director unexpectedly cried "Cut!" in mid-1970.

Rather than chronicle the late-Sixties American experience, this chapter will emphasize its mythic dimension. The political-social story has been told many times. For us the main point is that by 1968 religion as an institution was no longer leading as it had in the glorious days of King and the civil rights movement, or when Vatican II and novel secular theologies charged the spiritual air. But, as has sometimes been the case in human history, the times were religious even if the church was less conspicuous than a few years before.

Key Books

An article by Dale W. Brown in the *Christian Century* in November 1968, "The New Theological Radical," provides an interesting slant on developments. Citing an article by Richard Shaull, Brown speaks of a "shift from theological anthropology to a theology of messianism. This means that the new theological radical is more concerned about what it was that enabled the early Christians to turn the world upside down than about building bridges to secular philosophies." Probably speaking out of his own background in the Church of the Brethren with its ultimately "radical reformation" sources and style, the author goes on to write of "another mood of the new radicalism" suggested by the Niebuhrian phrase, "moral man and immoral society." This judgment, that society can be immoral, "represents a shift from concentration on building the great society to concentration on challenging the sick society."[2]

Brown speaks of the antidraft movement in this connection, implying that a theological shift parallels the social shift from the Great Society optimism of circa 1965 to the pathology of a 1968 society sickened by assassinations and Vietnam. The "radical" implication is clear and is rather different from what radical meant to some secular theology and servant-church people in that earlier year. Then radicalism inspired people to set aside transcendent theology and identify with the world; in 1968, as it had earlier for Mennonite, Anabaptist, and Quaker radical reformers, it meant recovering a transcendent standpoint from which the sin of the social world could be judged and its ways turned upside down. The church's role was to challenge, not to adapt.

Nonetheless, the church by 1968 was not challenging the world from the head of history's parade in the way it had in the palmy days of civil rights and the secular city. Then civil rights had been commanded by King and others of religious-pacifist bent and the antiwar movement led by Muste and the CALCAV group. The newsmaking events of Vatican II, sensational stories about the death of God, and the new ministerial world of the servant church had made religion seem a major player in a time of tumultuous change. The church expressed itself, as Gibson Winter had put it in *The New Creation as Metropolis*, not in individual piety that only subverted the gospel in Metropolis, but in "the engagement of the Church with the world."

But by early 1968 the church's engagement with the world seemed to be missing some strokes, and in any case religion was not the whole show. Jews had been disproportionately represented in the civil rights and antiwar movements; some of that enthusiasm had been lost through the alienation of segments of Judaism from mainstream, activist Christianity over the 1967 Six-Day War. Moves back toward spirituality in the old sense of individual piety or strong communal identification could be detected in both traditions. Muste and King were gone, civil

251

rights had become black power, and the antiwar movement—the moratorium and the Mobe—was more campus- than church-based and becoming ominously violent-radical on the fringes.

Both movements, civil rights and antiwar, had their ultimate roots in the radical peace-church tradition in America, A. J. Muste being at least the symbolic grandfather of both. But they had spread out from that seedbed to liberal Protestantism, Catholicism, and Judaism generally, on the way picking up enthusastic support from secular Old Left types, and thence (via groups like the SDS) connecting with the student and finally the secular world, where they now mainly lodged.

In somewhat the same way, as late as 1967 psychedelia and the counterculture were perceived by many as spiritual and visionary, however ominous the shadows lurking in their darker corners. By 1968 and 1969 that perception was definitely eroding as hippie crime and drug abuse drew more and more attention. Any remaining sympathy for the culture of the dropouts was shattered for many by the murders of the actress Sharon Tate, and later of Rosemary LaBianca, in August 1969; the crimes, apparently motivated by rebellion and twisted spirituality, were committed by Charles Manson and his tribe, who had crawled out of that drug-laden counterculture into the headlines.

By 1969–1970, then, Dale Brown's new Christian messianism against the establishment as a ministerial strategy seemed already one of those ideas that had flourished best before it was named. But it is significant that it was now being named—for while professional, institutional religion was no longer in the lead by 1968, on all sides religious *language* appeared the only tongue equal to the momentous moods and awesome happenings of those years. Not only messianism, but words like *charisma, apocalyptic, communion,* and *martyrdom* were heard or read almost more often on the street than in the secularized churches, and people talked about the counterculture's rediscovery of what might be called spontaneous traditionalism and transcendence. An important theme redolent of religous mysticism and eschatology was the negation of history, as we will see.

The search for a new way to be religious, in a way that went beyond both mid-decade secularism and traditionalist transcendence, was advanced in Michael Novak's *A Theology for Radical Politics.*[3] That book is interesting because the writer (a Catholic who here sounds like a rather alienated one) sees the task in a very different way from the perfectionist sectarianism behind Dale Brown's vision. The essay begins with a discussion of the current situation. The New Left people, Novak says with obvious sympathy, began in moral outrage and desperately sought a way to extract themselves from the system, and then to revolutionize it. They rightly yearn for fairness, for utopia, for love.

But though they may strive to be something like Albert Camus's "secular saint," they often fall down, because there is a dimension of depth they lack. Without that depth, they often end up arguing and parading their moral excellence like any other sect, no different from the *odium theologicum*[4] of the orthodox. "It is as difficult to be a secular saint as any other kind of saint" (51). Secular saints need to be made aware that no revolution can truly bear good fruits unless it starts all the way back at the beginning, and that means with the ultimate human question, "Who am I?" the question that links the human with the spiritual. Novak ends the book by saying, "The revolution is in the human spirit, or not at all" (128).

Because a real revolutionary ethic must begin at the beginning and not somewhere later along the line, the true enemy in Novak's eyes is history—the idea of historical drama, the notion of a call to humanity to remake the environment and exercise dominion over nature, culminating in seeing the historical figure of Jesus Christ as the sole source and standard of meaning in historical time. The latter gospel is intolerably narrow and parochial in Novak's view, and the concomitant idea of God as judge intolerably repressive.

Closely following Camus in *The Rebel*, Novak rejects both American pragmatism (because it seeks to make changes only within an accepted system) and "German ideology" (which Camus claimed was directed toward action as conquest rather than a "process of perfection"). The alternative is a return to nature—to a natural "Mediterranean" religion full of sun, the beauty of Earth, and the acceptance of nudity and biological life, including healthy sexuality.

This life harmonizes with the natural life of the universe and so has a quite different rhythm from history and the conquest-of-nature ideal. It is geared toward organic growth leading to a sort of finite perfection in each individual, and finally—going past "the myth of the objective observer"—it lurches toward a realization of the mystical identity of each soul with God. This oneness is expressed in the Upanishads' *Tat tvam asi*, "That art Thou." This is real religion. The same can be realized within Christianity and the use of its spiritual and liturgical traditions. Novak cites with particular appreciation Teilhard de Chardin. But the object of attachment is God, not the tradition. "Human first, Christian second," he says (112).

Novak accepts Marcuse's criticism of the technological society as totalitarian, masquerading as freedom through its fulfillment of false needs and its creation of false consciousness. But he rejects Marx, as he does Harvey Cox's secular city; the answer is not Marxist or secular but inward. It is here, not in some historical dialectic, that true revolution must commence, and its goal seems to be finally not another stage of history but the radical reversal of all history.

We appear now, in Novak's 1969 theology, to be at a stage where the secular idols of the mid-Sixties are shown to have feet of clay. Now the drive is on toward a recovery of the sacred, a reenchantment of the world like that sought by the spiritual counterculture, that would allow one to criticize and challenge the secular world even more thoroughly than could the New Left, and to reform it by pruning it back to its roots in soil and soul. The upshot has clear rapport with the incoming postmodernist mood. Like postmodernism's ultracritical deconstructionism, Novak's program appears to have a self-defeating ultimacy about it. The dreams and ideals of both are so utopian as to stifle much zeal for working toward day-by-day or year-by-year reforms on a pragmatic level.

A Theology for Radical Politics is covertly antiradical on the political level, whatever it may be on the theological. Coming out of late-Sixties burnout and despair, it strives to recover the original dream through a return to its original sources. But Novak's most radical book perhaps loses that primal vision by appeal to angelism beyond real human capacity, saying in effect, "If we can't have all this and heaven too, nothing is worth it." Revolutions may be made by persons of such passion, but they are not kept by them. Perhaps, in some convoluted way, here lie the sources of the neoconservatism for which Novak would later be celebrated, though at this point its face is well-concealed behind the radical gloss of *A Theology for Radical Politics*.

A comparable perspective is achieved, though with a very different language and conceptual framework, in a 1970 book (like Novak's, drawn from ca. 1967 lectures) by Thomas J. J. Altizer, *The Descent into Hell*.[5] The famous, or notorious, Death of God theologian here outlines his position as clearly and concisely as anywhere. The subtitle says much about it: *A Study of the Radical Reversal of the Christian Consciousness*. For Altizer, as for Novak and others of that *kairos*, the word *radical* is positive and definitive. The argument is so radically, one might say wildly, dialectic that the swing of dialectical categories becomes abstract and total. From Altizer's angle of vision, thesis and antithesis utterly determine what is happening in history, appearances notwithstanding.

Picking up another New Left term, Altizer says that we are in a "revolutionary situation," though characteristically meaning it not politically but religiously. A revolutionary situation is one in which established forms are closed to the future, and this he says is the situation of Christianity in the modern world. The need therefore is for an eschatological reversal of that dismal state. "A truly eschatological future, so far from being a culmination or organic fulfillment of the past, can become manifest and real only by shattering or bringing to a final end everything which is rooted in the past" (47). This means a reversal of Christian focus on heaven in favor of earth, negating God in favor of the death of God, and focusing on humankind represented by the radical Christ, so that the darkness of hell—the present secular world—is illumined by Christ and becomes heaven as well as hell. Just as the first appearance of Christ and the kingdom of God meant a radical reversal of religion from the transcendent God to God as Christ in this world, the Word become flesh, so the present revolutionary/ eschatological moment connotes the negation of God altogether so that the world becomes entirely secular but secretly sacred, hell without and heaven within, and death is one with life.

Altizer appears to be trying to make the increasingly sterile "revolutionary situation" in the America around him into something more religious than political; perhaps on that level it could still manage to bring off a dialectical reversal. But to do so requires that secular saints acquire a third eye and be able to perceive inward as well as social realities. Both Novak and Altizer, in these books, remain formally committed to the objectives of the secular gospel but subtly modify it so that the sacred canopies of nature, or even the wedding canopies of the marriage of heaven and hell, overshadow secularity—though seeable only by those who have eyes to see. But by making ultimate truth esoteric they also make it timeless (despite Altizer's undated talk of apocalypses and eschatons), and by making it timeless they detach it from the streets and leave the world as it is. And so it is in the early decades of postmodernism. In the modern world, at least trains and revolutions were clear-cut visible things that ran on schedule; now they are something else.

Another interesting title is John S. Dunne's *A Search for God in Time and Memory.* As is the case with most of Dunne's books (*The City of the Gods, The Way of All the Earth*), the superscription is a bit grander than what the book actually delivers.[6] The fresh autobiography-based theology of Augustinian scope and depth hinted at by the title is, in my view at least, never quite achieved. But I would like to work for a moment with Dunne's title because I think it contributes something to grasping the years of its provenance. One of Dunne's best paragraphs begins like this:

The modern life story, the story of appropriation, especially as it is told by Descartes and Hegel, is like the course of a recovery from sickness. It is a process in which a sickness is induced to destroy itself, as in fever therapy, and thus bring about health. The sickness is alienation, estrangement from oneself, from one's life, from reality. . . . The fever therapy lies in this, that doubt carried to the limit will end in the doubt of doubt, despair likewise will end in the despair of despair. It is as though disillusionment were to end at last in a disillusionment with disillusionment itself. (215)

The picture is clear. God is to be searched for in Shakespeare's "dark backward and abysm of time," in memories of childhood, perhaps, when earth seemed brighter and more intense of both pain and joy than after the world grew gray, or of youth when love and hope were fresh. God, or something we are prepared to call by that name, may give light only on the farther shore of doubt or desperation, or only after the exploration of disillusionment down to its darkest abyssal plains. Ultimate meaning is not something cranked up through reasoning, or known only through arbitrary, "straight-down" revelation, but more subtly by reflection on one's own life story.

How does Dunne's search fold into the late Sixties? First, in this *kairos* one finds, as did Novak, a passionate desire to deny history as significant story. I recall teaching in about 1969 an undergraduate history of religions course in which, when the students selected research topics, I noted that virtually all the projected papers were either about prehistoric religion or contemporary religious experience —nothing in between. I commented on this and was told in no uncertain terms, "We don't like history." It was, in the expression of the day, "not relevant." We need spiritually either to live in the present, or to go back to the beginning and start all over again.

So Novak had apparently heard also from his students at Stanford. But we human beings nonetheless need stories telling us why we are who we are. If the historical grand narrative is to be denied, what is there to fall back on but one's personal narrative? It was, therefore, an hour for personal stories: of how one was radicalized, what kind of psychedelic experiences one had, what life was like in the counterculture or the movement. Most of the memorable books stemming from those times that I will be citing are fundamentally autobiography, including the telegraphed messages of Yippies like Abbie Hoffman and Jerry Rubin.

It was much the same on the other side, in the much-heralded resurgent rise of Middle America. Its inhabitants did not come to their vision of America through reason or revelation either, so much as through a search of the times and the memories accessible to them.

They had known the depression, the war, the affluent society of the Fifties. They had knotted with less regret than others the cords of family relations and the bonds of rural town and suburbanity. If they idealized, that is what time and memory always do.

A popular and much-discussed book in those years was Albert Camus's *The Rebel*, already mentioned in connection with Novak's work.[7] In that essay, among much else, the great French existentialist novelist outlined four stages of "metaphysical rebellion," which can be concretized in "historical" political rebellion as well as in art and letters. They are dandyism, rejection of salvation, absolute affirmation, and nihilism. It is remarkable how well these stages interpret the Sixties political-cultural rebellion culminating in 1968–1969.

Dandyism is the preliminary stage, in which the rebel portrays his alienation by distinctive and self-admiring dress and life-style. "The dandy is, by occupation, always in opposition. He can exist only by defiance." His slogan is, says Camus quoting Baudelaire, "To live and die before a mirror" (47). Clearly dandyism represents the mod counterculture in its sartorial phase, in its 1967 Haight-Ashbury high.

But the rejection of salvation might be said to be the late-Sixties turning of the civil rights and antiwar movements from the spiritual, pacifistic nonviolence of the days when most of the leaders had "The Reverend" before their names, to this-worldly black power and the revolutionary mood epitomized by the Weatherman. The 1968 assassinations of King and Kennedy, and the Chicago upheaval, amounted to the assassination of the Holy Ghost. Perfectionist politics changed to demonology, satanizing adversaries and attaining ends not by the means that lead to salvation but "by any means necessary."

The affirmation of any means entails absolute affirmation. As Nietzsche realized, denying God can free one to deliver the world. In the process it frees one from bondage to good and evil, truth and falsehood, in sorting out one's means. The Yippies carried preliminary dandyism to its apex and—because words were for them jokes designed to save the world—issued the most absurd threats in the course of "revolution for the hell of it." The Weatherman with their bombings carried affirmation of revolutionary justice, as they interpreted it, beyond good and evil to the point of dehumanizing both their opponents and themselves in a world of political opposition without moral opposites.

But if one is acting out of a kind of affirmation that is based not on the ordinary humanizing center of judgment but only on a sense of transcendent mission, one is in effect acting out a part, playing a role. One has a strong sense of the late Sixties becoming theater on all sides, life lived before a mirror.

This is the final stage: nihilism, destruction for the sake of total renewal, something one instinctively realizes can only be done as theater. Bakunin, the Russian prophet of nihilism, intoned, "The passion for destruction is a creative passion," and so it was for some in America, as on the streets of Paris and elsewhere, about 1969. Camus spoke of Marx as a "prophet of justice without mercy." All this leads one to reminisce about themes borrowed from the cosmic stage drama of religious apocalyptic.

Nihilism is an unstable state, however. Bakunin notwithstanding, destruction of itself creates nothing but empty space. In that vacant air new dream castles can be built, or the old can reassert itself as lowering clouds. The faint odor of nihilism America inhaled around 1969 was mingled with reassertions of stability proffered by perfumers from the other side of the street, the alchemists of "Middle America" and of evangelical religion.

The conservative concoction they mixed at the very end of the Sixties was laced with nostalgia. It was not the old Victorian fragrance straight, however, but a synthesis of tradition and Sixties values. Most advocates of the old did not really expect to go back to the racial world of the 1950s or to pursue total victory in Vietnam. But their rhetoric, voiced by the likes of Spiro Agnew, presented itself as antithesis to the endgame of the radical Sixties. Deep called to deep, extreme to extreme, and the Sixties awakening blinked.

Harvey Cox came out in 1969 with *The Feast of Fools*, a rather different book from his *Secular City*.[8] Cox now celebrated the festive, playful aspects of religion. Features of festivity are described as "excess," "celebrative affirmation," and "juxtaposition." The festival must display sharp *contrast* with "everyday life"; it must be exceptional. (These features may be compared formally with those of *The Rebel* and the rebellious Weatherman, whose bombings certainly displayed excess, totalistic affirmation of their nihilistic mood, and contrast with ordinariness. But the means of expression in the festival is, needless to say, something else.)

The loss of festivity in the postmedieval and post-Reformation world, Cox insisted, has resulted in a diminishing of the wholeness of life. Compared to *The Secular City*, the tone of this book is postmodernism rather than modernism. Yet it is also a book of the late-Sixties moment of high-speed transition between the two, a moment between worlds reflected in the mood of negating all history. Cox cites Norman O. Brown's then fashionable view of history as "a cruel burden of repression." Brown followed Freud's contention that repression is the price of civilization, but he chafed under that repression rather than accepting it philosophically as did the father of psy-choanalysis—like many another late-Sixties person, he was ready to rebel.

Cox does not, like the early surrealists, say "Burn the Louvre!" Instead of embracing that immoderate extreme of the modernist metanarrative, he opted, through the medium of festival, for the postmodernist level playing field on which past and present are side by side. He favored appropriating from the past what one can use, and he affirmed that the role of festival was to permit controlled reenact-ments of the past, the affirmation of tradition as well as of the now, in an atmosphere of joy. The comic, he said, depends on discontinuity and the juxtaposition of incongruous entities. When social dissonance is pointed out, we can be surprised into the enjoyment of ambiguity, even of the tragic flaws of human nature. In a deep sense, the late Sixties were a very comic era.

The Regress of Progress

On August 30, 1968, a *Time* essay entitled "What a Year!" hit the newsstands. The year was only two-thirds over, and already it had recorded for history the Kennedy and King assassinations, student uprisings around the world, and the "Prague Spring" and its repres-sion. More would come: the same late-August issue also reported po-lice preparations in anticipation of riots rightly expected to be in store for the upcoming Democratic convention in Chicago.

"Until recently," we are told in the *Time* essay, "the U.S. had a boundless faith in steady progress, a growing sense of social justice, a belief that federal cash would solve the nation's remaining problems. Yet a decade that began with a quest for moral grandeur has bogged down in the effort to keep society from exploding." For all the Ameri-can faith in higher education so recently celebrated in *Time* as well as elsewhere, the country's youth had rebelled. The years had become times of big news and little solutions.[9] It would be hard to express more succinctly the crisis of transition from modernism to post-modernism.

Interestingly, it was the Far Left, presumptively the political-intel-lectual faction in the vanguard of change, that most clung to the mod-ern progressivism that was passing away—not only to the ideal of progress, but also to the ideal of the unitary state with its all-seeing leader. More concretely, it expressed itself on the extreme Left in adulation of Mao Tse-tung, the Chinese Communist dictator and revo-lutionary hero, who was then, in the context of the great proletarian cultural revolution, receiving near-divine honors. Shining-eyed Chinese masses held up the "Little Red Book" containing his thoughts like a talisman, chanted his name and slogans with revivalistic fervor, and reportedly were inspired in all their endeavors by his example. But if the Maoist cultural revolution was like a religion in its collective energy and its use of potent symbols, it was also, the essay remarked, like one of the stricter sort in that it tolerated no heresy.[10]

Time, in another of its perceptive essays of the era, spoke of the revolutionary mystique that led to rejection of rationalism and individual rights in favor of a "charismatic, quasi-religious style of leadership, the communion between the masses and a revered father figure, the traditional appeal that moves nations, the sense of a destiny transcending the individual." We have observed these were religious though not churchly times. But the essay warned that, while raising politics to virtually the level of religion may be attractive, it is far from desirable, as "the whole history of the twentieth century shows."[11] Presumably sacralized politics would result in "angelism," as Paul Tillich called aspirations for social or individual perfection beyond human capacity, and exceeding human grasp would quickly slide into Róheim's demonology.

Ironically, the Communist world was then where the modern still carried on, though probably the seeds of political communism's ultimate destruction lay in those years when it began to slip spiritually into the past. It still had appeal for some in the West, despite the brutal face it showed in the return of winter after the 1968 Prague Spring, but one feels that appeal was romantic, based more on visceral distaste for the realities of American life born of the civil rights and Vietnam struggle than on any likelihood that such free and independent spirits as these would find much joy in a real Eastern Bloc society.

The bad news, then, was the withering of the dream of progress through science, the advance of social justice, and higher education. Society had now become too complex and divided—too corrupted by its own perversions of such dreams into lust for unitary control, material excess, and Faustian knowledge that makes for power—for steady forward marches toward utopia. The good news could have been that with the withering of that dream came also (though it did not) the withering of those brutal means by which the twentieth century had too often tried to implement its dreams, as though the earthly paradise could be born of innocent blood and held in place by iron shackles. The mixed news was that some of the clearest souls, rightly impassioned beyond mere reason by the sight of injustice all around, still

260

had minds not entirely free from the enchantment of totalitarian politics as pseudoreligion but also had the passion to protest real evils near at hand.

The scale of disillusionment felt by people who had been seriously caught up in Sixties dreams, a despair that began with the traumas and tragedies of 1968, can hardly be overestimated. Those souls, many of them young and fervently committed students, seminarians, and members of the clergy, had been through three or four years of perhaps naive but intense hope that religion, church, and society were going to be deeply, radically changed within a few more years. It was now happening, they had surmised in 1966 or 1967, and the earthly eschaton was just about here.

At some point in 1968 or 1969, they had to confront the reality that it was not going to happen. It felt, in the words of a colleague of mine, like a "counterreformation" suddenly snapping into place. The new reality was often interpreted in terms no less dramatic or even apocalyptic than had been the preceding hopes. It was spoken of as the fruit of unprecedented repression, terror, fascism, or counterrevolution; as the abomination of desolation sitting and grinning where it ought not, right here in America. Little wonder the mood of activists quickly went sour, bitter, and violent. They were livid with anger at whomever or whatever had stolen victory from them when it seemed almost in their grasp; they suspected (not entirely without basis) devious plots against them; they sensed, though were not quite ready to admit even to themselves, that what had seemed the beginning was instead the end.

Yet it was more than just the end of the Sixties. It was the end of an era that had dominated the world at least since the Enlightenment. That was the era of belief in progress, that through science and technology, education and democracy, together with rising commitment to universal human welfare, the human condition would get better and better generation by generation. Despite the two world wars and the Cold War, this deeply rooted modern affirmation was only sustained by deferred wartime hopes and was well in place at the beginning of the Sixties. It was in fact further reinforced by the educational wonders and the civil rights successes of the early part of the Sixties, as we have seen.

But, feeding on the enhanced progressivist optimism of the postwar generation, and perhaps also registering deep-level anxiety that the progressivist window of opportunity was closing, the middle and late Sixties chose to try accelerating the rate of progress past even modern norms, finally to revolutionary-apocalyptic speeds—and suddenly the whole machine shattered and fell apart.

The moon landing of summer 1969 notwithstanding, since around spring 1970 the great fact of human consciousness has been the general absence of old-fashioned belief in progress. Changes, some of them good, have of course come since 1970: computerization, the end of the Cold War, the expansion in some places of human rights, especially to women and sexual minorities. But they do not add up to what progress entailed in the old secular eschatology, and they do not much modify the general gloom encircling late-twentieth-century humanity as it faces a future filled with far more dread than hope.

The old optimistic progressive eschatology had meant looking forward to a far better, almost godlike, life for everyone in a scientific, and democratic if not socialist, future. Now the tacit assumption seems to be that though the world may be girded several times over by fiber-optic networks, and computerized Virtual Reality may take the place of Sixties psychedelics, for as far into the future as one can see the planet will still be sorely overpopulated and ecologically ravaged, much of its people still sunk in deep poverty and as ready as ever to kill one another with anything from machetes to nukes. The change from the old-fashioned future became evident in fashionable dystopian movies of the seventies like *A Clockwork Orange, Soylent Green*, and *Bladerunner*. Through their gloom the hoofbeats of the postmodern four horsemen—now bearing names like demographics, AIDS, rampant nationalism, and environmental catastrophe—are heard approaching.

Anyone who remembers what progress and the future meant in, say, the 1930s and 1940s, the era, in spite of appalling depression and war, of the 1939 New York Worlds' Fair, and then of hopes for a brilliant, almost Buck Rogers postwar world, will know what the dimension of the change is.

From the religious point of view, it is of interest that midcentury writing on the future seemed to veer wildly between prognostications of paradise and holocaust. Depending on mood or predisposition, once could choose between Herman Kahn's future of abundance and leisure, in which a population of 6 billion with a per capita income of $18,000 was not beyond possibility, and Langdon Gilkey's estimate, following Robert Heilbroner's influential *Inquiry into the Human Prospect* (1974), that the same future would very likely bring only "a descent into the bleak cave of bare and unrelieved survival."[12] That was assuming one survived the even more pessimistic prospects of violent nuclear or ecological catastrophe. Mircea Eliade, in a paper *"Homo Faber* and *Homo Religiosus,"* very aptly pointed to how much these Seventies scenarios resembled traditional religious apocalyptic visions of earthly paradise and wrathful judgment.[13]

The Present Apocalypse

The mood of such a time was interestingly analyzed in a 1968 article by Earl Rovit, "On the Contemporary Apocalyptic Imagination."[14] Rovit paints the moral dimension of a season of open vision by noting that a frequent, deceptively simple question was in the air: Why not? It was at the root of every radical discussion. Why not mount this protest, break that law, throw another spanner in the gears of the system? Those two simple words were no less the gist of moral discourse. Why not? was so often the question that was also the answer when the topic was sex, drugs, dress or undress, life-style.

Why not? Rovit notes, is like a counterpoint to the immense Why? of the twentieth century. Why death camps? Why chronic dread of nuclear annihilation? Why, despite the unprecedented freedoms supposed to have been delivered by progress, is there so widespread a sense of loss of rational control over individual lives and the course of world events? Why? . . . Why? . . . the contradictions of modernity.

But Why? becoming Why not? is the world turned upside down, a desperate freedom asserting itself despite all the Whys? and ripping itself so violently from the womb as to tear the covers off the sky and reveal apocalyptic light. Apocalypse, Rovit says, is no more than a metaphor, but it "is our best model for viewing our contemporary human condition"; it is an "unspeakably powerful metaphor" that "invites all men to become saints or prophets." And there were plenty of both around in 1968, ready to herald, live out, or give a push to the end of the known world, not only in politics but also in art and literature and the sciences of consciousness; in all these the apocalyptic spirit of ultimacy, iconaclasm, and "breaking windows in order to let the fresh air in" was in vogue.

Its fashion of assault was omnivorous, uncompromising, and "treacherously sophisticated," according to Rovit. Apocalypse had fathered the movement for silence and outrage in the arts, for anarchy and violence in social and political affairs, for polymorphous perversity in psychology, for the death of metaphysics, and for the death of God in religion. Ultimately—and apocalyptic is never less than ultimate—it will accept nothing save spontaneity, immediacy of response, and the obliteration of all stabilities. In the late Sixties, sincere spontaneity was the great virtue; anything prepackaged was dead on arrival. Apocalypses, personal or cosmic, appear suddenly and (to all but the elect) unexpectedly, and to live under an apocalypse is to live close to the ultimate.

Though a metaphor, apocalyptic is the metaphor most open-ended of all—anything can happen during and after an apocalypse. The mood was, Rovit believed, based on the "new epistemology" of ESP, magic, hallucinatory drugs—all open-ended means of perception. Open-ended apocalyptic openings and occultism alike are characteristic of any time of the momentary falling away of horizons as one age transits to another. The late Sixties were, along with everything else, a season of burgeoning interest in the occult arts: ESP, tarot cards, astrology, witchcraft, and the like. As we have seen, these interests were surely an extension of the magical, mystical states of consciousness suggested by drug trips, and of the countercultural desire to bring forth wisdom and experience, old and new, leveling the field between what modernism labeled superstition and what it heralded as reason. It tried to find a third, perpendicular way between black reaction and the sunrise promises of progressivism.

There are apocalyptic dangers. Those wanting to break windows to let in fresh air can, as Rovit put it, become "hopelessly in love with the sound of smashing glass." It would be better to reinvent the sanctity of compromise, to relearn humility and that acceptance of limitations that is the strategy of humor.

Yet it is important to understand how one got radicalized and reached the point of contemplating revolution or of at least harboring sympathy for its proponents. Here are a couple of examples apart from students who may have been carried away by the glamor and the inflammatory rhetoric of the modern Jacobites.

The Native American spokesperson Vine Deloria, Jr., though the son of an Episcopal reservation priest and the graduate of a Lutheran seminary, came to the conclusion in *Custer Died for Your Sins* that Native Americans needed affirmation of their own spiritual culture far more than they needed the whites' religion or culture.[15] To be sure, Deloria liked to identify his own tribal peoples with the ancient Hebrew tribes, who also were shunted aside by more powerful peoples and made to taste the dregs of human existence, and who despite a four-hundred-year stay in Egypt managed to maintain the basic structure of their cultural and spiritual life.

But just as the Old Testament tribes became radicalized in their monotheism and sense of distinct spiritual identity under slavery, so must the American tribes. Deloria energized the Native American protest movement by pointing, more directly than any Native American writing for the general public before, to the whites' chronicle of exploitation. He was not sparing in his condemnations. "White culture destroys other culture because of its abstractness," he said. "It is not a culture but a cancer" (188).

Deloria's book is not just negativism, however. He looks toward the emergence of a new Native American tribalism, which he sees as an idea relevant to white culture as well, and which may be appearing in the counterculture. Even a corporation, looked at in the right way, is like a tribe. Both tribes and corporations are subgroups that combine internal cooperation with external competition.

A convert to a sort of new white tribalism was Robert A. McKenzie, pastor of St John's Presbyterian Church in Berkeley, who published "An Odyssey from Liberal to Radical" in the *Christian Century* of March 25, 1970.[16] The background was the People's Park struggle in Berkeley in 1969, when the city was filled with troops as though it were occupied enemy territory. City, county, and campus police, the National Guard, even a hundred highway patrol officers were present to control the disruptive tactics of students and street people.

People's Park, though it came to seem an almost metaphysical reality, was a small, nondescript, unused parcel of land in south Berkeley belonging to the University of California. The counterculturalists had "liberated" the tract, claiming it as a park, developing it with poignant little communal gardens and shelters. The state, asserting its property rights, removed these and surrounded the area with a wire fence.

Trouble began in earnest on May 15, 1969, "Bloody Thursday," when police tried to deal with demonstrators taking down the fence. They fired indiscriminate birdshot, killing one young man and blinding another. Then thousands of students and street people rampaged in the streets. The authorities responded, and soon the odor of tear gas was blowing on the wind. In a scene eerily reminiscent of Vietnam on the evening news, helicopters gassed a large part of the campus from the air.

In conversations around the dinner table, McKenzie's teenage son led him to accept the radical interpretation of these nightmarish events as tokens of establishment oppression. The minister joined an ad hoc clergy group, which found Richard York and his Free Church to be their best liaison with the People's Park Committee. As he moved out of a comfortable middle-class liberal worldview that had considered modern students to be not an oppressed class but quite privileged, McKenzie perceived the real issue was not relative benefits but the extent to which people were able to have a part in decisions that affect their lives. People's Park was not only property rights versus human rights in the abstract, it was property rights versus the right of the people in an affected community to decide whether they needed a park. The issue at People's Park was no less than the same issue as the draft or Vietnam on a small scale, for in those matters too the real question was whether those most affected by the war, the American draftees and the Vietnamese themelves, had any say in the decisions that perpetuated it.

The apocalyptic and revolutionary modes of the late Sixties were virtually the same thing. Revolution—as idea, as dream, as secular religion—is apocalyptic on earth. If apocalyptic is interpreted as it usually is by nonbelievers, as the ultimate in religious fantasy, then the age of reason and progress has also been a sublime age of apocalyptic fantasies of the spirit—so long as they are to be acted out as the shaking of the foundations here below, rather than as war in heaven. So it was that the modern era was also the era of great revolutions, not only scientific and technological but also political, from the French to the Russian and Chinese.

A revolution is simply an apocalyptic speeding up of the idea of progress, an endeavor to realize all the promises of modernism *now*. The revolutionary mystique appealed to moderns, who were characteristically impatient and, as we have seen, prone to those polarized, dualistic models of reality, the righteous against the children of darkness, that can seem so adequately to legitimate revolution. Revolution as righteous gesture also answered to the modern ideal of social justice, to be wrought out of such an apocalyptic struggle, and to the role of elites, idealized in the revolutionary activist vanguard.

For in the brief apocalyptic period of the late Sixties now under consideration, revolution was shimmering in the air, talked about, idealized, feared and hated, envisioned as a flaming sunrise heralding the apocalyptic consummation of Sixties hopes and dreams before they turned. But the bittersweet successes and revealing failures of the modern era's great revolutions surgically open for our inspection many of that age's profoundest dreams and contradictions, and so does dissection of the barren revolutionary reveries of the late Sixties.

Among the signs of the times was a change in heroes. The saints of early-Sixties activism, Gandhi and King, gave way in the latter part of the decade to men like Frantz Fanon, author of the radical Third World protest book *The Wretched of the Earth* and, as we have seen, inspiration of the Black Panther leaders; Herbert Marcuse, discussed earlier; and Ernesto (Che) Guevara, the Argentinian who had become an associate of Fidel Castro in his Cuban revolution and then executed in 1967 as he tried to spark a revolution in Bolivia. Also popular was Jules Debray, a scion of a prominent French family who had joined Che in Bolivia and was serving thirty years there for his part in the same uprising. Both men had written about revolution in the romantic radical vein, strong in their condemnations of capitalism, imperialism, and the United States.

266

Fired by the twin issues of black power and the war, frustrated activists in the United States, no longer sheep to pacifistic clerics, seized on those heroic martyrs. Che became an icon of joyous total dedication, immortalized in the slogan "Che Lives!" and featured on posters in a thousand undergraduate dorms. Debray, whose rather pedantic textbooks of revolution emphasized subversive urban activism, became the mentor of those who wished to make guerilla tactics the medium of protest and ultimately of change. Now the frontline strategists began to talk of skirmishes rather than demonstrations, and bombs rather than love balloons. But they would destroy themselves with their own weapons.

The revolutionary spirit, though fervently copied by the extreme Left in Europe and the United States, was especially associated in the late Sixties with the Third World, not least in Latin America, where Fidel Castro's successful Cuban revolution had sent out seismic-scale reverbations. No doubt there that mystique had something of the luminous but sometimes self-defeating romanticism and romantic heroism of the Hispanic world's most famous cultural icon, Don Quixote. Che Guevara evoked that quixotic spirit just before he was captured and executed by Bolivian troops in late 1967. Alluding to Cervantes, in his last letter to his parents Che wrote, "Once more I feel Rocinante's ribs under my heels. I'm taking to the road again with my shield on my arm." (But, as Alasdair MacIntyre commented, perhaps he should also have recalled Karl Marx's remark that "Don Quixote long ago paid the penalty for wrongly imagining that knight errantry was compatible with all economic forms of society.")[17]

Shootings and Chicago: Signs of the Times, 1968

The essence of the bitter years is that, while in the first half of the decade bad news came mixed with glad tidings, by 1968 and 1969, with the sole exception of the moon landing, the news was all bad and seemed to portend worse to come.

In the week beginning March 31, 1968, Lyndon Johnson curbed bombing in North Vietnam and withdrew from the presidential race, Martin Luther King was assassinated, and violence broke out in cities as a result, setting off more than five hundred urban fires. Johnson called a joint session of Congress to hear recommendations "in this hour of national need." The need was augmented by the killing of Robert Kennedy, a candidate for the presidency, on June 5.

Next came the disaster of the 1968 Democratic convention in Chicago. The beating of demonstrators on the streets, and the harassment of reporters and even delegates within the convention hall, produced a powerful reaction across the country, particularly in those not familiar with Chicago and its boss, Mayor Richard J. Daley. Chicago was, quite simply, a local-level dictatorship, and Daley was its dictator. He wanted to be a benevolent dictator and prided himself on making this city work, unlike some, but he was a dictator nonetheless and true to the type would resort to any means necessary to prove and sustain his power. The sort of "radicals" and "peaceniks" who wanted to intrude, however legally, on the serious proceedings of his own party were not to his liking, and he needed to show who was boss within the limits of his domain. The upshot was the display of a police state *modus operandi* surprising to some, though all too familiar to residents of ghettos, activist dissidents, and other minorities.

All during that last week of August 1968 apocalyptic scenes whirled across the nation's TV screens: Chicago police openly beating teenagers, girls as well as boys, till they fell bleeding to the pavement; delegates cheering a film in honor of the late Robert Kennedy; the mayor of Chicago jeering a U.S. senator; a young girl—recalling events only a few days before in Czechoslovakia—holding up a sign saying "Weclome to Prague." A state delegate chair was hauled off in handcuffs by guards. Masked National Guard soldiers, rifles ready, sprayed tear gas at demonstrators. Before the battle of Chicago was over more than 700 civilians and 83 police had been injured, and 653 persons were jailed. At the end, the party's nominee, Hubert Humphrey, tears filling his eyes, pleaded with America to pause and pray for itself.

Some liked what they saw on TV, especially the rising law-and-order crowd, sick of rebellion and protest. Daley received a flood of telegrams from across the country, the great majority supporting the police's handling of the demonstrators. George Wallace called the response "just right," and so did all those prepared to vote for him and his American Independent party. Others were appalled.

To be sure, as the *Christian Century* put it in an outraged editorial, "Some of the young protesters manifest a kind of militancy that is pathological if not nihilistic." Feeding on itself, the demonstration mentality had slid a long way toward nihilism since Nashville and Selma. But, as the editorial stated, the real blame lay with Mayor Daley for making police action the course of first resort.[18] It might have been better to let the demonstrators be, allowing what was juvenile in their actions to speak for itself.

There is much reason to believe that the trouble was in fact, as many claimed, a "police riot"—that the police, though sometimes unwisely taunted and goaded, went on a rampage, often singling out all longhairs for the club, on one occasion slashing the tires of some thirty cars simply because they bore McCarthy stickers. But this level of outrage called for scapegoats, and the people in power, together with Middle America, wanted them to be not the police or Mayor Daley but from the other side. The Yippies were chosen.

The Harlequin Underground

The Yippie or clowning protest and counterculture movement was an outgrowth of the Diggers, the free-spirited, free-food anarchists of Haight-Ashbury. The new movement picked up their insouciant defiance of legality and convention, in which "ripping off the establishment" was a virtue, and adopted their use of street theater demonstrations like burning money, showing again that the most nihilistic extremes can only be staged. But the Yippies, led by Jerry Rubin and Abbie Hoffman, made pranksterish display the central instrument of their politics. They strove for media coverage and wanted to be known for their outrageousness. The name Yippie (the name to justify the acronym, Youth International Party, came later) was adopted at a meeting on December 31, 1967, of Rubin, Hoffman, Dick Gregory, and others. But even before then, Jerry Rubin had asked for the permit and led the attempt to levitate the Pentagon at the November 1967 Washington demonstration. Before that, he had shown the political value of the put-on by appearing at a House Un-American Activities Committee hearing dressed as a Revolutionary War soldier, stoned and blowing bubbles.

In Chicago, August 1968, the Yippies came into their own. They prepared for the occasion, raising the gorge of Mayor Richard Daley's wrath with preliminary tongue-in-cheek announcements that they were going to put LSD into the city's water supply or, alternatively, would leave town for $100,000. During the convention itself, their "dummy agenda," as Todd Gitlin put it, "reads like a pastiche of John Birch and Marx Brothers fantasies of the anarchist left." They threatened to fake delegates' cards, set off smoke bombs in the convention hall, copulate nude on Chicago's beaches, release greased pigs, walk the streets dressed as Vietcong while burning draft cards en masse with the flames spelling out BEAT ARMY, and dose the Democratic delegates' food and drink with LSD.[19]

All this, intended as black, nihilistic humor, was not very funny except to those who shared the Yippies' marginal position. In the end the Yippie leaders were among the famous Chicago Seven (sometimes called the Chicago Eight if Bobby Seale, tried separately, is included) singled out by the Nixon administration for prosecution in connection with the Chicago troubles and tried in late 1969. The arraignments were an obvious attempt to isolate the movement's extremists. Abbie Hoffman, Jerry Rubin, Dave Dellinger, Rennie Davis, Tom Hayden, John Froines, and Lee Weiner, as well as the Black Panther Bobby Seale, made up the notorious seven or eight.

The government tried to center its case on conspiracy charges. The irreverent attitude of the defendents may be gauged by a typical response of Hoffman. When asked perfunctorily in what nation he resided, he answered, "The Woodstock Nation," and went on to explain that a nation is really a state of mind, such as the Sioux Nation, which many Native Americans might claim as their true identity. Needless to say, such repartee delighted some and infuriated others.[20]

The defendants' counsel, led by William Kunstler, took up a corresponding cultural defense. Said Kunstler, no doubt correctly so far as the government's real motives were concerned, "This is a political trial where their identities and values are on trial, not the criminal acts they may have committed."[21]

On another level, the Yippies personified the exuberant Sixties devotion to synaesthesia, street theater, signs, and condensed symbols, and more than others did so in the political arena. No one exemplifies the creation of counter-roles defrocking the old elite and their images so boisterously as the Yippies. In a large sense they are part of Sixties religion; they were the ritual clowns and tricksters of primal myth come back to life in the modern city.

The Religious Nonissue of 1968 and the Nixonian Lull

In spite of worlds coming to an end, the 1968 campaign went on. Even apart from Chicago, the election of that year was depressing for the religious community, if only because it seemed impossible to find in it a bright, clarifying religion issue like those of 1960 and 1964. The *Christian Century* produced an editorial on October 16 called "On Overcoming Disenchantment: The 1968 Election." It noted that both Humphrey and Nixon were "overexposed politicians," and that some radicals urged support of George Wallace on the "rather shamefully nihilistic grounds" that his success would sharpen the confrontation and help bring to ruin the established political system. Serious proposals in that direction indicate as much as anything the alienation and despair of the political year. But the *Century*'s editorialists, while granting that Wallace had considerable talent for such a task, were still sufficiently within the system to be able to say that "we cannot yet look upon every sign of ruin as a sign of hope." Rather, the liberal Christian periodical opined, what is needed this year is "a special kind of political maturity: the ability to overcome alienation when there are all too many alienating forces at work in the body politic."[22]

In the end, Richard Nixon won, and the Republicans were back in the executive branch. In the first half of 1969, an interesting lull in the intensity of protest emerged in the liberal religious community, though it turned out to be but the eye of the storm, and the real summer-of-1970 end of the Sixties was not yet at hand. At first many in the religious community seemed determined to give Richard Nixon a chance to entertain the national reconciliation he had so solemnly promised, despite the ominously rising law-and-order voices. It was as though a number of responsible minds were in post-1968 aftershock and now sensed that year, with its assassinations, violent demonstrations, and extremes of polarization, had gone too far.

So it was that on February 5, 1969, the *Christian Century* published a surprisingly commendatory editorial on Richard Nixon's inauguration, praising his desire, expressed in the inaugural address, to listen, to communicate, to be a peacemaker. The Quaker president had spoken of a "fever of words" afflicting the nation, and his own words seemed intended to bank fires, not ignite them. He urged a rest "from inflated rhetoric that promises more than it can possibly deliver; from angry rhetoric that fans discontents into hatreds; from bombastic rhetoric that postures instead of persuading." This language went down well with liberals who had supported the Sixties' reformist agenda but were increasingly disturbed by polarization in the nation, and by the uncompromising and confrontational, if not revolutionary, stance taken by the extreme Left.[23]

Interestingly, the first major religious critique of Nixon was directed not at policies but at the new president's rather naive religious inclusiveness, which suggested a lingering Fifties-type "brotherhood." His inauguration rites had been conspicuously interreligious, ostentatiously so, some sniffed, and had included Nixon's favorite preachers, Graham and Peale. These two may have had little in common theologically, but they shared the president's friendship and were both identified with conservative values.

Then came the Sunday morning White House services, which Nixon preferred to going out to church, and which were criticized in some quarters for mindless ecumenicity. For example, when a Jewish rabbi was the speaker, the hymns nonetheless included Christian praises to God as "Father, Son, and Holy Ghost." The *Washington Post* editorialized against such services as inappropriate in the political atmosphere of the White House.[24]

On the rethinking of radicalism, an interesting editorial in the *Christian Century* for March 5, 1969, was "Rebels, Amnesty and Property," which, no doubt to the surprise of many readers of this generally liberal journal, declared that "it is time to speak plainly to the mounting excesses of student rebelliousness on university campuses. It is also time to speak plainly to the specious moralism which attaches itself uncritically to the destruction of property, the demand for amnesty, and the insistence upon a student veto in all areas of university policy."[25]

Referring to the recent occupation and acts of destruction at the University of Chicago, the *Century* alluded not only to some $30,000 worth of damage to university property but also to the invasion of university administrators' offices and the saturnalia that followed, including the release of an unsigned letter of resignation by a vice-president, the scrawling of obscenities on the pictures of officials' wives, and the stealing and smashing of personal mementos of all kinds. The editorial roundly condemned these actions and took issue with some university chaplains who had called for amnesty for the student perpetrators of the takeover. The periodical agreed with Dean E. Spencer Parsons of Rockefeller Chapel at the university that the demand for amnesty revealed "a lack of moral seriousness about the relationship between acts and their consequences." On the other side a Lutheran chaplain declared that Parsons' statement continued "the unhappy tradition that the function of religious establishments is to support uncritically whatever establishments of power there are in the land, to condemn rather than defend the accused."

Undoubtedly, for real activists, the times did not call for politeness, or excessive tenderness toward the private feelings of such individuals as university administrators; the God of apocalypse was in the revolution of the times. In this exchange the religious though not churchly temper of the times is displayed; even men of the cloth spoke the language and voiced the concerns of revolution or antirevolution.

Black Religion, Black Power, Black Messiahs . . . and the National Council

Late in 1968, a group of African Americans were lingering over dinner at the Gateway Hotel in Saint Louis. Impatient, the white female cashier said to them, "Why don't you boys get out so I can go home?" Unfortunately for the Gateway, those particular "boys" were delegates to a conference of the National Committee of Black Churchmen. Incensed at what they took to be a racist slight, all four hundred delegates walked out of that hotel and finished their meeting in a nearby church.[26]

This incident typifies both the edgy racial mood and African American gains in the religious world by 1968. Blacks were in St. Louis because of immense advances in their position since, say, 1958. Black caucuses had been formed within most mainline denominations, and the St. Louis meeting drew black leaders from predominately white denominations such as the Methodist, United Church of Christ, and Episcopalian, as well as from the traditional African American denominations, and black nationalists interested in African spiritual roots like Ron Karenga of the Kwanzaa festival.

But though blacks had been given some highly visible national-level appointments in white churches, parish-level integration and acceptance of black leadership in largely white congregations was slow in coming, and unintentional offenses seemed to harry their every step forward. Increasingly blacks were talking about giving up on whites and on integration, as the black power set already had, and were looking toward tokens of a new separatism: revitalizing black congregations, black theology. And with so much changed, and so much unchanged beneath the surface, they were very touchy about slights.

The St. Louis meeting came in the wake of serious talk of black schism in the mainline predominately white denominations, replacing the racial unity ideal of only a year or so earlier. Blacks wanted control of inner city programs; they wanted black experience expressed in liturgies. The Reverend James Lawson, mentioned earlier in connection with the Nashville sit-ins and now president of the Methodist Black Caucus, spoke of desiring "a liturgy that is warm, vibrant, compassionate, and enthusiastic"—and black Methodists denounced the denomination's new hymnal for listing Negro spirituals under "American Folk Songs." If white churches did not listen to these issues of style and substance, it was bruited about, blacks, though they did not want schism, would be on their way out.[27]

The civil rights movement was supposed to have come to fruition in the late Sixties. The great victories over legal discrimination and on voting rights had been won, black heroes of the struggle were liberal national heroes, among young people there was even talk of interracial dating as chic. It was a time of changing roles among black Americans. Yet the mood was scarcely one of celebration.

For one thing, traditional black churches seemed to be declining. For many decades they had been the vital center of black life, the only black institution wholly controlled by blacks themselves. They had nourished leaders of the civil rights movement like King. But for a moment it seemed the very success of blacks in breaking out of the church-dominated ghetto might make the church seem obsolete. While churchgoers continued to sing the old hymns, black militants, the followers of Malcom X and the Black Panthers, were the names on the street; they were not traditional black Christians but closer to the new militant mood, Muslim or revolutionary Marxist. The only black ministers who appeared to have much influence were militants themselves who had taken up the black power cause and baptized it, like Albert B. Cleague of Detroit.

He exemplified the new mood and wrote *The Black Messiah*, a collection of sermons delivered at his Shrine of the Black Madonna in Detroit. A glance at this book suggests what an extraordinary move his nomination as president of the NCC in 1969 was in a body with the National Council's antecedents.[28] The controversial and militant Cleague was an avowed proponent of black power and a skeptic concerning King's nonviolence. The book's tone is well set by the first lines of the introduction: "For nearly 500 years the illusion that Jesus was white dominated the world only because white Europeans dominated the world. Now, with the emergence of the nationalistic movements of the world's colored majority, the historic truth is finally beginning to emerge—that Jesus was the non-white leader of a non-white people struggling for national liberation against the rule of a white nation, Rome" (3).

Evidence of this is found in the well-known mixing of races in the Mediterranean area, and the hundreds of shrines to black Madonnas all over the world. Cleague developed this theme in sermons that spoke, for example, of the Palm Sunday entry of the black Messiah into Jerusalem and alluded to the Pharisees as Uncle Toms. In a sermon entitled "Dr King and Black Power," preached just after King's assassination, Cleague paid eloquent tribute to the late civil rights leader, though he made no secret of his differences with King on nonviolence.

Cleague also held an annual service commemorating "Brother Malcolm," with whom he obviously felt spiritual kinship despite Malcolm X's being Muslim and he Christian. What they had in common was commitment to the "black revolution," and, as Cleague affirmed later in the introduction the *The Black Messiah*, "As black people, we have entered a revolution rather than the evolution or gradual change which white folks would like us to accept. We want to move fast enough to be able to see that we are moving" (5).

Here are a few more black theology writers of the day. According to Joseph C. Hough, Jr., in a thoughtful mediating book, *Black Power and White Protestants* (1968), blacks wanted to be seen as a community, not as whites in disguise; to this end token church integration was not the answer. The way to go was rather seeing the church, and para-church structures like the NCC Commission on Religion and Race (which lobbied for the civil rights bill in 1964) or the Delta Ministry, as mediators between the alienated ghetto community and white power. But unfortunately, it was no longer 1964.[29]

James H. Cone, of Union Theological Seminary, asserted in *Black Theology and Black Power* that black identity, the crux of the black power movement, must come first, then reconciliation. The sort of integration that would make blacks "honorary whites" is no answer. Blacks want to be respected as black men and women, and for no other reason. Black power is like Camus's Rebel, who says both no and yes: no to intolerable conditions, yes to what is worthwhile, and "there is a limit beyond which he shall not go." Black power then means complete emancipation for black people from all oppression whatsoever. Freedom now. All or nothing. And to assert this is an ethical act, like that affirmed in Paul Tillich's *Courage to Be*, Cone avers. It is not black racism but justifiable rage at injustice.[30]

All this is, for Cone, highly biblical and Christian. "Jesus' work is essentially one of liberation" (35). The kingdom of Heaven, he says, is not inward serenity but God at work in the fight against evil in the world. It is in the end an eschatological struggle of light against darkness for all humanity, for when blacks are liberated, whites are too.

Instead, revolution was the talk of the town on all sides. But that talk was not music to the ears of some Americans. Liberal whites were getting tired and discouraged, and nonliberal whites bitter. To many whites in Middle America, it seemed blacks wanted nothing but more and wanted it in a virtually blackmailing way. For many blacks, the problem was that the gains of the civil rights movement—especially in the northern cities—were mostly on paper; the money and the jobs were not there. They were ready to go for substance—even to the point of testing the limits for white liberals, on whom the black power people had already given up.

An example of the new boldness was the black manifesto presented by James Forman, now international affairs director of SNCC. The manifesto, an angry document formally entitled "Manifesto to the White Christian Churches and the Jewish Synagogues in the United

States of America and All Other Racist Institutions," had been drafted by Forman and adopted at the National Black Economic Development Conference in Detroit in April 26, 1969. It demanded $500 million in "reparations" from religious institutions for their implication in the "capitalist and imperialist power structure." The reparations money would be spent on such projects as southern land banks for cooperative black farms and for black publishing and TV ventures, a new black university, and a strike and defense fund. Until the demand was met, Forman said, blacks would engage in "total disruption of church agencies."

Almost immediately afterwards, Forman interrupted services at New York's Riverside Church and made an unscheduled appearance across the street at a meeting of the National Council of Churches General Board May 1–2. The intrusion was accompanied by rumors of an imminent occupation of NCC headquarters by promanifesto activists as a means of carrying out the disruption threat.

NCC officials responded with general sympathy for the justice of the manifesto cause, and the board authorized its executive committee to give serious consideration to the manifesto's demands while also assuring police protection in the event of an occupation attempt. But many churchpeople objected to the violent rhetoric of the document, claiming that it exaggerated both the wealth at the disposal of churches and synagogues and the power of denominational or NCC officials to dispense it. The board meeting collapsed in the face of the intrusion, dissolving for lack of a quorum before all agenda items had been completed.

The essential powerlessness of the great mainline, Fifties-type ecumenical agencies in the changing world of the late Sixties could hardly have been more dramatically demonstrated. Burdened by a limited mandate, bales of memoranda, and the faded ideal of Christian unity wrought through bureaucratic denominational cooperation, the late-Sixties NCC struggled on in a nation far different from that of its birth in 1950. At its best, it had in the Sixties provided a liberal voice and an umbrella for projects like the Delta Ministry, while serving as a lightning rod for rightist attacks on the mainline churches. But it was increasingly ignored by younger churchpeople, who tended to view it as a faceless nondenominational denomination with little identity.

On the face of it, the overall confrontation provoked by Forman and his followers bore little fruit. By August 1969 only $22,000 had come in. Yet the demand does seem to have served as a "catalyst of conscience," as *Newsweek* put it. Though rejecting the concept of reparations, the World Council of Churches nonetheless voted $500,000 in response—not to Forman but to all organizations of the oppressed whose purposes were "not inconsistent" with the WCC. The American Jewish Committee also rejected the black manifesto and its threat of violence but expanded aid to social programs. The Disciples rejected reparations as well but redeployed $30 million to fight poverty, and the Presbyterians topped that with $50 million.[31]

Joy at the National Council

Then, as a replay of the May confrontation, came the NCC's 1969 Assembly, which met November 30 to December 4 in Detroit. Despite the moribund state of the NCC, a bit of almost Yippie-style excitement was generated by this conclave in Cobo Hall.

First, the visual and audio environment had nearly caught up with the Sixties. The exhibition hall was decked with balloons and banners. The chief attraction was a "joy box," a blacked-out cubicle whose walls were lined with buttons, switches, and cords that turned on colored and flashing lights, bells, and other sensations—almost an ecclesiastical version of the psychedelic light shows so popular in the counterculture. The joy box was sponsored by Associated Parishes, a movement dedicated to the renewal of local churches. A modern jazz concert of sacred music conducted by Duke Ellington got staid bishops and other elders of the churches clapping their hands and stomping their feet. But there were less happy moments, and they basically centered around black power and the war.

Black delegates advanced two activist black churchmen for high office: Albert Cleague, the radical custodian of the Shrine of the Black Madonna in Detroit and, as we have seen, a fiery, provocative black nationalist, was proposed for president. The Reverend Leon Watts of New York was nominated for general secretary. Both blacks were defeated, but the bold moves again reminded delegates of the new world in which they lived.

Then James Forman arrived. He now called for the dissolution of the NCC, the reassignment of all its assets to black development, and the withdrawal of all overseas missionaries; and he added that "people who believe in the Black Manifesto will forever be a plague upon the racist white churches and synagogues of America."[32]

Next a draft resister appeared before the assembly requesting that it receive his draft card as a token of support for his position of conscience. His presence was unscheduled, like Forman's—such happenings occurred at the most solemn meetings in those days. When a resolution to take the card failed to receive the required two-thirds vote, the next unprogrammed entry into the agenda was of a churchly Yippielike group called Jonathon's Wake led by Stephen Rose, the author and activist editor of *Renewal*. A Jonathon's Wake member rushed up and poured red paint the full length of the speaker's table, saying, "The blood of the Vietnamese is upon you!" Then, after a resolution that the NCC would never use police power against supporters of the Black Manifesto lost amid an overwhelming number of abstentions, Rose ran back and forth across the hall shouting, "Crucify me! Crucify me!" (This bizarre scene offers a different image of Rose from the staunchly committed but sober and thoughtful reformist of the Mississippi Summer, *Renewal*, and the high Sixties generally, suggesting the frayed nerves, tension, and polarization of 1969.)[33] Finally Jonathon's Wake celebrated the "death of the NCC."[34]

The Underground Church

An interesting and significant movement of those years was the underground church. This was essentially church people meeting in homes, or sometimes in bars, shelters, or other unlikely places, for prayer and celebration of the eucharist, frequently using simplified, contemporary-language forms that emphasized the spiritual needs of activists in gritty, street-level settings. I attended a kitchen eucharist of this sort in 1968 or 1969 celebrated with common bread, an abbreviated plain-speech liturgy, and communion received by Roman Catholics and Episcopalians together.

What distinguished the underground church from conventional informal prayer meetings that many churchpeople have long held outside formal church services was, first, that they were frequently conducted by regular priests and ministers, often in defiance of established norms; second, that they were usually closely related to activist if not radical ministries; and third, that they were considered not only as supplement to the regular church but as a kind of protest against its apparent values. The late-Sixties underground church was like a catacombs perpetuation of the 1964–1966 years-of-secular-hope ideal of church and ministry, in a time when the above-ground church seemed uncertain, demoralized, and likely to slip back into old pieties.

In a book edited by Malcolm Boyd, *The Underground Church*, Robert E. Grossmann supported that perspective:

> A large number of Christians have become invisible. . . . This is not the first time that this phenomenon has occurred. Records mention a similar tactic almost two thousand years ago. It may seem more than a little romantic to make fanciful comparisons between a candle-lit

vigil in the catacombs and a clandestine worship in a high-rise apartment. But comparisons can be made, and they have to be neither romantic nor fanciful.[35]

In the same volume, the Reverend Layton P. Zimmer wrote of the ordinary church that it "is struggling, sacrificing even its own integrity, to sustain its organic life recognized in terms of buildings, stained glass, real estate, and homiletical whoredom." Malcolm Boyd himself said in the same book that "the Established Church seems to be a chaplain of the status quo," and "the underground church must, in a real sense, be seen as a radical and contemporary extension of what ... may be called Christian renewal." Zimmer adds that "the underground church is made up of men and women aware of a greater calling ... Christ was a revolutionary."[36] Malcolm Boyd put it vividly in his autobiography:

> The cry from the underground church is the cry for courage to face the future instead of the past; an ethic rooted in human need instead of eccesiastical legalism; a concern for people instead of statistics and things; and a passion for life rooted in Biblical faith instead of a passive living death masked by pasted-on smiles, incestuous concern for self-perpetuation of an organization, and yet more slick public-relations and fund-raising drives to create bigger and better real-estate interests.
>
> The cry from the underground church comes out of a curious common sense of loneliness. It is always more acute at times of celebration, and amid crowds and even family circles.[37]

The underground church was not always necessarily revolutionary in the political sense, but it was different and directly reflected the Sixties experience. It wanted to keep alive the power of the informal ecumenical eucharists at Selma. It concretized the servant-church mood of denigrating the denominational, institutionalized church and the latter's emphasis on professionalism and maintaining the structures. Certainly the spirit of Ruether's *The Church Against Itself*, in which ministry was defined as created moment by moment in encounter, was present in these occasional, situational bread breakings. The worship of the underground church was characteristically connected with underground ministries—to students, activists, and protesters, and in street work with dropouts and wanderers.

Even if the theological and often the social emphasis was different, the rise of charismatic groups must also be mentioned in connection with the underground church. During these years pentecostal activity grew rapidly in several mainline denominations—Episcopal, Presbyterian, and Lutheran as well as Roman Catholic. Quite frequently the pentecostal conventicles had in common with the underground church a disdain of the established church, a feeling that they represented instead the true apostolic spirit, manifested in this instance not so much by evangelical solidity with the poor and oppressed of the social activist sort as by the gifts of the Spirit tongues, healing, interpretation.

In the late Sixties, however, some Roman Catholic charismatic communities included strongly activist, post–Vatican II priests, nuns, and laity and so managed to combine both sides, though they later tended to become rather pietistic and protosectarian. Like the liberal underground church, the charismatics were regarded as divisive and troublesome by many establishment leaders, and in truth the clandestine spiritual communities of both came near to replacing the above-ground church in the loyalty of adherents. But both were a witness, full of yeast, to a new kind of life for the church.

In the Los Angeles of ultraconservative Cardinal McIntyre, the archdiocesan press was tightly censored, and few priests dared openly express other than conservative views. McIntyre was criticized elsewhere, though, for failure to oppose racism and for turning down an appeal to form a priests' council, as well as for being on the wrong side in his epic battle with the sisters of the Immaculate Heart. All this was grist for the underground church in that city. Until McIntyre's retirement in 1970, underground churchmanship was thought to be both larger and more secretive in the Los Angeles area than anywhere else, involving twelve thousand Catholics and fifty priests.

The underground rivers ran much in contrast to desertlike conditions on the surface, although a few famous above-ground churches, like Glide Methodist in San Francisco, acted like the underground church. But, as we have seen, attendance at Roman Catholic services was declining, and priests and nuns were leaving their callings, largely in reaction to *Humanae Vitae* and the general atmosphere of post–Vatican II letdown. Overall religious affiliation declined during 1968 from 64.4 to 63.2 percent of the population, and attendance over a busy decade, according to Gallup polls, fell from 49 percent of the population in an average week in 1958 to 43 percent in 1968. Although Protestant attendance was not declining as starkly as Roman Catholic in those few years after *Humanae Vitae*, certainly many Protestant churches felt wary and exhausted after the storms of the mid-Sixties and were hardly growing. An article by Walter D. Wagoner in the February 19, 1969, *Christian Century*, "Thoughts for Protestants to Be Static By," found four species of malaise abroad as the tumultuous decade reached its weary end: "theological exhaustion," "ecumenical doldrums," "parish bafflement," and "devotional emptiness."[38]

Against all this, the underground church was, for a few years, a holding action in the spirit of a few years before.

Above Ground: The Rise of Middle America

It is first of all important to realize that the Middle American of 1969 and 1970 was (like the hippie and the black power activist) an icon, a symbol, an archetype, not any particular person or even an aggregate whose boundaries could be drawn with any precision. And like the other Sixties ideal types, numerous people identified with Middle America once that image was unveiled, recognizing something important about themselves in the icon. When *Time*, on January 5, 1970, declared as Man and Woman of the Year the Middle Americans, it did for them what it had done two and a half years earlier for the hippie counterculture. And because Middle America was born as an antithesis, it was born at war.

Middle America was at war because it felt itself a culture under siege. Its predominant defining symptom was a fear that the American dream—itself a vague and seldom-achieved ideal—was being lost as unpatriotic radicals took over. The Middle Americans were people who, as veterans of the Great Depression and the war, as the inhabitants of the places the dropouts had dropped out from, felt the country was rightfully theirs—yet they were losing their grip on it. The radicals were getting all the glamorous publicity. The news media had Middle Americans saying things like, "This is the greatest country in the world. Why are they trying to tear it down?" Emotional needs bound up in that identity, they believed, were being neglected.

At least they were told this was how they felt by conservative politicians and preachers, and many of them believed it—though perhaps not quite as unquestioningly as appeared on the surface, where the confrontation seemed sharp and simple. Behind the scenes, Middle Americans knew as well as anyone else that there was no going back to 1960 and before. And they tended to blame themselves, in the end, for the youthful counterculture and the generation gap—saying either "We neglected them," or "We spoiled them."

At the same time, as hatreds and bombings accelerated, Main Street and blue-collar America did not want to go further. If things continued coming apart as they were, ahead loomed the abyss. Like the radicals, the middle recognized an apocalyptic moment at hand—but shrank from it. The other side might call for revolution, even as it

281

feared, with good reason, increasing surveillance and repression at home. Middle Americans were the kind of people for whom the Constitution was virtually scripture, and they could not imagine a different kind of government, nor could they really believe than an American government could be oppressive toward "good" people.

The lines were drawn on a number of issues that involved religion or crypto-religion. Praying was done in public schools despite the Supreme Court, in one New Jersey school by reading aloud invocations from the *Congressional Record*. Draconic bills against campus disturbance wended their ways through several state legislatures. There was a battle of bumper stickers—themselves largely a Sixties innovation, to the best of my memory—"Make Love Not War" vs. "America—Love It or Leave It" and "Spiro Is My Hero." Waving the flag and wearing it became a party sign. As the bumper sticker and the flag so well illustrated, it was a war of signs and slogans—of condensed symbols. The media loved such gestures as putting pictures of small-town Middle American drum majorettes beside shots of the notorious nude scenes in *Oh Calcutta!* or that uninhibited celebration of the counterculture, *Hair*.

It was also a battle of heroes. Instead of Che and Malcolm X, for Middle America it was Nixon and Agnew, Attorney General John Mitchell, John Wayne, and S. I. Hayakawa, the nemesis of San Francisco State's demonstrators. The image of toughness they all projected appealed to people frightened by rising crime rates, who saw the demands of black militants and white radicals as nothing more than blackmail.

The Apollo 11 and 12 successes were also music to the ears of Middle America, and their crewcut navigators further heroes. The moon landing cost some $26 billion, and liberals grumbled about better uses for so much money, but Middle America loved the astronauts. Eric Hoffer, the forklift philosopher who worked as a San Francisco longshoreman, called the moon's Tranquility Base "the triumph of the squares." (While capable of acute though tendentious insight, as in his classic blame-the-intellectuals study of the modern totalitarian mentality, *The True Believer*, Hoffer had not liked the Sixties and had become rather impatient as he gazed at its tempestuous days from his blue-collar perch, but there is no doubt he saw a good many things through the same lenses as did the working class with which he identified himself.)[39] To be sure, the moon landing, unlike the Vietnam War or the War on Poverty, did represent a clear American victory, and one achieved by clean-cut, short-haired young men Middle Americans could have been proud to call their own.

Middle America did indeed count in its ranks some wealthy people, such as the Texas millionaire H. Ross Perot, who organized a group called "United We Stand" to support the president on the war. But the bulk of those who identified with the icon were people like those for whom Hoffer spoke: veterans, blue-collar workers, the celebrated hardhats who wore the flag and countermarched against the peace people—heartland families, people whose lives and values seemed to them negated by what was going on, despite the radicals' claim to be on the side of the workers.

Middle America was not so much a political position or a party vote as a state of mind. Some Old Left union members, who might well have voted for Humphrey—or Wallace—in 1968 rather than for the Nixon-Agnew ticket, thought Middle American when it came to the all-important cultural symbols, like hair length and whether one wore the flag on one's hat or one's bottom.

Eric Hoffer no doubt spoke their minds when he later wrote in his diary, "The legacy of the 1960s: a revulsion from work; a horde of educated nobodies who want to be somebodies and end up being busybodies; a half submerged counterculture of drugs and drift still able to swallow juveniles (of every age) who cannot adjust to a humdrum existence."[40]

That was the problem, that image. For people who felt denied the education available to the Sixties generation, who knew what it meant to work day in and day out, who had long since adjusted to a humdrum existence, it was not the "horde's" moral values regarding race and war that revolted them. It was rather the implicit values of the student and countercultural moralizers, whose lives seemed anything but humdrum and work oriented, who appeared overeducated and overprivileged and probably oversexed as well, that grated on those whose life histories had been otherwise. They would not have seen any humor in the Yippies' threat to put LSD in the drinking water of Chicago, or Jonathon's Wake pouring red paint on the desk at the NCC Assembly; these would have been the destructive acts of overaged spoiled children.

No doubt it was partly the fault of the media, which naturally focused on the colorful bearded and beaded types in the demonstrations, on the draft card burnings, on the campus fires and barricades and shouting students in designer jeans, while ignoring the decent-looking clerics and grandmothers and even Wall Streeters who were saying the same things, at least about race and the war. But as usual symbol was almost all.

And there was more. Hoffer wrote: "The terrible 1960s were years of unprecedented abundance. From early 1961 to late 1969 this

283

country's economy went through 106 months of unbroken prosperity. The anarchy released by this affluent decade has increased enormously the weight of the human factor in social calculations. The fear of youth exploding in the streets is often preventing governments from making the right decisions in both domestic and foreign affairs" (143).

Hoffer was obsessed by the arrogance of Sixties leftist intellectuals, as he had been by earlier intellectuals in *The True Believer.* The Students for a Democratic Society (SDSers), he said through his rage, called the "common people" "Honky Swine." They reminded him of the sort of elitist European Marxists and privileged Soviet apologists he also despised. His case would have been better made had he also found occasion to mention how much the civil rights movement, for example, had benefited numerous "common people" of color. But as usual Hoffer deserves to be heard even at his most exasperating, for he had a way of putting in the most legitimating manner possible the middle-American case.

In his words one senses how newfound affluence, education, and sometimes immature moralism could look to survivors of another era who felt in need of time to catch up. They did not appreciate the irony of the extent to which the Old Left, including Communist functionaries from Berlin to Beijing, reacted with hardly less revulsion to the turbulence of 1968 around the world, having wanted a rational socialist order backed by plenty of state authority, not "flower power," "revolution for the hell of it," or a great cultural revolution. A few once Left-leaning intellectuals took one look as such phenomena as the student takeover of Columbia University and decamped for what came to be known as neoconservativism.

The late-Sixties Middle Americans were not really the same as those of the Bircher heyday either. They were more numerous and less cultish, embracing union members and ethnics who would have felt left out of what the Right meant back then, and who had probably voted for Kennedy and Johnson in 1960 and 1964. But they felt rejected by what the Left became in 1967 and 1968: black power, draft card burning, all those highly inflammatory symbols.

Thus, as Barbara Ehrenreich has pointed out, 1968 also meant a radical reshaping of the Right. The former Right, from Birchers to Goldwaterites, had been strongly anti-Communist and probusiness, but with a streak of antiauthoritarian individualism like that exemplified in the work of Ayn Rand. But the new Right, reacting against the New Left's antiauthoritarianism, "suddenly restyled itself as the defender of authority in all its manifestations—legal, familial, religious and military."[41] This governmental authoritarianism was not inconsistent with what one could legitimately have thought the Kennedy and

Johnson programs were all about. But by 1968 "authority" seemed more than ripe for transfer from the Left and from association with the modern progressive planned society and its imperial control missions, to the Right, where it would coexist in selected venues with postmodern questioning of such concepts of the state. The authoritarian Roosevelt-Johnson bureaucratic state was becoming the authoritarian Nixon-Reagan "traditional values" state.

The new identity really got under way in the 1968 presidential campaign, as Nixon and Agnew reached out to the Silent Majority and made the first tentative appeals to the "family values" and "traditional values" that were soon to become a staple of Republican rhetoric. With the other party identified with Chicago and profoundly divided over the war, they hardly had to say more. Indeed, as we have seen, after Nixon's inauguration, 1969 at first seemed calmer than that horrendous year, 1968. Nixon did liberal things about the draft (the lottery and the suspension of calls later in the year), ended the production of biological weapons, and started the SALT talks with the Soviet Union. But he obscured this pattern with increasingly polarizing rhetoric and actions like making Supreme Court appointments designed to appeal to conservatives, and weakening the voting rights bill. The pro-Middle America rhetoric, especially as uttered by Spiro Agnew, reached high decibels between fall 1969 and the great demonstrations of early May 1970 following the Cambodian incursion and Kent State—at that apocalyptic moment it was the Nixon-Agnew side that was forced to realize it was on the brink of a social abyss and had to take a step back. But the real Sixties were over.

The Angry Peace Movement

In its first issue of a new year, the cover of the *Christian Century* read "Vietnam, 1968. The Moral Issues Confronted," and confronted they were by a variety of authors, all presenting varying degrees of opposition to the war. Perhaps even more telling, many ads for anti-war rallies, petitions, and groups festooned the same magazine. If three or four years before it was civil rights, by 1968 it was certainly Vietnam.

In Washington, as well as in towns and cities across the land, doubts about Vietnam were perceptibly rising, and murmuring could be heard among Democrats about dumping Lyndon Johnson as the party's candidate that fall. At the end of March he resolved that question by dramatically withdrawing from the race. But the war issue continued to simmer, above all on for students.

Counterpoint: The Power of Evangelicalism

The rise of Middle America is inseparable from a turn-of-the-decade resurgence of evangelical Christianity. As *Time* stated in a June 1970 article on W. A. Criswell, the outgoing Southern Baptist president and staunch fundamentalist, "The sturdiest pulpits of Middle America stand in the 34,335 churches of the Southern Baptist Convention"—which with 11.5 million members was now the largest Protestant denomination in the country, though it was not when the Sixties began.* And there were other evangelicals and fundamentalists too; at least since the great revivals of the early nineteenth century, a quarter to a third of the U.S. population has been basically fundamentalist or evangelical in religious identity.

Evangelicals have not always been socially or politically conservative. Before the Civil War some, like revivalist Charles Finney, were leading abolitionists; at the turn of the century some, like William Jennings Bryan with his famous "You shall not crucify labor on a cross of gold" speech, were prominent populists. Those in the traditional peace churches—the Church of the Brethren, Mennonites, and Quakers (not all of whom are evangelicals)—have espoused pacifism and nonviolent tactics in season and out and, as we have seen, had a significant role in the background of both the civil rights and antiwar movements.

But demographically American evangelicals have tended to be strongest in the South and Midwest, and to be small town and rural rather than urban. They have been comfortable with neither the great liberal universities nor the centers of economic, cultural, and political power on the two coasts.

Theologically the differences between liberal and evangelical Christians can be summed up in their respective attitudes toward the language and values of the surrounding intellectual culture. Liberals generally believe the Gospel can and should be communicated in terms and concepts compatible with the best current science and philosophy. Evangelicals, though they may borrow homiletical images from popular culture, contend that the essence of the Gospel, matters such as the Incarnation and Atonement, are vitiated if they are presented in other than integral biblical language. This leads them to take the literal inspiration of the scriptures more seriously than liberals, to be very suspicious of radical restatements of traditional meanings like those of "secular theology," and to live in a separate religious culture possessing only a nodding acquaintance with mainstream intellectual life.

Needless to say, all this put them strongly at odds with the countercultural and radical Sixties. Like blue-collar America (which they often came out of), evangelicals were not necessarily opposed to quiet prag-

Counterpoint: The Power of Evangelicalism *Continued*

matic reform. Many had supported the New Deal and could come to terms with civil rights. But they commonly had a strong, Romans 13 respect for authority, the military, and "law and order"; embraced highly conventional sexual, family, and dress values; and looked warily at influences in education likely to undermine their spiritual culture. Like their opposites at the radical pole, they tended to view the world in polarized, light-versus-darkness terms. Most of what was new in the Sixties, then, sent out all the wrong signals to the evangelical subculture. From long hair to antiwar protests to meditation and occultism, not to mention drugs, it seemed another planet from theirs, and one in serious rebellion against God.

Yet the Sixties were also an opportunity for evangelicals, and not only because of their opposition. Evengelicals could recognize that, although in their eyes misguided, many counterculturalists were at least concerned about the spiritual quest. Evangelical preachers who could relate to hippies and talk their argot were quite successful in leading some of them them from drug and Eastern highs to those of Jesus. They laid the foundation for the Jesus movement of the early Seventies and pioneered a new churchly style, the youth-oriented, hip-talking, gospel-rock evangelical or Pentecostal church, or equivalent street or coffee-house ministries.

In a larger sense too the Sixties ended with evangelicalism on the brink of opportunity. When a dominant culture appears strong and stable, clearly the way the future is going, as scientific, democratic modernism did in most of the first half of the twentieth century, subcultures like evangelicalism that refuse to accept its conceptual language are marginalized and may well be objects of ridicule. But when culture is in flux as it was in the Sixties, those with an outside point of reference may come to have a strong position. They will appeal especially to those in the middle who feel ill at ease with what is going on—Middle America.

On another level, attempts at reconciliation were made. The most influential evangelical journal of the time was *Christianity Today*, founded in 1956 as an alternative to the politically and theologically "Leftish" *Christian Century*. The founding editor was Carl Henry; when he retired from this position in 1968, the magazine had a circulation of 160,000. In good evangelical fashion, Henry emphasized individual conversion and biblical authority. But he rejected the fundamentalist position that ethics is purely a matter of private morality, though on the other hand he condemned liberals who felt the institutional church should identify itself with particular social and political policies. We have noted this periodical's position in relation to

Continued

Counterpoint: The Power of Evangelicalism *Continued*

the Civil Rights Act of 1964 and the 1967 riots. The church, *Christianity Today* thought, should enunciate biblical principles pertaining to current social issues but leave the decisions to individuals. (Perhaps it is not entirely irrelevant to note that in 1968 a much-discussed topic was whether Billy Graham, very influential in *Christianity Today*'s establishment and known to be a friend of Richard Nixon, would publicly endorse him as a presidential candidate. He did not.)

Although little appreciated at the time, the Sixties ended with evangelicals set up for their surge into mainline respectability, and for their much-vaunted political influence, in the Seventies and Eighties. But they came out of the Sixties changed like everyone else. They were no longer a straight-laced, isolated subculture that rising suburbanites dropped as soon as they could in favor of a better denomination, but something at times almost like a new early Franciscanism or Wesleyanism of street ministries, gladsome music, preachers in Levi's, and postmodern leveling—even if evangelicalism's issues were not those of the secular gospel Sixties and were often labeled, in the rough way such labels are usually applied, conservative and dogmatic.

*"Bickering Baptists," *Time*, June 15, 1970, 54.

Typical of the state of affairs on liberal campuses was the situation at Harvard. According to a poll reported early in 1968, 94 percent of Harvard seniors said they opposed U.S. policy in Vietnam; 59 percent said they would make a determined effort to oppose the draft, 22 percent asserting they would flee the country or go to jail rather than do military service. Perhaps that figure overstates what would actually have happened, but it is clear the war was extremely unpopular among students.[42] Many of the clergy were with them. Early in the same year, thirteen hundred ministers signed a statement on "Conscience and Conscription" supporting resistance to the draft. Some two thousand marched in Washington and stood in silence for five minutes at the Arlington National Cemetery in a "silent outcry" against the war.

Peace marches, which were becoming an annual spring and fall tradition, took place in many cities on April 27, 1968. (In Chicago the marchers of spring were attacked by Mayor Daley's police, a preview of events in August when the Democratic convention met in that city.)

But in 1968, just as many blacks were no longer in the corner of Martin Luther King's nonviolence, so now not all antiwar activists were necessarily pacifists. Some believed in fighting—for the other side, or at least against the system. They were revolutionaries; admirers perhaps of Che or Mao, or they were Weathermen, or "just revolutionaries for the hell of it." Defiance and apocalypse was in their blood.

Something was changing, and some religionists fell under the spell of this new sincerity and total dedication, as it presented itself, to justice and the overthrow of injustice by any means necessary. In not a few parsonages, the move was away from pacifism and toward endorsing righteous anger and feeling good about violence. According to O. Carnell Arnold, who looked on the trend with a dubious eye in an article entitled, "Fight Fiercely, Christians!" violence had found a place among the Christian sacraments, amid such catchwords as "God is in the revolution of our time," and "Jesus was a revolutionary."[43]

A *Time* cover story for June 7, 1968, highlighted "The Graduate, 1968" calling these young people "cynical idealists." Regarding religion, despite secular and even revolutionary theology, this troubled and troublesome generation tended to dismiss institutional churches as irrelevant or unimportant, yet according to Michael Novak of Stanford, one found "more religion among students who act on their conscience than among those who sit in church every Sunday seeking to be blessed." Sincerity was registered as an important virtue, and the activist, not to mention the revolutionary, seemed nothing if not sincere.[44]

Student protests accelerated at home and abroad in 1968. The streets of Paris were filled with young insurgents to an extent that made some observers think of a new French Revolution. In the United States, some campuses were virtually in the hands of the revolution. In May, for example, two Columbia Universities occupied the same space at the same time, one run by the administration, the other by striking students. The latter Columbia constituted perhaps 4,900 scholars out of 17,500 total. Each camp possessed its own buildings and telephone exchange; the regular faculty tried to carry on with their regular courses, while the strike faction offered a curriculum of 128 "liberation" classes.

Colleges and universities remained the scenes of increasingly angry and violent demonstrations in the 1968–1969 and 1969–1970 academic years. The issues were several, centering around race and war. Opposition to the Vietnam War and the draft was joined by protests against campus involvement in military and corporate research, by requests for student participation in academic policy decision making, and especially by black student demands for liberalized admissions on behalf of minorities, black studies programs and faculty appointments, and support of Third World causes. Many activists saw the causes as all connected: "liberation," including revolutionary liberation against American "imperialism" abroad in such places as Vietnam, was one with the racism and corporate greed of the establishment at home. It was as though the universities were a surrogate for society and all its ills, despite most major campuses being far more liberal in tone than society as a whole.

Demonstrations by the Black Student Union and the Third World Liberation Front at San Francisco State at the beginning of 1969, for example, led to confrontations between stone-throwing students and baton-wielding police. Over 150 were arrested. The engagement greatly enhanced the stature of acting president S. I. Hayakawa, who stoutly resisted the militants. During the spring semester of 1969, black militants seized buildings at Cornell, Stanford, and Columbia, demanding black studies programs and admissions policies favoring blacks. At the City College of New York, black activists laboring on behalf of black and Puerto Rican admissions disrupted the South Campus to the extent that it had to be sealed off. At Brooklyn College there was a rash of fires, and Queens College was closed after black students vandalized the library. At Harvard 173 were arrested for criminal trespass after wild demonstrations.

These events in the spring of the year, of which the preceding are only a sampling, presented a dilemma to white liberals, especially academics. They had supported the civil rights movement from Greensboro to Selma but were uneasy with "nonnegotiable" demands, supported by strikes, sit-ins, and takeover attempts, for appointments and curricular changes in their own bailiwicks. Understandably, they had little enthusiasm for disruption and destruction around those ivied halls and cherished a belief that professors should be named and courses established in accordance with academic due process, and not for political or racial reasons.

Bolstered by conservative officials like President Nixon and California governor Ronald Reagan, academic administrators took an increasingly hard line against disruptive demonstrations, even though it often put them in a no-win position: repression of student uprisings was popular with the general public while tending to create more protests on campus. The protests led to problems, particularly at state universities subject to the passions of local politicians. After conspicuous demonstrations or strikes and statehouse backlash, some schools confronted budget cuts and heavy faculty turnover. But the mood continued into the decade's end. Commencement 1969 was anticommencement day in many schools. Graduates wore armbands protesting the war, and at Brown a third turned their backs on Henry Kissinger as he received an honorary degree. The real question, and a burning one, was, Whose university is it? The students'? Minorities'? The faculty's? Or the government's?

Students for a Democratic Society was an important campus activist group across the country and the power behind many of these disturbances. We have observed that it was founded in 1960 as a youth organization by the moderately socialist, AFL-CIO–sponsored League for Industrial Democracy, but it quickly acquired a life of its own as it became one of the first groups to swing into action against the Vietnam War. Not noted for meticulous organization or rhetorical consistency, the SDS was less a conspiracy than a contagious spirit in a time of campus effervescence and turmoil. (Countering charges of Communist infiltration, students joked that "the Communists can't take over the SDS; they can't find it.") But it did have a program, or at least issues, based on the famous Port Huron statement of 1962, and it had strong personal ties to the civil rights movement; many of its leaders, like Tom Hayden, had been beaten and jailed in that cause in places like Mississippi and Georgia. A major SDS theme was participatory democracy, the right of everyone involved, whether students in a university or recruits for an army, to have a part in shaping policies that affect them. Another, of course, was racial justice, including equal access to education at all levels, and holding teach-ins on minority and Third World issues. Together with opposition to the war, these issues preoccupied the SDS as they did many others.

In churches and synagogues, sympathy for draft resistance brought in a revival of the ancient right of church sanctuary. A growing number of liberal, antiwar churches, probably more Unitarian than any other denomination, offered public sanctuary to draftees who opposed the war and held conscientious objections to serving. Sympathetic clergy spoke of sanctuary as a concept going back to Mosaic law. It decreed that fugitives from the laws of the world could take refuge at the altar of God, who would protect them if innocent. The same concept was given partial recognition in the Justinian Code of the Byzantine Empire, and in the practice of medieval Europe. Although this ancient right had long been dormant and had never been tested in U.S. courts, some said it was now once again apposite, at a time when human law seemed so flagrantly to conflict with many consciences.

Churches could not of course offer full security. FBI agents walked through not a few church doors with arrest warrants. The Reverend Harold R. Frey, a United Church of Christ pastor who headed

Massachusetts's Commitee of Religious Concern for Peace, said, "We are not trying to protect these boys. We are not harboring them against the law. What we are doing is setting up a platform where their ethical and moral convictions can be made public." But the gesture naturally produced consternation on the part of the government officials, knowing that apprehensions on church territory made them look bad. That in turn made many of the clergy feel good, as the practice showed the church to be once again a force capable of moral confrontation.[45]

The mood of conscience and confrontation in those days is well illustrated by the antiwar Berrigan brothers, Daniel and Philip, both priests and certainly the two most radical and revolutionary priests the U.S. Roman Catholic church had yet produced. The clerical pair's specialty was robbing draft boards of their precious records. Philip once poured blood on the Baltimore board's papers. In May 1968 they burned draft files in Catonsville, Maryland. They were arrested, of course, but that was hardly a setback, for they knew the trial would only give them a platform and whip up more publicity for the cause. "Maybe one way of getting free these days is going to jail," said Daniel.[46]

A little later, Philip Berrigan wrote a memorable article about his jailhouse experience called "Violence: A Prisoner's View." He told of being thrown together with a man convicted of manslaughter and other charges who would break into fits of uncontrollable weeping. Pulling out of them, Berrigan's fellow inmate would say he wished he could go to Vietnam, where his brother was, instead of doing jail time. He boasted he'd "feel more like a man getting one of them little mothers in my sights" and argued that "somebody's got to stop them commies. If I had my way, we'd walk in there and clean 'em out!" Even to the point of using the Bomb.[47]

Berrigan, incarcerated for a very different attitude toward the war, first tried rather self-righteously to change this unhappy man's mind. He got nothing for his pains but blank inarticulate incredulity. In time the priest came to see that he was taking unfair advantage of a man of limited capacity and deep emotional anguish and realized that here was his chance to transcend the debate and relate in a different way to the casualties of society who fill its jails. "By exposing himself freely to the punishment society inflicts on its victims," Berrigan concluded, "the Christian can give meaning to their powerlessness."

Then came the great protests. Disappointment in the Nixon administration brought an impassioned throng of some 250,000 to the capital in October 1969 with banners, balloons, and flags, including the Vietcong emblem. Comparable crowds filled the streets of other cities. The *Christian Century* editorialized: "There is a resurrection to

proclaim. The peacemakers are alive and well again in America."
After eighteen months of unsuccessfully trying to allow the political
process of change to work, "the unyielding conscience of young
America has brought us back to life again. On October 15 the bells
tolled and the candles were lit." At a time when apologists for the Far
Left and the Far Right appealing to violence seemed nearly to have
taken over by default, the spirit of nonviolent activism appeared once
more in place.[48]

It was the most massive antiwar demonstration in U.S. history to
date, and its religious, though often extra-ecclesiastical, dimension
needs to be appreciated. Traditionally religious symbols, like bells
and candles, were widely used. The moratorium had a Memorial Day
or All Saints' Day aspect as the names of Americans killed in Vietnam
were solemnly read out in churches and campus auditoriums. Religious assemblies held special services.[49]

The antiwar faction was then angered by the administration's lack
of sympathetic response. That undoubtedly contributed to a winter
and spring of unrest, and the even greater outburst of the Days of
Concern the next May.

In fact, the violence that marked the last stage of the movement—
roughly October 1969 to May 1970—began just before the October 15
Mobe, on October 8. That was the four Days of Rage in Chicago set up
by members of the radical faction of the SDS headed by Mark Rudd,
and known as the Weatherman. Those outrageous days were scheduled to coincide with the continuing trial of the Chicago Seven.

Charging toward the Drake Hotel, where Judge Julius Hoffmann of
the trial was said to live, about a hundred men armed with clubs,
chains, and metal pipes, chanting "Ho, Ho, Ho Chi Minh," and "The
only direction is insurrection, the only solution revolution," clashed
in the streets with police and the National Guard. They were accompanied by a hundred women in helmets—the Women's Liberation
Army. Much glass was broken, including windows in the Chicago
Historical Society, and some blood was spilled. But generally the Chicago police, in contrast with 1968, dispelled the riot with admirable
professionalism and restraint. The worst casualty was in the reputation of radicalism; not a few sympathizers who had been appalled by
events of the previous year had to acknowledge that now it was the
radical side that looked like crazies out of control.

The Days of Rage had a telling religious consequence. It turned
out that while the Weatherman's street fighters were in town, they had
slept dormitory-style in four Methodist churches in the upscale suburb of Evanston. In late September the Weatherman had contacted the

Evanston United Methodist Parish, a coalition of six churches, asking for housing during their four-day stay in Chicago. The parish council left it up to the individual churches. One had refused; one had given accommodations in private homes only; four—after informal meetings or formal votes or just on the minister's own initiative—had offered housing. Between 200 and 250 Weatherman members moved in. Even when the rampage began, they were not asked to leave. Afterwards, parishioners were quick to turn on the ministers of those churches, charging them with naively opening their sanctuaries to vandals and "subversives."

The ministers responded with such justifications as that of the Reverend Dale Nelson, of Covenant Methodist Church, who told a hostile congregation in his next sermon that "the church must be open to one and all regardless of a person's political views and affiliations." Others spoke of the hope of changing them from "destructive, violent revolutionaries into constructive, peaceful revolutionaries" or invoked, as in the draft cases, the right of church sanctuary. Bishop Thomas N. Pryor of the Chicago United Methodist area carefully distinguished between denouncing the violence and ministering to those who perpetrated it, neither absolving the Weatherman nor condemning the ministers who provided shelter and godly advice.[50] But justified or not, the obvious difference between this giving of shelter and earlier offerings of sanctuary to pacifistic civil rights workers or draft resisters testified to the changed nature of 1969.

That was just the beginning. To name only a few of the other bombings and burnings of those last months: an elegant town house in Greenwich Village that was apparently being used as a factory for homemade bombs; two black militants killed when their car was blasted in Maryland; a thirty-foot hole blown in a courthouse in nearby Cambridge, Maryland, where the militant H. Rap Brown had been scheduled to stand trial, until he disappeared; a bank in Santa Barbara, California, near the branch of the University of California there; and some ninety-three more bombings in New York City alone. Not all were necessarily related to the Weatherman or other radical organizations, but undoubtedly many were. The Greenwich Village explosion in March 1970 took the lives of three of the Weatherman; thereafter the group went underground.

Then came the Kent State killings of four student protesters by the National Guard on May 4 and the May 1970 Days of Concern. Hundreds of thousands again gathered in an outpouring even greater than the Mobe in October 1969, schools were closed, some thirty ROTC buildings on campuses across the nation were burned or bombed, and on May 14 two more students were killed at Jackson State College in Mississippi. On May 27, thirty-nine members of the clergy in Evanston, Illinois, site of the infamous SDS lodging, said the nation was "perilously close" to dictatorship, based on military involvement in Southeast Asia and now Cambodia.

For weeks after Kent State and the Days of Concern, letters to editors across the nation, in both religious and secular journals, were full of anguish, anger, tears, penitence, defiance. It was an incredible outpouring of national passion. As we have indicated, the Nixon administration did not come out well, at least in the eyes of those liberals who had been willing to give it a chance. A *Christian Century* editorial entitled "A Shattered Trust" summed up the discouraging story by writing, "To trust a President is an awesome and, usually, a very necessary thing. . . . The oldest complaint against Richard Nixon is that he cannot be trusted. However, so ugly was the legacy of Lyndon Johnson and the Democratic Party—in Vietnam, in the cities, and on the campuses—that many who were not normally Nixon supporters were persuaded that his election might be salutary. . . . Now that trust has been broken."[51]

The last major episode in the 1969–1970 cycle of violence was on August 24, 1970, when the army's mathematics research building at the University of Wisconsin was blasted, killing a graduate student who had been working late. According to Todd Gitlin, he was the antiwar activists' first innocent victim, and "in the illumination of that bomb the movement knew sin."[52]

The dramatic antiwar escalation of 1969–1970 was also the last hurrah of the movement on campus. As we have noted, scores of campuses closed early that spring of 1970, and the movement never recovered from the long summer vacation. By the time students returned in September they, and numerous off-campus radical activists, seemed sobered. They now had to weigh their lives against the possibility of being shot by the National Guard as at Kent State or Jackson State, and they had to balance any commitment to the counterculture against drug-related crime, the Charles Manson killings, and the University of Wisconsin bombing, among other chilling considerations. The stakes were too high. Many turned from alternative politics to alternative life-styles, switching the Sixties off and the gloomy, inner-directed Seventies on.

To be sure, antiwar protest continued into the early Seventies on the streets and in the political world. The Out Now rally of April 24, 1971, brought a half million demonstrators to the nation's capital. Those most concerned (on the American side) finally became also those most active; according to the government's own figures, more than half of all soldiers during 1970–1971 became involved in some form of resistance activity—a remarkable and unprecedented level of disaffection that virtually paralyzed the armed forces of the United States and certainly contributed to the final end of the sorry Vietnam mess a few years later.[53] All this was continued by other means in the McGovern campaign of 1972, and the ultimate expression of Sixties endtime bitterness was Watergate and the Nixon resignation of 1974. But these surly events were picking up the pieces after the Sixties balloons has expanded and burst by mid-1970.

Catholic Conservatives and Controversies

In the early part of 1968, liberal priests, nuns, and laity in the Roman Catholic church were visibly continuing strong efforts to maintain the spirit of Vatican II. One sign was the formation of a national Federation of Priests' Councils, drawn from a large number of post–Vatican II diocesan councils. These local councils were clerical senates with advisory powers in their dioceses. Sometimes they seemed almost clerical trade unions; one in Providence, Rhode Island, won a 100 percent increase in priests' salaries.

Advances of this sort were balanced by losses. The different mood of the post–Vatican II church from the Fifties and very early Sixties is illustrated by the decline of contemplative orders, such as the Trappists, Carmelites, and Poor Clares, whose members were presumably little concerned about salaries. The Trappists were now down 50 percent from the numbers that they had enjoyed a decade or so earlier, buoyed by Thomas Merton's books. These "spiritual" monks and nuns were adversely affected by the Peace Corps mentality—the feeling that real religion meant working in the world—by the slowness of monastic orders to incorporate post–Vatican II changes, and by the new plethora of options for those seriously interested in the spiritual life.[54]

On the other hand, women theologians within Catholicism, virtually unheard of before except for those classified essentially as mystics (Julian of Norwich, Teresa of Avila), came to the fore with stunning new perspectives on the meaning and message of the church. Besides Rosemary Ruether and Mary Daly, discussed elsewhere, there was Sidney Callahan, wife of Daniel Callahan, the executive editor of *Commonweal*. In *Beyond Birth Control*, Callahan (the mother of six) argued—prior to *Humanae Vitae*—that the Vatican not only should approve of contraception but should also abandon puritanical and repressive attitudes toward sex in marriage generally. Strong sexual desire, she said, is not immoral but human and natural—*naturalness* being a key word in Catholic discourse because of its implication of consistency with natural law.[55]

But at the same time, conservative Roman Catholics were soldiering on in what must have seemed to them, and certainly seemed to everyone else, a near hopeless effort to hold back the tide. At the end of June 1968, some 350 delegates gathered in Minneapolis for the Fourth National *Wanderer* Forum, sponsored by the ultraconservative Catholic magazine of that name. Those gathered were able to enjoy, for a change, the traditional Latin Mass, and to exchange sentiments of nostalgia for the old-fashioned Catholicism of rosaries, fish on Friday, unquestioned papal authority, and militant anticommunism. Several speakers and delegates stressed the last point; representatives from such groups as the Young Americans for Freedom and the Cardinal Mindszenty Foundation clearly wished to put conservative Catholics in the same camp as the John Birch Society and the (Protestant) Christian Anti-Communist Crusade—organizations battered by the Sixties but unbowed. Orators of this stripe claimed that liberalism in the church was humanism in disguise and only paved the way for Communist infiltration.[56]

What was perhaps significant was that such charges were made not by unbending clerics, of whom few were in evidence, but by lay speakers such as Lola Belle Holmes, who identified herself as a former undercover agent for the FBI in the Communist party, and L. Brent Bozell, editor of another conservative Catholic magazine, *Triumph*, and brother-in-law of William Buckley.

There is precedent and moral justification for such loyal opposition within the church. Nonetheless the protest seemed a Sixties kind of thing: appeal to romantic, hierarchical traditions of other times and places, in some mystic, idealized East or Middle Ages; protest and leveling attitudes toward the institution in the present. It was almost as though the ultratraditionalists were becoming yet another underground church.

But the great event for the Roman Catholic church in 1968, which led to a tremendous upheaval and came near to undoing all the advances of Vatican II, was the encyclical *Humanae Vitae* (On Human Life) issued by Pope Paul VI on July 29. In this document the pope took the advice of his most conservative consultants to condemn all methods of birth control except rhythm. In so doing he rejected the conclusions of his own commission to study the subject, which in 1966 had voted seventy to fourteen in favor of easing the church's stand on contraception, and he also ignored the urgent pleas of a number of leading theologians, as well as the near unanimous opinion of the non-Catholic world.

The encyclical was narrowly based on natural-law considerations, in traditional Roman Catholic theology held to reflect the will of God as Creator. If the obvious purpose of the sexual organs is procreation, then any act intended to thwart that purpose artificially is contrary to nature and so to nature's Maker. The pope took into account arguments against the traditional position: the population explosion, sex as having as a natural purpose the expression of love as well as procreation, the economic hardships faced by couples with unwanted children. But in the end he rejected them, for "it is not licit, even for the gravest reasons, to do evil so that good may follow therefrom, even when the intention is to safeguard or promote individual, family or social well-being." He also cited abuses that supposedly would follow from widespread contraception: marital infidelity, loss of respect for women, the possibility of civil authorities making birth limitation mandatory.

For numerous Catholics and others the document was simply out of touch with the realities of their lives and, even more tellingly, with the moral judgments of their own consciences. Certainly its tone seemed in little rapport with the times. The now condemned Pill, as we have seen, was one of the defining creators of the Sixties, with their sexual revolution and reaction against arbitrary-seeming moral norms. Perhaps one could not expect a pontiff to embrace a sexual revolution so far as extramarital sex was concerned, but *Humanae Vitae* also appeared to reverse the momentum of Vatican II; though not explicitly endorsing contraception, Vatican II had strongly affirmed the principle of responsible parenthood and the right of couples to decide for themselves the size of their families. Had Paul VI issued this encyclical at the commencement of his reign it might have been accepted, but too much had happened since 1963.

It was lack of faith in the right and ability of married couples to form their own consciences in these matters that galled many, along with the idea that the encyclical was entirely the work of rather elderly celibates. Some women noted that, although the pope had argued that contraception lowered respect for women, the encyclical was addressed to "Venerable Brothers and Beloved Sons," with no evidence that women, though manifestly involved in the issue, were either consulted or directly spoken to. Certainly the encyclical was not popular in the United States. John A. O'Brien found that 54 percent of U.S. Catholics opposed *Humanae Vitae*, while only 28 percent favored it, and 18 percent had no opinion.[57]

Finally, also in the wake of Vatican II and its renewed emphasis on collegiality in the church, serious questions were raised about the manner in which the edict was issued. For the pope to put out his own view as the magisterium of the church (and so binding on Catholic consciences) a position at odds with the great majority of his own commission and by all appearances with the consensus of the church at large seemed a reversion to monarchical papacy that liberals found disturbing. Some, like Franziskus Cardinal Konig of Vienna and the Dutch Catholic hierarchy, issued statements circumspectly encouraging Catholics to follow their own consciences nonetheless. J. John Palen, perhaps thinking of antiwar Democrats and Republicans eating their hearts out in hawk-dominated parties, complained that "the plight of the Catholic liberal is parallel to that of the political dissenter in national party politics" versus the organized "machine" of bishops and priests bound to support the pontiff whatever their private reservations. An editorial in the *Christian Century* entitled "Catholicism's Authority Crisis" emphasized that the real crisis lay not in *Humanae Vitae*'s teaching on contraception, which in any case was likely to be ignored, but in the authority by which it was issued.[58]

Charles Curran of Catholic University in Washington, D.C., was quoted as saying, "Papal authority really needs to be demythologized and brought under limits." James T. Burtchaell of Notre Dame added, "The Pope, I think, is a victim of the overexpectation everyone has of the papacy, namely, that it ought to be able to solve every crisis right away even if it hasn't the answer. On this particular issue we see the whole system falling on its face." (Not surprisingly, conservatives also saw the issue less in substantive terms than as a test case of papal primacy. They hailed the encyclical as a vigorous reassertion of the pope's authority. L. Brent Bozell, editor of *Triumph*, declared that "any person who refuses submission to an authoritative teaching of the Supreme Pontiff on faith or morals is a schismatic.")[59]

In the United States, 172 Catholic theologians and others, led by Curran and including all six American lay members of the pontifical birth control commission, signed a statement rejecting the encyclical. "We conclude," they said, "that spouses may responsibly decide according to their conscience that artificial birth control in some cases in permissible and indeed is necessary to preserve and foster the value and sacredness of marriage." The Association of Washington Priests, representing some one hundred clerics, formally endorsed this petition, and various other Catholic organizations took similar positions. Demonstrations appeared on Catholic campuses and outside St. Patrick's Cathedral in New York.[60]

The Pill and the sexual revolution were ultimately to diminish as unmitigated goods even in the eyes of liberals, especially after the emergence of AIDS. But the real issue surrounding *Humanae Vitae* was as much authority as contraception. Many felt the spirit of Vatican II had been betrayed and were now little inclined to trust anyone claiming to speak for the church. The damage had been done, so far as traditional views of Catholic authority were concerned. The church did not go into major schism over *Humanae Vitae,* though some left. But that was largely because most remaining Catholics were prepared to stay on their own terms, following their own consciences on this matter—and, precedent set, perhaps on others, such as abortion. Unintentionally, a pope acting in an authoritarian manner had created a church whose temperament was much less authoritarian than ever before on the grass-roots level. The encyclical undoubtedly did much to stir up the general atmosphere of mistrust, betrayal, and malaise that permeated nearly all quarters of the Roman Catholic church by the late Sixties.

The Immaculate Heart of Mary (IHM) controversy finally came to a climax. Early in 1970 the implacably conservative archbishop of Los Angeles, Cardinal McIntyre, retired. More or less simultaneously the order divided into two parts. About 315 of its 380 nuns followed their president, Anita Caspary, in asking dispensation from their vows and forming a new secular organization, the Immaculate Heart Community, devoted to "the service of man in the spirit of the Gospels." It would be involved in teaching, public health, and social work. The Vatican dispensed them, although it had refused to admit the changes the sisters had previously sought in the order's prerogatives. But, in the words of Fr. Edward Heaton, secretary of the Congregation of Religious in Rome, "When it became obvious that these ladies no longer wanted to operate within the framework of the religous community, there was nothing else to do but permit them to get out." The remaining nuns stayed in the order under its old rules.[61]

I had the privilege of knowing several IHM sisters both as graduate students at my university and as friends during this tumultuous period. It was remarkable to watch these bright and determined women emerge from the cloister as if from a chrysalis and appear one day as smartly dressed sophisticated professionals, going to work nine to five and serving sherry to friends in modish apartments after hours. Some became interested in vogues of the period, from astrology to pop art and secular theology. A very few resisted change, one nun stubbornly refusing to wear anything but the old habit. Some drifted into marriage. But almost all, I would say, retained two distinctive characteristics: a fresh, perceptive insider/outsider view of the world, and a deep anger at their treatment by the church they had served. The inner fires of rage could be banked for long periods but never completely went cold.

The Immaculate Heart rebels who left were far from alone. On February 23, 1970, Anita Caspary, their leader, shared the cover of *Time* magazine with James Shannon, former auxiliary bishop of St. Paul-Minneapolis and a leading progressive, once heralded as perhaps the first "intellectual" to become a U.S. bishop in the twentieth century. He had given up his office in 1968 and subsequently married. In the feature article, "The Catholic Exodus: Why Priests and Nuns Are Quitting," the numbers were significant. Some three hundred priests left in 1966 and 1967 alone. But even more significant was the quality and manner of their leaving. Instead of the typical quiet, individual defections of unsuited clerics, these were highly public departures of persons among the best and the brightest.[62]

They formed ex-priests' or ex-nuns' organizations and frequently remained nominally within the church but, both before and after exiting the priesthood or sisterhood, increasingly worked out of their own definitions of Christian life. The leavers included Edward J. Sponga, who had been head of a Jesuit university in Scranton, Pennsylvania, and rector of the famous Jesuit training center Woodstock College; and Joseph F. Mulligan, former dean of Fordham University's Graduate School of Arts and Sciences.

Obviously something new was going on. The *Time* article noted that Vatican II had been called the first council of the church that did not produce a schism. But in fact, though it left behind no Nestorians or Old Catholics, it produced a "psychological schism" of monumental proportions. The conciliar renewal effort had, ironically, led up to the present situation by making more and more obvious to those within the church attuned to the progressive wave the unbearable tension between their obligation to an "ancient, troubled structure" and the changing turbulent world around them whose emergent Sixties values were, to many, not always bad.

Not a few modern priests wanted to be living a free, secular-city kind of Christian life but instead found themselves caught up in the creaking machinery of a baroque institution. The council had liberated the church's laity in far more ways than it had its priests. Laypeople were now praised as the church's heroic frontline and their marriages celebrated, but the clergy were left under authoritarian control and celibate, and with male and female roles rigidly defined.

Andrew Greeley, in a 1969 article in the venerable *American Eccle-*

siastical Review, a journal for priests, noted that there has been no serious systematic research on why priests leave the priesthood, but he ventured some impressions. First and fundamentally, defecting priests were deeply, chronically unhappy, out of loneliness, discouragement, and frustration. Second, they have a view of the outside world that leads them to expect life to be better there. In this, Greeley avers, they were naive: about the world, about sex and marriage, about theology, about human society. If they think they will automatically be more "relevant" or be able to do more good as a government bureaucrat, a university professor, or even a social worker than as a pastor, some of them may be in for a rude surprise, Greeley contended—or if they think marriage is always happier than celibacy.[63]

Subsequent issues of the same periodical indicated the persistence of the problem, however. An article by George A. Schlichte, "The Vanishing Priest, A Sign from God to Change Our Ways," pointed to the cruel dilemma of postconciliar inwardly changed priests surrounded by a changed laity, caught in a structure still unchanged from the past. David M. Knight, SJ, in "Celibacy as a Personal Response," argued for it as a free option for priests.[64]

Finally, in assessing the changes in the Roman Catholic church, a later sociological survey of Catholics by Andrew Greeley provides some helpful figures and interesting insights. In *American Catholics since the Council: An Unauthorized Report*, published in 1985, Greeley first noted the changing demographics of America's Catholic population. Thus, for example, before the council years a smaller percentage of Catholics than Protestants went to college; since then almost 50 percent *more* Catholics per capita than Protestants have done so. Also, until around the council years most Catholics were within two or three generations of immigrant forebears and largely lived in urban ethnic enclaves; in the 1950s and 1960s younger urban Catholics, like many others, moved to the suburbs and rapidly shed much of their ethnic character. All this meant a change in the Catholic religious personality that was not so much due *to* the Council as *parallel* to it. Yet that social change was congruous with many of the council's values. Younger Catholics were much more independent and self-confident about their personal spiritual lives, not to mention their relationships to the church, than earlier generations.[65]

This did not mean they left the church. Greeley found in the 1970s that about 15 percent of those raised Catholic had left, a figure consistent with findings both before and after the council. But significant changes obtained in Catholic *belief* patterns. In 1963 70 percent of Catholics said they believed in divine papal authority; by 1974 that figure had shrunk to 32 percent. In 1966 about 67 percent of Catholics went to Sunday mass regularly; in 1969, the year after *Humanae Vitae*, the percentage began to decline precipitously, sinking to around 50 percent in 1975. Then the decline stopped as suddenly as it had begun. No parallel decline marked Protestant church attendance in the same period. Greeley was convinced that the birth control encyclical—together with the crisis of church authority it generated—was almost alone responsible.

This conclusion was ambiguously reinforced by his finding that only about 12 percent of polled Catholics accepted the birth control teachings. This meant, Greeley argued, that 16 percent of Catholics stopped attending church because of *Humanae Vitae*—and that 38 percent continued to go even though they did *not* accept it. They were thus becoming "selective" or "do it yourself" Catholics. They had during the Sixties become postmodern Catholics who were little enamoured either of a monolithic institution or any need for rigorous consistency and instead lived mainly out of a pluralistic subjectivity that felt free to draw what it could use from both tradition and modernity, leaving the rest.

This is no doubt reflected in Greeley's most interesting discovery of all: a big change in what he refers to as Catholic "religious imagination" since Vatican II. The selective Catholics say that they experience themselves as "close" to God and think of God primarily as "loving." Allowing respondents to choose from a list of divine attributes those closest to their own ideas and experiences, Greeley found that the images, pictures, and stories of God post–Vatican II were generally more benign, more gracious, and more affectionate than the judgmental and legalistic set that might have been picked before. More significant, the more selective these Catholics were in their religious practice and belief, the more they chose the benign images. "The more Catholics imagine God as mother, lover, spouse and friend," Greeley concluded, "the more likely they are to make their appeal to God over the heads of institutional church leaders" (199). This is a situation about which those same leaders can do little, Greeley warned, for if they try to go back to a fire and brimstone religion they will simply be rejected.

The Finger Pointing Back from the Moon

What about the religious response to the landing of the first humans on the moon on July 20, 1969? There is a Zen saying that when a finger is pointing at the moon, one should not look at the finger, but at

Counterpoint: The World Council of Churches at Uppsala

Another significant event was the July 1968 meeting of the World Council of Churches at Uppsala, Sweden. Or perhaps one should say non-event, for despite much anticipation Uppsala demonstrated, like the Blake-Pike plan and the feeble drift of the National Council of Churches, that Fifties-style ecumenism was no longer religion's cutting edge, but a paper-clogged backwater.

This conclave was expected to show that the World Council of Churches was no longer the "stepchild of mainstream Western Protestantism." Eastern Orthodoxy was now the body's largest single bloc. Fifteen nonvoting Roman Catholic delegates were present, together with Southern Baptists and other observers from the evangelical tradition. And most importantly, some 260 members were from the Third World. Martin Luther King was scheduled to give the opening address, and it was expected that "North versus South" together with the "theology of revolution" and strident condemnations of the United States on Vietnam would emerge as explosive issues riveting attention on the Swedish city.

But King was assassinated three months before the opening gavel. Some Asian and African delegates hinted at the need for revolution, but no speaker advocated violence. Although the failure of the Third World to gain much attention or its spokespersons to be very outspoken was a disappointment to some, it should have been realized that the churches they came from were often small and cowed by their own governments, or else the local church leaders selected as delegates were in fact also establishment figures in their home Third World countries. One would not expect to find many revolutionary firebrands among such people. Expectations that had been shaped by the freewheeling, revolution-talking mood of some smaller church gatherings, including the NCC, and that continually measured Uppsala against it, were bound to be disappointed.

Placards were carried by youth participants at one of the teach-ins held concurrently with the assembly bearing messages like "Christ Is Still Too Revolutionary for the Church," and "Christ Works Alone in the Third World While the Churches Worship." But as Alan Geyer pointed out, "The ecumenical establishment was never really in danger of destruction at Uppsala, except . . . through boredom." To be sure, the WCC approved a call for the United States to cease bombing North Vietnam and for both sides to end the war on the ground—a resolution toned down from what the U.S. delegation itself wanted. The Eastern Orthodox contingent blocked the admission of a woman to the six-member presidium of the council, softened calls for

---

Counterpoint: The World Council of Churches at Uppsala *Continued*

family planning, and vetoed appeals for Marxist-Christian dialogue by the council. In the end the council produced little more than ten tons of quickly forgotten memorandums, reports, and statements.[*] The Assembly Message was based on the theme, "I Make All Things New" and referred to newness in worship, the relation of religion to scientific work, the need to renew social and economic systems. But to those familiar with ecumenese it sounded like standard rhetoric, barely equal at best to a world preoccupied with real and often frightening newness all around.

[*]Alan Geyer, "Old and New at Uppsala," *Christian Century*, August 21, 1968, 1031–1037; "Explosive Hope," *Newsweek*, July 15, 1968, 75; "Ten Tons of Talk," *Newsweek*, July 29, 1968, 99–100.

---

the moon to which it is directed. But in this case the significance was quite opposite; few found much of real interest in the rocky, dead world of Earth's satellite as such, but that human beings had not only pointed at it but followed their fingers to land on it was seen as of profound importance. Everyone knew the lunar landing was essentially a mythological event that happened to be true, comprised of hard nuts and bolts and sturdy flesh as well as human spirit.

In the 1990s, as one watches videos of the epochal event, one vicariously participates in an adventure inherently gripping yet already oddly dated in mentality and means, like a tale from Homer. Despite the 1969 talk of the heroic venture of Michael Collins, Neil Armstrong, and Edwin "Buzz" Aldrin as only the first step in a great human exploration of the universe, one feels intuitively it was rather the last great moment in an era now closed.

Not only the backdrop of Cold War, space race, and what one knows was simultaneously happening in Vietnam and the cities periodizes the Sixties astronauts and their stentorian announcement on the lunar surface, "We come in peace for all mankind." The Anglo names, all the white faces and male voices in control central as well as on the earth's satellite, the constant references to "man" and "mankind," and the stark, laconic, oppressively unemotional diction thought suitable to military-technological ventures ("lunar orbit insertion," "rocks with angularity") contrast mightily with the counterculture down below, and with what has since transpired on the blue-and-white marble in the sky the astronauts had left behind.

Above all, of course, is the knowledge that, after the sixth manned mission in the Apollo-Saturn series in December 1972, little more on the same scale was to come, despite orbital and unmanned ventures, and that while those $26 billion garnered some rocks of great scientific interest and produced some interesting photo opportunities, they didn't make much difference to the course of human events.

The Apollo-Saturn missions were isolated adventures like Odysseus's, not new Columbian voyages. Their countdown started in the Kennedy era, when we thought we could do anything and continued in the secular-city years when we believed humankind could be remade and technology was still good; but when time came for blastoff, the spirit that launched the Eagle was already cause for nostalgia.

Like the Vietnam War and the early civil rights movement, the moon landing was a supreme and last expression of the American modernist spirit, of the America of Roosevelt and Truman, of Clark Kerr, John F. Kennedy, and Lyndon Johnson, an America bold, masculine, comfortable with power and vast governmental projects, invincibly confident in its technological skill and its righteous use thereof, believing in progress forever. The postmodernist thinker Jean Baudrillard, pursing his argument that the contemporary world is dominated by technological simulations of reality rather than actual encounters with it, wrote:

> For what is the ultimate function of the space race, of lunar conquest, of satellite launching, if not the institution of a model of universal gravitation, satellisation, whose perfect embryo is the lunar module: a programmed microcosm, where *nothing can be left to chance?* Trajectory, energy, computation, physiology, psychology, the environment—nothing can be left to contingency, this is the total universe of the norm—the Law no longer exists, it is the operational immanence of every detail which is law. A universe purged of every threat to the senses, in a state of asepsis and weightlessness—it is this very perfection which is fascinating. For the exaltation of the masses was not in response to the lunar landing or the voyage of man in space (this is rather the fulfillment of an earlier dream)—no, we are dumbfounded by the perfection of their planning and technical manipulation, by the immanent wonder of programmed development.[66]

But Middle America, still more than half modern, and no doubt inspired in some such Baudrillardian manner by the laconic technical genius of the astronaunts and the multibillion-dollar program behind them, cheered the astronauts on as bearers of the American values of courage and creative enterprise, not to mention American spiritual faith.

Even the subsequent failure of Apollo-Saturn 13 in April 1970 produced a reactivation of what was left of civil religion. The return of three defeated astronauts, James Lovell, Fred Haise, and John Swigert, at least led to a successful splashdown that was played up as a triumph. The three were widely pictured in prayer, and their brush with death emphasized—until a few days later when they were supplanted in the media by four real deaths at Kent State.

Other religionists were not so sure what myth was being played out, putting Apollo 11 in the context of references to Babel and Prometheus.[67] *Life* magazine in July 1969 made a fascinating and perhaps unconscious juxtaposition of two wildly contrasting mythologies by placing, between its July 4 and July 25 cover stories on the lunar project and its fabulous technology, a July 18 special on "The Youth Communes." This issue featured on its face not shiny spaceships but a rustic nineteenth-century-looking scene displaying bearded men in buckskin, women barefoot and in long print dresses. Inside, the same counterculture figures are shown living in teepees, hoeing gardens, or bathing nude in rivers and ponds. Alongside them were a couple of other mythological texts, one on "What We Hope Apollo 11 Will Tell Us about the Moon," and one on the Nixon-era mania for U.S. flag decals.

And what about the costs? There were those who thought of the moon in terms of Lewis Mumford's "mad rationality," or Captain Ahab's "All my means are sane; my motives and object mad," sentiments that some thought might apply to Vietnam as well. Already the technocrats were projecting a Mars landing in 1986 at a cost of $57 billion, compared to the moon's mere $26 billion. Ian Barbour opined that the benefits of this venture paled against the material and spiritual costs of an Earth with so many needs, and a widening gap of rich and poor.[68]

In the end, the much-vaunted Sixties technological triumphs—psychedelics, the Pill, all the expensive high-tech military hardware in Vietnam, and the moon venture—have been less important to history than they seemed at the time. (No doubt a moral lies in the observation that what changed life in the United States more than anything else in the Sixties was instead nonviolent social action.) And along with the triumph of intrusive technology on the moon, where human footprints have been left for the ages, came a growing awareness of ecological ethics as a branch of natural theology.[69]

The clash of comparative mythologies also produced church and state issues. Does the First Amendment apply to outer space? The celebrated atheist Madalyn Murray O'Hair filed suit in federal court in Austin, Texas, to ban all religious practices by American astronauts on Earth, in space, or around the moon. She had been offended by

Col. Frank Borman's reading Genesis from Apollo 8 while circumnavigating the moon on Christmas 1968. But then, as the *Christian Century* put it in a memorable line, "Now come Americans United for Separation of Church and State seeking to undo Mrs. O'Hair's space suit." Americans United (like the *Century*) opposed O'Hair's position on the grounds that Borman's delivery was a "free exercise of religion," involving no compulsion.

An evangelical perspective on space exploration was offered by *Christianity Today* for July 18, 1969, which featured an interview with Dr. Rodney W. Johnson, a NASA scientist and conservative Christian. He declared the moon landing an aspect of the human vocation to "subdue the earth," saying of the home planet that "our escape from it shows our mastery over it." Dr. Johnson further remarked that glorifying God is not always explicit in the space program but perhaps present "in a subconscious way," since most astronauts have faith in God. Then, intriguingly, he commented that "the most frightening thought regarding space exploration is that we might encounter a form of life with a higher intelligence." This could mean that God "had made beings superior to us and didn't tell us about it." But on the other hand the discovery of any life, high or low, beyond Earth could well have the effect of "encouraging unregenerate man to reflect on who he is and where he came from," and this could lead to conversion and commitment to Christ. It could also, in Johnson's view, somehow lead "man" to "begin to discover that our social welfare programs do *not* provide the peace of mind he seeks."[70]

The Counterculture Carries On

The countercultural hippie scene was deteriorating in its homelands—the Haight-Ashbury and similar enclaves in most major cities. In July 1968 there gathered "what may be the flagging flower world's last great love-in" in Boston: thirteen hundred "nomads" assembled on Boston Common. The conclave led to conflict; the hippie ranks were allegedly "infiltrated" by criminal types, drug dealers and their ilk, and the tribe was forced to evacuate the Commons at night. The hippies held a candlelight parade to protest and also produced, to the delight of the news cameras, a gorgeous but nonbinding "hippie wedding."[71]

But as the hippie life-style degenerated on the streets, other aspects of what it had brought back to life were moving into general popular culture. The fresh and free hippie attitudes toward sex and nudity were not without their nondropout enthusiasts; the media in

Counterpoint: New Mythologies, Easy Rides in Space and Time

The eminent French critic Michel Butor noted in 1967 that science fiction is "the normal form of mythology of our time."* The emphasis should in fact be on the religious connotations of the word *mythology*, for one of the more profound shifts in religious consciousness that center around the Sixties has been the creation of new mythologies from the fabrics of science fiction and fantasy. What the Apollo missions did not do at the time may eventually be done on the mytho-religious level by the subconscious workings of images from *Star Trek* and *Star Wars*.

Yet it should also be observed that Butor declared science fiction to be "a fantasy framed by a realism"—that is, it accepts as its operating premise the universe as defined by modern science, which for its readers at least is reality. Within that sometimes elastic framework the new genre creates fantasies worthy of the religions of yore. Therefore, Butor says, the sci-fi spaceship differs from the unscientific magic carpet of *The Arabian Nights* and, one might add, from religious supernatural realities like resurrections and ascensions.

Perhaps the Scheherazade who first imagined a magic carpet, or the evangelists who recorded the raising and rising of Jesus, accepted a worldview into which those marvels could fit without strain. But though of course those stories are still told, moderns have preferred to place their *new* maps of heaven and hell in another mounting, one that evokes instead the mystique of the laboratory and the observatory.

Nonetheless, the new science fiction mythologies, no less than those of gods and titans, deal with the deepest enigmas faced by the human psyche, and with its profoundest dreams and fears. Here is where the Sixties as a time of shifting religious imagination come in, for in its yeasty atmosphere the new mythologies of science fiction and fastasy took firm root in popular culture, and that may yet turn out to be among the most far-reaching religious developments of the decade.

We have noted the explosive popularity of such works as Heinlein's *Stranger in a Strange Land* and Tolkien's *Lord of the Rings*. The Sixties were a time of powerful growth in the science fiction and fantasy genre generally, and that growth clearly had meaning related to spiritual change, though cause and effect are not always easy to sort out. (To gauge the growth of the genre, we may note that in 1951, just 15 science fiction novels were published in the United States; in 1985, the figure was 1,332, of which 715 were new and 617 reprints. Furthermore, new science fiction

Continued

Counterpoint: New Mythologies, Easy Rides in Space and Time *Continued*

constituted the largest single fiction-publishing category in the country with 20 percent of the market. The major late-twentieth-century science fiction films have included some of the greatest box office hits of all times, beginning with the 1969 epic *2001* and going on to *E.T.*, the *Star Wars* series, and *Close Encounters of the Third Kind.*)

A 1985 survey by Peter Lowentrout, distributed among readers of all ages but of course containing a large Sixties generation contingent, found that frequent readers of science fiction were less likely to be regular church attenders but more likely to believe in psychic phenomena or the "Force" of *Star Wars* than the norm. Lowentrout concluded that science fiction and fantasy have provoked, or are the result of, a "displacement" of the religious drive into nonconventional, more imaginative, and more privatized directions. This conclusion is reinforced in a study of science fiction by William Sims Bainbridge, in which he found that what readers preferred most of all were "stories that convey a sense of wonder," clearly a crypto-religious appeal, though for these readers the Bible, along with "occult literature," lurked at the bottom of a list of forty popularity categories.**

With this in mind, let us look first at the 1969 film *2001: A Space Odyssey*, directed by Stanley Kubrick, story by the famous British science fiction writer Arthur C. Clarke. This is a picture of mythic dimensions that inculcates a powerful but unconventional sense of spirituality, and whose images create unparalleled feelings of mystery and awe. The film, behind all the cosmic wonder it evokes, is a parable on a fundamental problem of the decade. In a twist on the modernist science versus religion conundrum, in which science was often presented not only as truer but also as facilitating a more advanced moral vision than its outworn rival, the problem in *2001* is the rapid pace of technological advance, now culminating in humans on the moon, versus the slower rate of human spiritual evolution.

The film commences with a remarkable scene of primal man as carnivorous hunter discovering the first tool—a bone with which to kill more game—and the transformation of that primal implement into its ultimate outcome, a shining space station. The action moves to an expedition to Jupiter to discover the secret of a mysterious rectangular monument found on the moon. On the way the ship's computer, HAL 9000, kills all but one of the earthly crew, perhaps in a reversal of the original killing that set human technology on its fantastic course; they are guilty of "human error," and Hal's program is to maintain the security of the mission at all costs. At the end are scenes clearly intended to represent human transcendence

Counterpoint: New Mythologies, Easy Rides in Space and Time *Continued*

over the technological level altogether, and to act out a futuristic mystery drama of death and rebirth. For some viewers these episodes conveyed that initiatory meaning; for others they were unnecessarily obscure.

A summary of the story does not do justice to the visual (and audial, with its famous use of Richard Strauss's *Also Sprach Zarathustra* and Johann Strauss's *Blue Danube*) feast that the film is. For 1969, the special effects were phenomenal; combined with the strange imagination of the story they were capable of effecting an almost psychedelic intoxication. Even more important, in its role of Sixties parable, *2001* touched all corners of the decade's conundrums. It celebrated the wonder of science while suggesting the parricidal possibilities of its progeny. But also, in line with the subjective visionary side of the Sixties, it made the universe not only an astronomical but also a spiritual wonderland; an infinity not only of mind-boggling beauty, potency, and distances, but also of transformative possibilities for us its children, and even death did not finally limit its power. The Sixties dream of true human transformation remains alive in this end-of-the-decade film, but it seems now that it will not happen merely in the secular city nor in the "real time" of the lunar mission, but that ultimate transfiguration will require some movement outside the circles of ordinary space and time altogether, followed by the return of a wise child; all this effectively removes it to the realm of timeless myth.

The film *2001* hinted at the counterculture's dream of speeding up spiritual evolution by the use of psychedelics but left these prospects properly ambiguous. We may recall that the Tate-LaBianca murders by mad counterculture mystics occurred only a few days after the moon landing.

As religious vehicle, *2001* can be compared to another important 1969 movie, *Easy Rider*. The protagonists in this saga hate time and want to get outside of it. They circle around in several Sixties-type backwaters and confront the place where time must have a stop—death—but because they do not return from that undiscovered country they leave the mystery as great as before, and because they are not transfigured they leave the Sixties as ambiguous as before. This saga of two bikers, Billy and Captain America, suggests that, though the Sixties dream was still thought to be there somewhere, the frustrations were adding up and the search was getting desperate by 1969.

The two motorcyclists are looking for something and set off for such goals as California or New Orleans but tend to turn aside for something

Continued

Counterpoint: New Mythologies, Easy Rides in Space and Time *Continued*

else before they get there. Or if they do reach a destination, like Mardi Gras in New Orleans, they decide that isn't really where it's at and move on. On the way they spend time in a commune where prayers are said before meals and take LSD in a churchyard where the psychedelic effects are mixed with crosses and tombstones. Like 1969, they hated time and history; the characters have no particular background or beginning, and the pair end up shot dead by hostile rednecks. Before they set out, Captain America had torn off his watch and thrown it to the ground. It's 1969: the means are there, the hatreds are there, the wild wandering impulses are there, but the clocks are stopped and the directional compass is swinging wildly. One knows it can't go on.

*Michel Butor, "Science Fiction: The Crisis of Its Growth," *Partisan Review*, Fall 1967, 595–602.
**Peter Lowentrout, "The Influence of Speculative Fiction on the Religous Formation of the Young," *Extrapolation*, 28, 4 (1987): 345–359; William Sims Bainbridge, *Dimensions of Science Fiction* (Cambridge, Mass.: Harvard University Press, 1986), 229–231. Quote from 229.

---

these years were full of attention to "the sex explosion," ranging in concerns from a vast exfoliation of nude entertainment to new attention to homosexuality, as well as the post-Pill relaxation of taboos against premarital and extramarital sex.

On another front, the late Sixties saw an explosion of interest in the quasi-magical esoterica by which the counterculture had defined its awareness of nonrational realities. Sales of crystals, amulets, horoscopes, and tarot cards boomed, and chatter about them was chic in many circles. Mystical religions, from Zen and transcendental meditation to Scientology and ceremonial magic, grew exponentially as many people, no longer counting on the revolution or the Aquarian Age, found private refuges where they could maintain Sixties spiritual values in the upcoming Dark Ages.

But perhaps the new occultism was not so unfamiliar after all. A *Time* essay on "That New Black Magic" noted that TV commercials verge on magic. How, it asked, does a deodorant differ from a love potion? And "already the incantations of New Left and New Right extremists echo the irrational chants of sinister shamans."[72]

By 1968, the hippie phenomenon was receiving full scholarly attention. A special winter 1968 issue of *Religion in Life*, for example, devoted a section to it.

Carl Bangs, in "The Hippies: Some Historical Perspectives," first recalled Will Herberg's reference to them as "the Adamites of our time." The Adamites were a second-century sect mentioned by Augustine, Epiphanius, and John of Damascus; they allegedly worshipped in the nude, lived in isolation, rejected marriage, practiced continence, and believed themselves to be in paradise. Bangs also compares the hippies to St. Anthony of Egypt, who attained visionary experience by means of deprivation and fasting, and mentions other dissident spiritual perfectionist dropout movements (the Montanists, early Franciscans, Quakers, Anabaptists) and other facets of radical reform including the Diggers, who as we have seen were putatively revived in Haight-Ashbury. Apparently intrigued by the hippies' relative openness to nudity, Bangs notes that other religious radicals too have practiced nudity as a sign of radical dissent and Adamic perfection.[73]

Other writers were less interested in the remote antecedents of the movement. Alan J. Moore, in "The Revolt against Affluence," points to its rejection of marriage and the family, and Paul R. Woudenberg, in "The Egoism of Flower Power," to an "I" mysticism centering on the authority of the self and concomitant rejection of authority.[74] As always when approached by sensitive religious writers, the hippie movement was seen to be in a venerable tradition, expressing valid religious protest against a largely corrupt and corrupting society, and endeavoring to set foot on a genuine spiritual quest—yet seriously flawed by egoism and lack of self-discipline. Spoiled by an affluent, consumerist "buy now, pay later" society, they might say, hippies wanted and expected too much too soon in the spiritual realm, as their parents had in the material. But the fact remains that, in a day of anger and cynicism, few others could even talk about peace and love without hypocrisy or shame.

Certain aspects of hippie culture, like the use of marijuana, were undergoing scrutiny by religious moralists. For example, Joseph Fletcher of *Situation Ethics* fame said the legitimacy of its use depended on the situation, like social drinking, and many of the clergy condemned strict laws on the model of Prohibition against the weed. Some acknowledged that pot and other drugs were by now a problem even in divinity schools. Others perhaps would not have even used the word *problem*; perhaps recalling the Good Friday experiment a few long years earlier, they were willing to countenance chemical ways of access to mysticism, even though still denouncing their use as a way of life.[75]

Then came the books. Two that appeared in 1968 were *Voices from the Love Generation*, edited by Leonard Wolf, and Nicholas von

Hoffman's *We Are the People Our Parents Warned Us Against.*[76] Both contain extensive firsthand accounts of the new scene and are pretty cynical about it, Von Hoffman's especially, in contrast to the *LSD and the Search for God* mood of only a year or two before. The authors now are not afraid to portray hippiedom as perhaps based not on love, but on dope and crime to get it. Yet the "perhaps" is still there—the writers were honest enough to realize how hard it was to get into the hippie world even if one were a citizen of it, as these writers were at least part of the time. Many paths wended their ways through the counterculture. Some dropouts were truly mystical, some just incoherent. All had drugs in common, though their significance could vary tremendously. One woman described the ecstasy of tripping nude in the woods, while other counterculturalists talked grimly of the unsavory, gun-carrying drug dealers and suchlike who lurked on the fringes of paradise.

On another level, Ralph Metzner, sometime companion of Timothy Leary at Millbrook, in *The Ecstatic Adventure* presented an anthology of acid experiences by more mature explorers of the art, such as André Malraux, Aldous Huxley, and the Millbrook set (including a scientist who solved problems in theoretical physics while high), and others who talked of sex and even going through childbirth under the influence. This was a different acidic world than that of the Wolf and von Hoffman kids on the street.[77]

Thus for its high priests, as for some Christian moralists, the psychedelic dream was still there. Along with the continuing acid idealism of Metzner's *Ecstatic Adventure* was that of Metzner's even more true-believing colleague Timothy Leary. The latter had updated the utilitarian "hedonic calculus" to "hedonic engineering," which he defined as "designing one's life for pleasure through chemical turn-ons and turn-offs." He considered hedonism morally valid; it was the antipleasure society that was "uptight" and therefore becomes repressive and, in compensation for its frustration, warlike. And about 1970 Alan Watts wrote an essay, "The Future of Ecstasy," putatively dated January 6, 1990, that begins, "It wasn't until thirty years ago, in the 1960s, that there began to be any widespread realization that ecstasy is a legitimate human need—as essential for mental and physical health as proper nutrition, vitamins, rest, and recreation."[78] The counterculture believed this. The trouble was that its members didn't always get ecstasy, and that could make them angry and very desperate.

And there were religious ministries to hippies. Though some Evangelicals challenged the countercultural world directly, other clerics did so more obliquely, as if in a postmodern world without oppo-

314

sites. One example was the Reverend Richard York, pastor of the Free Church that ministered to the nonstudent hippie population clustered around Telegraph Avenue just south of the University of California in Berkeley, after Haight-Ashbury in San Francisco one of the largest of such enclaves.

York, an Episcopalian, kept a journal of people he encountered in this work; it is sufficient to dispel any illusions one might have about what could lie behind the counterculture's surface glamor and freedom. "A young man who has taken 100 cough drops and is standing on the street convulsing and foaming at the mouth from the overdose. . . . A 16-year-old heroin addict who can't get medical attention for severe gonorrhea because it is the weekend. Clinics are closed and he is a minor. . . . A girl who is pregnant, unmarried, needs surgery, hasn't eaten in two days and has no place to sleep. She feels she will have to deal in drugs to pay for her baby because no one will hire a hippie. . . . A boy who tried to slash his wrists and whose parents don't want him. . . . A boy who is vomiting in my living room from a poison someone sold him saying it was LSD."[79]

Nonetheless, York's work was based less on confrontational preaching than on affirming the strong features of the counterculture and building on them. Take, for example, the hippies' notable capacity for festive celebration. On a festival of the Blessed Virgin Mary in the Episcopal calendar the Free Church made a large papier-mâché image of the Virgin, engaged rock bands, solicited food, pulled in over a thousand people from off the "Avenue," and held a "Christian-hippie-happening" in honor of Our Lady. All the five senses of those present could feast on the rich brocade vestments and liturgical folderol, the incense wafting in the air, the clerics washing the feet of hippies, the free food, and the balloons released that were inscribed "Love," "Peace," and "Mary." Two not totally disparate cultures met and kissed. One imagines that the Harvey Cox of *The Feast of Fools*, if not of *The Secular City*, would have loved it.

Richard York's own admission to the priesthood on March 9, 1968, which received wide publicity as a "hippie ordination," was a no less memorable happening. Again there were rock bands; the ordinand's new vestments were in paisley-hip style, and everyone wore flowers; clergy of many denominations joined the bishop in laying hands on the new priest; girls tossed rose petals over the congregation; and at the end a huge pink and white balloon bobbed up and down above the assembly. In his sermon, the Reverend John Brown warned York not to so identify himself with the community he served as to have nothing left of his own to offer it—one might say, to preserve the messianic role.

A word must be said about the biblical musical dramas of Andrew Lloyd Webber and Timothy Rice, especially *Joseph and the Amazing Technicolor Dreamcoat* (1968) and *Jesus Christ Superstar* (1971). The last especially, though technically after the Sixties, wonderfully captures something of the essence of Sixties spirituality in its portrayal of Jesus: revisionist, controversial, earthy, youthful, rock music-oriented, and in the end a passive suffering servant in a cruel world he never made.

But the triumphant countercultural event of the last Sixties years was Woodstock, the greatest camp meeting of the Love Generation, and the last.

The Woodstock Art and Music Fair, held at a Catskill farm on a rainy August weekend in 1969, was first of all a statistical epic: 400,000 people (at least), four thousand injuries, six hundred acres, six hundred toilets, a hundred miles of traffic, thirty performing groups, six wells, four miscarriages, three births, three deaths, $2 million lost, and an inch of rain.[80]

The figures only begin to testify to the significance of Woodstock, however. At the time, the media saw it as a portent of the future. *Time* called rock music "one long symphony of protest" and spoke of the rock festival as "an art form and social structure unique to our time," inaccessible to adults, and predicted that this strange generation, after "doing its thing" in mysterious seclusion at such places as Woodstock, would "change the world"—but how?[81]

But in fact Woodstock was the climax and denouement of the counterculture as a distinct entity, at once its defining moment and the beginning of its reaggregation into straight society. As one watches Woodstock again on videos, one picks up numerous signs of crypto-religious performance and community formation: the shamanlike ecstasy of the singers as they worked up to greater and greater intensity of feeling expressed in rapid dancelike and trancelike motions, the passing of marijuana joints around a circle like Holy Communion, the edenic nude bathing, the pilgrim simplicity of life in tents and sleeping bags, the pervasive flavor of eroticism, the distinctive garb, the reiterated self-definition of the assembly by singers and announcers as "children" (like children of God, like a transfigured Love Generation, set over against the parental establishment generation with its rules and wars).

A separate, set-apart community was thus defined in numerous ways. The peaceful sustenance of so many more than expected was almost a miracle, like the feeding of the five thousand. Religiously, Woodstock was half early-Franciscans, half return to some antinomian paradise. It was a pilgrim band celebrating what Victor Turner called *communitas*, the spirit of antistructure, I-Thou relationships ideally achieved at festival and on pilgrimages. Even the logistics disaster that Woodstock was, with the rain and temporary population explosion, had its spiritual side: troubles make people work together and create community. Wavy Gravy (Hugh Romney) said from the stage, "There's always a little bit of heaven in a disaster area," and Andrew Kopkind wrote, "Woodstock must always be [our] model of how good we will all feel after the revolution."[82]

But the revolution was delayed, and Woodstock was the end of the counterculture, because by now most young people thought of themselves as counterculture, dressing hip and listening to rock music, so it was nothing special. The great majority at Woodstock were in fact not real dropout hippies but regular youths out for the weekend, ready to go back to a reasonably normal Monday-morning life as students or even salaried workers. They would always keep something of Woodstock in their hearts, but that would be while they were making it in the system, not overthrowing it. Revolution for them was just something you sang about, and now the Beatles, on their new "Hey, Jude" disc, paeaned a song called "Revolution" that stressed that the real revolution was not destruction but upbuilding, in one's heart rather than on the streets.

Furthermore, Woodstock had its shadow side at a place called Altamont in California near San Francisco in November 1969. Here, at a Rolling Stones concert, the Hell's Angels motorcycle gang was retained to keep order and overdid it almost on the scale of the Chicago police at the Democratic convention. The crowd was high, spacy, crowding closer and closer; the Angels, trying to keep them back and taking offense at the nudity of a few, left one dead and many bleeding. What was most appalling were scenes, some recorded on film, showing the stoned indifference of fans to beatings going on in their midst, even blocking access to doctors, as the music rocked on. Altamont, together with the Tate-LaBianca murders and the increasing despair of Haight-Ashbury, showed a counterculture, despite Woodstock, winding down and discovering sin.

More Books

Tom Wolfe's *Electric Kool-Aid Acid Test* (1968) deserves mention as the great Sixties counterculture novel, portraying in thinly fictionalized form the story of Ken Kesey and the coming of the acid culture. Kesey is compared to religious figures like Jesus and the Buddha, and

Counterpoint: God Coming Back to Life in New Styles of Ministry

While church attendance was shrinking in the late Sixties, unlike attendance at quasi- or pseudoreligious rock concerts, and ecclesiastical life was often tired and drowned out by what was happening in the streets, the old religious institutions were still alive. Vitality was reflected in fresh approaches to ministry here and there, wherever fatigue was not the last word.

In a Christmas 1969 story, *Time* wrote of new ways the churches and synagogues, despite declining numbers and all the talk of secularity, were fervently trying to be "relevant." As society appeared to be falling apart, understandable differences appeared between those who saw the church's role as "prophetic," pointing toward the future, and those who wanted it to be a "stabilizer," keeping reassuring traditions alive in a tempestous time. But the more interesting ministries to which this article and other sources referred were those that came under Dale Brown's messianic role. They were prepared not just to build bridges to the secular world but also to preach to it, judge it, if possible turn it upside down, on behalf of something other than that world. Significantly, on the Protestant side the exciting new ministries were now sometimes outside the liberal churches that had borne the heat and burden of the day in the mid-Sixties theological and activist struggles. They instead spotlighted fresh, spirited new contenders from other quarters.*

One example was the Reverend Arthur Blessitt, a Baptist evangelical who preached to large crowds in counterculture strongholds and ran a storefront center on the Sunset Strip in Los Angeles. His rap was full of hip jargon: "Jesus is just the best trip, man. You don't have to drop acid to get high—all you have to do is pray and you go all the way to heaven." Blessitt had a long string of successes in getting kids off drugs, and his unabashed street-level fundamentalism was a major precursor of the "Jesus People" movement of the early Seventies.

There were other signs: burgeoning Pentecostalism, a growth in Christian and other religious communes, new musical experiences like that of largely black St. Francis de Sales Roman Catholic Church in New Orleans, where Catholic rituals were accompanied by piano and songs from the traditional black church repertoire.

But liberal and mainstream Protestant churches too were by now trying out the new ideas on the grass-roots level. The October 1969 issue of the *United Church Herald* listed a number of one-sentence responses by ministers and church leaders on the new worship trends, indicating ways they hit the ecclesiastical grass roots. Here are a few:

Counterpoint: God Coming Back to Life in New Styles of Ministry *Continued*

Because worshippers (our customers) are older, we please them with the traditional. But this repels the younger.

A vociferous minority are offended by sameness. What can I do with the conservative/avant-garde tension in my church? Help!

We're moving with talk back, vocal responses, folk music, passing the peace, lay leadership. But it's not spontaneous. We're arranging it.

Hand clapping, jazz, alleluias can turn them off as quickly as solemn anthems, dull sermons, stiff necks.

Innovation at 9:30 and tradition at 11:00 is our pattern. People can choose.**

All these tokens of new life convinced many that God was not dead after all. News media now started to talk of the death of the Death of God. A significant Christmas 1969 article by Roy E. Benson was titled, "Time to Meet the Evangelicals?" In the last years of the Sixties, he said, mainline and evangelical Christians are meeting each other going in opposite directions. Time to talk?***

    *"The New Ministry: Bring God Back to Life," *Time*, December 26, 1969, 40–45.
    **"Alterations: Words on Worship for Today," *United Church Herald* 12, 10 (October 1969): 8m–9m.
    ***Roy E. Benson, "Time to Meet the Evangelicals?" *Christian Century*, December 24, 1969, 1640.

---

his disappearance in midcourse is like the profoundly enigmatic and spiritually significant disappearance of Leo in Herman Hesse's *Journey to the East.* In the book is thus a good portion of extrainstitutional, countercultural religiosity, together with youthful self-consciousness, wonderful hip jargon, and Wolfe's incomparable carnival-in-a-madhouse style.

In *The New Immorality* (1968), Brooks R. Walker, a Unitarian minister, describes current cultural phenomena such as wife swapping, premarital and extramarital intercourse, and pornography. Walker criticizes both the sheer sensuality of the *Playboy* philosophy and the situation ethics attitude that love is the only norm. But the author had no real solution, saying that we are in a moral "interregnum." For now it is enough just to celebrate the present pluralism.[83]

Peter L. Berger's *A Rumor of Angels* (1969) represents an attempt by the critical author of *The Noise of Solemn Assemblies* and the sociologist coauthor of *The Sacred Canopy* to speak for the other side, confronting "the alleged demise of the supernatural" with signs that the biblical God is still around and coming unawares behind such signs as the existence of hope, the existence of evil, the comic dimension of human life.[84] Like Harvey Cox and others, Berger saw presentiments that the secular was wearing thin, and light was beginning to show through.

The Church and the Second Sex (1968) was by Mary Daly, a young radical-feminist Catholic author who here first outlined the "case against the church."[85] She lines up misogynist quotes from even the greatest saints, theologians, and bishops, presenting potent evidence of a built-in subordination of women in conventional Catholic understandings of priesthood, marriage, and even in such rules as those against girls serving at Mass like boys. Daly moreover saw little hope in the "pedastal peddlars" who exalted a few women like Mary, or women in the abstract, so much that they denied women's real humanity and so their human equality with men. She put more trust in the "winds of change" evident in the papacy of John XXIII and Vatican II, and in their spirit made some "modest proposals" for partnership and coeducation between males and females in the church, such as that priests and sisters should attend the same seminary classes, together with reform in the direction of less hierarchy and more leveling.

As modest as the proposals may have been, this book nearly cost Daly her job as an instructor at Boston College, a Jesuit institution, and precipitated one of the great academic confrontations of spring 1969. When it appeared that her contract would not be renewed for the following fall, clearly as a result of the book's publication, a series of great demonstrations arose, complete with student petitions containing over twenty-five hundred names, picketing of the president's house, graffiti, teach-ins with professors coming in from other institutions to participate, local witches arriving to hex the college, and of course TV cameras rolling and front-page stories in the Boston and New York papers. In a later edition of the book, in a new introduction that describes these events, Daly speaks of the "archetypal" quality she came to sense in this confrontation, a sense that seemed to pervade many late-Sixties battles. Eventually, in late summer, the administration suddenly and without explanation relented, and she was rehired. But she later described herself as a "post-Christian" feminist.

Rosemary Radford Ruether's *Radical Kingdom* is an ambitious work by an already familiar feminist writer.[86] It is an inevitably incomplete but impressive survey of the significance of radicalism in Western

culture from the radical reformers of the sixteenth century to the Sixties' New Left, making important connections between the radicals of
one generation and another along the way. Though clearly aware of
the dangers of revolutionary totalitariansim, as in Stalinism, Ruether's
heart is obviously with sincere and spirited revolutionaries. "Revolution," she says toward the very end, "breaking the bonds of the possible, is essential to man's affirmation of his life against every stasis,
including the stasis of liberal affluence. . . . The time of revolutionary
expectation is the time when men come closest to experiencing the
spirit dwelling in the community of man. In such a time of struggle
one feels closest to one's brother. One glimpses what true fraternity
and community might mean" (287–288). This is one of the most judi-
cious though sympathetic books to come out of a moment when revolution was in the air, and lines like those just quoted help us to
understand why revolution was so often felt to be fraught with profound religious and spiritual meaning.

Weatherman (1970), edited by Harold Jacobs, consists of papers
by people in the movement, plus some critical pieces, to make up a
document reflecting 1969–1970 on the extreme Left.[87] The tone is
strong and serious, but the Weatherman's pedantic anger and radicalism are generally vented through all the right jargon. The volume ends
with communiqués on the 1970 bombings and the story of how the
movement went underground.

Charles Reich's *Greening of America* (1970) was one of those books
that makes a big splash in its time but soon enough becomes nothing
but a tag line.[88] People still talk about the "greening" (or some other
coloring) of something, but I imagine few of them could fairly summa-
rize the contents of Reich's book. *Greening* was an attempt to interpret
the new youth culture sympathetically. Like its spokespersons, Reich
was radical enough to say that America was not working and was
dealing death to its own people and around the world. Liberal reformism was not the answer because it offers no truly new way of life. But
that new way was in fact breaking through all around.

The paradigm Reich uses to explain this is three consciousnesses.
Con I was America at its beginning, a mentality of harsh individualism. Con II was the corporate and also the liberal, New Deal mind that
tries to create organizations for social benefit but actually dehuman-
izes to make for a robot society. The next level, Con III, however, was
starting to peek through. Out of a feeling of betrayal by Con II, young
people were finding a new self-affirmation and a reaffirmation of childhood ideals. The foundation of Con III is liberation of self—not in a

selfish sense, but as a postulation of the absolute worth of each individual.

Although at first too much celebrated, then too much denigrated, and finally too much ignored, *Greening* is a preview of postmodernism and its dilemmas. It was premature, and like so many such books too optimistic in tone. It forgot that radical pluralism and self-affirmation can bring their own ills of indifference, that the theoretical affirmation of the absolute worth of all individuals can in practice be such a utopian ideal as to reduce other humans to idealized abstractions and amount mostly to one's own self-affirmation. In such a state the concrete reformism of Con II might well be preferred. Yet *The Greening of America* was a significant book appearing at the very end of the Sixties, a good symbolic statement of how far we had come since the last Eisenhower year, 1960.

Theodore Roszak's *Making of a Counter Culture*, one of the classics of instant Sixties interpretation, presented the young as "technocracy's children," but profoundly alienated from a world devoted primarily to the production of products and technocracy's own self-perpetuation. For them, the system is like a robot that has gone out of control and is willing to risk even the extermination of its human creators to maintain the momentum.

Against this, "the counterculture is . . . that healthy instinct which refuses both at the personal and political level to practice such a cold-blooded rape of our human sensibilities."[89] Like others, Roszak speaks of the present as "an historical emergency of absolutely unprecedented proportions" (47). To handle the emergency, the counterculture comes as "an invasion of centaurs," questing for "a Holy City that lies beyond the technocracy." The "centaurs" represent primitive human instincts. They confront technological society with "the experience of radical culture disjuncture" and challenge with their subjective utopias "the myth of objective consciousness" that underlies the dominant culture (49).

The Making of a Counter Culture, cast in the polarized apocalyptic mode characteristic of the day, may seem a bit overheated a few decades later. But it is, with the works of Herbert Marcuse and Paul Goodman, among the best contemporary philosophical interpretations of the counterculture by a writer with first-class intellectual credentials. Roszak's antitechnological view of it is one-sided but important.

Thomas A. Harris's *I'm O.K.—You're O.K.: A Practical Guide to Transactional Analysis* (1969) is a characteristic work of popular psychology, typical of the thirst for secular salvation through neat models of psychic entities and their positionings.[90] Here the point is to get the parent, the adult, and the child within each of us lined up and all affirming each other. Perhaps it was a way for those eternal, Peter Pan children of the counterculture to save the best of Cockaigne while transiting back into adulthood and even parenthood.

The Dramatic Structure of the Final Scene

In the final scene of a masterful play, several things happen. The conflict and tension is screwed to the tightest point imaginable, then suddenly resolved and released. The characters are seen to be transformed by what they have passed through, and like Prospero in abjuring "this rough magic" may look back on former means and ends with a new wisdom. And around them dawns, as for Caesar's heirs, a new day in which fresh glories are to be parted out. In the end, the logic of the drama becomes personal, not formal; it is the story line that prevails over the didacticism. In the final scene the God found in time and memory, in flashbacks to one's own personal days of penance and pentecost, eclipses the God of the philosophers and moves luminously to center stage.

The great drama of the religious Sixties was, to use words echoing those of John S. Dunne, a story of a recovery from sickness by means of a disease induced to destroy itself. The sickness, as he put it, was alienation, estrangement from oneself, from one's life . . . a sickness many felt in that glorious and terrible decade in the form of alienation from their society, their nation, even their world. And what is that estrangement, in the deepest analysis, but alienation from another part of oneself?

The fever therapy prescribed by Dunne was doubt and despair carried to the limit so they at last cancel themselves out. So it was in the sanitaria of the Sixties end-time, but the resolution was less visible in society as a whole than in individual life narratives. The fever was less acute, whether for healing or ill, in the Seventies, but one could hardly say American society then displayed much health. The best of those who thought deeply on the things of the spirit came out of the Sixties much shaken and with many hopes and idols shattered, but with new eyes to see the sacred in odd and incidental ways.

The high Sixties had been a golden age for theologians. The position of the Catholic *periti* at Vatican II was unparalleled; the leading Protestant (as well as Catholic) theologians were given prominence by such media as *Time* magazine and treated like serious, normative national intellectual voices. Even the radicals, those of the Death of

God camp, were widely publicized and enjoyed a certain scandalous success.

By the end of the Sixties, however, their theological dramas in the sun had played out. Once the Vatican II Council fathers had packed their bags, the papacy and curia found ways to reassert their customary authority and conservatism, notably in the *Humanae Vitae* episode. Protestants, now bereft of such greats as Tillich and Barth, and caught between pietism and secular/sacred apocalypse, looked aside to scan the barren plains for a burning bush in some new direction. Harvey Cox, in *The Feast of Fools*, saw one in the medieval holy play the too-serious modern world had forgotten, now being recovered by the counterculture's up-to-date mysticism.

Robert McAfee Brown, in a contribution to the *Christian Century*'s "How My Mind Has Changed" series, stated that he had come to believe very much in "the pseudonyms of God"—"the strange names he uses in the world to accomplish his purpose when his self-proclaimed servants let him down." Though he acknowledged no personal attraction for the secular or Death of God theologies, Brown—like Cox in *The Feast of Fools* and Peter Berger in *A Rumor of Angels*— had now discovered God at work in "an infinitely wider variety of activities than I had earlier believed" and called for different language to cover the realities behind such worn-out terms as *revelation* or *atonement*.[91]

But the talk of the death of the Death of God that began to be heard around as the Sixties endgame was played appears too simple. The God who came back in 1969 was not the God of the 1950s. He was a God hip to the new things of the Sixties. He was at home in the secular city as well as in joyously playful liturgical trips as lavish as Richard York's; he was sometimes revolutionary and sometimes traditionalist; he could even be psychedelic. He was also found in the most unexpected of everyday encounters, in the comic and the strange, outside the church as well as in official revelation. This God was not proved or revealed so much as simply seen when the eye was clear.

The radical seekers of the Fifties like Merton, Huxley, and Watts had perforce turned to the language of venerable mystical traditions almost exclusively. Now the talk of God, even by those at theological odds with the radical side of the Sixties, was laced with the new jargon of highs, trips, and liberation. The upshot was the evangelicalism and mysticism of the Seventies: the Jesus People, the "born again" talk, the high-point popularity of Transcendental Meditation and the Divine Light Mission, and strong residual interest in Zen and Yoga and the like. This all took the increasingly instutionalized forms described in Steven Tipton's *Getting Saved from the Sixties* (1982).

Though present hope seemed a little faded by the Sixties' end, that was all the more reason to take it off the streets and interiorize it in spiritual adventures. The capacity to riot, to demonstrate, to hold summers of love, and to sail off on ontological explorations was what was left—but now all within the mind.

Chapter 6

Getting It Together:
Final Reflections on the Sixties

A savage place! as holy and enchanted
As e'er beneath a waning moon was haunted
By woman wailing for her demon-lover!
And from this chasm, with ceaseless turmoil seething,
As if this earth in fast thick pants were breathing,
A mighty fountain momently was forced. . . .

It flung up momently the sacred river . . .
Through wood and dale the sacred river ran,
Then reached the caverns measureless to man,
And sank in tumult to a lifeless ocean.
—*Coleridge, "Kubla Khan"*

Though but a few years in ordinary surface time, the Sixties undoubt-edly had deep measureless sources and will have consequences as far reaching. There will long be those for whom that decade was a time when a sacred fountain was allowed to spume forth momently, even as others judge it a time of cultural congress with a demon-lover.

Our concern, however, is not to assess the Sixties in the apocalyp-tic terms with which the era was ever-ready to view itself, but to look back at its significance from the perspective of a little distance, a quarter-century or so at the time of writing.

What will the final upshot of the Sixties be? By the Nineties sev-eral results had appeared. First came the reaction of the Nixon-Reagan era. But I am now writing ten days after the 1992 election, when, as has been widely remarked in the press, for the first time a president and vice-president born after World War II were chosen. Now the mystique of that great and good war that so framed the mentality of Sixties Middle America and indirectly influenced the counterculture as well is finally slipping out of conscious, living memory so far as the power generation is concerned. Instead we have leaders whose forma-tive years were shaped by the Sixties, not in reaction to them, and in Bill Clinton a one-time antiwar protester in the White House.

Parallels to all this abound in religion. The much-celebrated resur-gence of evangelicalism in the Seventies and Eighties was no doubt a religious backlash against the Sixties comparable to the general political conservatism of the same decades. But if the thirty-year-cycle theory of American history, proposed among others by Arthur Schlesinger, is of any merit, the Nineties should be another radical decade in politics, religion, and society, like the Thirties or Sixties.[1]

Mainstream religion, long comfortably yoked to basically modernist views of human life and society even when it criticized aspects of them with reformist zeal, was caught in the Sixties between two roles: that longstanding familiar one by which religion was basically part of the establishment, a relationship that was compromising perhaps but one in which religious institutions often could be truly helpful; and an internal view that religion ought somehow also to be independent of any kingdom of this world, able to identify with the marginal as well as the elite and to look at things from an inside/outside observation post . . . to be, in Thomas Merton's words, "a guilty bystander." American religion did not so much solve this conundrum as bypass it.

The result is that it underwent what Phillip E. Hammond has called "the Third Disestablishment in America," or what we might call the post-Sixties establishment of postmodern religion. Let us recapitulate the discussion of Hammond's and Wade Clark Roof's findings presented earlier. After the first disestablishment, the constitutional separation of church and state in the Bill of Rights, and the second, the dethroning of Anglo-Protestant hegemony in the Sixties and after, according to Hammond a third has taken place, founded on increased personal autonomy in religion and corresponding decline in traditional forms of parish involvement, "and—what is culturally more relevant—the meaning of that involvement has been significantly altered."[2] This is like what Greeley more provocatively called a shift in religious imagination.

Based on a 1988 sociological survey of religion in four states (Massachusetts, North Carolina, Ohio, and California), Hammond found this new sense of personal autonomy in religion strikingly expressed in very "loose-bonding" views of personal relationships to religious institutions. No fewer than 88 percent agreed that "a person can be a good Christian/Jew without attending church/synagogue," and 76 percent that "an individual should arrive at his or her own religious beliefs independent of any church or synagogue." It is not surprising that the percentage of persons who switch religions, or switch from a natal faith to none, is rising, up to 30 percent in California. Since the Sixties, then, religion has been far more a matter of personal autonomy, and less a question of denomination or family tradition, than for a long time. Subjectivity is supreme, and believers show a readiness to switch religion and church affiliation for subjective reasons.

Wade Clark Roof has generally supported these findings with his own, presented in *A Generation of Seekers*. He notes a radical boomer shift from an ethic of self-denial to an ethic of self-fulfillment—to the notion that it is important to "find meaning," to "grow," and to find "self-expression." This is one of those basal presuppositions that joins both those of the postwar generation who have taken conservative religious paths and those given to spiritual experimentation. In both cases, self-fulfillment as a priority obviously requires a subordination of consistency and self-abnegation; therefore the presence of plural options, and willingness to test them, is necessary. Along with this is a feeling that it is important to have belief in oneself and faith that strength comes from within, whether by the power of Christ or otherwise; clearly this also mandates ability to change and experiment according to one's inner compass.

Yet Roof observes that "commitment" is also seen as an important value. Boomers seek ways to modify the quest for self with showing concern for others as well, and to make reliable commitments to important others and groups. Indeed, in one 1988 survey in which respondents were asked to evaluate a list of changes from the time of their parents' generation, the largest number, 83 percent, said the greater openness and willingness to share personal feelings was the most important change for the better. At their best, postmodern religious communities are experienced as places where that sort of openness and communication can occur. This means, in short, that they remain important, even though the meaning of church and temple may have changed over the generations.[3]

It is not to be supposed, however, that all this necessarily means religionists are becoming more liberal in the conventional sense of the word. It is true that, on the one hand, in Hammond's survey 43 percent agreed one can be a good Christian or Jew and still doubt the existence of God; that around 25 percent believe in reincarnation, not an orthodox Judeo-Christian doctrine; and some 15 percent say they practice a meditation technique "like that taught by Transcendental Meditation, Zen, etc." But over against this must be set the 40 percent who believe the Bible is the literal word of God, and the fact that conservative Protestant churches have been the chief beneficiaries of the church switching.

Clearly something else is going on than the liberalizing or "conservatizing" of American religion in the sense those terms might have had a generation or two ago. The kind of conservative Protestant churches that are growing fastest are not so much those of the rural, hardshell stereotype, but smoothly run suburban institutions with easy music, upbeat and not highly judgmental preaching, and a great amount of emphasis on small groups and gifts of the spirit, together with personal physical and psychological healing phrased in biblical language. They are highly supportive of families in a stressful world and come at people and problems less in terms of "God commands" than of "God loves and heals," though they may inculcate some highly traditional moral values.

I would say that they are not so much liberal or conservative as postmodern. Some adherents may be computer programmers or airline pilots—easy manipulators of the wondrous technology that came ultimately out of the modern era—who have no problem setting those skills, and that world, alongside speaking in tongues or speaking with comparable technical expertise on biblical prophecy. From the modern perspective, that would represent an unconscionable lapse of rational consistency, above all in one of the technological elite. But the postmodernist has not only no serious commitment to rational consistency, but apparently no concept with the least bit of rigor to it of what that might mean. She or he works instead out of radical personal autonomy, defined in effect as ability to name and practice truth—or rather truths—entirely in subjective terms, and these may in fact mean different names and practices in different areas of life. Thus contemporary postmodern religion can, for many people, be both liberal in its personal autonomy and looseness toward traditional religious institutions, and evangelical when—as is often the case—that style of faith best warms and heals the heart. From the postmodern perspective modern, rational concepts of objective truth have no more relevance to healing the heart, or to understanding evangelical and other kinds of neotraditionalist faith, than they do to understanding quantum theory or the postmodern atom.

I do not present this material because I am so deluded as to think that such attitudes toward religion are entirely new. The protean style in American religon, whether under evangelical or New Age auspices, may actually be a reversion to something older on these shores than the 1950s apotheosis of mainline Protestantism and Cardinal Spellman-style Roman Catholicism, which for many observers seems to be a baseline.

In the last century Alexis de Tocqueville, in reporting that America's rampant religious pluralism was a concomitant and facilitator of its democracy, indicated also that Americans "enjoy explaining almost every act of their lives on the principle of self-interest properly understood," and "not only do the Americans practice their religion out of self-interest, but they often even place in this world the interest which they have in practicing it. . . . [P]reachers in America are continually coming down to earth. Indeed they find it difficult to take their eyes off it. The better to touch their hearers, they are forever pointing out how religious beliefs favor freedom and public order, and it is often difficult to be sure when listening to them whether the main object of religion is to procure eternal felicity in the next world or prosperity in this."[4] The "user-friendly" religion of the Sixties-and-after postmodern establishment seems, in its pluralism and lack of internal rigor or consistency, to have nothing on this observation.

Tocqueville also perceptively observed that when, as in America, religion is a voluntary association, this can well work to its advantage, but it must learn how to compete and to accept that a considerable number of people will freely move from one religious association to another. "Though American Christians are divided into very many sects, they all see their religion in the same light. This is true of Roman Catholics as well as of other beliefs. . . . Thus, by respecting all democratic instincts which are not against it and making use of many favorable ones, religion succeeds in struggling successfully with that spirit of individual independence which is its most dangerous enemy."[5]

What then was new in the Sixties? First of all, novelty like so much else can exist and become an important reality simply by definition. Nothing is more fundamental to the Sixties mentality than its own belief that the decade was a radically new time. That credo was extrapolated from the genuine postwar transformation of society, which had demographically skewed the society toward youth with no living memory of prewar society. By 1960 the new order had loosened many things, such as the tight ethnic communities that had characterized much of Roman Catholicism and Judaism before. This may well have produced a new version of the frontier fluidity in American religion Tocqueville had observed in 1831, manifesting itself in the do-it-yourself, "self interest properly understood" faith of early Americans. Now that same openness was back as the new, more easygoing "religious imagination" of Greeley's post–Vatican II Catholics and their Protestant and Jewish equivalents. The Sixties brought a return of the repressed, of something of the young Republic's individualistic revivalism, experimentalism, and denominational reshuffling later covered over with Victorian consistency and modernist rationalization.

Of course, for many of its most influential denizens, the Sixties were fully and consummately a modern period when Marx, Freud, modern science, or neo-orthodoxy were accepted as universal truth, and reform, revolution, social justice, and national purpose were all taken seriously. So also was the role of the modernist elite—the psychoanalyist, the cleric, the professorial expert, the revolutionary cadre, the reformist hero, the general in Vietnam.

Yet the Sixties were also the first postmodernist era. Antitheses, if one may use Hegelian language, of all the modernist theses showed up on the doorstep. Modernism's rationalism and elitism were accused of being mutually supportive, if not one and the same thing, and were challenged from underground, by the nonrational in the basements of the mind and the non-elite on the margins of the world. In those years the great modernist institutions, from university to established church and state, were challenged as never since the Enlightenment onset of modernism, and precisely on the grounds that their claims to be the last word of progress and the holders of the master keys were spurious.

In place of those audacious claims was projected precisely those notions most threatening to the modern mindset, the equal validity of the primitive, of the nonrational, and of disunited knowledge. Tacitly or explicitly, the Sixties' free marketplace of ideas wanted all its stalls, old or new, drugstore or headshop, hardware or horoscope emporium, to be set up side by side.

The emergent postmodern age was now without a broadly accepted worldview that connected technology, politics, and religion. Instead the world witnessed the flourishing of disparate ecological, feminist, and liberationist spiritualities, of mystical, shamanist, and occultist paths, of resurgent fundamentalisms and religous nationalisms. At the time the lack of a center seemed to be no great lack.

But let us get back to the Sixties. I would like to present four models—no doubt all true, or none—by which the progress of Sixties religion can be interpreted.

In the first model, *the dominant paradigm moves from mainline to nonconformist religion, in various forms.* We observed that the decade opened in 1960 with a clear if unstated image that there was "first-team" religion, Anglo-Protestant, Episcopalian, Presbyterian, and the like, to which others were in greater or lesser degrees of marginalization. The Sixties challenged that hierarchy by bringing to the fore a succession of nonconformist alternatives as where the action was: first the peace church tradition as background for the civil rights and antiwar movements, then the occult/mystical counterculture model, then the ideal of charismatic spontaneity and informality (even in Roman Catholicism, though the style had been pioneered by Protestant nonconformists) in worship, and finally the emerging evangelicalism of the decade's end.

What this meant was nothing less than that the mainline, establishment, ultimately state-church pattern in both Protestant and Catholic religion, which though theoretically abandoned by the American republic had enjoyed a long-lingering half-life, was finally decisively rejected in the Sixties as a viable American option.

The second model is *the "discovery of the world" as a model for theology and practice.* The quest for "relevance," that is, for religion that makes a difference in the world, was an important Sixties theme. The trouble was that the location of the world to which one would be relevant kept shifting. Perhaps that unpleasant realization had to do with postmodernist subversion of the underlying concept. The modernist idea was that the world is a definite place that is there all the time; it is only the human mind that is likely to be shaky. In the image of Richard Rorty, the modern concept is that valid knowledge can be found only when the mind is trained to "mirror" reality. But as Hans Christian von Baeyer, explicating the current world of atomic physics, has put it, "Studying the atom is like scrutinizing the surface of a mirror. If you scrutinize it too closely, you suddenly realize that you are looking at yourself."[6]

So it was that secular theologians, and Catholics who wanted to be relevant, kept discovering that whenever they believed they had pinned down the world as an object of religious concern, something seemed to pop up that had been left out: festival; the comic; human yearning for tradition, for mystical transcendence, or for the distant and the past.

The third model is *the rediscovery of natural religion,* as over against revealed religion. Divine revelation was theoretically the sine qua non of the neo-orthodox Protestantism and pre–Vatican II Roman Catholicism of the Fifties, though their seamless robes of pure doctrine were certainly beginning to fray on the suburban fringes. But the Sixties, though superficially purchasing a hundred new revelations, went a long way toward natural religiosity, in the sense of religion that finds and celebrates the divine already implanted in the human heart and the natural world.

Natural religion believes this innate presence may be tapped by a normal quickening of spiritual sensitivity, which can be aided by various techniques or insights but does not require extraordinary grace. Faith in nature and nature's God may affirm hidden ("occult") natural forces that go beyond reason as ordinarily understood, including trust in psychic energies and powers of mind that seem almost magical. But ultimately these realities depend on little-known laws of nature and so are not strictly supernatural entities; their employment postulates religion less as response to "straight-down" revelation than as a gracious tool to be engaged therapeutically for this-worldly healings of self and society.

Natural religion in America has a lengthy tradition, as Catherine Albanese has demonstrated.[7] At least from the Christian theological point of view, such was the faith and cult of the Native Americans; the reaffirmation of their spiritual heritage, including the use by some of them of psychedelic substances, was an important Sixties theme. Even Jonathan Edwards hallowed the footsteps of the Creator in nature and noted their tracking by the new science, and the New England Transcendentalists found themselves in a new world of such splendid natural beauty, and of so promising a future, as almost to mock the fallen cosmos of their Puritan forebears. Nineteenth-century movements from Spiritualism to Freemasonry were natural religions in our present sense, in that they were based essentially on the human discovery of spiritual and moral realities outside the received revealed scriptures and transmitted outside the ecclesiastical establishments related to them. Or, at best, they were based on new revelations through such persons as Emanuel Swedenborg and Anton Mesmer, and their spiritual grandchildren in the ranks of Mesmerists, Transcendentalists, and Spiritualists.

The Sixties, as many recognized, meant a reversion to that American tradition after a season of drifting away from it in favor of the European Reformation or the Middle Ages; perhaps this even had something to do with the American sacredness acknowledged by various Death of God and counterculture spokespersons. It also meant a recovery of American natural religion's social conscience, embodied in times past in the likes of Thoreau or Andrew Jackson Davis.

Thus the Sixties meant social ministries on behalf of natural human needs, and natural mysticisms related to the congenital potentialities of the human mind (the "human potentials movement" was significantly named), though everyday ecstasy might be enhanced by certain products of chemical science or "scientific" meditation. (The word *science* is generously used in the literature of transcendental meditation and Krishna Consciousness, as it is in that of secular theology.) Further, there was of course an emphasis on nature as such, leading down to the ecotheology and the creation spirituality of Matthew Fox and others in the Eighties and Nineties. Needless to say, secular theology and the Death of God, though originally offshoots of Barthianism, in the end had nothing left to offer but natural religion under an apocalyptic sky.

But the trouble with nature, including human nature, is that while it can seem wondrous and perfect in a timeless moment of mystical rapture, hear the ticking of a clock and it slips back into the light of common day. Introduce time, and the canker begins to eat the rose, the tiger raises its claw to savage the lamb, and the Buddha's ancient enemies, old age, sickness, and death, show their pale faces.

Natural religion is then caught in a conundrum. Either it must transcend the nature it reveres and bring time to a stop, or grant that in time the Perfect and the Possible are in a race like that of Achilles and the tortoise, which the Perfect will seem to win only to lose as the seconds advance. Once the ideal is achieved, the transcendent vision framed, it commences to decay.

So it was for the apocalyptic Sixties. Its victorious moments—in civil rights, at Vatican II, in secular and Death of God theology, in the counterculture's countless Cockaignes—were followed by as many mornings after, and the Sixties end-time hatred of history can be well understood. But the gradualist, reformist Sixties of the Great Society and what was left of ecumenism could never match the human yearning for natural Elysian Fields the spiritual Sixties unleashed.

Finally, the fourth theme is the *theme of freedom.* In innumerable arenas, the Sixties were searching for what its people conceived to be greater freedom: freedom from limits imposed by race (civil rights), from the involuntary servitude of the draft (the antiwar movement), from conventional sexual limits (the Pill), from the earth itself (space exploration). There was the inner freedom sought by the counterculture mystic and the evangelical convert, and the outer freedom of the dropout and the wanderer.

The trouble was that "freedom" can be as slippery a concept as "world," and it is well known that countless strikes for freedom have ended with the seeker in greater bondage than before. Yet, without attemped jailbreaks, much about the architecture of the jail would have never been discovered. In the course of the Sixties' tries at escape from conventional religion, several important things were learned, or relearned, about religion, discoveries that greatly enhanced what Greeley termed "religious imagination."

First came what we may call the "people revolution" in religion. The new symbols in religious rhetoric and rite were of community, the people of God, of faith as a communal and popular affair. As we have seen, church, meetinghouse, and synagogue were swept by this revolution in the word used and the sign seen. Symbols of hierarchy, from dark suits and clerical collars to archaic languages, gave way to non-elite tokens like jeans and guitars, the ecclesiastical equivalents of Andy Warhol pop art. Even more dramatic were the liturgical changes

334

that put people around the altar and leveled the prestige of establish-ment-type (though not free-lance charismatic) star preachers and aca-demic theologians. The social activism of the decade cut both ways, since it did often depend on prestigious leadership, but it put its elites in a different role than before.

Second, the Sixties brought a rediscovery of radical subjectivity as the real wellspring of religion. This was part of neoromanticism, and so like a return to Schleiermacher (who enjoyed a popularity boomlet among theologians at the end of the decade). But it also had to do with the vogue for Marx on the New Left, and his deriving of "conscious-ness" from socioeconomic status. And of course it had to do with drugs and meditation and, for Middle America, the evocative power of traditional symbols. It was expressed in the recovery of the primitive, in fashionable Jungianism, in the conscious or unconscous prestige of the shaman and the shamanlike performances of rock stars such as Jim Morrison of the Doors. It was one with the quest for freedom, for it was assumed that to be truly free was to be able to "do one's own thing" and live out of one's subjectivity. Radical subjectivity drew from the requirements of a time of transition but showed staying power.

So the new religious imagination conceived of a church or temple that was egalitarian, concerned with subjectivity, driven by feeling rather than highly consistent doctrine: and it imagined a God who himself enjoyed rich subjectivity and was not very legalistic. This God was apparently also easy with pluralism, well aware that Americans are not likely ever to be very much alike in religion. That Sixties God is pretty much the God that has been worshiped ever since in this corner of the world, whether by liberals or conservatives, Catholics, Protestants, or Jews.

Some may protest, however, that this is the God that has really been worshiped in America for a long time, as Toqueville bears wit-ness, and that the Sixties were not so much a revolution as a restora-tion, a recovery of the deity known diversely before by Jefferson, Thoreau, or the frontier revivals with all their youthful purity and spirit intoxication.

The Sixties, in other words, may not have been so much an aber-ration as a restoration, the real aberration being American religion as it reconstructed itself in the late nineteenth and twentieth centuries through the Fifties, amid the immense traumas of urbanization, indus-trialization, and two world wars. In a certain sense, the characteristic Sixties religious style was like a recovery of the more fluid, sentimen-tal, charismatic, psychic, magical, communalistic, and righteous-pro-phetic style of the first decades of the Republic, perhaps especially the

1840s and 1850s, the "sentimental years" and the heyday of the covered-wagon Western migration. These were also years when New England transcendentalism was in flower, with its restless idealism and orientalism, and the air was full of progressivist exaltation so sharp as to be almost apocalyptic, and communes were being formed and exciting new religious movements like Spiritualism and Mormonism were talked about. At the same time, the nation was increasingly divided over war (e.g. Thoreau's famous essay on civil disobedience in the context of the Mexican war) and race and slavery, and the moral passion of the abolitionists was in the air.

In the light of that past, if it be a usable past, the Sixties were not so much as they chose to view themselves—the hinge of history and a time of new, unprecedented consciousness—as a relapse to a classic American way of being in history, one that has always liked to experience any given present time as a *novus ordo seclorum*, a new world order, ripe with judgment and new possibilities.

Perhaps so. The world is a caricature of itself, Santayana once remarked. It is not what it seems to be, much less what it pretends to be.

Notes

Chapter 1. Magic Is Afoot, War is Prophesied: Foundations of the Sixties

1. Todd Gitlin, *The Sixties: Years of Hope, Days of Rage* (New York: Bantam 1987), 409-411.

2. As caught up as I was at the time with sympathetic enthusiasm for the campus demonstrations against the Cambodian "incursion," I have since worried not a little over to what extent they, by forcing the U.S. withdrawal from that weak and vulnerable state, may ultimately have a share of responsibility for the genocidal Khmer Rouge's coming to power there in 1975. Their killing fields made Kent State look like pikers. The archetypal images from the Sixties remain; so do the questions.

3. Wade Clark Roof, *A Generation of Seekers: The Spiritual Journeys of the Baby Boom Generation* (San Francisco: Harper Collins, 1993), especially 243-260.

4. Jean-François Lyotard, *The Postmodern Condition: A Report on Knowledge*, trans. Geoff Bennington and Brian Massumi (Minneapolis: University of Minnesota Press, 1984), ix.

5. See Karl Jaspers, *The Origin and Goal of History*, trans. Michael Bullock (London: Routledge & Kegan Paul, 1963).

6. Paul Ricoeur, "The Symbol Gives Rise to Thought," in *Literature and Religion*, ed. Giles B. Gunn (New York: Harper and Row, 1971), 214.

7. Gilbert K. Chesterton, *Heretics* (London: Bodley Head, 1905), 180.

8. Jean Gebser, *The Ever-Present Origin* (Athens: Ohio University Press, 1985), 481; John W. Murphy, *Postmodern Social Analysis and Criticism* (New York: Greenwood, 1989), 20.

9. Robert J. Lifton, "Protean Man," in *The Religious Situation: 1969*, ed. Donald Cutler (Boston: Beacon, 1969), 816; John Orr and F. Patrick Nicholson, *The Radical Suburb: Soundings in Changing American Character* (Philadelphia: Westminster, 1970).

10. John H. Redekop, *The American Far Right: A Case Study of Billy James Hargis and the Christian Crusade* (Grand Rapids, Mich.: Eerdmans, 1968), 144.

11. John Kenneth Galbraith, *The Affluent Society* (Boston: Houghton Mifflin, 1958).

12. Cited in Walter H. Capps, *The Unfinished War: Vietnam and the American Conscience* (Boston: Beacon, 1982), 60.

13. Cited in W. J. Rorabaugh, *Berkeley at War: The 1960s* (New York: Oxford University Press, 1989), 46.

14. "The Gossiping Guru," *San Francisco Oracle* 1, 4 (December 16, 1966): 11 [73]. Page numbers for the Oracle in brackets are from the bound facsimile edition. Allen Cohen, ed., *The San Francisco Oracle: Facsimile Edition* (Berkeley, Calif.: Regent, 1991).

15. Allen Ginsberg, "Renaissance or Die," *San Francisco Oracle* 1, 5 (January 1967): 14 [102].

16. See, for example, Victor Turner, "Betwixt and Between: The Liminal Phase in Rites of Passage," in *The Forest of Symbols* (Ithaca, N.Y.: Cornell University Press, 1967), 93-111, and *The Ritual Process: Structure and Anti-Structure* (Ithaca, N.Y.: Cornell University Press, 1977). The concept is from Arnold van Gennep's classic, *Rites of Passage*.

17. Chester Anderson, "Notes for the New Geology," *San Francisco Oracle* 1, 6 (February 1967): 2 [116].

18. Ibid., 23 [137].

19. "The Gathering of the Tribes," *San Francisco Oracle* 1, 5 (January 1967), 2 [90].

20. Cited in Rorabaugh, *Berkeley at War*, 31.

21. Allen Ginsberg, "Renaissance or Die," *San Francisco Oracle* 1, 5 (January 1967): 15 [103].

22. "Changes," *San Francisco Oracle* 1, 7 (April 1967): 2q [150]. This issue gives the complete transcript of this conversation, held on Alan Watts's houseboat in Sausalito, California, in great secrecy.

23. Paul A. Robinson, *The Freudian Left: Wilhelm Reich, Geza Róheim, Herbert Marcuse* (New York: Harper and Row, 1969), 122.

24. Norman O. Brown, *Life against Death: The Psychoanalytic Meaning of History* (Middleton, Conn.: Wesleyan University Press, 1959), and *Love's Body* (New York: Random House, 1966); Herbert Marcuse, *Eros and Civilization* (Boston: Beacon, 1955), *One-Dimensional Man* (Boston: Beacon, 1964), and *An Essay on Liberation* (Boston: Beacon, 1969); Philip Rieff, *The Triumph of the Therapeutic: Uses of Faith after Freud* (New York: Harper and Row, 1966), 254.

Chapter 2. 1960–1963: The Fifties under Pressure

1. William H. Whyte, Jr., *The Organization Man* (New York: Simon and Schuster, 1956), 406. See all of chapter 27, "The Church of Suburbia."

2. For a chilling portrayal of this period through the experience of one person who was a target, see Robert Newman, *Owen Lattimore and the "Loss" of China* (Berkeley and Los Angeles: University of California Press, 1992). See also Ellen W. Schrecker, *No Ivory Tower: McCarthyism and the Universities* (New York: Oxford University Press, 1986). Both books implicitly make very clear the extent to which the anti-Communist campaigns of the Fifties and early Sixties were also struggles between regions and between social and educational classes, with the hegemony of a privileged, WASP Eastern establishment often the real if unspoken target of embittered posses based well west of the Appalachians. Schrecker points out, quite rightly, that despite the claims of some observers, McCarthyism, at least a good deal of the time, was not populism in the usual sense of the term but partisan politics. The sort of Republicanism it embodied, however, had a great deal to do with the movement of the GOP's ideological as well as electoral base substantially south and west, in unconscious preparation for that party's Goldwater, Nixon, and Reagan eras.

3. John Patrick Diggins, *The Proud Decades: America in War and in Peace, 1941–1960* (New York: Norton, 1988), 114–115.

4. Nathan Glazer, *American Judaism*, 2d ed. (Chicago: University of Chicago Press, 1972), 109.

5. "Golf Anyone?" *Newsweek*, March 25, 1963, 104–105.

6. Thomas Merton, *The Seven Story Mountain* (New York: Harcourt, Brace, 1948).

7. Aldous Huxley, *The Perennial Philosophy* (New York: Harper, 1945).

8. Aldous Huxley, *The Doors of Perception* (New York: Harper, 1954); Evans Wentz, ed., *Tibetan Book of the Dead* (New York: Oxford University Press, 1927).

9. Alan Watts, *The Glorious Cosmology* (New York: Random House, 1962) and *The Way of Zen* (New York: Vintage, 1957).

10. Alan Watts, *Behold the Spirit* (New York: Pantheon, 1947) and *The Supreme Identity* (New York: Pantheon, 1950).

11. Richard Kapleau, *The Three Pillars of Zen* (New York: Harper, 1966).

12. Alan Watts, *In My Own Way* (New York: Random House, 1973), 309.

13. Jack Kerouac, *The Dharma Bums* (New York: Viking, 1958), 157.

14. I sometimes use masculine rather than gender-inclusive terms in this book in reference to members of the clergy, in recognition of the fact that, while there were ordained women in a few denominations in the Sixties, their numbers were not large and their influence on the events in this narrative was, unfortunately, also small. Most Sixties people would have thought of the ordained ministry, priesthood, or rabbinate as a male domain. But women theologians, usually not formally ordained, were becoming more and more important in the decade, as I hope to show.

15. "Blake's Second Thoughts," *Time*, January 29, 1965, 89.

16. Rose K. Goldsen, Morris Rosenberg, Robin M. Williams, Jr., and Edward A. Suchman, *What College Students Think* (New York: Van Nostrand, 1960). Cited in *Newsweek*, April 25, 1960, 104.

17. Ellwood, *History and Future of Faith* (New York: Crossroad, 1988).

18. Barry Goldwater, *The Conscience of a Conservative* (Shepherdsville, Ky.: Victor, 1960). See the cover story on Goldwater and the new conservatism in *Time*, April 10, 1961. A box on the John Birch Society points out that its members have a "violent distaste for the social concerns of the nation's churches." The story also indicates that the campus resurgence of conservatism may be largely a matter of perception; educators reported that Goldwater was a popular speaker, that students in 1961 were more individualistic than before and willing to see intellectual conservatism as respectable but were not necessarily "converted" in large numbers. Hugo W. Thompson, in "College Students and the Church," *Christian Century*, March 22, 1961, 355–357, also saw the alleged campus swing toward conservatism as something everyone talked about but for which there was little hard evidence. But he perceived the same apathy I have already mentioned toward church if not religion. "Many students, seeing institutions as contrary to the Christian spirit, feel the church is merely one of society's conventions." Despite their nonradicalism, they saw preachers as belonging to the parental generation, their defense of religion and the church as professional, like lawyers of their clients, and their views on social issues as not necessarily better informed than those of others. Religious vocabulary was a serious problem. But on the other hand students wanted meaning, and Thompson said they were drawn to whatever seemed truly authentic, whether Zen, existentialism, Buber, Bonhöffer, or others. Here we see, perhaps, a generation on the brink, still quiescent but inwardly preparing to make the unexpected leap into the tumultuous questing and activism of the mid-Sixties. As early as 1962, some rise in campus activism in support of the sit-ins and freedom riders was observed (*Time*, February 23, 1962, 74). A perceptive early view of things to come was Kenneth Rexroth, "The Students Take Over," *Nation*, July 2, 1960, 4–9, who cites civil rights activism and campus opposition to ROTC (Reserve Officers' Training Corps).

19. For a contemporary survey of those groups, see Arnold Forster and

Benjamin R. Epstein, *Danger on the Right* (New York: Random House, 1964). See also "Thunder on the Far Right," *Newsweek*, December 4, 1961, and Redekop, *The American Far Right*. The last contains extensive further bibliography to date of publication.

20. "The Air Force Credo," *Nation*, March 5, 1960, 198–199.

21. John A. Stormer, *None Dare Call It Treason* (Florissant, Mo.: Liberty Bell, 1964). This book sold well over a million copies its first year in print, the superheated Goldwater election year. For a devastating critique of its sources and misinformation see "A Package of Political Poison," *Christian Century*, October 14, 1964, 1263–1264, excerpted from an editorial in the *Minneapolis Tribune* of September 20. The book also prompted an October 22, 1964, picketing of Republican headquarters in Kansas City by Methodist ministers to protest the party's sale of the volume with its "false witness" against their church and the NCC (*Christian Century*, December 2, 1964, 1506).

22. The early and middle Sixties produced a considerable run of popular and semipopular reaction books targeted at the Right. Most had similar, if not repetitious, chapters on the Birchers, Hargis, Schwarz, and so on. Most were written in a caustic, critical, exposé manner, suggesting that the literary public, at least, was by now ready to classify these worthies as humbugs, charlatans, or nuts. Some bring out anti-Semitic links. Examples include Edward Cain, *They'd Rather Be Right* (New York: Macmillan, 1963); Ralph E. Ellsworth and Sarah M. Harris, *The American Right Wing* (Washington, D.C.: Public Affairs Press, 1962); Forster and Epstein, *Danger on the Right*; Richard Hofstadter, *The Paranoid Style in American Politics* (New York: Knopf, 1966); Donald Janson and Bernard Eisman, *The Far Right* (New York: McGraw-Hill, 1963); Harry and Bonaro Overstreet, *The Strange Tactics of Extremism* (New York: Norton, 1964); Mark Sherwin, *The Extremists* (New York: St. Martin's, 1963); and Brooks R. Walker, *The Christian Fright Peddlers* (Garden City, N.Y.: Doubleday, 1964).

23. See also Leola McKie, "Rightist Binge in Omaha," *Christian Century*, October 16, 1963, 1270–1271, on the climate of fear and suspicion that developed in this city after Frederick Schwarz's Christian Anti-Communism Crusade came to town. The most respectable outgrowth of its efforts in Omaha was the American Citizens Forum, Inc., which presented four principal speakers in the weeks following, including William Buckley, who was overly intellectual for his audience, and the "actor" Ronald Reagan. On the Christian Anti-Communism Crusade, see Forster and Epstein, *Danger on the Right*, and "Crusader Schwarz," *Time*, February 9, 1962, 18–19.

24. Sherwin, *The Extremists*, 110.

25. Eric Lincoln, *The Black Muslims in America* (Boston: Beacon, 1961).

26. "The Growing Churches," *Newsweek*, October 24, 1960, 120.

27. "The Protestant Future," *Time*, April 28, 1961.

28. See Richard G. Hutcheson, Jr., *God in the White House* (New York: Macmillan, 1988), 52–55.

29. "Protestants and a President's Faith," *Newsweek*, March 14, 1960, 33.

30. James A. Pike with Richard Byfield, *A Roman Catholic in the White House?* (Garden City, N.Y.: Doubleday, 1960). The book is an adequate summary of the issues. It takes a cautious stand, pointing out that the Jesuit John Courtney Murray's "American interpretation" was not the official one. The latter, as expounded by conservatives like Cardinal Ottaviani in the curia, still held that the state need not give all religions the same rights, and that the church can, for the good of souls, call upon the state to inhibit the growth of

error, and to support Catholic education and institutions exclusively. In 1960 policies such as these were still in full operation in countries like Spain and Portugal. Pike could not have then known how soon Vatican II and encyclicals of John XXIII would discard these anachronistic ideas and render that part of his argument obsolete.

31. Some were not so sure, however. Louis H. Bean, a noted analyst of elections, contended that the Kennedy victory was the "result of Catholic pride winning over Protestant prejudice." His study convinced him that even more Catholics than usual voted for the Democratic candidate, giving JFK the margin of victory, and Protestants voting the other way for religious reasons were not sufficient to offset that edge. Lest anyone read this result with a jaundiced eye, Bean reminded readers that pride is not prejudice ("Why Kennedy Won," *Nation*, November 26, 1960, 408–409).

32. John Cooney, *The American Pope: The Life and Times of Francis Cardinal Spellman* (New York: Times Books, 1984), 271.

33. "Church and President," *America*, January 13, 1962, 461–462.

34. John Courtney Murray, *We Hold These Truths* (New York: Sheed and Ward, 1960), 148. On Murray, see J. M. Cudihy, *No Offense: Civil Religion and Protestant Taste* (New York: Seabury, 1979), 64–100.

35. Xavier Rynne, *Vatican Council II* (New York: Farrar, Straus and Giroux, 1968), 454–466.

36. Peter Hebblethwaite, *Pope John XXIII* (Garden City, N.Y.: Doubleday, 1984), 467–488. See also chapter 2, "How Pacem in Terris was Born," in Giancarlo Zizola, *The Utopia of Pope John XXIII*, trans. Helen Barolini (Maryknoll, N.Y.: Orbis, 1978), 3–10.

37. *Pope John XXIII: Journal of a Soul*, trans. Dorothy White (New York: McGraw-Hill, 1964), 239.

38. James H. Smylie, "The First Amendment and Bishop Pike," *Christian Century*, October 31, 1962, 1316–1318.

39. William Hamilton, "The Victory Was Video's," *Christian Century*, November 30, 1961, 1409–1410.

40. Martin E. Marty, "Protestantism Enters Third Phase," *Christian Century*, January 18, 1961, 72–75, and *The New Shape of American Religion* (New York: Harper and Row, 1959).

41. John Howard Griffin, *Black Like Me* (Boston: Houghton Mifflin, 1961).

42. For chronology see Lester A. Sobel, ed., *Civil Rights 1960–66* (New York: Facts on File, 1967).

43. Woodrow A. Geier, "Sit-ins Prod a Community," *Christian Century*, March 30, 1960, 381.

44. Ibid., 379; J. Robert Nelson, "Vanderbilt's Time of Testing," *Christian Century*, August 10, 1960, 921.

45. Martin Oppenheimer, *The Sit-In Movement of 1960* (New York: Carlson, 1989), 45–47, 80–82. On the Nashville affair, see 124–130.

46. See Emily Stoper, *The Student Nonviolent Coordinating Committee: The Growth of Radicalism in a Civil Rights Organization* (New York: Carlson, 1989).

47. "Now the Kneel-in," *Newsweek*, August 22, 1960, 60.

48. Five major black organizations were active in civil rights at this time: the venerable National Association for the Advancement of Colored People (NAACP), founded in 1909 and most concerned with action in the courts; the National Urban League, led by Whitney Young and chiefly involved in community organization; the Congress of Racial Equality, founded in 1942 and

now led by James Farmer, a disciple of Gandhi and original organizer of the freedom rides; the Southern Christian Leadership Council, vehicle of King's mission, founded in 1956 after the Montgomery boycott and now the mainspring of the Birmingham action; and the Student Nonviolent Coordinating Council, led by James Forman, formed in 1960 to promote sit-ins and voter registration and considered the most reckless and activist of all. On CORE see August Meier and Elliott Rudwick, *CORE: A Study in the Civil Rights Movement, 1942–1968* (New York: Oxford University Press, 1973). Although much older than SNCC, CORE also became radicalized in the movement of the early Sixties, reached its zenith in the Mississippi Summer of 1964, and declined thereafter.

49. "God's Armor," *Newsweek*, September 25, 1961, 101.

50. Ellen Naylor Bouton and Thomas F. Pettigrew, "When a Priest Makes a Pilgrimage," *Christian Century*, March 20, 1963, 363–365.

51. "Myth in the Gospel," *Time*, February 24, 1961, 48.

52. Taylor Branch, *Parting the Waters: America in the King Years, 1954–63* (New York: Simon and Schuster, 1988), 326–327.

53. "The Need to Speak Out," *Time*, February 23, 1962, 74.

54. Watts, *The Joyous Cosmology*, 3.

55. Walter N. Pahnke, "Drugs and Mysticism," *International Journal of Parapsychology* 8, 2 (1966); reprinted in Bernard Aaronson and Humphrey Osmond, *Psychedelics: The Uses and Implications of Hallucinogenic Drugs* (Garden City, N.Y.: Doubleday, 1970), 145–165. "Drugs and Mysticism" was originally Pahnke's 1963 Ph.D. dissertation at Harvard. Rick Doblin, "Pahnke's 'Good Friday Experiment': A Long-Term Follow-Up and Methodological Critique," *Journal of Transpersonal Psychology* 23, 1 (1991): 1–28. Pahnke died in 1971; otherwise, he might have done this follow-up himself. On the Good Friday experiment see also "Instant Mysticism," *Time*, October 25, 1963, 86–87.

56. Timothy Leary, "The Religious Experience: Its Production and Interpretation," lecture delivered at a meeting of Lutheran psychologists and other interested professionals, sponsored by the Board of Theological Education, Lutheran Church in America, in conjunction with the Seventy-first Annual Convention of the American Psychological Association, Philadelphia, August 30, 1963. Published in *Psychedelic Review*, no. 3, and reprinted in *The Psychedelic Reader*, ed. Gunther M. Weil, Ralph Metzner, and Timothy Leary (New Hyde Park, N.Y.: University Books, 1965), 191–216. See also Timothy Leary's two autobiographical works, *High Priest* (New York: New American Library, 1968), and *Flashbacks: An Autobiography* (Los Angeles: Tarcher, 1985). *High Priest* contains Leary's rather jaundiced account of the Good Friday experiment, 291–296.

57. J. M. Dechanet, *Christian Yoga* (New York: Harper, 1960); Dom Aelrad Graham, *Zen Catholicism* (New York: Harcourt, Brace & World, 1963).

58. Leary, *High Priest*, 296–297: "It started with Fred Swain, World War II Air Force major, who became a Vedanta Hindu monk in 1948, and who lived in an ashram near Boston. He started hanging out at the house and he told us about Hinduism and the psychedelic pantheon of gods and his guru and yoga. Fred had gone to Mexico the year before and had a far-out mushroom trip with Maria Sabrina in the mountains of Oaxaca.

I started visiting the Vedanta ashram. It was a surprise and delight to discover this group of holy, mature, sensible people who had renounced the world in pursuit of the visionary quest. The Hindu Bibles read like psychedelic manuals. The Hindu myths were session reports. The ashram itself was a turn-on."

59. "The Pope Today," *Newsweek*, April 18, 1960, 75.

60. "Modernizing the Mass," *Time*, December 13, 1963, 55.

61. See the special issue of the *Christian Century* on the council, January 10, 1962.

62. Pierre Teilhard de Chardin, *Phenomenon of Man* (New York: Harper, 1959).

63. A Guillaumont et al., trans., *The Coptic Gospel of Thomas* (New York: Harper, 1959); Robert M. Grant, *Gnosticism and Early Christianity* (New York: Columbia University Press, 1959) and *The Secret Sayings of Jesus* (Garden City, N.Y.: Doubleday, 1960); Jean Doresse, *Secret Books of the Egyptian Gnostics* (New York: Viking, 1960).

64. Nikos Kazantzakis, *The Last Temptation of Christ* (New York: Simon & Schuster, 1960); Robert A. Heinlein, *Stranger in a Strange Land* (New York: Pubnam, 1961).

65. Mircea Eliade, *Images and Symbols* (New York: Sheed & Ward, 1961), 31, 5.

66. Irenaeus Rosier, *I Looked for God's Absence* (New York: Sheed & Ward, 1960).

67. Thomas Merton, *Disputed Questions* (New York: Farrar, Straus & Cudahy, 1960).

68. H. Richard Niebuhr, *Radical Monotheism and Western Culture* (New York: Harper, 1960); Vance Packard, *The Waste Makers* (New York: McKay, 1960), *The Hidden Persuaders* (New York: McKay, 1957), and *The Status Seekers* ((New York: McKay, 1959).

69. Daniel Bell, *The End of Ideology* (New York: Collier, 1961).

70. Daniel Bell and Irving Kristol, eds., *Confrontation: The Student Rebellion and the Universities* (New York: Basic Books, 1969), 94, 105–106.

71. Madeleine Slade, *The Spirit's Pilgrimage* (New York: Coward-McCann, 1960).

72. Norman Cousins, *Dr. Schweitzer of Lamberéné* (New York: Harper, 1960).

73. Paul Goodman, *Growing Up Absurd* (New York: Random, 1960) and *Utopian Essays and Practical Proposals* (New York: Random, 1962), xvii.

74. Paul Tillich, *Christianity and the Encounter of the World Religions* (New York: Columbia University Press, 1963).

75. See A. Campbell Garnett, "Is Modern Theology Atheistic?" *Christian Century*, May 31, 1961. Garnett complains, citing the Chicago debate, that Tillichian terms like "being itself" or "ultimate reality" simply veil a nonpersonal God incapable of life or love; such arguments would be heard with increasing rancour as secular Christianity, and finally public rather than veiled proclamations of the Death of God, gathered steam.

76. Will Herberg, *Protestant Catholic Jew* (Garden City, N.Y.: Doubleday, 1956; Robert McAfee Brown and Gustave Weigel, *An American Dialogue* (1960); Robert McAfee Brown, *The Spirit of Protestantism* (1961); Gustave Weigel, *Catholic Theology in Dialogue* (1961).

77. Martin E. Marty, "Submerged in Suburbia," *Christian Century*, March 22, 1961, 360–362.

78. Peter Berger, *The Noise of Solemn Assemblies* (Garden City, N.Y.: Doubleday, 1961).

79. Karl Barth, *Evangelical Theology: An Introduction* (New York: Holt, Rinehart & Winston, 1963).

80. John A. T. Robinson, *Honest to God* (Philadelphia: Westminster, 1963); John D. Godsey, *The Theology of Dietrich Bonhoeffer* (Philadelphia: Westminster, 1960); Martin Marty, ed. *The Place of Bonhoeffer* (New York: Association Press, 1962)

81. John McQuarrie, *Scope of Demythologizing: Bultmann and His Critics* (New York: Harper Torchbooks, 1960); Charles S. McCoy, "The Plight of American Theology," *Christian Century*, July 11, 1962; Reinhold Niebuhr, *The Nature and Destiny of Man* (New York: Scribner, 1941–1943).

82. William Hamilton, *The New Essence of Christianity* (New York: Association Press, 1961), 55–56, 109.

83. Norman Vincent Peale, *The Tough-Minded Optimist* (Englewood Cliffs, N.J.: Prentice-Hall, 1961).

84. Herman Wouk, *This Is My God* (Garden City, N.Y.: Doubleday, 1959); Gershom G. Scholem, *Major Trends in Jewish Mysticism* rev. ed. (New York: Schocken Books, 1961).

85. Betty Friedan, *The Feminine Mystique* (New York: Norton, 1963); Rachel Carson, *Silent Spring* (Boston: Houghton Mifflin, 1962).

86. *Christian Century*, December 4, 1963, 1487.

Chapter 3. 1964–1966: The Years of Secular Hope

1. Robert E. Fitch, "The Sexplosion," *Christian Century*, January 29, 1964, 136–138.

2. Peter A. Bertocci, "Extramarital Sex and the Pill," *Christian Century*, February 26, 1964, 267.

3. Joseph Fletcher, *Situation Ethics* (Philadelphia: Westminster, 1966).

4. "Facing the 'Black' Facts," *Newsweek*, February 10, 1964, 55. A later story, "POAU in Crisis," *Newsweek*, October 5, 1964, 102–105, noted that Protestants and Other Americans United, an organization concerned with maintaining separation of church and state, and often considered to maintain especial vigilance against Roman Catholicism and its alleged violations of the wall of separation, was in considerable difficulty as old attitudes on both sides fell precipitously in the Vatican II atmosphere.

5. "Pius, Hitler, and the Jews," *Newsweek*, March 2, 1964, 78–79.

6. Robert Wuthnow, *The Restructuring of American Religion: Society and Faith Since World War II* (Princeton, N.J.: Princeton University Press, 1988), 155.

7. *Time*, "On the Fringe of a Golden Era," January 29, 1965, 56.

8. Ibid., 57B. As the twentieth century closes, and the golden era has become the Age of Limits, one may well ask what went wrong. More to the point of this study, why, only a couple of years later, had the lack of intergenerational conflict become youthful rebellion or the "generation gap," and boasts of educational excellence turned to confessions of failure as campus after campus was disrupted by often violent demonstrations culminating in the Kent State shootings. As described in 1964, teenagers were the heirs of a modernist paradise, all its fondest dreams of unlimited universal education, health, affluence, modern views of child raising, and democracy being fulfilled in them right here in America. Yet they wanted something else, or perhaps more accurately saw and experienced something else, from Saigon to Selma.

9. Joanna Moore, "Hattiesburg and Central Illinois," *Christian Century*, March 11, 1964, 340–341.

10. "NCC Draws Battle Lines," *Christianity Today*, March 27, 1964, 616. See also "W.C.C. Sends Mission to Mississippi Delta," *Christian Century*, May 20, 1964, 660.

11. Doug McAdam, *Freedom Summer* (New York: Oxford University Press, 1988), 67.

12. Stephen C. Rose, "The Churches and Mississippi," *Christian Century*, July 15, 1964, 909–910.

13. Rose, "The Churches and Mississippi," 909; Sally Belfrage, *Freedom Summer* (New York: Viking, 1965), 11–12.

14. For this story see Seth Cagin and Philip Dray, *We Are Not Afraid: The Story of Goodman, Schwerner, and Chaney and the Civil Rights Campaign for Mississippi* (New York: Macmillan, 1988).

15. Quoted in Mamie E. Locke, "Is This America? Fannie Lou Hamer and the Mississippi Freedom Democratic Party," in *Women in the Civil Rights Movement*, ed. Vicki L. Crawford et al. (Brooklyn, N.Y.: Carlson, 1990), 34.

16. Cited in Jacquelyn Grant, "Civil Rights Women: A Source for Doing Womanist Theology," ibid., 39. See also Kay Mills, *This Little Light of Mine: The Life of Fannie Lou Hamer* (New York: Dutton, 1992).

17. On disillusionment, see McAdam, *Freedom Summer*, 136. The main complaint was that churches seemed comfortable with an idealized vision of America in which the realities of Mississippi were unacknowledged. Eric D. Blanchard, "The Delta Ministry," *Christian Century*, March 17, 1965, 337–338; and in the same issue, 340–342, Wilmina Rowland, "How It Is in Mississippi," a firsthand account of four months in the Delta Ministry.

18. *Christian Century*, July 1, 1964, 851

19. Hubert H. Humphrey, "?" *Christian Century*, September 23, 1964, ; "The 1964 Religious Issue," *Christian Century*, October 7, 1964,

20. "Goldwater Yes or No?" *Christian Century*, July 8, 1964, 879–883; William Stringfellow, "God, Guilt and Goldwater," ibid., September 2, 1964, 1079–1083; "The Churches' Mandate," editorial in ibid., November 18, 1964, 1419.

21. "Pulpits and Politics," *Newsweek*, November 2, 1964, 90–91.

22. "Selma, Civil Rights, and the Church Militant," *Newsweek*, March 29, 1965, 75–78.

23. Margaret Halsey, "Integration Has Failed," *Christian Century*, December 28, 1966, 1596.

24. This article, like the other important religion stories cited in *Time*, reflects the serious religious interests of Henry Luce, the magazine's opinionated but intelligent and intellectually curious founder, raised in China of missionary parents. At the time of his death on February 28, 1967, nearly a year after the notorious article, he was said to have been corresponding with an old friend about the Death of God issue.

25. Karl Marx's saying that "religion . . . is the opium of the people" is common coin. The context of the expression is less well known but deserves to be cited in a discussion of secular theology. From Karl Marx, "Toward the Critique of Hegel's Philosophy of Right," in *Basic Writings on Politics and Philosophy: Karl Marx and Friedrich Engels*, ed. Lewis S. Feuer (Garden City, N.Y.: Doubleday 1959):

> Man makes religion, religion does not make man. In other words, religion is the self-consciousness and self-feeling of man, who either has not yet found himself or has already lost himself again. But *man* is no abstract being, squatting outside the world. Man is *the world of man*, the state, society. This state, this society produce religion, a

perverted world consciousness, because they are *a perverted world.*
. . . *Religious* distress is at the same time the *expression* of real distress and the *protest* against real distress. Religion is the sight of the oppressed creature, the heart of a heartless world, just as it is the spirit of an unspiritual situation. It is the *opium* of the people.
The abolition of religion as the *illusory* happiness of the people is required for their *real* happiness. The demand to give up the illusion about its condition is the *demand to give up a condition which needs illusion.* The criticism of religion is therefore *in embryo the criticism of the vale of woe,* the *halo* of which is religion. (262–263)

26. Peter L. Berger, *The Sacred Canopy* (Garden City, N.Y.: Doubleday, 1969), 107.
27. Karl Barth, *Römerbrief* (Bern: G. A. Bäschlin, 1919).
28. Dietrich Bonhöffer, *Letters and Papers from Prison* (London: SCM Press, 1953), 122. It should not be forgotten that Barth had an important role in inspiring and shaping the Barmen Declaration of 1934 by which certain German pastors and theologians courageously expressed their moral outrage at nazism and laid the foundations of the confessing church, which refused to kneel to the new idols of race and the totalitarian state. The neo-orthodox concept of God as Other, infinitely above all such transient objects of attachment as race or state, was important to this act.
29. Dietrich Bonhöffer, *Letters and Papers from Prison*, 1953, 166.
30. Citation, attributed to the *New York Herald Tribune*, on the cover of the 1966 New American Library edition of McLuhan's *Understanding Media*.
31. See "Understanding McLuhan," *Newsweek*, February 28, 1966, 56–57; and Marshall McLuhan, *Understanding Media: The Extensions of Man* (New York: McGraw-Hill, 1964).
32. Robinson, *Honest to God* (Philadelphia: Westminster, 1963), 78. Quotations in the next paragraph are from 67–68.
33. Ibid., 102; David L. Edwards, *The Honest to God Debate* (Philadelphia: Westminster, 1964).
34. James A. Pike, *A Time for Christian Candor* (New York: Harper & Row, 1964). A couple of years later Pike presented a compensatory positive assessment of Jesus and his role in *What Is This Treasure?* (New York: Harper and Row, 1966).
35. Pike, *A Time for Christian Candor*, 113–114; "The Relevance of Faith and Myth in Twentieth Century Life," *Time*, November 11, 1966, p.
36. This diocese comprises the San Francisco Bay area and a strip of coastline running south from it. There are several other dioceses in California.
37. For Pike's impassioned response to the heresy charges, and restatement of his beliefs, see *If This Be Heresy* (New York: Harper and Row, 1967). Interestingly, in view of his developing concerns, the longest chapter in the book is on life after death and is replete with material from the annals of psychic research. See also William Stringfellow and Anthony Towne, *The Bishop Pike Affair* (New York: Harper and Row, 1967).
38. James Pike, *The Other Side* (New York: Doubleday, 1968).
39. Based in part on Paul A. Laughlin, "James A, Pike," in *Twentieth Century Shapers of American Popular Religion,* ed. Charles H. Lippy (New York: Greenwood, 1989), 334–342.
40. Joseph Fletcher, *Situation Ethics*, 13; Harvey Cox, ed., *The Situation Ethics Debate* (Philadelphia: Westminster, 1968), 242, 263.
41. Ronald Gregor Smith, *Secular Christianity* (London: Collins, 1966).

42. Gibson Winter, *The New Creation as Metropolis* (New York: Macmillan, 1963).

43. Harvey Cox, *The Secular City* (New York: Macmillan, 1965).

44. The entire sentence reads, "There is a certain validity to the Marxist assertion that existentialism is a 'symptom of bourgeois decadence,' since its categories of *Angst* and vertigo seem increasingly irrelevant to the ethos of the new epoch. In the age of the secular city, the questions with which we concern ourselves tend to be mostly functional and operational" (ibid., 80–81).

45. Harvey Cox, *The Secular City: Twenty-fifth Anniversary Edition* (New York: Macmillan, 1990). In the new preface Cox recognizes that, when the book was first written, he did not adequately take into account the critiques of religion of feminist or black theology—which have special loci in the American city—or the persistence of positive (and negative) religion in new forms, or the changes, mostly bad, that have happened to the city since then. But he holds that the fundamental thesis is still valid, citing again little-noticed lines on 145: Secularization "is not the Messiah. But neither is it anti-Christ. It is rather a dangerous liberation."

46. "1966 Paperback Bestsellers in the Bookstores," *Publishers Weekly,* January 30, 1967, 43–46. Other top paperbacks in 1966 reflected a wide-ranging and remarkable publishing era. In addition to the other two works in the Tolkien trilogy, *The Two Towers* and *The Return of the King* (578,000 copies together), among popular culture or religiously significant titles were Jeanne Dixon's *A Gift of Prophecy,* by the psychic who claimed to have predicted the Kennedy assassination; Robin Moore's *Green Berets*; Frank Edwards's *Flying Saucers: Serious Business;* A. S. Neil's *Summerhill,* on radical education; Robert Short's *Gospel According to Peanuts*; Hermann Hesse's *Siddhartha* (New York: New Directions, 1951); Joseph Fletcher's *Situation Ethics*; Boris Pasternak's *Dr. Zhivago*; and Marshall McLuhan's *Understanding Media.* See also Robert Sklar, "Tolkien and Hesse: Top of the Pops," *Nation,* May 8, 1967, 598–560. Sklar notes the profoundly different mood of the work of these writers from that of such books favored by Fifties youth as J. D. Salinger's *Catcher in the Rye* and William Golding's *Lord of the Flies.*

47. Hermann Hesse, *Siddhartha* (New York: New Directions, 1951); *Damien* (New York: Harper & Row, 1965); *Steppenwolf* (New York: Modern Library, 1963); *The Journey to the East* (New York: Noonday, 1956).

48. Paul van Buren, *The Secular Meaning of the Gospel* (New York: Macmillan, 1963).

49. Thomas J. J. Altizer, *The Gospel of Christian Atheism* (Philadelphia: Westminster, 1966).

50. In Thomas J. J. Altizer and William Hamilton, *Radical Theology and the Death of God* (Indianapolis: Bobbs-Merrill, 1966), 157–169. Originally published in *Theology Today,* January 1966.

51. Reinhold Niebuhr, *Moral Man and Immoral Society* (New York: Scribner, 1932); *The Nature and Destiny of Man* (New York: Scribner, 1941–1943).

52. Kenneth Boulding, *The Meaning of the Twentieth Century* (New York: Harper and Row, 1964). Boulding says that we are moving from a civilized to a postcivilized society that will be the age of the mass media, of automation, of a constantly accelerating rate of change. He wrote that the "great transition" the present moment demands will call for a new kind of human personality, perhaps the secular Christian Hamilton prophesied. Hamilton fails to mention that Boulding makes plain that the transition will be hard, if it is made at all. Boulding saw three roadblocks to a scientific paradise, and he described them

in chapters entitled, "The War Trap," "The Population Trap," and "The Entropy Trap."

53. William Hamilton, "New Optimism," 165

54. Altizer and Hamilton, *Radical Theology*, 9.

55. Ibid., 87.

56. To be sure, the Sixties Death of God theology has had a postmodernist future in the work of deconstructionist theologians like Mark Taylor, Robert Sharleman, and Ray Hart. In my view, however, their work, though sharing a sense that traditional ontological constructions of God are no longer viable, lacks the vibrant apocalyptic tenor of Altizer and Hamilton particularly—a sense that experiencing the death of God is a radically now event linked to a dramatic present-moment historical *kairos*—and so they are not quite in the same camp as those Sixties writers.

57. Richard L. Rubenstein, *After Auschwitz: Radical Theology and Contemporary Judaism* (Indianapolis: Bobbs-Merrill, 1966), 204, 263.

58. Irving Shushnick, "Save Earth Now!!" *East Village Other* 1, 22 (October 15–November 1, 1966), 11.

59. In Robert Houriet, *Getting Back Together* (New York: Avon, 1972), 335–336.

60. See Robert S. Ellwood, "ISKCON and the Spirituality of the 60s," in *Krishna Consciousness in the West*, ed. David G. Bromley and Larry D. Shinn (Lewisburg, Pa.: Bucknell University Press, 1989), 102–113.

61. David Michael Jacobs, *The UFO Controversy in America* (Bloomington: Indiana University Press, 1975), 200–202.

62. "The Servant Church," *Time*, December 25, 1964, 45–49; "U.S. Protestantism: Time for a Second Reformation," *Newsweek,* January 3, 1966, 33–37.

63. Malcolm Boyd, *Are You Running With Me, Jesus?* (New York: Holt, Rinehart and Winston, 1965).

64. C. S. Lewis, *Letters to Malcolm: Chiefly on Prayer* (New York: Harcourt, Brace and World, 1964), 5. Significantly quoted in an article in the conservative Episcopal periodical, *The Living Church*, July 12, 1966, by Darwin Kirby: "A Backward Glance at a Forward Movement," 14–15.

65. Jay Stevens, *Storming Heaven: LSD and the American Dream* (New York: Atlantic Monthly Press, 1987), 209.

66. New York's.

67. Timothy Leary, Ralph Metzner, and Richard Alpert, *The Psychedelic Experience: A Manual Based on the Tibetan Book of the Dead* (New Hyde Park, N.Y.: University Books, 1964). The *Psychedelic Review* commenced in June 1963 and continued for some ten issues through 1969, after which it was absorbed by the *Journal for the Study of the Unconscious*. The best articles from the first four issues were published in Weil et al., *The Psychedelic Reader.*

68. For example Bobby Seale of the Black Panthers, interviewed in the *East Village Other*, condemned the psychedelic culture: "I am opposed to any kind of idealism and metaphysical moonism or spookism. I am opposed to getting caught up in wishes and dreams. I don't think that psychedelic trips kill pigs. . . . [Psychedelics] hamper and hinder the masses in their struggle toward the truly revolutionary consciousness." Allen Katzman, ed., *Our Time: An Anthology of Interviews from the East Village Other* (New York: Dial, 1972), 281.

69. Quoted in "What the Council Did," *Newsweek*, December 20, 1965, 60. The Sixties were a golden age of Protestant theology professors as well. As we

have seen, elder theological statesmen like Barth, Tillich, and the Niebuhrs were revered public figures, and young tigers of the trade like Harvey Cox, Robert McAfee Brown, or the Death of God set were regularly making news. In both great wings of Christendom, a perceived need for fundamental rethinking, and a widespread regard for education as schools and universities grew at unprecedented rates, made it the hour of the theologian. As never before, at least since the Reformation, what was "just theory" yesterday—a squabble of monks—might hit the parishes and the front pages tomorrow. The behind-the-scenes religion story since the Sixties has been the effort of the church's professional administrators—popes, Curialists, bishops, and hardly less their Protestant equivalents in many denominations—to get theologians with disconcerting ideas back into their universities and seminaries and keep them there, while maintaining a steady hand on the wheel. By and large these efforts have been successful, though as we shall see at some cost.

70. Nancy Zaroulis and Gerald Sullivan, *Who Spoke Up? American Protest against the War in Vietnam, 1963–1975* (Garden City, N.Y.: Doubleday, 1984), 25.

71. Mitchell K. Hall, *Because of Their Faith: CALCAV and Religious Opposition to the Vietnam War* (New York: Columbia University Press, 1990), 9.

72. Nat Hentoff, *Peace Agitator: The Story of A. J. Muste* (New York: Macmillan, 1963), 14. The words are those of Professor John Oliver Nelson of Yale.

73. "The Demonstrators: Why? How Many?" *Newsweek*, November 1, 1965, 25–34.

74. "Battle of Conscience," *Newsweek*, November 15, 1965, 78.

75. See Mitchell K. Hall, *Because of Their Faith: CALCAV and Religious Opposition to the Vietnam War* (New York: Columbia University Press, 1990). A CALCAV ad in the *Christian Century*, December 21, 1966, for a January 31–February 1, 1967, vigil and workshop in Washington lists the following sponsors by name: Bennett; Heschel; Brown; Coffin; Fr. John McKenzie of Notre Dame; Rabbi Maurice Eisendrath, president of the Union of American Hebrew Congregations; Methodist bishop John Wesley Lord; Rabbi Jacob Weinstein, president of the Central Conference of American Rabbis; Sister Mary Corita of the Immaculate Heart of Mary order and a well-known artist; Harvey Cox; Fr. Joseph F. Mulligan, dean of the graduate school of Fordham University; Fr. Donald Campion, former editor of the Jesuit periodical *America;* and Fr. Peter Riga, professor at St Mary's College.

76. Zaroulis and Sullivan, *Who Spoke Up?* 1–3. Between 1965 and 1970, eight Americans burned themselves to death in protest against the war. Morrison and Alice Herz (another Quaker, a Jewish-background refugee from Hitler's Germany, and eighty-two at the time of her self-immolation in March 1965) were made into major heroes in North Vietnam, their names celebrated in songs and on huge posters; Morrison even had a Hanoi street named for him and a postage stamp issued in his honor.

77. Gitlin, *The Sixties*, 195–197.

78. John C. Bennett, *Foreign Policy in Christian Perspective* (New York: Scribner's, 1966), 36.

79. Harold E. Fey, "Inconsistent Application," *Christian Century*, July 27, 1966, 936.

80. Paul Ramsey, "Vietnam: Dissent on Dissent," *Christian Century*, July 20, 1966, 909–913.

81. Hall, *Because of their Faith*, 30.

82. Martin Luther King, Jr., *Why We Can't Wait* (New York: Harper and Row, 1964).

83. Malcolm X, with Alex Haley, *The Autobiography of Malcolm X* (New York: Grove, 1964, 1965).

84. Malcolm X, *Malcolm X Speaks* (New York, Grove, 1966).

85. Morton Kelsey, *Tongue Speaking: An Experiment in Spiritual Experience* (Garden City, New York: Doubleday, 1964).

86. Dag Hammerskjöld, *Markings* (New York: Knopf, 1964).

87. Robert McAfee Brown, *Observer in Rome* (Garden City, N.Y.: Doubleday, 1964).

88. Schubert Ogden, *The Reality of God & Other Essays* (New York: Harper & Row, 1966).

89. Thomas Merton, *Seeds of Contemplation* (Norfolk, Conn.: New Directions, 1949); *The Waters of Siloe* (New York, Harcourt, 1949); and *Ascent to Truth* (New York: Harcourt, 1951).

90. Ibid., *Gandhi on Non-Violence* (New York: New Directions, 1965), *The Way of Chuang Tzu* (New York: New Directions, 1965), *Conjectures of a Guilty Bystander* (Garden City, N.Y.: Doubleday, 1966), *Mystics and Zen Masters* (New York: Delta, 1967), *Faith and Violence* (Notre Dame, Ind.: University of Notre Dame Press, 1968), *Zen and the Birds of Appetite* (New York: New Directions, 1968).

91. Herbert Marcuse, *One-Dimensional Man* (Boston: Beacon, 1964).

92. "Impresario Religioso," *Time*, September 30, 1966, 62.

Chapter 4. 1967: The Year of the Avatars

1. "The Inheritor," *Time*, January 6, 1967, 18–23.

2. "The CIA and the Students," *Time*, February 24, 1967; quotes from "The Silent Service," *Time*, February 24, 1967, p.17.

3. It is only fair to add that, however one now assess Luce's politics, *Time*'s major religion stories in the 1950s and 1960s, incomparable reflections of both the zeitgeist and Luce's own serious interest in the subject, set a standard for religion writing unequalled in national mass journalism before or since. Because of *Time*, and to a slightly lesser degree its rival *Newsweek*, millions were reasonably aware of and able to respond to the great theologians and religious movements of those contentious times who would undoubtedly not have been familiar with them otherwise; in this sense the newsmagazines made as well as reported religous history.

4. "Obedient Rebel," *Time*, March 24, 1967, 70–76, quote from 74.

5. "Three Tales of the CIA," *Ramparts*, April 1967, 15–28.

6. Thomas Moore, ed., *A Blue Fire: Selected Writings by James Hillman* (New York: Harper and Row, 1989), 123.

7. "The New Radicals," *Time*, April 28, 1967, 26–27.

8. "The Home Front War," *Newsweek*, May 8, 1967, 31–36.

9. "Youth: The Hippies," *Time*, July 7, 1967, 18–22; "The Vietnam War and American Life," Special Issue of *Newsweek*, July 10, 1967.

10. "The Arts: Protest on all Sides," in "The Vietnam War and American Life," Special Issue of *Newsweek*, July 10, 1967, 83–86.

11. Reinhold Niebuhr, *The Irony of American History* (New York: Scribner, 1952).

12. Thomas A. Langford, "Campus Turmoil: A Religious Dimension," *Christian Century*, February 8, 1967, 172–174.

13. Charles Perry, *The Haight-Ashbury: A History* (New York: Random House, 1984).

14. Theodore Roszak, *The Making of a Counter Culture* (Garden City, N.Y.: Doubleday, 1969).

15. Walter Anderson, *The Upstart Spring: Esalen and the American Awakening* (Reading, Mass.: Addison-Wesley, 1983).

16. Warren Hinckle, "The Social History of the Hippies," *Ramparts*, March 1967, 5–26 (origin of the word "hippie" is not from this article).

17. Ken Kesey, *One Flew over the Cuckoo's Nest* (New York: Viking, 1962); Tom Wolfe, *The Electric Kool-Aid Acid Test* (New York: Farrar, Straus & Giroux, 1968).

18. "Schneck," "Flex, Reflex," *San Francisco Oracle* 1, 2 (October 1966), 3 [33].

19. Ibid. This event was the enactment of that called for in a statement printed in all capital letters on the back of the previous issue of the *Oracle*, which declared: "Political action will take place October 6, 1966 (666....The mark of the ascension of the beast) the date the California law prohibiting the possession of L.S.D. comes into effect. The day of the fear produced legislation against the expansion of consciousness. At 2:00 P.M. in the Panhandle at Oak and Masonic we will gather and walk to the Park District Station to affirm our identity, community and innocence from influence of the fear addiction of the general public and symbolized in the law."

And, as a kind of coda, the statement ended: "Bring the color gold . . . bring photos of personal saints and gurus and heroes of the Underground . . . bring children . . . flowers . . . flutes . . . drums . . . feathers . . . bands . . . beads . . . banners . . . flags . . . incense . . . chimes . . . gongs . . . cymbals . . . symbols . . . joy."

20. "The Button Pushers," *Newsweek*, March 27, 1967, 88.

21. Lewis Yablonsky, *The Hippie Trip* (New York: Pegasus, 1968), 35–36.

22. Timothy Miller, *The Hippies and American Values: The Utopian Ethics of the Counterculture* (Knoxville: University of Tennessee Press, 1991), 88.

23. Rasa Gustaitis, *Turning On* (New York: Macmillan, 1969), 104–111. This book is based on a 1967 exploration.

24. Yablonsky, *The Hippie Trip*, 186.

25. "The Hippies," *Time*, July 7, 1967, 18–22.

26. Harvey Cox, "God and the Hippies," *Playboy*, January 1968, 94. Cited in Miller, *The Hippies and American Values*, 17.

27. Lester Kinsolving, "A Rector, a Church, and the Hippies," *Christian Century*, May 17, 1967, 667–668.

28. Richard John Neuhaus, "American Religion and the War," *Worldview* 10 (October 1967): 9–13; Robert McAfee Brown, Abraham J. Heschel, and Michael Novak, *Vietnam: Crisis of Conscience* (New York: Association Press, Behrman House, and Herder and Herder, 1967), 84.

29. Hall, *Because of Their Faith*, 56–57.

30. William Sloane Coffin, Jr., *Once to Every Man: A Memoir* (New York: Atheneum, 1977), 234.

31. Nancy Zaroulis and Gerald Sullivan, *Who Spoke Up? American Protest against the War in Vietnam, 1963–1975* (Garden City, N.Y.: Doubleday, 1984), 108.

32. Martin Luther King, "A Time to Break Silence," in *A Testament of Hope: The Essential Writings of Martin Luther King, Jr.*, ed. James Melvin Washington (San Francisco: Harper & Row, 1986), 231–244.

33. Ibid., 110–111.

34. Ibid., 104–105.

35. Herbert L. Bergsma, *Chaplains with the Marines in Vietnam, 1962–1971* (Washington, D.C.: History and Museum Division, Headquarters, U.S. Marine Corps, 1985), 149–151.

36. "A Question of Priorities," *Time*, September 8, 1967, 13–14.

37. Report by Marjorie Swann in *Direct Action*, the newsletter of the New England Committee for Nonviolent Action. Reprinted in Alice Lynd, ed., *We Won't Go: Personal Accounts of War Objectors* (Boston: Beacon, 1968), 242–243.

38. Norman Mailer, *The Armies of the Night* (New York: New American Library, 1968).

39. William L. O'Neill, *Coming Apart: An Informal History of America in the 1960s* (New York: Times Books, 1971), 344.

40. Mailer, *Armies*, 120.

41. James Kavanaugh, *A Modern Priest Looks at His Outdated Church* (New York: Trident, 1967).

42. For further information on these and other Catholic traditionalist groups, see Karl Pruter and J. Gordon Melton, *The Old Catholic Sourcebook* (New York: Garland, 1983), 109–122.

43. "Liturgy in Headlines," *America*, January 21, 1967, 79.

44. Hubert Horan, "A Missionary's Predicament: How Far to Adapt?" *America*, August 26, 1967, 197–200.

45. "How U.S. Catholics View Their Church," *Newsweek*, March 20, 1967, 68–77.

46. Daniel Callahan, "The Renewal Mess," *Commonweal*, March 3, 1967, 621–625.

47. "The Cool Generation and the Church: A Commonweal Symposium," *Commonweal*, October 6, 1967, 11–25. Quote from 12.

48. Philip Gleason, "Our New Age of Romanticism," *America*, October 7, 1967, 372–374.

49. Karl Rahner, *Belief Today* (New York: Sheed & Ward,1967), 97. Italics in original.

50. Ibid., *The Christian of the Future* (New York: Herder & Herder, 1967), 50–52, 73–76.

51. Hans Küng, *The Church* (New York: Sheed & Ward, 1967), and *Structures of the Church* (New York: T. Nelson, 1964).

52. James Kavanaugh, "A Modern Priest Looks at his Outdated Church," excerpts from the book, *Look*, June 13, 1967, 54–58; and "Speaking Out," *Saturday Evening Post*, December 16, 1967, 10.

53. Vincent Yzermans, ed., *American Participation in the Second Vatical Council* (New York: Sheed & Ward, 1967). See also Cooney, *The American Pope*, 274–278, where Spellman's role at the council is regarded as "defensive" and "obstructionist."

54. Rosemary Ruether, *The Church against Itself* (New York: Herder & Herder, 1967), 219.

55. Peter Riga, *The Church and Revolution* (Milwaukee: Bruce, 1967), v.

56. John M. Gessell, "The Riots—Our National Response," *Christian Century*, August 23, 1967, 1063–1065. Would that Gessell's sentiment had come to pass. As it happens, I am writing these words only a few miles and a few weeks away from the great 1992 riots in Los Angeles, and cannot help reflecting on how nearly identical Gessell's words are to those spoken by Los Angeles's

civic and religious leaders twenty-five years later—as though nothing had been learned or forgotten in the intervening quarter-century.

57. Fred M. Henley, "Riots and Revolution: From Boston 1770 to Detroit 1967," *America*, August 12, 1967, 150–153. Quote from 150.

58. "The Rising Tide of Violence," *Christianity Today*, August 18, 1967, 28–29. Quote from 29.

59. Arlie E. Porter, "Detroit: Before and After," *Church in Metropolis*, no. 15 (Winter 1967): 13–17.

60. William S. Logan, "Interfaith Emergency Center," ibid., 13–14.

61. "The Crisis in the Nation," ibid., 6.

62. "Statement of United Presbyterian Commission on Religion and Race," ibid., 8.

63. See "General Convention," *The Living Church*, October 1, 1967, 6–8, and October 8, 1967, 4–6.

64. "Statement of United Presbyterian Commission of Religion and Race," *Church in Metropolis* (Winter 1967), 8.pp.

65. Stokely Carmichael and Charles V. Hamilton, *Black Power: The Politics of Liberation in America* (New York: Vintage, 1967), 53.

66. Frantz Fanon, *The Wretched of the Earth* (New York: Grove, 1963). Frederick Douglass is quoted from "West India Emancipation Speech," August 1857.

67. Thomas B. Morgan, *Among the Anti-Americans: Why They Don't Like Us* (New York: Holt, Rinehart, and Winston, 1967), 4.

68. Thich Nhat-Hanh, *Vietnam: Lotus in a Sea of Fire* (New York: Hill and Wang, 1967).

69. Jurgen Moltmann, *A Theology of Hope* (New York: Harper & Row, 1967).

70. Dean Peerman, ed., *Frontline Theology* (Richmond: John Knox Press, 1967); Donald R. Cutler, ed., *The Religious Situation, 1968* (Boston: Beacon, 1968).

71. Thomas Luckmann, *The Invisible Religion* (New York: Macmillan, 1967).

72. Adam Clayton Powell, Jr., *Keep the Faith, Baby* (New York: Trident, 1967). See also Charles V. Hamilton, *Adam Clayton Powell, Jr.: The Political Biography of an American Dilemma* (New York: Atheneum, 1992).

73. Stephen E. Rose, *The Grass Roots Church* (New York: Holt, Rinehart & Winston, 1967).

74. Ibid., *Alarms and Visions: Church and the American Crisis* (Chicago: Renewal magazine, 1967).

75. William Styron, *Confessions of Nat Turner: A Novel* (New York: Random House, 1967). The next year John Henrik Clarke's *William Stryon's Nat Turner: Ten Black Writers Respond* (Boston: Beacon, 1968) was published in riposte to this work. The anger that many black militants and intellectuals felt toward the novel by an obviously sympathetic white writer is an indicator of the polarized atmosphere of the period. The black writers argued that Styron was inaccurate in implying that Turner's was the only serious black slave insurrection, that it was put down with the help of "loyal" slaves, that most slaves were complacent and toadied to their masters; Styron allegedly failed to understand that blacks had one language for talking to whites and another for conversing with each other.

76. Thomas J. J. Altizer, *The New Apocalypse: The Radical Christian Vision of William Blake* (East Lansing: Michigan State University Press, 1967), xi.

77. Joseph Washington, *The Politics of God* (Boston: Beacon Press, 1967).

Special: Judaism in the Later Sixties

1. Eugene B. Borowitz, "God-Is-Dead Theology," *Judaism* 15, 1 (Winter 1966): 85–94.

2. Nathan Rotenstreich, "Secularism and Religion in Israel," *Judaism* 15, 3 (Summer 1966): 271.

3. Arthur Hertzberg, "Israel and American Jewry," *Commentary* 44, 2 (August 1967): 69–73.

4. Lucy S. Dawidowicz, "American Public Opinion," *American Jewish Yearbook 1968* (New York: American Jewish Committee of Philadelphia and Jewish Publication Society of America, 1968), 221.

5. Nancy Weber, "The Truth of Tears," ibid. (originally printed in *Village Voice*, June 15, 1967).

6. Jacob Neusner, *Death and Birth of Judaism: The Impact of Chrsitianity, Secularism, and the Holocaust on Jewish Faith* (New York: Basic Books, 1987), 279.

7. Editorial, "National Council Position on Middle East," *Christian Century*, June 21, 1967, 804–805. Quote 804.

8. See Dawidowicz, "American Public Opinion," 219, and the collection of articles in the special issue of the *Christian Century* on the Middle East, August 2, 1967.

9. Lucy S. Dawidowicz, "American Public Opinion," in *American Jewish Yearbook, 1968* (New York: American Jewish Committee, 1968), 198–229. Quote 220.

10. Msgr. George G. Higgins, cited in Dawidowicz, "American Public Opinion," 220–221; Henry P. Van Dusen, letter to the editor, "'Silence' of Church Leaders on Mideast," *New York Times*, July 7, 1967, 32.

11. A. Roy Eckhardt and Alice L. Eckhardt, "Christians and Arab Ideology," *Christian Century*, August 2, 1967, 993.

12. Marshall Sklare, *America's Jews* (New York: Random House, 1971), 222.

13. Michael P. Lerner, "Jewish New Leftism at Berkeley," *Judaism* 18, 4 (Fall 1969): 473–478.

14. Reuven Kimelman, "A Jewish Peace Demonstration," *Judaism* 18, 3 (Summer 1969): 356.

15. Leonard K. J. Fein et al., *Reform Is a Verb: Notes on Reform and Reforming Jews* (New York: Union of American Hebrew Congregations, 1972), passim.

16. Richard J. Israel, "The Rabbi on Campus," *Judaism* 16, 2 (Apring 1967): 186–192.

17. Herbert Weiner, *9¹/₂ Mystics: The Kabbala Today* (New York: Holt, Rinehart and Winston, 1969).

18. The question of what all this has meant in depth in terms of American Jewish identity has been interestingly studied in Sara Bershtel and Allen Graubard, *Saving Remnants: Feeling Jewish in America* (New York: Free Press, 1992).

19. Richard N. Levy, "The Reform Synagogue: Plight and Possibility," *Judaism* 18, 2 (Spring 1969): 159–176.

20. Bernard Reisman, *The Chavurah: A Contemporary Jewish Experience* (New York: Union of American Hebrew Congregations, 1977), 9.

21. Milton Himmelfarb, "Relevance in the Synagogue," *Commentary* 45, 5 (May 1968): 42–46.

22. Levy, "The Reform Synagogue."

23. Based on Abraham J. Karp, *Haven and Home: A History of the Jews in America* (New York: Schocken, 1985), 320–323.

24. Earl Raab, "The Black Revolution and the Jewish Question," *Commentary* 47, 1 (January 1969): 23–33.

25. For a valuable look at Jewish "civil religion" and its Sixties and recent permutations, see Jonathan S. Woocher, *Sacred Survival: The Civil Religion of American Jews* (Bloomington: Indiana University Press, 1986).

Chapter 5. 1968–1970: The Bitter Years

1. "R.F.K.," *Christian Century*, June 19, 1968, 807.

2. Dale W. Brown, "The New Theological Radical," *Christian Century*, November 13, 1968, 1431–1434. The Richard Shaull article is "Theology and the Transformation of Society," *Theology Today*, April 1968.

3. Michael Novak, *A Theology for Radical Politics* (New York: Herder and Herder, 1969).

4. Hatred of rival theologians.

5. Thomas J. J. Altizer, *The Descent into Hell: A Study of the Radical Reversal of the Christian Consciousness* (Philadelphia: Lippincott, 1970).

6. John S. Dunne, *A Search for God in Time and Memory* (New York: Macmillan, 1969), *The City of the Gods* (New York: Macmillan, 1965), and *The Way of All the Earth* (New York: Macmillan, 1972).

7. Albert Camus, *The Rebel*, trans. Anthony Bower (Harmondsworth, England: Penguin, 1965). (This translation was first published in 1953; first published in French in 1951).

8. Harvey Cox, *The Feast of Fools* (Cambridge, Mass.: Harvard University Press, 1969).

9. "What a Year!" *Time*, August 30, 1968, 21.

10. See Donald E. McInnis, "Maoism: The Religious Analogy," *Christian Century*, January 10, 1968, 39–42.

11. "Anti-Revolutionaries," *Time*, June 28, 1968, 42–47.

12. Langdon Gilkey, *Reaping the Whirlwind.* (New York: Seabury Press, 1976), 79.

13. Mircea Eliade, "*Homo Faber* and *Homo Religiosus*," in *The History of Religions: Retrospect and Prospect*, ed. Joseph M. Kitagawa (New York: Macmillan, 1985), 1–12.

14. Earl Rovit, "On the Contemporary Apocalyptic Imagination," *American Scholar* 37 (Summer 1968): 453–468. See also "Anti-Revolutionaries," *Time*, June 28, 1968, 42–47.

15. Vine Deloria, Jr., *Custer Died for Your Sins* (New York: Macmillan, 1969).

16. Robert A. McKenzie, "An Odyssey from Liberal to Radical," *Christian Century*, March 25, 1970, pp.362–363.

17. Alasdair MacIntyre, "Marxism of the Will," *Partisan Review* 36, 1 (Winter 1969): 128–133.

18. "Chicago's Blitzkrieg," *Christian Century*, September 11, 1968, 1127.

19. Gitlin, *The Sixties*, 322. For the full story of the Yippies, see 230–238, 320–328.

20. See Jerry Rubin, *We Are Everywhere* (New York: Harper and Row, 1971). This book, written in Cook County jail, gives Rubin's story of the conspiracy trial.

21. "The Chicago Defense," *Newsweek*, January 5, 1970, 15–16. Quote 15.

22. "On Overcoming Disenchantment: The 1968 Election," *Christian Century,* October 16, 1968, 1298–1299.

23. "Nixon as Peacemaker," *Christian Century,* February 5, 1969, 171.

24. "God and the White House," *Newsweek,* July 14, 1969, 57.

25. "Rebels, Amnesty, and Property," *Christian Century,* March 5, 1969, 307.

26. "Is God Black?" *Time,* November 15, 1968, 78.

27. "A Black Schism," *Newsweek,* March 4, 1968, 90.

28. Albert B. Cleague, *The Black Messiah* (New York: Sheed and Ward, 1968).

29. Joseph Hough, *Black Power and White Protestants* (New York: Oxford University Press, 1968).

30. James H. Cone, *Black Theology and Black Power* (New York: Seabury, 1969).

31. "Catalyst of Conscience," *Newsweek,* August 29, 1969, 49.

32. "Joy Box with No Joy: The N.C.C. at Detroit," *Christian Century,* December 17, 1969, 1601–1605.

33. Rose quickly recovered to continue his distinguished career in the coming decades.

34. "Joy Box," 1601.

35. Robert E. Grossmann, "The Invisible Christian," in *The Underground Church,* ed. Malcolm Boyd (New York: Sheed and Ward, 1968).

36. Layton P. Zimmer, "The People of the Underground Church," ibid., 14; Malcolm Boyd, ibid., 6–7.

37. Malcolm Boyd, *As I Live and Breathe: Stages of an Autobiography* (New York: Random House, 1969), 256.

38. Walter D. Wagoner, "Thoughts for Protestants to Be Static By," *Christian Century,* February 19, 1969, 249–251.

39. Eric Hoffer, *The True Believer* (New York: Harper & Row, 1951).

40. Ibid., *Before the Sabbath* (New York: Harper and Row, 1979), 64.

41. Barbara Ehrenreich, "Living Out the Wars of 1968," *Time,* June 7, 1993, 74.

42. "'Hell, No!' at Harvard," *Newsweek,* January 29, 1968, 26.

43. O. Carnell Arnold, "Fight Fiercely, Christians," *Christian Century,* June 19, 1968, 812–814.

44. "The Cynical Idealists of 1968," *Time,* June 7, 1968, pp.78–83. Quote 79.

45. "The Concept of Sanctuary versus the Draft," *Time,* June 28, 1968, 78.

46. "The Berrigan Brothers: They Rob Draft Boards," *Time,* June 7, 1968, 62.

47. Philip Berrigan, "Violence: A Prisoner's View," *Christian Century,* August 14, 1968, 1011–1013.

48. "The Ides of October," *Christian Century,* October 29, 1969, 1369.

49. See, for example, Thomas M. Gannon, "A Report on the Vietnam Moratorium," *America,* November 1, 1969, 374.

50. "Sheltering the Weathermen," *Christian Century,* November 5, 1969, 1411.

51. "A Shattered Trust," *Christian Century,* May 13, 1970, 587.

52. Gitlin, *The Sixties,* 408.

53. David Cartright, "GI Resistance during the Vietnam War," in Melvin Small and William D. Hoover, eds., *Give Peace a Chance: Exploring the Vietnam Antiwar Movement* (Syracuse, N.Y.: Syrcacuse University Press, 1992), 117.

54. "Woe behind the Walls," *Time*, February 9, 1968, 66.
55. "The Rib Uncaged," *Time*, April 19, 1968, 70–71. See Sidney Callahan, *Beyond Birth Control: The Christian Experience of Sex* (New York: Sheed & Ward, 1968), published in 1969 under the title *Exiled to Eden: The Christian Experience of Sex.*
56. "Foot Soldiers of Orthodoxy," *Time*, July 5, 1968, 48.
57. John A. O'Brien, "'Humanae Vitae': Reactions and Consequences," *Christian Century*, February 26, 1969, 288–289.
58. J. John Palen, "Catholicism, Contraception, and Conscience," *Christian Century*, September 11, 1968, 1132; "Catholicism's Authority Crisis," *Christian Century*, September 25, 1968, 1191–1192.
59. All cited in "Pope Paul's Bitter Birth-Control Pill," *Newsweek,* August 12, 1968, 78.
60. "The Pope and Birth Control: A Crisis in Catholic Authority," *Time*, August 9, 1968, 40–42.
61. "The Immaculate Heart Rebels," *Time*, February 16, 1970, 49–51.
62. "The Catholic Exodus: Why Priests and Nuns Are Quitting," *Time*, February 23, 1970,
63. Andrew Greeley, "Why They Leave," *American Ecclesiastical Review* 161, 4 (October 1969): 251–257.
64. George A. Schlichte, "The Vanishing Priest, A Sign from God to Change Our Ways," ibid., 334–343; David M. Knight, SJ, "Celibacy as a Personal Response," ibid., 375–385.
65. Andrew M. Greeley, *American Catholics since the Council: An Unauthorized Report* (Chicago: Thomas More, 1985).
66. Jean Baudrillard, *Simulations*, trans. Paul Foss, Paul Patton, and Philip Beitchman (New York: Semiotext[e], 1983), 62–63.
67. Conrad Hyers, "Ambivalent Man and His Ambiguous Moon," *Christian Century*, September 10, 1969, 1158–1162.
68. Ian Barbour, "On to Mars?" *Christian Century*, November 19, 1969, 1478–1480.
69. For one example, see Richard L. Means, "Ecology and the Contemporary Religious Consciousness," *Christian Century*, December 3, 1969, 1546
70. "Space, Science, and Scripture," *Christianity Today*, July 18, 1969, 931–934.
71. "Love-in in BossTown," *Time*, July 12, 1968, 18–19.
72. "That New Black Magic," *Time*, September 27, 1968, 42.
73. Carl Bangs, "The Hippies: Some Historical Perspectives," *Religion in Life*, Winter 1968, 498–508.
74. Alan J. Moore, "The Revolt against Affluence," *Religion in Life*, Winter 1968, 509–518; Paul R. Woudenberg, "The Egoism of Flower Power," ibid., 519–525.
75. "The Morality of Marijuana," *Time*, August 16, 1968, 58.
76. Nicholas von Hoffman, *We Are the People our Parents Warned Us Against*, (Chicago: Quadrangle Books, 1968); Leonard Wolf, ed., *Voices from the Love Generation* (Boston: Little, Brown, 1968).
77. Ralph Metzger, *The Ecstatic Adventure* (New York: Macmillan, 1968); and see "Among the Flower People," *Newsweek*, June 3, 1968, 94–96.
78. Leary is cited in Miller, *The Hippies and American Values,* 19. Alan Watts, *Cloud-Hidden, Whereabouts Unknown* (New York: Random House, 1973), 35.
79. "The 'Free' Church of Berkeley's Hippies," *Christian Century*, April 10, 1968, 464–468.

80. Cited in "Comment," *United Church Herald* 12, 11 (November 1969): 34.

81. "Message of History's Biggest Happening: Woodstock Music and Art Fair," *Time*, August 29, 1969, 32–33.

82. 69. Cited in Miller, *The Hippies and American Values,* 83.

83. Brooks R. Walker, *The New Immorality* (Garden City, N.Y.: Doubleday, 1968).

84. Peter Berger, *A Rumor of Angels* (Garden City, N.Y.: Doubleday, 1969).

85. Mary Daly, *The Church and the Second Sex* (New York: Harper, 1968).

86. Rosemary Radford Ruether, *The Radical Kingdom* (New York: Harper and Row, 1970).

87. Harold Jacobs, *Weatherman* (Berkeley, Calif.: Ramparts, 1970).

88. Charles Reich, *The Greening of America* (New York: Random House, 1970).

89. Roszak, *The Making of a Counter Culture,* 47.

90. Thomas A. Harris, *I'm O.K.—You're O.K.: A Practical Guide to Transactional Analysis* (New York: Harper & Row, 1969).

91. Robert McAfee Brown, "Discoveries and Dangers," *Christian Century,* January 14, 1970, 40–45.

Chapter 6. Getting It Together: Final Reflections on the Sixties

1. Arthur Schlesinger, *The Cycles of American History* (Boston: Houghton Mifflin, 1986).

2. Phillip E. Hammond, *Religion and Personal Autonomy: The Third Disestablishment in America* (Columbia: University of South Carolina Press, 1992), 139.

3. Roof, *A Generation of Seekers,* 44–47.

4. Alexis de Tocqueville, *Democracy in America*, trans. George Lawrence (Garden City, N.Y.: Anchor, 1969), 403. See Lisle Dalton et al., "Bringing Tocqueville in: Remedying a Neglect in the Sociology of Religion," *Journal for the Scientific Study of Religion* 31, 4 (December 1992): 395–407.

5. Tocqueville, *Democracy in America,* 448–449.

6. Richard Rorty, *Philosophy and the Mirror of Nature* (Princeton, N.J.: Princeton University Press, 1979). Hans Christian von Baeyer, *Taming the Atom: The Emergence of the Visible Microworld* (New York: Random House, 1992), 75.

7. Catherine Albanese, *Nature Religion in America: From the Algonkian Indians to the New Age* (Chicago: University of Chicago Press, 1991).

Bibliography

This bibliography lists selected books of lasting historical value for the study of religion in the Sixties. It does not attempt to name all sources relevant to that subject that are cited in the text, nor does it list most books of the day mentioned in the "Books" section of each chapter, nor all books footnoted only in connection with short topical discussions within the text.

Aaronson, Bernard, and Humphrey Osmond. *Psychedelics: The Uses and Implications of Hallucinogenic Drugs*. Garden City, N.Y.: Doubleday, 1970.

Altizer, Thomas, and William Hamilton. *Radical Theology and the Death of God*. Indianapolis: Bobbs-Merrill, 1966.

Anderson, Walter. *The Upstart Spring: Esalen and the American Awakening*. Reading, Mass.: Addison-Wesley, 1983

Avens, Roberts. *Imagination Is Reality: Western Nirvana in Jung, Hillman, Barfield, and Cassirer*. Dallas: Spring, 1980.

Baudrillard, Jean. *Simulations*. Translated by Paul Foss, Paul Patton, and Philip Beitchman. New York: Simiotext(e), 1983.

Belfrage, Sally. *Freedom Summer*. New York: Viking, 1965.

Bellah, Robert, and Charles Glock. *The New Religious Consciousness*. Berkeley and Los Angeles: University of California Press, 1976.

Blumberg, Rhoda Lois. *Civil Rights: The 1960s Freedom Struggle*. Rev. ed. Boston: Hall, 1991.

Braden, William. *The Age of Aquarius*. Chicago: Quadrangle, 1970.

———. *The Private Sea: LSD and the Search for God*. Chicago: Quadrangle, 1967.

Branch, Taylor. *Parting the Waters: America in the King Years, 1954-63*. New York: Simon and Schuster, 1988.

Brown, Norman O. *Love's Body*. New York: Random House, 1966.

Brown, Robert McAfee; Abraham J. Heschel; and Michael Novak. *Vietnam: Crisis of Conscience*. New York: Association Press, Behrman House, and Herder and Herder, 1967.

Capps, Walter. *The Unfinished War: Vietnam and the American Conscience*. Boston: Beacon, 1982.

Chatfield, Charles. *The American Peace Movement: Ideals and Activism*. New York: Twayne, 1992.

Clecak, Peter. *America's Quest for the Ideal Self: Dissent and Fulfillment in the 60s and 70s*. New York: Oxford University Press, 1983.

Coffin, William Sloane, Jr. *Once to Every Man: A Memoir*. New York: Atheneum, 1977.

Cohen, Allen, ed. *The San Francisco Oracle*. Facsimile ed. Berkeley, Calif.: Regent, 1991.

Collier, Peter, and David Horowitz. *Second Thoughts: Former Radicals Look Back at the Sixties*. New York: Summit, 1990.

Cox, Harvey. *The Secular City*. New York: Macmillan, 1965.

———. *The Feast of Fools*. Cambridge, Mass.: Harvard University Press, 1969.

DeBeneditti, Charles, and Charles Chatfield. *An American Ordeal: The Antiwar*

Movement of the Vietnam Era. Syracuse, N.Y.: Syracuse University Press, 1990.

Dickstein, Morris. *The Gates of Eden: American Culture in the Sixties*. New York: Basic Books, 1977.

Forster, Arnold, and Benjamin R. Epstein. *Danger on the Right*. New York: Random House, 1964.

Friedan, Betty. *The Feminine Mystique*. New York: Norton, 1963.

Gaskin, Stephen. *Haight-Ashbury Flashbacks: Amazing Dope Tales of the Sixties*. Berkeley, Calif.: Ronin, 1990.

Gitlin, Todd. *The Sixties: Years of Hope, Days of Rage*. New York: Bantam, 1987.

Goodman, Paul. *The New Reformation*. New York: Random House, 1970.

Gottleib, Anne. *Do You Believe in Magic? The Second Coming of the Sixties Generation*. New York: Random House, 1987.

Gustaitis, Rasa. *Turning On*. New York: Macmillan, 1969.

Hall, Mitchell K. *Because of Their Faith: CALCAV and Religious Opposition to the Vietnam War*. New York: Columbia University Press, 1990.

Hammond, Philip. *Religion and Personal Autonomy*. Columbia: University of South Carolina Press, 1992.

Hampton, H., and S. Fager. *Voices of Freedom: An Oral History of the Civil Rights Movement*. New York: Bantam, 1990.

Harrison, Hank. *The Dead Book: A Social History of the Grateful Dead*. New York: Links, 1973.

Hillman, James. *Archetypal Psychology*. Dallas: Spring, 1985.

Hoffman, Abbie. *Steal This Book*. New York: Pirate Editions, 1971.

Horowitz, Irving. *Ideology and Utopia in the U.S. 1956–1976*. New York: Oxford University Press, 1977.

Hough, Joseph. *Black Power and White Protestants*. New York: Oxford University Press, 1968.

Kessler, Lauren. *After All these Years: Sixties' Ideas in a Different World*. New York: Thunder's Mouth, 1990.

King, Martin Luther. *Why We Can't Wait*. New York: Harper and Row, 1964.

Koerselman, Gary. *The Lost Decade: A Story of America in the 1960s*. New York: Lang, 1981.

Laing, R. D. *The Politics of Experience*. New York: Pantheon, 1967.

Leamer, Laurence. *The Paper Revolutionaries: The Rise of the Underground Press*. New York: Simon and Schuster, 1972.

Leary, Timothy. *High Priest*. New York: New American Library, 1968.

———. *Flashbacks: An Autobiography*. Los Angeles: Tarcher, 1983.

———. *The Politics of Ecstasy*. New York: Putnam, 1968.

Leonard, George. *Walking on the Edge of the World*. Boston: Houghton Mifflin, 1988.

Lyotard, Jean-François. *The Postmodern Condition: A Report on Knowledge*. Trans. Geoff Bennington and Brian Massumi. Minneapolis: University of Minnesota Press, 1984.

McAdam, Doug. *Freedom Summer* (New York: Oxford University Press, 1988).

McPherson, Myra. *Long Time Passing: Vietnam and the Haunted Generation*. Garden City, N.Y.: Doubleday, 1984.

Mailer, Norman. *The Armies of the Night*. New York: New American Library, 1968.

Makower, Joel. *Woodstock: The Oral History*. New York: Doubleday, 1989.

Marcuse, Herbert. *One Dimensional Man*. Boston: Beacon, 1964.

Meier, August, and Elliott Rudwick. *CORE: A Study in the Civil Rights Movement 1942–1968*. New York: Oxford University Press, 1973.

Merton, Thomas. *Seeds of Destruction*. New York: Farrar, Straus and Giroux, 1980.

Michener, James A. *Kent State: What Happened and Why*. New York: Random House, 1971.

Miller, Timothy. *The Hippies and American Values*. Knoxville: University of Tennessee Press, 1991.

Moore, Thomas, ed. *A Blue Fire: Selected Writings by James Hillman*. New York: Harper and Row, 1989.

Needleman, Jacob. *The New Religions*. Garden City, N.Y.: Doubleday, 1970.

Neises, C. P., ed. *The Beatles Reader*. Ann Arbor, Mich.: Pierian, 1984.

Norman, Philip. *Shout! The Beatles in Their Generation*. New York: Simon and Schuster, 1981.

Novak, Michael. *A Theology for Radical Politics*. New York: Herder and Herder, 1969.

O'Brien, Geoffrey. *Dream Time: Chapters from the Sixties*. New York: Viking, 1988.

O'Neill, William. *Coming Apart: An Informal History of America in the 1960s*. New York: Quadrangle/ New York Times Book Co., 1971.

Oppenheimer, Martin. *The Sit-in Movement of 1960*. New York: Carlson, 1989.

Peck, Abe. *Uncovering the Sixties: The Life and Times of the Underground Press*. New York: Pantheon, 1985.

Perry, Charles. *The Haight-Ashbury: A History*. New York: Random House, 1984.

Perry, John W. *The Far Side of Madness*. Englewood Cliffs, N.J.: Prentice-Hall, 1974.

Reich, Charles. *The Greening of America*. New York: Random House, 1970.

Rieff, Philip. *The Triumph of the Therapeutic*. New York: Harper and Row, 1966.

Robinson, John A. T. *Honest to God*. Philadelphia: Westminster, 1963.

Roof, Wade Clark. *A Generation of Seekers*. San Francisco: Harper Collins, 1993.

Rorabaugh, W. J. *Berkeley at War: The 1960s*. New York: Oxford University Press, 1989.

Roszak, Theodore. *The Making of a Counter Culture*. Garden City, N.Y.: Doubleday, 1969.

Rubin, Jerry. *Do It! Scenarios of the Revolution*. New York: Simon and Schuster, 1970.

Rynne, Xavier. *Vatican Council II*. New York: Farrar, Straus and Giroux, 1968.

Small, Melvin, and William D. Hoover, eds. *Give Peace a Chance: Exploring the Vietnam Antiwar Movement*. Syracuse, N.Y.: Syracuse University Press, 1992.

Sobel, Lester A., ed. *Civil Rights 1960–66*. New York: Facts on File, 1967.

Stevens, Jay. *Storming Heaven: LSD and the American Dream*. New York: Atlantic Monthly Press, 1987.

Stoper, Emily. *The Student Nonviolent Coordinating Committee: The Growth of Radicalism in a Civil Rights Organization*. New York: Carlson, 1989.

Stringfellow, William, and Anthony Towne. *The Bishop Pike Affair*. New York: Harper and Row, 1967.

Tipton, Steven M. *Getting Saved from the Sixties*. Berkeley and Los Angeles: University of California Press, 1982.

Turner, Victor. *The Forest of Symbols*. Ithaca, N.Y.: Cornell University Press, 1967.

———. *The Ritual Process: Structure and Anti-Structure*. Ithaca, N.Y.: Cornell University Press, 1977.

Vahanian, Gabriel. *Death of God*.

Viorst, Milton. *Fire in the Streets: America in the 1960s*. New York: Simon and Schuster, 1979.

Washington, Joseph. *The Politics of God*. Boston: Beacon, 1967.

Weil, Andrew. *The Natural Mind*. Boston: Houghton Mifflin, 1972.

Weil, Gunther M.; Ralph Metzner; and Timothy Leary, eds. *The Psychedelic Reader*. New Hyde Park, N.Y.: University Books, 1965.

Westby, David. *Clouded Vision: The Student Movement in the U.S. in the 1960s*. Lewisburg, Penn.: Bucknell University Press, 1976.

Whalen, Jack, and Richard Flacks. *Beyond the Barricades: The Sixties Generation Grows Up*. Philadelphia: Temple University Press, 1989.

Whitmer, Peter O., with Bruce Van Wyngarden. *Aquarius Revisited: Seven Who Created the Sixties Counterculture*. New York: Macmillan, 1987.

Wilson, Bryan. *Contemporary Transformations of Religion*. London: Oxford University Press, 1977.

Winter, Gibson. *Suburban Captivity of the Churches*. Garden City, N.Y.: Doubleday, 1961.

Wolf, Leonard, ed. *Voices from the Love Generation*. Boston: Little, Brown, 1968.

Yablonsky, Lewis. *The Hippie Trip*. New York: Pegasus, 1968.

Zaroulis, Nancy, and Gerald Sullivan. *Who Spoke Up? American Protest against the War in Vietnam, 1963–1975*. Garden City, N.Y.: Doubleday, 1984.

Index

About the Author

Robert Ellwood is professor in the School of Religion, University of Southern California. He has published over a dozen books, including *The History and Future of Faith* and *Islands of the Dawn*. He is editor of the Prentice-Hall Series in World Religions and is an associate editor of *American National Biography*, published by the American Council of Learned Societies. He has served as an Episcopal clergyman and Navy chaplain.